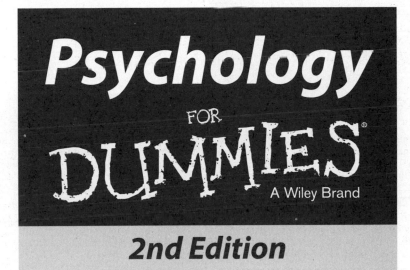

Psychology

FOR

DUMMIES®

A Wiley Brand

2nd Edition

by Adam Cash, PsyD

Psychologist

FOR

DUMMIES®

A Wiley Brand

Psychology For Dummies® 2nd Edition

Published by
John Wiley & Sons, Inc.
111 River Street, Hoboken
NJ 07030-5774

www.wiley.com

Contents at a Glance

Table of Contents

Introduction

● ●

So you've bought *Psychology For Dummies.* How does that make you feel? Hopefully, you're feeling pretty good. And why shouldn't you be? You're going to discover all kinds of interesting information about the basics of human behavior and mental processes.

Everybody is interested in psychology. People are fascinating, and that includes you! Humans often defy explanation and evade prediction. Figuring people out can be pretty hard. Just when you think that you've figured some-one out, bang, he surprises you. Now I know that some of you may be think-ing, "Actually, I'm a pretty good judge of people. I've got a handle on things." If that's the case, that's great! Some folks do seem to have a more intuitive understanding of people than others. For the rest of us though, there's psychology.

About This Book

Psychology For Dummies is an introduction to the field of psychology. I tried to write this book using plain English and everyday examples with the hope that it will be real and applicable to everyday life. I've always felt that tack-ling a new subject is more enjoyable when it has real-world importance. Psychology is full of jargon, so much jargon that it even has its own diction-ary, aptly named *The Dictionary of Psychology* (Penguin Reference Books). This book is for those of you who are interested in what people do, think, say, and feel, but want the information presented in a clear and easily under-standable manner.

The information in this reference is not intended to substitute for expert psy-chological, healthcare, or medical advice or treatment; it is designed to help you make informed choices. Because each individual is unique, a psychologist, healthcare practitioner, or physician must diagnose conditions and supervise treatments for each individual health problem. If an individual is under a psy-chologist's or physician's care and receives advice contrary to information provided in this reference, the psychologist's or physician's advice should be followed, as it is based on the unique characteristics of that individual.

Conventional language for psychologists can sound like gibberish to someone who has never had a psychology class. As I state earlier in this chapter, I try to stay away from jargon and technical language in this book. You may come across an attempt at a joke or two. I tend to take a lighter approach to life, but sometimes people don't get my sense of humor. If I try to crack a joke in the text and it bombs, please don't be too harsh. I'm a psychologist after all, and I don't think we're known for our sense of humor. I hope I don't come across as insensitive or cavalier either — that is certainly not my intention.

Sometimes, talking about psychology can be pretty dry, so I try to liven things up with examples and personal stories. I make no references to any patients I've ever had in therapy. If there appears to be a resemblance, it's purely coincidental. In fact, I took great care in preserving the privacy and confidentiality of the people I have worked with.

Foolish Assumptions

You can find a lot of psychology books out there. Most of them are either too technical and specialized or cover too narrow an area of psychology. Here are some of the reasons why I think *Psychology For Dummies* is the book for you:

- ✔ You've got a lot of questions about people.
- ✔ You've got a lot of questions about yourself.
- ✔ You're thinking about going into the field of psychology.
- ✔ You're currently studying psychology or a related discipline, such as social work or counseling.
- ✔ You're interested in psychology but don't have the time or the money to take a psychology course.
- ✔ You've got people all figured out, and you want to see if I'm on track.

Icons Used In This Book

Throughout this book, you find icons in the margins. They're there to help you easily find certain types of information. Here's a list of the icons you see:

When you see this one, I'm asking you to engage in a little psychological experimentation. In other words, you're the guinea pig when you run across this icon. What would psychology be without its guinea pigs? Don't worry — the experiments are harmless. No shocks, I promise.

When you see this icon, I'm trying to emphasize a bit of information that may come in handy someday.

With this creative piece of art, I'm trying to alert you to information that is a "must know" if you're going to learn psychology.

Don't forget it. When you see this icon I am reminding you of the highlights from that section. It flags the "if you learn just one thing from this chapter" type of stuff, so pay attention.

This icon flags discussions that may rise above the level you need to basically understand the topic at hand. These sections can safely be skipped without harming your comprehension of the main point.

Beyond the Book

In addition to the chapters in this print book, you'll find lots more *Psychology for Dummies* information on the Web at www.dummies.com/extras/psychology. For free!

There's just too much good information out there, and I want you to learn as much as you can about psychology. But there was only so much space I had to work with in print. So I put the rest online for you.

Check out the eCheat Sheets for quick access to information about the differences between psychologists and other mental health professionals and coping with psychological crises.

You'll also find three extra online "chapters" — full articles on the following topics:

- ✔ "Ten Ways the Internet and Psychology are Intersecting" deals with the psychology of the Internet and cyberpsychology.
- ✔ "Applying Psychology for a Better World" covers behavioral economics and forensic psychology.
- ✔ "Exploring Human Differences: Culture, Gender, and Sexuality" is a look at the differences that make us unique as individuals and groups.

For fun, you can also take a couple of mock tests to check out your intelligence and personality!

Where to Go from Here

Psychology is a broad field. I think you'll find that the organization of this book lets you check out what you're interested in and leave the rest of the stuff behind, if you want.

Use the table of contents and index to see what grabs your interest. If you're new to the subject, by all means start with Chapter 1 and go. But you don't have to read it cover to cover. Kind of like a cafeteria — take what you like and leave the rest.

But hey, if I can write an entire book on psychology, I think you can read an entire book on this stuff. Besides, I think you'll like it. Psychology is a great subject. Enjoy!

Part I
Getting Started with Psychology

In this part...

✔ Understand what psychology is and get an overview of the field.

✔ Get in touch with your inner armchair psychologist by exploring the concept that we are all "acting" psychologists, analyzing and assessing human behavior every day.

✔ Find out about the professional practice of psychology with an introduction to its scientific nature and the different approaches psychologists use to investigate and understand people.

✔ Get to know the ethical guidelines that psychologists are expected to follow during treatment and in applied psychology.

Chapter 1

Seeing the Purpose of Psychology

. . . .

In This Chapter

▶ Defining psychology

▶ Understanding how people work

▶ Figuring out how psychology can help

. . . .

Most people I know have a certain idea in mind when they think about psychology.

I'm a psychologist. But what's that? Someone who knows and studies psychology, but is that all there is to it? When I get together with family and friends during the holidays, it seems like they still don't know exactly what I do for a living.

Some of my patients have said, "All you do is talk. Can't you prescribe some medicine for me?" Still others grant me seemingly supernatural powers of knowledge and healing. I wrote this book to clear up some misconceptions about psychology.

What Is Psychology?

What are some of the ideas that come to mind when people think about the topic of psychology? It depends on whom you ask. Sometimes, I imagine myself as a guest on a television talk show. I'm bombarded by questions from the audience that I can't answer. My heart starts to pound. I begin to sweat. I start to stand up so that I can run off the set, but then something comes to me that keeps me in my seat. I imagine asking the people in the audience what they think psychology is and why they think a psychologist can answer questions about psychology.

Whys, hows, and whats

Before I provide a definition of psychology, I want you to take a few minutes to jot down some of your ideas on what psychology is.

Why did this book catch your eye?

Are you looking for answers? Looking for advice?

What's the question you're asking here?

"Why do people do what they do?" is the question that lies beneath many of the other questions people ask psychologists. Whether you're a professional psychologist, a researcher, or a layperson, this one simple question seems to be the root issue.

Here are some examples of the motivating questions that drive the discipline of psychology:

- ✔ Why did that shooting happen?
- ✔ Why can't I stop feeling sad?
- ✔ Why did she break up with me?
- ✔ Why are people so mean?

Basically, psychology is a branch of knowledge that focuses on *people,* either as individuals or in groups.

Other fundamental questions of psychology center on the "how" of things:

- ✔ How can I get excited about my marriage again?
- ✔ How can I get my 2-year-old to stop throwing tantrums?
- ✔ How does the mind work?

Still other questions deal with the "whats":

- ✔ What are emotions?
- ✔ What is mental illness?
- ✔ What is intelligence?

These why, how, and what questions comprise the intellectual and philosophical core of psychology.

Therefore, *psychology* can be defined as the *scientific study of human behavior and mental processes.* Psychology attempts to uncover what people do along with why and how they do it.

Building a person

When I try to imagine all the reasons that people do what they do and figure out how various behaviors and mental processes come to pass, I often run with a "mad scientist" approach. I've always thought that one of the best ways to answer the what and why and how questions would be to build a person. Well, not actually build one like Dr. Frankenstein did — out of parts and brains and electricity — but to create a blueprint of a person's mind and behavior.

In therapy, when people try to explain a particular behavior or situation to me, I often say, "Can you make it happen, now? Can you show me?" For example, a parent may be telling me how his child hits him when he tells the child to do something. And I'll say, "Show me. Make it happen." The most common response is a puzzled or disturbed look on the parent's face.

The point is, if they can cause it to happen, then they can un-cause it to happen, too. And that means they understand why and how it's happening. This is a type of reverse psychological engineering for figuring out the "why" and "how" of human behavior.

I envision psychology reaching a pinnacle when it can list all the ingredients of the human mind and all the determinants of behavior. Maybe the field can figure it all out through that reverse engineering process mentioned earlier. Or, at the very least, maybe psychology will figure out people, and all the information that experts gather can be stored or formulated into an *algorithm* for making people that, one day, a super-intelligent robotic life form can utilize to re-create the human species thousands of years after it becomes extinct. I did say mad scientist, right?

Yes, this is the kind of blueprint or overlay I use to understand what psychology is: What are the ingredients of a person — mind, thoughts, emotions, perceptions, dreams, fears, personality, and brain — and what is the purpose of each ingredient? I'm not alone. Many psychologists engage in reverse engineering of the mind and behavior by looking at all the parts and how they work together to create . . . well, you.

Finding the function

A first principle of my mad-scientist vision of psychology is that building a human requires you to know what the person's function is. After all, engineers don't build things without knowing what they're supposed to do. Only with a purpose in mind can you know what to build and what features and materials need to be considered.

So, what's the function — the purpose — of a human being?

Like all other carbon-based living organisms on planet Earth, human beings are "staying alive" machines. (Admit it; you instantly thought of the Bee Gees, didn't you, or John Travolta in that white bell-bottom suit?) I'm not saying there is no meaning to life. Quite the contrary; I'm saying that the function of life is to be alive, to stay alive, and to perpetuate life. What's the meaning of it all? Wrong book; try *Philosophy For Dummies* or *Religion For Dummies*.

The field of psychology concerns itself with the study of the "how" of life — the behavior and mental processes of being alive, staying alive, and perpetuating life.

Checking the Parts List

From a psychological standpoint, what does the human machine need in order to fulfill its function of existing, staying alive, and perpetuating? Well, if you've ever put together a do-it-yourself piece of furniture, you know that the instructions usually start out with a parts list.

Psychological science has already put together quite an impressive psychological parts list:

✔ **Bodies** (and all the subparts — see Chapter 3 for more)

- Brains

- Hearts

- Hormones

- Genes

- Motor skills

✔ **Minds** (and all the subparts — see Chapters 4–8)

- Consciousness

- Sensations and perceptions, including vision, hearing, taste, smell, touch, balance, and pain

- Thinking, which manages attending, remembering, forming concepts, problem solving, deciding, and intelligence

- Communicating, including verbal and nonverbal expressions such as body language, gestures, speech, and language

- Motivations

- Emotions

✔ **Personality** (see Chapter 9)

- ✔ **Gender and sexuality** (see the free online article "Exploring Human Differences: Culture, Gender, and Sexuality" at www.dummies.com/extras/psychology)

- ✔ **Social skills and relationship skills** (see Chapters 10 and 11)

Just like putting together that desk from IKEA seemed a lot easier on paper than it actually turned out to be, assembling this list of psychological parts is daunting as well. Psychologists are still trying to understand each component in relative isolation and figure out how they all fit together. It's the crux of what remains a formidable task in developing a comprehensive human science.

Troubleshooting

Imagine that I've assembled my human being, switched it on, and let it loose to go about its primary function of surviving. I think I've equipped it with all it needs in order to survive.

But then it happens — change. That's right, something unexpected happens, and my human begins floundering, struggling, and verging on failing to achieve its primary function. How could I have forgotten that the world is not a static place?

My creation is dealing with the environment in ways that I should have anticipated. So I go back to the drawing board to add the following functions and abilities (yep, more parts):

- ✔ **Learning:** Ability to learn from the environment

- ✔ **Context:** Ability to grow and develop in response to the environment

- ✔ **Adaption:** Ability to cope with change, stress, and illness

Humans need parts and procedures.

Whew, this is getting complicated.

Finding Professional Help

Often, a person's parts are all assembled, and he's learning, growing, adapting, and adjusting to the best of his individual ability — but something's "off" or he's just not functioning properly. This is where physicians, psychotherapists, counselors, social workers, educators, and consultants enter the picture.

The tools and procedures that health care providers use to diagnose, fix, and maintain people include the following and other areas of research and practice:

- ✔ **Diagnostics:** Among the specialties of diagnostics are abnormal psychology (covered in Chapter 13) and psychological assessment and testing (see Chapter 14).

- ✔ **Biomedical therapies:** Treatment for various psychological conditions may include medication and/or physiological therapies (see Chapter 3).

- ✔ **Psychological therapy and intervention:** Psychoanalysis, cognitive-behavioral therapy, and humanistic therapies (see Chapters 15–18).

- ✔ **Applied psychology:** Using psychological science to solve a wide range of human problems and issues. (See the free online article "Applying Psychology for a Better World" at www.dummies.com/extras/psychology.)

Putting It into Practice

Psychology is the scientific study of human behavior and mental processes. In case you were wondering (and worried), I am not engaged in an actual "build a human" project. But I'd have a very solid foundation and a good blueprint to get started if I ever decided to try. Each of a person's parts, processes, and sources of help represents a chapter or section of *Psychology For Dummies,* 2nd Edition.

Psychology began as a type of philosophy, a mostly subjective, speculative, and theoretical way of thinking about human beings. But, as a result of the enormous contributions of such people as William James, Wilhem Wundt, Edward Thorndike, B. F. Skinner, Albert Bandura, Jean Piaget, Phillip Zimbardo, Robert Sternberg, Albert Ellis, and many, many others, it has matured over the last 100 years into an objective science. Psychology's experimentation methods and statistical analyses continue to grow increasingly sophisticated.

Psychology has evolved from a study of intangible thought and consciousness to the study of material subject matter — as in brains and test scores — thanks to modern technological advances such as psychological testing instruments, EEG, and MRI.

This fascinating field continues to mature as its practitioners become more sophisticated in their understanding of how the environment and human differences (such as culture and ethnicity, gender, and sexual orientation) impact the mind and behavior.

Chapter 2

Making Sense of What People Do: Psychology Essentials

*1*n a way, each of us is an amateur psychologist of sorts. Professional psychologists aren't the only ones who try to figure people out. When I started taking psychology courses, I had my own ideas about people. Sometimes I agreed with the theories of Freud and others, and sometimes I disagreed wholeheartedly. I'm not alone. Most people seem to have specific ideas about what makes others tick.

Psychology covers a topic we all have experience with — people. It's pretty hard to say the same thing about chemistry, astronomy, or electrical engineering. Of course, we all encounter chemicals every day, but I can't remember the last time I asked, "How do they get that mouthwash to taste like mint?" However, a psychologist may ask, "What happens inside a person so that her toothpaste tastes like mint?"

One of the best places to catch armchair psychologists (people who speculate without systematic evidence) in action is the local coffeehouse or watering hole. People love talking about the whys and the wherefores of other people's behavior. "And then I said. . . ." "You should have told him. . . ." Hanging out in public social spaces is much like being in group therapy sometimes. People work hard at figuring out other people.

Psychologists sometimes call this armchair psychologizing *folk psychology* — a framework of principles used by ordinary people to understand, explain, and predict their own and other people's behavior and mental states. In practice, everyone uses a variety of psychological notions or concepts to explain individuals' mental states, personalities, and behaviors. Two concepts in particular that people tend to rely on are *beliefs* and *desires.* That is, most people assume that people have beliefs and that they act on those beliefs. So when you wonder why people do what they do, it's easy; it's because of their beliefs.

Yet folk psychology isn't the only tool in the bag of an armchair psychologist. People also explain other's behavior in terms of luck, curses, blessings, karma, fate, destiny, and other non-psychological terms. Using these explanations isn't necessarily a bad thing. It's pretty hard to explain from a psychological perspective why someone wins the lottery. Explaining why someone continues to buy tickets when they keep losing, however, is a question for psychology.

In this chapter, you find out how psychologists go about their business, including how overarching theories frame the questions they ask and the variables they look at. You also get a look at the various branches of psychology that include more than what people typically think of such as clinical psychology. Finally, you see how the discipline of psychology works to be as scientific as possible by basing its knowledge on research and statistical methods, which shores up its credibility among the other scholarly disciplines.

Finding a Framework

At a very basic level, psychology is a branch of knowledge. Psychology exists among and interacts with other scientific and scholarly disciplines in a community-like environment of knowledge, and contributes a vast collection of theories and research to help answer questions related to human behavior and mental processes. A number of other fields of study — physics, biology, chemistry, history, economics, political science, sociology, medicine, and anthropology — attempt to use their own perspectives to answer the same basic questions about people that psychology addresses.

One comment I get from students from time to time is, "What makes you think that psychology has all the answers?" My answer is, "Psychologists are just trying to provide a piece of the puzzle, not all the answers."

To enable psychology to contribute to the community of knowledge about people, over the years, psychologists as a group have come up with a basic set of *broad theoretical perspectives,* or frameworks to guide the work of psychology. These broad theoretical frameworks are sometimes referred to as *metatheories.* The lion's share of psychological research is based on one or more of these broad frameworks or metatheories.

Each metatheory provides an overarching framework for conducting psychological research and comes with a different point of emphasis to figure out what people do, and why and how they do it. Other perspectives represent hybridized approaches, such as motivational science and affective neuroscience. But for now, I'm just sticking with the basics.

In this section, I describe the most common metatheories psychologists use when they find a behavior or mental process they're interested in researching. Work typically begins from within one of these theories.

Biological

The biological approach centers on the biological underpinnings of behavior, including the effects of evolution and genetics. The premise is that behavior and mental processes can be explained by understanding genetics, human physiology, and anatomy. Biological psychologists focus mostly on the brain and the nervous system. (For more on biological psychology, see Chapter 3.) Neuropsychology and the study of the brain, genetics, and evolutionary psychology are included within the biological metatheory.

For an example of biology's impact on behavior, just think about how differently people act when they're under the influence of alcohol. Holiday office parties are good laboratories for applying the biological perspective. You walk into the party and see Bob, the relatively quiet guy from accounting, burning up the cubicles. Bob's transformed into a lady's man. He's funny. He's drunk. Do you think Bob will remember?

Psychoanalytic/Psychodynamic

The psychoanalytic/psychodynamic metatheory emphasizes the importance of unconscious mental processes, early child development, personality, the self, attachment patterns, and relationships. This approach explores how these mental and developmental processes interact with the challenges of life and everyday demands to affect the person you are and how you behave.

Sigmund Freud founded psychoanalysis in the early 1900s; since then, hundreds of theorists have added to his work. The later theories are typically labeled *psychodynamic* because they emphasize the dynamic interplay between various components of mind, the self, personality, others, and reality. Object Relations Theory and Self Psychology are two specific theoretical perspectives that fall within the psychoanalytic/psychodynamic metatheory. (For more on psychoanalysis/psychodynamics, flip to Chapters 9 and 15.)

Behaviorism

Behaviorism emphasizes the role and influence of a person's environment and previous learning experiences to understanding behavior. Behaviorists don't traditionally focus on mental processes per se because they believe that mental processes are too difficult to observe and measure objectively.

In the framework of behaviorism, the "why" of behavior can be explained by looking at the circumstances in which it occurs and the consequences surrounding someone's actions. Classical conditioning and operant conditioning are ways of understanding behavior and they lead to behavior modification, a specific approach to modifying behavior, and helping people change that comes from the metatheory of behaviorism (see Chapter 8 for details on some behavior-modification techniques that are based on classical and operant conditioning).

Cognitive

The cognitive framework centers on the mental processing of information, including the specific functions of attention, concentration, reasoning, problem solving, and memory. Cognitive psychologists are interested in the mental plans and thoughts that guide and cause behavior and affect how people feel. Intelligence testing and information-processing theories are examples that fall within the cognitive metatheory.

Whenever someone tells you to look at the bright side, they're coming from a cognitive perspective. When something bad happens, most people feel better if the problem gets solved or the issue is resolved. But how should you feel if nothing changes? If circumstances don't change, do you have to feel bad forever? Of course not; in most cases, people can change the way they think about a situation. You can choose to look on the bright side — or at least not look solely at the downside. That's the gist of cognitive therapy.

Humanistic and existential

The humanistic and existential metatheory emphasizes that each person is unique and that humans have the ability and responsibility to make choices in their lives. I'm not a victim of circumstance! I have choices in my life. Humanists believe that a person's free choice, free will, and understanding of the meaning of events in his or her life are the most important things to study in order to understand behavior. The works of Victor Frankl, Rollo May, and Fritz Perls and the study of spirituality and religion are examples that fall within this framework.

In your own life, have you ever felt like just another nameless face in the crowd? Has your life ever seemed as if it's controlled by the winds of chance? How did it feel? Probably not very good. Feeling like you have choices — and making good choices — gives you a sense of true being and affirms your existence. That's the case with most people anyway, and psychologists who work within the humanistic and existential metatheory believe that behavior is simply a result of choice.

Sociocultural

The sociocultural approach focuses on the social and cultural factors that affect behavior. This is all about the enormous power of groups and culture on the why, how, and what of behavior and mental processes.

Tattoos and body piercings are good examples of this power. At one point in mainstream culture, people who got ink and piercings were perceived to be acting outside of the status quo, so "status quo" people weren't lined up outside the tattoo or piercing parlor. Nowadays, both are widely accepted, and even Mr. Status Quo may have a tat or piercing (or two or three).

Social and cross-cultural psychology fall within the sociocultural metatheory.

Feminism

Feminist psychology focuses on the political, economic, and social rights of women and how these forces influence the behavior of both men and women. Although feminism had some earlier influence, the feminist perspective in psychology gained momentum during the women's movement of the 1960s.

One issue in particular that has caught the attention of feminist researchers and clinicians is eating disorders. From the perspective of feminists, eating disorders are largely the consequence of excessive pressures to be thin that mass media and culture place upon females of all ages. Feminists draw attention to the fashion magazines and female role models in popular culture.

Postmodernism

The Postmodern metatheory questions the very core of psychological science, challenging its approach to truth and its focus on the individual. Postmodernists propose, for example, that in order to understand human thinking and reason, we need to look at the social and communal processes involved in thinking and reason. Reality is not something out there independently; it is something that humans, as a community, create.

Postmodernists make the argument that people in powerful positions have too much to say about what is "real" and "true" in psychology, and they advocate a *social constructionist* view of reality, which states that the concepts of "reality" and "truth" are defined, or constructed, by society. These concepts, according to this framework, have no meaning apart from the meanings that society and its experts assign to them. Narrative and constructionist theories are examples that fall within the metatheory of Postmodernism.

Working with the Biopsychosocial Model

Over the years, each of these metatheories has enjoyed its day in the sun, only to be put on the shelf when the next big thing came along. This revolving door of explanatory frameworks makes it tough to sort through the different metatheories and choose the best one for finding the answers you're seeking. Where do you begin?

One alternative to picking a metatheory is to combine several views together, thus adopting an integrationist approach. The *biopsychosocial model* of psychology represents a popular attempt at integration.

The basic idea behind this model is that human behavior and mental processes are the products of biological, psychological, and social influences. Biopsychosocialists try to find out how these influences interact to produce behavior. They believe that any explanation of behavior and mental processes that doesn't consider all three primary factors (body, mind, and environment) is incomplete.

Feeling out the role of the body

As material beings, humans are made of flesh and bones. Any discussion of thoughts, feelings, and other psychological concepts that doesn't factor in biological makeup and function, especially the brain and nervous system, ignores the fundamental facts of human existence.

Take the mind for example. Most people agree that they have a mind and that others (well, most others) have one too. But where does this mind exist? Psychologists accept that the mind exists in, or is synonymous with, the brain. The biological metatheory is integrated into the biopsychosocial model because of this component. You may say that, just as digestion is what the stomach does, "mind" is what the brain does.

Thinking about the role of the mind

When most people think about psychology, they have this aspect of the biopsychosocial model in mind (no pun intended). Thoughts, feelings, desires, beliefs, and numerous other mental concepts are addressed by the biopsychosocial model through analysis of the role of the mind.

What if this book was about botany? Would the biopsychosocial model apply? Only if you believe that plants have minds. In other words, it'd be a stretch! This highlights the uniqueness of the biopsychosocial model of psychology: The mind is central to understanding behavior and mental processes.

Behaviorists neglect the mind. Biological psychologists study the mind as the brain. By considering a person's mental state in the context of the biological systems and social environment, biopsychosocial psychologists get a broader view of a person's behavior and mental state than those who focus exclusively on one aspect of the three-part model.

Observing the role of the outside world

Brains don't work and minds don't think in a vacuum. Behavior and mental processes are embedded within a context that includes other people and things in the environment in which people live. Therefore, the social aspect of the biopsychosocial model also includes parent-child relationships, families, communities, and culture.

Other people have enormous power in shaping and influencing an individual's behavior and mental processes. If you're unsure, consider the detrimental effects that negative social events or experiences, such as physical or sexual abuse, can have on a person. Overlooking the impact of a person's interaction with family and friends is to neglect reality.

Do behaviors and mental processes vary across cultures? Let me put the question to you this way: If I only conducted research with white, middle-class, college students, can I state that my results apply to all people? Definitely not. This subject has been a hot topic in psychology over the last 30 years or so. Technological advances help make our world a smaller place and different cultures come into contact with each other more often than ever before, making a person's social life increasingly complex. Thus, just as the influence of family and friend relations is critical, it is also vital that psychologists consider cultural differences.

So it's safe to say that the culture in which an individual is raised as well as the cultures he experiences or adopts throughout life impact his behavior and mental processes.

Cultural influence needs to be addressed in psychology for at least two reasons:

- ✔ **Science seeks objectivity and truth.** Everyone is vulnerable to cultural bias, and psychologists are no exception. Therefore, psychology should try to identify the influence of culture on their own thinking, theories, and research in order to provide the most objective and complete picture of reality possible.

- ✔ **Accuracy depends on the relativity of truth in a specific culture.** So, just because research with Americans shows that using baby talk to communicate with infants stunts the growth of mature speech, this doesn't mean that these findings hold true in other countries.

Resolving the Nature versus Nurture Debate

Consider professional athletes, those elite performers who are lucky enough to get paid to play games for a living. How much luck do you think is really involved? A common misconception about professional, elite athletes is that their natural raw talent accounts for their success. Yet anyone who has worked with or known one of these individuals will tell you that hard work has a lot to do with his success.

So which is it? Talent or hard work? This question lies at the heart of a long-running debate within psychology; it's known as the *nature versus nurture* debate. Talent versus hard work. Inborn ability versus learning and effort.

Nature refers to the concept that behavior and mental processes are innate, inborn, and hard-wired and will unfold over time as a person develops and her genetic blueprint is revealed. *Nurture* refers to the idea that behavior and mental processes are not inborn and instead are learned from the environment in which people live.

Both perspectives have their proponents. John Locke, a 17th-century British philosopher, espoused the concept of *tabula rasa,* the "blank slate" and believed that, given the right learning experiences, a person can become anything in life. On the other side is Charles Darwin, the father of evolution and nature advocate, who believed that a person's destiny is found in his biology and genes.

A quote by John Watson, considered by some historians as the founder of behaviorism, epitomizes this perspective:

> Give me a dozen healthy infants, well-formed, and my own specified world to bring them up in and I'll guarantee to take any one at random and train him to become any type of specialist I might select — doctor, lawyer, artist, merchant-chief, and, yes, even beggarman and thief, regardless of his talents, penchants, tendencies, abilities, vocations, and race of his ancestors. I am going beyond my facts and I admit it, but so have the advocates of the contrary and they have been doing it for many thousands of years.
>
> — John B. Watson, *Behaviorism,* 1930

Most modern psychologists consider this debate over. The simple answer is that both nature and nurture impact a person's behavior and level of success. This means that making sense of what people do and why they do it is ultimately accomplished only by investigating and understanding the relative contributions of innate biological influences and learned environmental influences.

Branching Off

Fundamentally, psychologists are scientists who are armed with metatheory, the biopsychosocial model, research, and data as they go about their business. There are three main types of psychologists:

- ✔ **Experimental psychologists** spend the majority of their time conducting research and teaching, and they often work in academic settings. Experimental psychology covers a wide range of topics, but individual researchers typically have a specialty such as social psychology or developmental psychology.

- ✔ **Applied psychologists** directly apply research findings and psychological theory to everyday settings and problems. Applied psychologists work in a wide variety of settings, such as business, government, education, and even sports. Popular areas of applied psychology include Industrial/Organizational Psychology, Forensic Psychology, and Military Psychology.

- ✔ **Clinical psychologists** study, diagnose, and treat psychological problems.

Of course, some psychologists fit in more than one of these categories, for example, clinical psychologists conducting research.

The American Psychological Association states that in order for an individual to be considered a psychologist, he or she must possess a doctoral degree (a PhD, PsyD, or EdD, for example), and although requirements may vary from country to country, this is a generally accepted standard in much of the world as well. And nearly all US states require the individual to obtain a license to practice psychology, which typically involves taking an intensive licensing exam. In the United Kingdom, the British Psychological Society requires doctoral-level training in order to practice as a clinical psychologist, and practitioners are regulated by the Health and Care Professions Council.

Considering ethics

Human conduct is guided by codes of behavior known as *ethics*. Simply put, ethics refers to the prescribing of *right* behavior and the proscribing of *wrong* behavior. In addition to psychologists being guided by the principles of science, they are also guided by their own code of ethics, their own understanding of right and wrong behavior.

The *American Psychological Association (APA;* visit its website, www.APA.org*)* is the largest organization in the world representing psychology as a profession. Other countries, including the UK, have their own professional bodies, with similar regulatory frameworks. The mission of the APA is to advance the field of psychology and to benefit society. The APA's *Ethical Principles of Psychologists and Code of Conduct* is the ethical rule book for psychologists. The main components of this rulebook are the "General Principles" and specific "Ethical Standards." The Ethical Standards are numerous and cover topics ranging from resolution of ethical dilemmas to competence, education and training, and therapy.

Although all the ethical standards are important, the one that is often considered tantamount is the ethical principle of *confidentiality* — that information of a research participant or therapy client information is kept private and there are limits on how and when it can be disclosed to a third party. The APA's code is enforceable for members of the association, and a breach of the code can result in expulsion from the association. Most state licensing boards in the United States have adopted the APA's code as their guide and standard as well and can enforce compliance through various forms of disciplinary action including revoking licenses.

Generally speaking, the code of ethics is shaped by several overarching principles that compel psychologists to act in the best interest of the people they are working with or for (for example, clients, patients, students, or research subjects) and to avoid any harm. They are expected to act responsibly and with best practices in mind, with honesty and integrity. Basic human rights and dignity should be respected and justice should be preserved and pursued.

Seeking Truth

It seems that I've always been looking for *the* truth. When I was in college, I frequented a little bookstore near campus that specialized in spiritual, philosophical, and popular-psychology books. At least once a week, I would peruse the shelves looking for something interesting. The books were arranged by topic: metaphysics, Eastern wisdom, Western wisdom, Buddhism, Taoism, Judaism, Islam, Christianity, new age, channeling, and so on. I read books from every section. I was searching for some kind of ultimate truth, some kind of answer.

One day, I realized that I had sampled works from every section in this bookstore, but I still wasn't satisfied. Then, I had a strange thought: This bookstore is full of opinions! How was I supposed to find the answers or the truth when I was only getting opinions? Many of the books contained testimonials, logical arguments, and stories, but very little, if any, evidence or proof. If I questioned something, I simply had to take an author's word for it and trust it was true. But they couldn't all be right because some authors contradicted or criticized others. So who *was* right?

I guess I'm just one of those people who needs proof. It would be an exaggeration to say that I'm finding all the answers in psychology, but, as a field, psychology makes a serious effort to establish the truth of its claims with proof, or *empirical evidence,* which comes from applying the *empirical method,* an approach to truth that uses observation and experiment.

Psychology, as the scientific study of human behavior and mental processes, uses the empirical method. It relies on data and information obtained from research, experimentation, observation, and measurement. The empiricist motto is *Show me the data.* This is not to deny the importance of theory. But theory is insufficient as a working position for reliable psychologists.

Psychologists act responsibly when they are working with empirical evidence and less responsibly when not. These scientists are expected to base their work on solid data and information, not opinion.

From an empirical perspective, just because a psychologist says something doesn't make it true. A psychologist is compelled to base her claims on empirical evidence gathered from research and statistical analysis. Is it really worth paying for a psychologist's services to treat depression or a phobia, for example, if what she is saying and doing is just based on her opinion? What makes her the expert? You expect professionals to possess a credible amount of specific knowledge about their area of expertise, and this knowledge and expertise should be based on empirical evidence.

The authority of these experts is maintained through the ways in which they know and investigate their subject matter.

Words like *knowledge* and *truth* can be tricky sometimes. Knowing where psychologists' knowledge comes from is an important first step in learning about psychology. In this section, I explore the different ways that psychologists gather evidence and try to substantiate the truth of their claims and knowledge. Specifically, I describe scientific research and theory development, the two primary tools psychologists use to establish expertise in human behavior and mental processes.

Applying the scientific method

Most everyone has an opinion about the behavior and mental processes of others and ourselves. "She left you because you're emotionally unavailable." "If you don't express yourself, it just stays bottled up inside." We're full of answers to the why, how, and what questions regarding people. But how do we really know that not talking about feelings leads to bottling them up? I may think that not expressing feelings allows them to drift away like clouds on a windy day. Who's right? You may be thinking that it doesn't matter, but we've got this whole group of psychologists who claim to be experts on these matters. On what grounds can they make this claim to expertise?

Psychologists strive to maintain their expertise and knowledge through the use of three forms of knowledge acquisition or ways of knowing:

- **Authority:** Utilized to transmit information, usually in a therapy setting or the education and training process. Patients and students don't have time to go out and research everything that they're told. They have to take someone's word for it at some point.

- **Rationalism/logic:** Used to create theories and hypotheses. If things don't make logical sense, they probably won't make sense when researchers use the scientific method to investigate them.

- **Scientific method:** Used as the preferred method of obtaining information and investigating behavior and mental processes. Psychologists implement the scientific method through a variety of different techniques.

Let me be perfectly clear: Not everything that psychologists do, talk about, and believe is based on scientific research. A lot of stuff is based on the authority of well-known personalities in the field. Other knowledge is based on clinical experience without any systematic investigation. A good-sized chunk of information that's out there is also purely theoretical, but it makes sense on rational or logical grounds.

The vast majority of psychologists prefer to use the scientific method when seeking truth because it's seen as a fair and impartial process. When I do a research study, I'm expected to outline exactly what I'm doing and what it is I claim to be looking for. That way, if people want to try to prove me wrong, they can repeat my work, step by step, and see if they get the same results. If knowledge is based on authority alone, I can never be sure that the information I receive is unbiased and trustworthy. When the scientific method is in place, a theory that doesn't match the empirical results experienced in a research study is labeled inaccurate. Time for a new theory!

Scientists should never change their experimental data to match their original theory; that's cheating!

Developing a good theory

A *theory* is a set of related statements about a set of objects or events (the ones being studied) that explains how these objects or events are related. Knowing this is important because a significant amount of psychological knowledge is based on theory. Theories perform two main functions: They combine what is already known into a simpler package of knowledge and they help psychologists plan future investigations: Theories *summarize* and *guide*.

Theories and hypotheses are similar but not exactly the same thing. Psychologists test theories by studying their logical implications. Hypotheses are specific predictions based on these implications. You can add new information to theories, and you can use existing theories to generate new ones.

Not every theory is a good theory. In order for a theory to be good, it must meet three criteria:

- ✔ **Parsimony:** It must be the simplest explanation possible that still explains the available observation.
- ✔ **Precision:** It must make precise, not overly large or vague, statements about reality.
- ✔ **Testability:** It must lend itself to scientific investigation. There must be some way to show that the theory can be wrong. It is easy to collect more information consistent with one's theory. It is braver to be a scientist: to examine situations that may prove one's theory wrong.

Researching Matters

Psychologists use two broad categories of research when they want to scientifically evaluate a theory: descriptive research and experimental research. In this section, I describe these approaches and dig into matters related to statistics, understanding cause and effect in correlational studies, and the fascinating placebo effect.

Understanding descriptive research

Descriptive research consists of observation and the collection of data without trying to manipulate any of the conditions or circumstances being observed. It's a passive observation of the topics being investigated.

Descriptive studies are good for developing new theories and hypotheses and are often the first step for a researcher investigating things that haven't been studied much. However, they don't help much if you're interested in cause and effect relationships.

If I'm only interested in the content of bus-stop conversations, I may video-tape people talking to each other at a bus stop and analyze the video. But, if I want to know what causes people to talk about certain subjects at bus stops, I should conduct an experiment.

Doing experimental research

Experimental research involves the control and manipulation of the objects and events being investigated in order to get a better idea of the cause and effect relationships between the objects or events.

Say I have a theory about bus-stop conversations called the "five-minute or more rule" that states, "Strangers will engage in conversation with each other only after having been in each other's presence for five or more minutes." My hypothesis is, "After five minutes, apparent strangers will engage in a conversation beyond the simple pleasantries and greetings afforded to strangers." That is, I am hypothesizing that after strangers at a bus stop have been there for five minutes, they will start having a conversation. How can I test my hypothesis?

I can just hang out at a bus stop and watch to see if it happens. But how do I know that my five-minute-or-more rule is behind my observations? I don't. It maybe any number of things. This is a problematic issue in research I like to call the z-factor. A *z-factor* is something affecting the hypothesis that I am unaware of or not accounting for. It is an extraneous variable that I need to control in order to have confidence in my theory. Some possible z-factors in the bus-stop study may be culture, age, and time of day. Good research studies try to eliminate z-factors or extraneous variables by controlling for their influence and factoring them out of the explanation.

A descriptive or observational study won't account for z-factors, so instead I set up an experiment in which *I* approach people at bus stops and try a variety of things to test my hypothesis. I may go up and try to talk to someone after two minutes. I may wait for ten minutes. I may conduct studies during a thunderstorm or while dressed in particular ways, and I would try to prove my hypothesis wrong! I seek to find that people have conversations at bus stops before five minutes. If this is the case, then the five-minute rule is inaccurate. The more often I fail to prove my five-minute-or-more rule wrong, the more it deserves my confidence.

This is confusing. Why would I try to disprove my hypothesis instead of just proving it right? In any scientific investigation, I can never really prove a hypothesis true. Instead, I set out to disprove the opposite of my hypothesis. For example, people once thought the earth was flat. Everything observed at that time was consistent with this idea. However, someone came along and provided evidence that disputed this idea, which showed the flaw in the thinking. If I have a hypothesis and I keep finding evidence for it, I can be more and more confident in my hypothesis but never really know for sure. But if I can find just one example that contradicts my hypothesis, then this casts doubt on my hypothesis. If I say all swans are white, what happens when I find one black swan? The notion that all swans are white is false!

Measuring one, measuring all with statistics

Good psychology is based on solid theory and good data, whether the data is obtained through observation or experimentation. And psychology claims to make statements about all people. That is, psychologists claim that their research applies to people in general most of the time. They seek the truth as it applies to all people. But without conducting research on everyone on Earth, how can psychologists possibly make this claim?

A branch of mathematics called *statistics* comes riding in on a white horse to enable a psychologist to make claims about humanity based on studies and research conducted on only a few dozen or a couple hundred people. After a theory is developed, the scientific method dictates that that theory then be put to the test, either through observation or experimentation. Again, we run into the problem of not being able to observe or experiment with everyone and this is where statistics helps out.

Statistics is concerned with the rules of data collection and analysis. Generally, two types of statistical analyses are used in psychology, descriptive and inferential:

- **Descriptive statistics** refer to the direct numerical measurement of characteristics of a *population* such as how many of something there are, what the average number of some phenomenon is, or what the range of a particular value of something is. I am describing what is there, but not going beyond the data. If I conduct descriptive statistics on all swans to test my hypothesis that all swans are white, I would have to describe every swan. Formally, a *population* is defined as a well-defined, complete collection of things, objects, and so on. A descriptive analysis requires a description of the entire swan population.

> ✔ **Inferential statistics** comes to the rescue when I can't measure all swans, because this approach allows me to measure a *sample* of swans, a subset of the swan population, and then make inferences or estimates about the population as a whole from the sample that was drawn.
>
> Inferential statistics solves the measurement dilemma as long, of course, as you follow some basic rules such as *randomization* and appropriate *sample size.*

Randomization allows researchers to make inferences about a population based on the way a sample is chosen. Every member of the population must have the same chance of being in the sample.

Collecting a random sample ensures that the population is well represented. If you don't randomly choose the people to measure, then you can fall prey to *sampling bias,* choosing in a way so that some members of the population are less likely to be included than others. Sampling bias prevents you from being able to make statements about an entire population.

This issue often comes up in the use of polls during election season. A pollster claims that a result from measuring a sample extends to the population of likely voters, and critics are quick to point out that the sample consisted of 20- to 25-year-old graduate students at a liberal arts college in the Northwest. Is this a representative sample of likely voters?

Another key ingredient to ensuring that your sample is representative of the population is *sample size,* the number or *n* of individuals in your sample. Certainly the larger the sample the better because you get closer to measuring the population more directly and less inference is required. Of course, the size of your sample, your *n*, is determined by logistics and practicality so you typically have to settle for something much smaller than anything approaching the total population.

This brings up a pet peeve for psychologists, and scientists in general, known as the "N of One" problem. Everyone gets advice and information from friends about dieting and nutrition. My buddy tried the "caveman diet" and swears he lost 40 lbs. My officemate was on the "cupcake" diet and lost 20 lbs. My cousin was on the "carbs only" diet and gained 100 lbs. These people are offering data from their own experience. However, they have only sampled one individual from the population, themselves. They have a sample size of one. So, from a statistical perspective, how likely is it that their sample represents the population as a whole? Not likely at all. Correspondingly, this is why most people are more likely to trust advice if the same data comes from multiple people.

Relating variables: Correlation versus causation

A *variable* is the thing, characteristic, behavior, or mental process that is being measured or observed. Psychologists are interested in how variables relate, that is how do the things that are measured affect, impact, or alter each other? How does child abuse affect school performance? How does work stress affect depression? How does obsessive thinking affect relationships? In research, there are two types of variables, *independent* and *dependent*. A *dependent variable* is the thing that is impacted or altered as a function of the independent variable. The *independent variable* impacts the dependent variable as it changes.

My pulse and heart rate go way up when I am involved in a near-miss car accident situation. The dependent variable is my heart rate. The independent variable is the near miss. So, the near miss *causes* my heart rate to go up. This is a *causal relationship*. The value of the dependent variable is directly caused or influenced by the independent variable.

Does that mean that if two variables are related that there is a causal relationship? No, sometimes variables can be involved in a non-causal manner known as a *correlation* or a correlational relationship. A *correlation* exists between two variables when the value of one is related to the value of the other but not necessarily in a causal manner. For example, a semifamous correlation is that the crime rate tends to be higher in the summer months. So, there *is* a relationship between heat and crime rate; when one is high, the other is too. But does that mean that hot weather *causes* crime to go up? Not necessarily, it can be rather that youth and adolescents have more free time on their hands and therefore get into more trouble and commit more crime. This is conjecture of course and is just to prove the point that simply because hot weather and crime are related does not mean that one causes the other to happen. Correlation, not causation.

Doing nothing is something: The placebo effect

Psychologists want to test the impact of independent variables on dependent variables. They may want to test the impact of a new medication (independent variable) on levels of anxiety (dependent variable). This can be done by comparing people with anxiety who get the medication with those who do not. If anxiety goes down (or up), then maybe the medication is helping (or making things worse). This is considered a simple experimental and control group approach. An experimental group is the group that is getting the independent variable, and the control group is not; it is getting nothing in essence.

This is a solid experimental approach but there is another variation of this approach that is often used to help make the impact of the independent variable stand out more. This is done by using a *placebo group* in addition to the control group. A *placebo* is a decoy variable of sorts, a fake independent variable that is not expected to have an impact on the dependent variable, but the person in the study thinks it is an actual treatment or independent variable. Of course, some psychologists fit in more than one of these categories, for example, clinical psychologists conducting research.

From the preceding anxiety example, there would then be three groups, the medication group (independent variable group), the no-medication group (control group), and the placebo medication group (another control group). So, if at the end of the experiment the findings are that the medication group's anxiety went down substantially, we can conclude the medication worked right? This can be said only in contrast to the no-medication group. But with the placebo group, another level of confidence exists because sometimes in studies like this both the independent variable and the placebo group show change. That would shed doubt on the trustworthiness of the finding from the independent variable group. But if the independent variable group shows change and *neither* the control group nor the placebo group showed change, we can be that much more confident in that finding.

What is interesting about this, however, is that the placebo group quite often shows change or improvement. This is known as the *placebo effect,* when an experimental effect is related to the presence of the placebo. For example, it is amazing how often a sugar pill (placebo) produces reductions in anxiety in experimental subjects. This truly fascinating phenomenon is one that scientists from all fields are trying to learn more about but have not quite figured out yet.

The rest of this book introduces you to various theories and research. There's a lot of stuff in here! Because psychology is about people, some people may argue that everything about people is psychology. I couldn't write a book about everything. This is not *Everything About People For Dummies.* In establishing a way to decide what to put in the book and what not to, I used scientific research and theory as my measuring rod. The information you find in this book is considered part of legitimate psychological science and theory.

Part II
Picking Your Brain (And Body)

Check out more about how psychology can be applied to help in different corners of society in the free article "Applying Psychology for a Better World" at www.dummies.com/extras/psychology.

In this part...

- ✔ Explore the basics of biological psychology, including coverage of the basic structures of the nervous system and the important role that biology plays in psychological knowledge.

- ✔ Navigate the varieties of conscious awareness and its important role in psychology.

- ✔ Find out how you touch, see, hear, and sense the world and how the senses shape our perception of the world around us.

- ✔ Take a glimpse at psychopharmacology and the ways chemistry can help alleviate some psychological problems.

- ✔ Discover how to change the brain without neurosurgery.

Chapter 3

Hardware, Software, and Wetware

. . . .

. . . .

*P*sychology can seem pretty abstract, seemingly having more in common with philosophy than biology. In this book, I introduce you to all kinds of psychological concepts — thoughts, feelings, beliefs, and personalities among them. But have you ever wondered *where* all of these things exist? If I need to find a thought or feeling, where do I look?

One place that seems logical to look for these psychological concepts is inside the human mind. But where is a person's mind? The quick response for many people: It's inside my skull, in my brain! So, I wonder, if you opened someone's skull and could gaze upon the brain, would you see various kinds of thoughts, feelings, and other psychological stuff tucked away in there? Definitely not. You'd see a wrinkled and convoluted mass of grayish-pinkish-whitish tissue. There are no visible thoughts, feelings, or beliefs. Yet you know they exist because you experience them every day.

The question of where the mind, the home of psychological concepts, exists is an age-old philosophical question. Is the mind in the brain? Is the mind somewhere other than the brain? Are the brain and the mind the same thing? Most scientists today hold the position that the mind and the brain are one and the same. Scientists taking this position, known as *monism*, believe that the key to understanding the human mind, with all of its psychological concepts, lies in understanding the body, specifically the nervous system.

Psychologist Neil Carlson states, "What we call the 'mind' is a consequence of the functioning of the human body and its interactions with the environment." This is a powerful idea — the key to unlocking the mysteries of such psychological concepts as thinking and feeling lies in a thorough understanding of biology.

The idea that all of human psychology can be reduced to biology is known as *biological reductionism.* This idea seems to insult the esteemed sense of free will, self-awareness, and consciousness. I mean, how can all this complex stuff going on inside my mind be reduced to a hunk of flesh resting between my ears? If you feel this way, maybe you're not a *biological reductionist.* But for the sake of this chapter, I'm going to be one. I focus on human biology as the pathway to understanding human psychology.

In this chapter, you're introduced to the major components of biological psychology, including related body systems, the brain, and the chemical messengers of the brain. The role of genetics in understanding behavior and mental processes is covered as well. The chapter closes with a discussion of medications and newer forms of brain-based treatments for mental disorders.

Believing in Biology

People haven't always believed that human behavior and mental processes are the consequences of biology. In the times of ancient Greeks and Romans, human behavior was seen as the consequence of supernatural forces, namely the whims and passions of the gods. But somewhere along the line, suspicion grew that maybe the human body had something to do with it. Where would such a radical idea come from?

The history of research in this area is long, but at the core of all the research is a very simple observation: Changes in a person's biology result in changes in her behavior and mental processes.

Take alcohol consumption, for example. No question that people act differently when under the influence of alcohol. They may flirt, dance like an idiot, get emotional and sentimental, or even become angry and violent. Alcohol has a chemical effect on the brain; it alters the biology of the drinker's brain. It goes something like this:

Alcohol consumption→chemical effect on brain→thinks he's Don Juan

What about more serious changes in biology like brain damage? People who suffer from brain damage can exhibit drastic changes in their personality and thinking. They may go from being very organized to very messy. Or a once very laid-back, easygoing person may fly into a rage at the slightest frustration. They may have difficulty with memory or understanding.

I think you probably have an intuitive understanding that what goes on within your body has an effect on your behavior and mental processes. *Biological psychologists* are a group of psychologists who have extended this intuitive belief and these casual observations, using techniques and methods of modern science to investigate the idea that changes in biology lead to changes in psychology.

Although a lot of this seems logical, you may be thinking that there must be more to you than biology. And I say, that's just the dualist in you acting up. Try not to struggle with it too much, at least while you read this chapter. Even if you think you're more than just cells and molecules, you can still benefit from the research of biological psychology.

Did you read about the *biopsychosocial model* in Chapter 2? (If not, you may want to check it out. Trust me — it's a good chapter.) That model proposes that human psychology is a function of the three important levels of understanding:

- ✔ The biological level
- ✔ The psychological level
- ✔ The social level

This chapter focuses on the biological level, and the remainder of the book focuses on the other two. But you need to find out how the three levels interact — that is, how biology influences psychology, how psychology influences biology, and so on — to really get a handle on behavior and mental processes.

A useful metaphor for describing how the different levels interact is the modern computer. You may know that a computer has at least two functional components: hardware and software. The hardware consists of the actual physical components of the computer: the processor, hard drive, wires, CD-ROM, and various other components. The software includes the operating system, a word-processing program, and various other tools you use to actually work on a computer.

In this metaphor, the hardware of a computer represents the biological level of understanding. This is the physical body, specifically the nervous system. The software represents the psychological level, and the interface between the user and the software represents the social level. The hardware is useless without software, and vice versa. So, see, even if you're not a monist, you can still respect the role that biology (hardware) plays in psychology (software).

The word "wetware" in the title of this chapter represents the actual physical substance of the brain. Most people don't have "hard" ware in their brains (wires, plastic, silicon, and so on); instead, they have "wet" ware (neurons, tissue, and chemicals, for example). To stay consistent in my metaphor, I really focus on the wetware level of psychology in this chapter. Specifically, I introduce the wetware of the human nervous system as well as the endocrine system, genetics, and medications.

Recognizing the Body's Control Room

The human nervous system consists of two large divisions: the *peripheral nervous system (PNS)* and the *central nervous system (CNS)*. The CNS includes the brain and spinal cord. The PNS includes the nerves outside the CNS; they are in the rest (the periphery) of the body.

The basic building blocks of the nervous system are nerves, neurons, and neurotransmitters and glial cells. The nerves are, essentially, bundles of neurons, like a box of spaghetti is a bundle of individual strips of pasta. The neurons are individual nerve cells. Usually, they receive signals from other neurons, evaluate those signals, and then transmit new signals to other parts of the nervous system.

Electrical changes allow signals to be transmitted within a neuron: Because these electrical changes involve the movement of chemical ions, the transmission system is called an electrochemical system. Neurotransmitters are chemicals that play a critical role in transmitting signals between neurons. The glial cells are cells within the nervous system that play a variety of support roles for the neurons; they protect neurons from damage, repair them when they are damaged, and remove damaged or dead tissue when it can't be repaired ("taking out the trash").

The nervous system is a living part of the body and, therefore, has the same basic needs as any other body part; it needs fuel and immune protection. The components of the nervous system stay alive and healthy by the circulatory system and other regulatory body functions. The specifics of the support systems for each division of the nervous system are described in more detail within each division's corresponding section in this chapter.

If you've studied any physics, chemistry, or biology, you may remember that the building blocks of life begin with atoms (operating under the laws of physics); atoms are grouped in particular ways to make up molecules that then form compounds. Compounds combine to create cells, and cells build tissue, and eventually an entire person is standing there! So if you really want to be a reductionist, you can just study physics and do away with all other branches of science. Or, you can look at human behavior and mental processes from a molecular level. This is the focus of the field of *neurobiology*.

Typically, however, biological psychology begins at the cellular level of study. Two types of cells appear in the nervous system, *supporting cells* and *neurons*. In this section, you discover the main divisions of the human nervous system, the brain, and how the brain is organized.

Tiptoeing into the periphery

Of the two divisions of the body's nervous system, think of the peripheral nervous system (PNS) as a system of connections that make it possible for the brain and spinal cord to communicate with the rest of the body. Two sets of nerves are involved:

- **Spinal nerves:** These nerves carry neural signals both to and from the spinal cord. Sensory nerves carry information from the body to the central nervous system: For example, they carry signals from sensors in your foot when somebody steps on your foot. Motor nerves carry signals from the central nervous system to the body; they cause the muscles in your limbs to move (raising your hand).

- **Cranial nerves:** These nerves are involved in the muscular (motor) and sensory processes, except that they are connected directly to the brain itself, not to the spinal cord. Cranial nerves support functions occurring in your face and head, including seeing and hearing, blinking and speaking.

In addition to these two sets of nerves, the PNS contains a subsystem known as the *autonomic nervous system (ANS).* The autonomic nervous system helps regulate two specific types of muscles (smooth and cardiac) and the glands in our body. The ANS is involved in automatic, or involuntary, action. Bodily organs, reflexive muscle contractions, and even the dilation of our pupils are all automatic behaviors governed by the ANS. There are two very important divisions of the ANS:

- **Sympathetic nervous system (SNS):** The sympathetic branch of the ANS is involved in energetic activation of the body when it needs high levels of energy. For example, when you are confronted with a life-threatening situation, your sympathetic nervous system kicks in and gives you the energy to either take on the challenge or flee the situation.

- **Parasympathetic nervous system:** The parasympathetic branch of the ANS deactivates the SNS after it has been engaged. This action is sometimes called the *relaxation response* because the activity of the SNS is relaxed, or turned off, and then returns to normal functioning.

Moving to the center

The CNS consists of both the brain and the spinal cord. Although the spinal cord is critical, the focus of this section is on the brain, which is considered to be the underlying physical foundation for psychological functioning. It is, literally, the command center for behavior. The brain, with billions of cells and sophisticated networks, is among the most complex biological structures known to scientists.

Throughout the history of studying the brain, many attempts have been made to understand exactly what it is made of and how it works and is organized. So far, the simplest way to think of the brain (the "city") is in terms of these different levels:

- **Structural:** Basic anatomical divisions of the brain, identified by their major functions (the "neighborhoods")
- **Network:** The pathways that connect different parts of the brain and allow them to interact (the "roads")
- **Neural:** Cellular and microcellular functions (the "houses and furniture")

Essentially, everything people do involves the brain. What happens, though, when some part of the brain gets damaged? The behavior and mental processes associated with the damaged portion of the brain are adversely affected, which affects related functions. Clinical neuropsychologists are particularly interested in the behavioral and mental consequences of brain injuries.

The brain can be damaged in numerous ways:

- **Closed-head injuries:** These injuries occur when someone sustains a blow to the head but the skull is not penetrated. A common form of closed-head injury is a *contrecoup* injury — the injury occurs to the part of the brain opposite from where the individual was struck. For example, if you're hit in the back of the head, this could cause the front of your brain to hit the inside of your forehead, and you may sustain damage to your frontal lobe, thus affecting your organizational and planning abilities. Even though the skull is not broken, serious damage can occur if the brain bleeds or swells resulting in pressure and additional damage beyond the site of injury.

- **Open-head injuries:** These injuries occur when the skull is either penetrated or fractured; both closed-head and open-head injuries can lead to serious brain damage.

- **Other brain disorders:** Degenerative diseases such as Alzheimer's can produce brain damage in the form of atrophied (for example, a reduction in size or loss of cells) brain tissue and cellular death. Strokes (a blood clot or bleed in the brain) and other vascular accidents also can result in brain damage by denying parts of the brain blood and oxygen, causing cellular death.

Running Like a Well-Oiled Machine: Body Systems

Structurally, there are three main divisions of the brain: *forebrain, midbrain,* and *hindbrain.* Each of these divisions consists of many substructures that are involved in various behaviors and activity.

The brain is a complex, integrated system. All of its components work together to produce the complexity of human behavior. The concept of *localization* refers to the idea that there are specific parts of the brain for specific components of behaviors. Various parts work together to produce vision, hearing, speech, and so forth. Neurological techniques such as post-mortem brain examination, CT (co-axial tomography) scans, MRI (magnetic resonance imaging) scans, and PET (positron-emission tomography) scans have been used to identify and explore these systems.

Forebrain

The human forebrain is involved in a wide range of mental processes, including the sensing, perceiving, and processing of information. It is also involved in thinking, problem solving, organizing, and language functions.

The human forebrain consists of four sections:

✔ **Cerebral cortex:** If you think of the brain as a mushroom, with a top and a stalk, then the cerebral cortex is the top of the mushroom. It's divided into two halves, called *cerebral hemispheres* (the left and the right — pretty creative, I know). These halves are connected by a bundle of nerve fibers known as the *corpus collosum.* Without the corpus collosum, the halves wouldn't be able to communicate with each other.

Figure 3-1 shows the four major divisions of the cerebral cortex and their corresponding functions:

- **Frontal lobe:** Planning, organizing, coordinating, and controlling movements (in an area known as the primary motor cortex), reasoning, and overall monitoring of the thinking process

- **Parietal lobe:** Sensation, spatial and somatosensory (bodily) awareness

- **Temporal lobe:** Hearing, language, and other verbal activity

- **Occipital lobe:** Vision

Figure 3-1:
The lobes of
the cerebral
cortex.

✓ **Limbic system:** Located on the underside of the mushroom top (the cerebral cortex), the limbic system is involved in learning, memory, emotional behavior, and mating or reproduction.

✓ **Basal ganglia:** This part of the brain is involved in controlling movement.

✓ **Thalamus:** This "neural switchboard" is a relay station for the different parts of the brain. However, it is more than simply a connection. It analyzes inputs to construct organized outputs.

✓ **Hypothalamus:** The hypothalamus takes part in the control of the endocrine system and works with the limbic system to control behaviors such as aggression, eating, protection, and mating.

Midbrain

The midbrain is involved in the auditory and visual processes and in motor control.

The midbrain consists of the following divisions and their respective areas of responsibility:

✓ **Tectum:** Auditory and visual systems

✓ **Tegmentum:** Sleep, arousal, attention, muscle tone, and reflexes

Hindbrain

The hindbrain is involved in the autonomic functions of the body such as heart rate and breathing as well as the coordination of movement.

The hindbrain includes two divisions with assigned duties:

- **Cerebellum:** Motor movement and its coordination
- **Pons:** The bridge connecting the cerebellum to the rest of the brain
- **Medulla:** Vital functions of the body such as the cardiovascular system, breathing, and the movement of skeletal muscles

Finding Out About Cells and Chemicals

At the neural level of the brain is what many brain scientists consider to be the fundamental unit of the brain and the nervous system: the *neuron*, a specialized cell that provides the foundation for brain functioning: communication among nerve cells. Actually, there is another important type of cell in the brain: the *glial cells*. Glial cells provide the basic structure to the nervous system and nourish the neurons. But neurons are the star of the brain show according to most scientists.

A neuron is considered the information cell; it's involved in the processing and storage of information. Neurons contain the following parts:

- **Soma:** The cell body of the neuron containing the nucleus and supportive structures of the cell, including the mitochondria
- **Dendrite:** Projections from the cell body that receive information from other neurons
- **Axon:** The nerve fiber that conducts the electrical impulse
- **Terminal button:** The end of the axon involved in neurotransmitter release and signaling to other neurons

The center of action in the brain happens at the cellular level, when a neuron is activated and fires. Neurons become activated by input from other neurons, which in turn impacts the other neurons in a given network. Simply put, when information from the environment (or inside the brain itself from other neurons) comes into the brain through the sensory organs and activates a particular neuron (or, more often, a set of neurons), an *action potential* is created.

Action potentials are the movement of electrochemical energy through a neuron toward its terminal button, toward other neurons. Something called the *all-or-none law* states that neurons are either "on" or "off"; they are either firing an action potential or not. After a neuron is activated, it fires. If it's not activated: no action, no fire!

Some people consider the firing of a neuron (the action potential) to be an electrical process; others say it's a chemical process. In essence, however, it's both. The action potential consists of electrical energy that's created and activated by the exchange of positive and negative chemical ions between the inside and the outside of the neuron. It's electrochemical.

When a neuron is not firing, it is considered to be in the state of a *resting potential* and its electrical charge is more negative on the inside relative to the outside. There are more negatively charged ions inside than outside. But when a neuron receives a signal from another neuron, gates in the cell *membrane* (its covering) open and positive ions rush into the negatively charged inside of the cell. Chemistry and physics point out that positive charges move toward negative charges; they attract! So as the inside of the cell spikes to the positive, the action potential is created and the neuron "fires"! In many ways, the action potential is an electrical disturbance in the axon that travels along the axon, like the fire moves down a lit fuse of a firecracker.

When the action potential occurs, the cell cannot fire again for a short period of time. During this refractory period, small pumps in the cell membrane work to reset the neuron by moving positive ions back out of the cell, returning the chemical balance of the neuron to its original state to prepare for another round of action.

In this section, you discover more about how a neural signal travels from one neuron to another in a process called *synaptic transmission*.

Crossing the divide

As an action potential speeds through a neuron toward its terminal button, how does it propagate that signal to other neurons in the network? Before I can answer, you need to know that neurons don't actually connect to each other in a physical sense. There are gaps between them known as *synapse*, spaces between axon terminals of one neuron (the neuron sending the signal) and the dendrites of the next neuron (the neuron receiving the signal); this is where inter-neuronal communication happens through chemical messengers called *neurotransmitters*. Figure 3-2 shows a neuron and a synapse. Although they are only millionths of an inch apart, the sending neuron throws its "message in a bottle" into the sea-napse, where it drifts to the other shore (the receiving dendrite). The message says, "Please hear me; please fire!" Dramatic stuff!

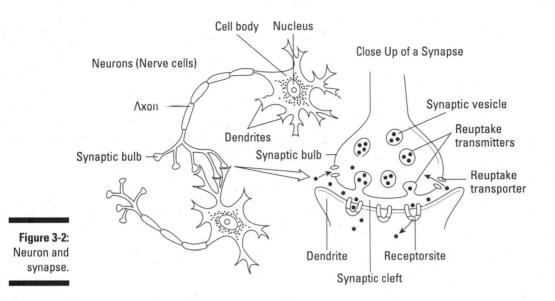

Figure 3-2:
Neuron and
synapse.

Neurotransmitters are stored in the axon of the sending cell. An action potential stimulates their release into the synapse. They travel (actually drift) to a receiving neuron in which specialized docks known as *receptor sites* are present. Different shaped neurotransmitters have different docks.

Basically, neurotransmitters have one of two effects; they either *excite* the receiving neuron (make it more likely to fire) or *inhibit* the receiving neuron (make it less likely to fire). Some neurotransmitters are excitatory and some are inhibitory. Whether a particular neuron fires (transmits a signal) depends on the balance between excitatory and inhibitory neurotransmitters.

Following the docking process, neurotransmitters are either broken down by enzymes or reabsorbed by the sending neurons in a process called *reuptake*. These two processes clear neurotransmitters from the synapse after they have done their job (enough, already!). This is critical to prepare the cells for the next neural communication. And neurotransmitter manipulation is a primary mechanism of action for most psychiatric medications (find information on the actions of medications in the "Understanding Psychopharmacology" section later in this chapter).

Scientists have discovered more than 100 neurotransmitters in the human brain. Many, including the following, play a major role:

- **Glutamate:** The most common excitatory neurotransmitter

- **GABA:** The most common inhibitory transmitter; involved in eating, aggression, and sleep

- **Acetylcholine:** A common neurotransmitter with multiple excitatory and inhibitory functions; involved in movement and memory

Another group of four chemically similar neurotransmitters modify behavior in many ways. These neurotransmitters are particularly important regarding psychological disorders:

- **Serotonin:** An inhibitory transmitter that is involved in balancing excitatory transmitters as well as mood, sleep, eating, and pain

- **Dopamine:** Can be either inhibitory or excitatory and is implicated in attention, pleasure and reward, and movement

- **Epinephrine:** An excitatory transmitter related to stress responses, heart rate, and blood pressure

- **Norepinephrine:** An excitatory transmitter involved in energy regulation, anxiety, and fear

Branching out

An estimated 86 billion neurons live in the human brain and form trillions of connections among themselves. So you can think of the brain as a massive collection of nodes in a well-connected network. Just exactly how information is kept and processed in the brain remains the focus of incredible amounts of neuroscience research, but here's what scientists do know.

The brain is a "massively parallel" information-processing system (flip to Chapter 6 for more about information processing). If each neuron was connected to only one other neuron, the neuron system would be considered "massively serial." Compared to electronic signals, neural signals travel very slowly (like 5–100 mph), so it is efficient to do many things at once — called *parallel processing*. Think of it like finding a person who is lost in a large national park. The search party probably doesn't stay together and follow each other on the same path (serial processing); instead, they "branch out" (parallel processing) to cover more ground in the same amount of time. Likewise, the brain, with its billions of neurons and trillions of connections, uses the branching-out method to process, store, and find information among its cells and cell clusters.

Not every neuron is connected to every other neuron, but neurons are connected to multiple others that form clusters or networks involved in particular psychological processes and behaviors. For example, if seeing a red ball activates neurons #3, 4, 192, X, A, and 56, then the network for "seeing a red ball" would be called 3-4-192-X-A-56. Neuroscience researchers are working hard to map the brain and its networks in order to connect cell clusters to respective mental functions and behavior. The International Consortium for Brain Mapping (ICBM) is one such group of scientists that is dedicated to this endeavor.

Activating brain change

Have you ever scratched your nose and noticed that your foot stopped itching? Okay, well, that's a slight stretch, but there is something called *phantom limb syndrome* in which people who have lost a limb (an arm or leg for example) continue to report feeling sensations from that limb such as pain, cold, touch, and so on. How can this be? The limb is gone so where are the sensations coming from?

In his book, *Half a Brain is Enough: The Story of Nico,* Dr. Antonio Battro tells the story of a boy named Nico who has a very significant portion of his brain surgically removed to control seizure activity (a drastic but sometimes necessary surgery for individuals with intractable seizures). However, after having that large portion of his brain removed, Nico remains relatively normal and maintains a fair amount of brain functioning — as if the brain tissue had not been removed. Why does Nico remain relatively unimpaired while working with half a brain?

Both phantom limb and Nico's brain demonstrate what brain scientists refer to as *neuroplasticity* — the notion that the brain's neural networks and connections continually reorganize. At one point in time, scientists believed that the brain's organization was "fixed," but this is simply not the case. The brain can change its size and connections throughout a person's lifetime: this ability is called *neuroplasticity*.

The ability for the brain to update itself in response to new stimulation and input represents the neurobiological foundation of learning. In phantom limb syndrome it was found that the neural networks devoted to the lost limb (arm, leg, and so on) had been co-opted by neurons and networks proximal to it such as neurons associated with sensation in the in nearby body parts. So, when the face had a sensation, the neurons that were previously associated with the lost limb were being stimulated, and other parts of the brain interpreted the sensations as coming from the limb.

In Nico's case, the functions performed by the lost brain cells from surgical removal were taken over by neighboring or other cells and networks. Other parts of the brain essentially learned how to do the functions once performed by the lost cells. In both cases, phantom limb and Nico, the brain essentially rewired itself in response to new inputs and learning experiences.

Neuroplasticity is good news for people who lose brain tissue through trauma or disease. But what about growing new brain cells? After all, new skin cells grow after a cut. Does this happen in the brain?

For many years scientists believed that it was not possible to grow new neurons or brain cells. However, research has shown that *neurogenesis* (regeneration of nerve cells) is possible in specific regions of the brain, particularly the lateral ventricles and the hippocampus. More research is being conducted to see if this process is happening in other parts of the brain as well. If neurogenesis is found to be more widespread or possible in other brain areas or if scientists can find a way to stimulate the process, manipulate it, or otherwise impact it, then there may be a great ray of sunshine for people who now suffer from diseases or trauma such as Alzheimer's, stroke, traumatic brain injury, or spinal cord injury. However, the science and research is very preliminary in this area and much more work needs to be done before such a thing is possible.

Finding Destiny with DNA

I look a lot like my father's father. But do I act like him, too? Does your personality come from your parents? Do people inherit intellect and good looks? The field of psychology known as *behavioral genetics,* the study of the role of genetics and heredity in determining mental processes and behavior, investigates these questions.

The brain influences behavior. The endocrine system influences behavior. But what about your genetic makeup? Scientists have answered this question with a resounding "yes"; genetics do matter! Research implicates genetic contributions to cognition and intelligence, personality, and even psychopathology.

Genetic contributions to psychology have been traditionally performed using *twin and adoption studies*, in which identical twins (who share a common genetic code) who've been adopted separately at birth and raised in different environments are compared for some psychological construct or disorder (such as the presence of ADHD). This testing setup allows for the control of the influence of different environments, so if the identical twins show similar findings on the construct in question, then it is deduced that it must be due primarily to their genetic similarities — DNA. Research continues to evolve, and other techniques, such as large-scale DNA sampling and gene manipulation, push the field of behavioral genetics.

Researchers are looking for *genetic markers* for particular behaviors, including disorders. A genetic marker is a gene with a known location on the human genome. Genetic markers for such disorders as autism, schizophrenia, and reading disabilities have been found. Just keep in mind that the presence of a genetic marker in a person's genome does not guarantee that he will have a particular trait or disorder; it simply increases the odds of such.

Although the complexity of behavioral genetics leaves much to be discovered, one thing is clear: genes matter. But where do these inherited traits, behaviors, and mental processes come from? How do gene-behavior relationships come about? Evolution.

Evolutionary psychology is a branch of psychology that says human psychology (behavior and mental processes) is the result of the evolutionary process of natural selection. *Natural selection* is the process by which specific genes become more or less common in a population of a species through reproduction and mating. In other words, genes that contribute to survival are more likely to be passed on than those that don't. After all, if your genes help you live long enough to pass them on to your offspring, then those genes perpetuate. If they don't, and you don't perpetuate, then your genes don't survive either.

Evolutionary biologists look at biological phenomena (such as opposable thumbs and walking upright) as adaptations that thrived. Evolutionary psychologists take the same approach with psychological phenomena such as language, memory, attention, visual perception, happiness, and so forth. Finding out how these psychological phenomena helped our ancestors adapt as a way to explain why they exist in us today is a matter of extreme interest. An evolutionary psychologist, for example, may look at attachment theory (see Chapter 10) and propose that the behaviors and mental processes underlying the mother-infant bonding process evolved over time to the state they can be observed today because these behaviors and processes enable the human species to survive.

Understanding Psychopharmacology

The use of medications in the treatment of mental disorders (such as schizophrenia and major depressive disorder) gained significant prominence over the last half of the 20th century. (For more about mental disorders see Chapter 13.) Prior to that, medications were used to a lesser extent, along with psychotherapy, psychosocial, and behavioral treatments. But advances in research and drug development led to the creation of more effective drugs, which in turn spurred an increase in their use. Hundreds of drugs have been developed that are used to target the specific symptoms of a particular mental disorder. The primary goals of pharmacotherapy are to produce improvements in behavior and thinking, alleviation of suffering, and enhancement of functioning.

Many brain systems involved in the symptoms of mental illness involve one particular neurotransmitter, and drugs used for the treatment of a particular illness are designed to affect the functioning of that specific neurotransmitter. The sleep difficulties and appetite disturbance often seen in major depressive disorder, for example, are thought to be related to the limbic system. For these symptoms, most drugs for depression target the neurotransmitter serotonin.

In this section, I describe common symptoms of and treatment for depression, schizophrenia, and anxiety, three of the better known mental disorders, pointing out various medications and their biological mechanism of action.

Easing depression

Medications that are used to treat depression are called *antidepressants*. Most antidepressants affect one or both of two neurotransmitters: *norepinephrine* and *serotonin*. Basically, there are two major classes of antidepressant medications (although there are some that don't fit in either class, such as Wellbutrin, Remeron, or Effexor) differentiated by their mechanism of action:

- ✔ **Tricyclic antidepressants:** Block the presynaptic neuron's re-absorption of mostly norepinephrine (NE). This allows for a functional "increase" in the level of NE in the synapse and prolongs the activation of the postsynaptic neuron when stimulated by NE.

- ✔ **Selective serotonin reuptake inhibitors (SSRIs):** Block the re-absorption of serotonin rather than NE and have the similar effect of prolonging activation. Some of the more popular brands of SSRIs are Prozac, Paxil, and Zoloft.

Shushing the voices

The experience of auditory hallucinations or feeling like someone is out to get you can be extremely troubling. These are common symptoms of the mental disorder schizophrenia. One of the most powerful treatments for some of the symptoms of schizophrenia is the use of *antipsychotic medications*.

Antipsychotic medications have a specific effect on the neurotransmitter dopamine. The *dopamine dysregulation hypothesis* of schizophrenia holds that the symptoms of psychosis result from disruptions in the action of dopamine in the brain. Antipsychotic medications block the postsynaptic receptor sites of dopamine. This blockage keeps dopamine from being able to activate the postsynaptic neuron and has been found to reduce the presence of psychotic symptoms substantially.

Unfortunately, antipsychotic medications, as do all medications, don't just affect the neurotransmitters in the brain areas theorized to be implicated in the disorder. Most medications also affect other brain areas and can often lead to very unpleasant side effects. Side effects associated with antipsychotic medication can include weight gain; repetitive, involuntary motor movements (known as tardive dyskinesia); or sexual dysfunction, to name just a few. The experience of these side effects often leads people to stop taking their medication, which can have serious negative consequences. This situation keeps drug researchers searching for even more selective drugs.

Relaxing

Anxiety disorders are the most common mental disorder in the United States. Millions of people suffer from intolerable worry, panic attacks, and disabling phobias. The good news is that medications can help with these symptoms.

Anxiolytic medications are drugs designed to relieve the symptoms of anxiety disorders. Psychiatrists and family physicians prescribe one class of Anxiolytics, *benzodiazepines,* quite often. Benzodiazepines affect the neurotransmitter GABA, which has a suppressing effect on the central nervous system. In other words, it slows things down in the brain.

Benzodiazepines are very effective in reducing anxiety. Unfortunately, they are also highly addictive. Benzodiazepines have a near-immediate effect and often produce sedation and an overall feeling of calmness. These feelings are highly pleasurable, and patients sometimes don't want to stop taking these medications even after their anxiety disorder has been successfully medicated. Table 3-1 gives an overview of some frequently prescribed medications.

Table 3-1	Major Medication Groups	
Medication	*Problem*	*Common Example*
Antidepressants	Depression	Prozac
	Panic disorder	Zoloft
	Obsessive-compulsive disorder	Paxil
	Insomnia	Benzodiazepines (Xanax)
	Generalized anxiety disorder	Benzodiazepines
	Panic disorder	Benzodiazepines
Antipsychotics	Schizophrenia	Haldol
	Mania	Zyprexa
Mood stabilizers	Mania	Lithium
	Bipolar disorder	Depakote
Stimulants	ADHD	Ritalin

Undergoing No-Knife Brain Surgery

Changes in biological functioning can and do result in psychological changes. Medications have a direct biological effect on the brain. Neurosurgeons lesion, excise, and cut brain tissue. But imagine a day when doctors can change your brain directly without a pill or surgery.

Dr. "Bones" McCoy of *Star Trek* used to use a device that he placed on the head of patients with neurological conditions. Using some form of energy field, the device alleviated all sorts of conditions, including brain injury and bleeding. Well, Dr. McCoy, that day has arrived!

Transcranial Magnetic Stimulation (or TMS) is a technology right out of *Star Trek*. TMS devices are placed on the head and use electromagnetic pulses to activate specific parts of the brain. This technique is being used to treat migraines, stroke symptoms, hallucinations, and even depression.

For depression, TMS stimulates the brain's frontal lobe and limbic system, parts impacted by the disorder. The medical world is excited and hopeful about the prospects of TMS as a treatment for a broad range of other disorders.

Chapter 4

Conscious Beings

- -

- -

S ince the beginning of time, human beings have been trying to alter their consciousness. For some, it may seem like a way to get in touch with a reality greater than themselves. For others, it may simply be a way to escape the harsh realities of a bad home or a meaningless job. Psychologists define *consciousness* as our current state of awareness of external and internal stimuli. A *stimulus* is anything in an environment (an event, situation, or object) that triggers a psychological response.

Being conscious is like having a light on in the brain. When the light is off, you're unconscious. Consciousness allows you to monitor yourself and your environment, giving you greater control over your actions and behaviors. But if you've stood on a busy street corner in a large city, you've realized that there's a heck of a lot going on around you at any given time. Only so much awareness is available. Consciousness has its limits. The quantity or amount of material in your awareness, along with the content of that material, defines your state of consciousness in any single moment.

In this chapter, I introduce you to consciousness, both normal and altered states. You learn about sleep, its stages, and that ever so interesting phenomenon, dreaming. Finally, you learn how consciousness can be manipulated or altered with meditation and hypnosis.

Exploring the Horizons of Awareness

Consciousness is an elusive concept. You know it's there, but it's hard to put your finger on it. My consciousness exists as my inner voice and my awareness of myself, my surroundings, and my experience. But, I'm typically not aware of numerous mental processes, bodily sensations, and things going on in my mind. For example, I don't usually hear my heart beating as I'm walking down the street, but I can hear it when I try to hear it. When I become conscious of something that I was unconscious of before, I become *aware* of it. I pay attention to it.

One of the best ways to think about the psychology of consciousness is to think about the absence of consciousness. For example, a person in a *coma* — a state of extreme unawareness or lack of consciousness — is essentially disconnected from the world around her, lacks self-awareness, cannot be roused, and exhibits no voluntary movements or behavior. She does not react to stimulation from the outside.

I once heard that the entire idea of vampires and the undead came from medieval observations of dead bodies. I don't exactly know why people were digging up dead bodies, but when they did, they found that their hair and fingernails had continued to grow. Sometimes, the bodies would utter a deep groan when someone moved them. What was going on?

Scientifically speaking, hair and nails continue to grow for a short period of time after death, and the groaning sound could have been caused by leftover air in the body's chest cavity passing over the vocal chords when the chest was compressed. But medieval grave robbers attributed life to the bodies based on these observations. They believed that the cause of these phenomena was the conscious action and deliberation of the dead person, not reflexive byproducts of physiology and anatomy.

As elusive as consciousness has been for scientists, there have been attempts to clarify understanding by classifying so-called "states" or levels of awareness based on the content, objects, or "stuff" of that awareness and also by looking at the behavior and responsiveness of a person.

Attempts to pin down consciousness include the following classifications and ways of measuring or determining the presence of consciousness:

- **Normal consciousness:** Awake, responsive to environment in speech and behavior with some fluctuations relative to concentration and attentiveness.

- **Confusion:** Atypical thinking with altered speed, clarity, and coherence, including inattentiveness and disorientation, lowered awareness of immediate environment, and distractibility, which is sometimes referred to as delirium.

- **Drowsiness and stupor:** Mental and physical activity substantially reduced, with difficulty sustaining wakefulness and/or ability to be aroused only by intense and continuous effort.

- **Coma:** Appearance of being asleep and incapable of responding to external stimuli.

✔ **Subjective experience of your own awareness:** Have you ever had a dream in which you knew you were dreaming? Really, you were aware that you were asleep. Being aware of your own awareness involves realizing or being aware that you are either awake or asleep.

✔ **Others' observations of deliberate actions:** One of the most important features of consciousness is that it mediates our behavior. Sometimes I act impulsively and reflexively; I don't think about what I'm doing, I just do it. Other times, there's a step of conscious deliberation, an act of will, before acting. In that case, I am consciously analyzing what I am going to do. Willful, or voluntary, acts are a signal of conscious awareness. Consciousness is attributed to acts of deliberation and intention. When someone does something willfully, it is assumed he is conscious.

✔ **Measurement of the brain's electrical activity:** Consciousness can be observed physiologically, in addition to behaviorally, through the measurement of brain activity. Different EEG (electroencephalogram — a special machine that measures the "brain waves" or electrophysiological activity of the brain) measurements of electrical activity in the brain correspond to different levels of observable consciousness.

Antonio Damasio, neurologist and neuroscience professor at the University of Southern California, considered by many to be the foremost authority on consciousness, says that emotions, feelings, and a sense of self are central to consciousness. He famously refers to consciousness as the "movie within the movie" of our life. Damasio's classification of consciousness is as follows:

✔ **Consciousness of the Proto-Self:** Awareness of bodily states and "here and now" moment-by-moment awareness

✔ **Consciousness of the Core-Self:** Considered "core consciousness" including a sense of "me" or "selfness," if being in the present

✔ **Consciousness of Autobiographical-Self:** Awareness of a linear timeline of the core self over time in both past and future

Planes with faces, pets with agendas

Believe it or not, children's cartoons represent a challenge of sorts to our concepts of consciousness. How? Everything in a cartoon is a conscious being — from toasters and shoes to trees and animals. One of my favorite cartoons when I was younger was about a family of airplanes: Poppa Plane, Momma Plane, and so on. Each of the planes had its own little personality. The attribution of consciousness to inanimate objects is called *animism* and the attribution of human traits to inanimate objects is called *anthropomorphism*. Most of us are pretty sure that machines and plants don't possess consciousness, but what about animals? I know plenty of pet owners that swear that their little buddy has deep thoughts of his or her own. They get pretty upset when I suggest that little Scruffy is just a bundle of routines and reflexes, acting without conscious deliberation. He's probably not thinking, "Should I bury this bone here or over by the garage?"

Catching some zzzzs

Sleep represents a change in consciousness. When I'm asleep, I am unconscious. Sleep is characterized by a change in brain wave activity, also called *electrophysiological activity*. Sleep, as a level of consciousness, can be distinguished from other levels of consciousness by measuring the electrophysiological energy of the brain with an EEG. When someone is awake and alert, his brain emits a wave with a frequency of 13 to 30 hertz (Hz), called *beta activity*. When awake but relaxed, the brain shows *alpha activity* — a frequency of 8 to 12 Hz.

Generally, sleep is divided into four stages with one *substage*. Each stage is characterized by specific brain activities.

✔ **Stage 1:** When you close your eyes and begin to relax, getting into sleep mode, your brain waves are at an alpha frequency. As you drift deeper into Stage 1, your brain waves become less regular, and they have a higher amplitude. This is *theta activity*, 3.5 to 7.5 Hz. This stage is a transition period between being awake and asleep, and it lasts approximately 10 minutes.

✔ **Stage 2:** During Stage 2 sleep, brain wave activity is irregular and contains spikes of very high-amplitude EEG waves called *K-complexes*. There are also short bursts of 12 to 14 Hz waves called *spindles*. You are sound asleep at this stage, but you may think you're not actually sleeping. My wife wakes me up while I'm sleeping in front of the television set all the time to tell me that I'm snoring, but I always tell her I wasn't sleeping. I must have been snoring while awake. I don't know which is worse — snoring while asleep or awake!

✔ **Stage 3:** Stage 3 is characterized by the presence of high-amplitude, low-frequency waves (3.5 Hz), which are an EEG signal of *delta activity*. Stage 3 lasts about an hour and a half.

✔ **Stage 4:** This stage is signaled by the presence of more theta waves interrupting the smooth waves of delta. During Stage 4, your eyes begin to move back and forth very rapidly, which is called *rapid eye movement (REM)*. *REM sleep* is characterized by the presence of beta activity. Here, part of the brain is active but disconnected from skeletal muscle systems; however, you *are* asleep.

You dream during REM sleep. After you reach this stage, usually about an hour and a half into the whole sleep process, the rest of the night is characterized by alternating periods of REM sleep and non-REM sleep (activity of Stages 1, 2, and 3).

Understanding tired brains, slipping minds

I don't necessarily know why other people sleep, but I usually sleep because I'm tired. For the most part, researchers still don't know why people sleep, but some believe that sleep has a *restorative* function. Research that looks at the effects of a lack of sleep, or sleep deprivation, suggests that people engage in sleep so that the body can restore what was lost or damaged during waking hours.

When people have difficulties sleeping, they may be suffering from a formal *sleep disorder* in which there are abnormalities in the amount, timing, or the mental activity or behavior of the sleeping person. There are two broad categories of sleep disorders: *dyssomnias* and *parasomnias:*

- ✔ **Dyssomnias** consist of difficulties in the amount, quality, or timing of sleep. *Insomnia* is a common type of dyssomnia in which people have difficulty either falling to sleep or staying asleep. *Hypersomnia* is a condition of excessive sleepiness. Anybody with infants or young children at home? Can you say "hypersomnia"? *Narcolepsy* involves repeatedly falling fully asleep just out of nowhere. It can be in the middle of driving, during a conversation, or in the middle of lecture. Quite inconvenient!

- ✔ **Parasomnias** consist of the activation of bodily actions at the wrong time. For example, *nightmares* are a type of parasomnia that involve the inappropriate activation of cognitive process or thinking during sleep characterized by extremely frightening dreams in which a person feels threatened or in danger. *Sleepwalking disorder* is another parasomnia that involves getting out of bed during sleep, walking around, having a blank stare on one's face, looking awake but being unresponsive, and being extremely difficult to awaken. I used to get out of bed, unlock the door, and walk down the street. Still other people have been known to engage in some pretty sophisticated behavior while sleepwalking — ranging from making a sandwich to driving to the next town. There are even famous court cases where defendants have claimed that they committed murder while sleepwalking. In 1994, for example, Michael Ricksgers claimed that he accidently killed his wife while sleepwalking. The jury didn't buy it. *Sleep apnea,* a parasomnia characterized by abnormal pauses in breathing or abnormally low breathing rates, has been shown to have important health consequences such as high blood pressure and heart attacks.

Sleep deprivation is a big problem in today's do-more, fast-paced, and stimulation-packed 24-hour lifestyle. And the consequences of sleep disorders can be significant, ranging from slowed thinking, low alertness, poor work performance, and irritability. This does not mean that people who are sleep deprived are akin to zombies or the "walking dead." It's not quite that dramatic, but sleep deprivation has been related to an experience of feeling brain dead or having impaired thinking and cognition, feeling mentally more slow, and of being in a mental fog. So get to sleep! After you finish reading, of course! Ultimately, the long-term health effects of sleep disorders are only now being appreciated. A good source of information on sleep disorders is the National Center on Sleep Disorder Research website at `www.nhlbi.nih. gov/sleep`.

Arriving at Work Naked: Dreams

I once had a dream that I told a group of attractive women that my name is "Lion's Den." Maybe there's meaning behind it, or maybe it was just mental gibberish. I think if you ask most people, they would tell you they believe that dreams have either symbolic or prophetic importance. Dreams represent another altered state of consciousness, and some psychologists have postulated that dreams have meanings that can be interpreted. I'm not sure what my Lion's Den dream meant or what my dream persona was trying to convey, but perhaps he thought it was impressive to be a place where lions live.

Psychoanalysis has probably provided the most comprehensive look at the psychological importance of dreams and dreaming. Freud and other psycho-dynamic psychologists make a simple point: Dreams have deeper meanings than their surface content suggests. If I have a dream about getting a new car, it means more than I want a new car. It can mean any number of things, but the meaning is something unique to my psychological makeup, something idiosyncratic. The car may represent a repressed desire to be free; the car is a symbol of movement.

Psychoanalysts believe that the contents and processes of dreams represent deep, unconscious conflicts, desires, and issues. Dreams are hard to decipher; they're often convoluted, and they don't make much sense. In *The Interpretation of Dreams,* Freud states that dreams often represent our attempts to fulfill wishes that we're not consciously aware of. Through the technique of dream interpretation, a psychoanalyst helps a patient get to the bottom of the meaning of his or her dreams.

Understanding the meaning of many dreams is oftentimes not that complex. They can simply be reflections of events, worries, or experiences that are at the forefront of our minds. Yet other times the "true" meaning of a dream is extremely difficult, if not impossible, to discover. Dreams and their meanings are very personal and subjective phenomena. But just because dreams and their symbolic meanings are difficult to analyze scientifically, it shouldn't take away from anyone's belief that his dreams have some deeper meaning. The process of discovering the meaning of dreams in therapy, whether factually correct or not, can be an exciting and often helpful experience.

Regardless of whether dreams have meaning or not, some psychologists propose that they serve a vital biological function. Based on the restorative theory of sleep (see the "Catching some zzzzs" section earlier in this chapter), dreams are the byproduct of the brain reorganizing and storing the information gathered over the course of a waking day. This explanation actually allows for the possibility that dreams can be interpreted because they relate to real events and situations; therefore, they can have meaning.

Altering Your Consciousness

People have been deliberately trying to alter their consciousness since the beginning of human history. Human beings have used meditation, medication, religious rituals, sleep deprivation, and numerous other means to alter their levels of everyday awareness.

Psychologist and author Stanley Krippner identified more than 20 states of altered consciousness. One of the more common states is dreaming, and among the more intriguing altered states of consciousness identified by Krippner are these four states:

- **Rapture:** An intense feeling of overpowering emotion, experienced as pleasurable and positive. People have reported experiencing rapture after sex, ritualistic dancing, religious rituals, and the use of psychoactive substances.

- **Trance states:** An alert but very suggestible state. An individual in a trance is focused on a single stimulus and oblivious to much of everything else going on around her. People in trances sometimes report that they feel "at one" with the world. Religious rituals, chanting, hypnosis, brainwashing, yoga, and even music can induce trance states.

- **Daydreaming:** Rapid thinking unrelated to an individual's current environment. Daydreaming can often result from boredom, sensory deprivation, and sleep deprivation.

- **Expanded consciousness:** Increased awareness not typical of everyday experience and awareness. People try all kinds of ways to "expand" their consciousness from using drugs to sensory deprivation. There are four levels of expanded consciousness:

  - **Sensory:** An altered experience of space, time, and other sensory phenomena.

  - **Recollective-analytic:** An experience in which individuals develop novel ideas and revelations about themselves, the world, and their role within the world.

  - **Symbolic:** Identification with a historical figure or famous person accompanied by mystical symbols such as having a vision of a crucifix or an angel.

> • **Integral:** A religious and/or mystical experience usually involving God or some other supernatural being or force. The person usually feels merged with or at one with the universe. This state has sometimes been called *cosmic consciousness.* Krippner and other experts believe that very few people are actually capable of attaining this level of consciousness.

Mind on the mind (meditative states)

Meditative states of consciousness are considered an atypical form of consciousness but not necessarily abnormal or maladaptive. As with other states of consciousness, the focus of or object of attention differs with meditation. There is an intense concentration and focusing of attention upon a particular facet of experience, mental activity, or physical experience.

The meditative state has often been referred to as watching yourself think. The purpose or goal is to engage in the practice as a form of mental training to increase a person's ability to concentrate, stay calm, and be aware. It's also used as a positive coping strategy in the face of distress or adversity.

Meditation is considered to be a mental enhancement technique. There are many different forms of meditation that differ in subtle ways; the focus of meditation may be one's own thoughts (as in mindfulness to the sensations of the body in body-scan meditation) or on a statement or phrase repeated over and over (as in religious chanting or some prayer).

Practicing meditation has been associated with positive health benefits such as reduced stress and muscle tension. It has been used in conjunction with psychotherapy for depression and posttraumatic stress disorder (PTSD). Although historically associated with Buddhism, many consider meditation to be a nondenominational and non-religious practice and applicable to medical-, educational-, athletic-, and even business-related goals. Besides, why should the Buddhists have all the fun?

It seems that people have been trying to alter their conscious awareness since the dawn of civilization. In the next section, you explore the fascinating ways people attempt to alter or change their consciousness. For some, altered consciousness is delivered through the use of mind-altering drugs. For others it can come in the form of hypnosis.

Getting high on conscious life

Perhaps one of the most common methods for altering consciousness is the use of drugs. Drug use is an ancient phenomenon as well as a contemporary practice. Archaeologists have found traces of cocaine in mummified bodies from ancient Egypt.

Some people claim that one of the purposes of taking drugs is to gain added insight into the concept of consciousness itself. Most people who have used drugs report that they do so in order to get *high* or intoxicated.

The state of being high actually represents a change in consciousness, perhaps going from a level of awareness that induces negative feelings to a different level of awareness where an individual no longer feels "bad." The idea that drugs are an escape rings true, if you consider that many mind- and mood-altering drugs trigger a transition from one state of consciousness to another.

Not all drugs necessarily have an impact on consciousness. I don't recall feeling altered the last time I took an aspirin or antibiotic. Drugs whose main effect is the alteration of consciousness are called *psychoactive drugs*. Common psychoactive drugs and substances include LSD, PCP, marijuana, cocaine, amphetamines, barbiturates, ecstasy, and alcohol.

Although some people consider drug use for the claimed purpose of expanding their consciousness to be a good thing, as a health professional I feel compelled to warn you of many of the negative effects of psychoactive substance use and abuse. Addiction, brain damage, mental illness, psychological distress, and social and legal problems are common consequences of psychoactive drug use. With these in mind, I strongly caution anyone considering the use of drugs to avoid them, and I argue that seeking higher states of consciousness without the use of substances is far more enlightening.

Being naturally high

Stanley Krippner defines an altered state of consciousness as a mental state that is subjectively experienced as representing a difference in psychological functioning from an individual's normal, alert, waking state. The importance of the subjectively experienced difference can be illustrated by a story told by Baba Ram Das in his book *Be Here Now* (Crown Publishing Group).

Baba Ram Das's original name was Richard Alpert. Alpert was a psychology professor at Harvard in the 1960s, where he and Timothy Leary conducted experiments with LSD. Timothy Leary's most famous saying was "Turn on, tune in, drop out." Eventually, both Alpert and Leary were fired.

Ram Das traveled to India to seek the path of Hindu wisdom and to find out if anyone could explain why LSD seemed to have such a profound effect on consciousness. One day, Ram Das encountered a very wise and respected guru. Ram Das asked the guru if he could explain the effects of LSD. The guru asked for some LSD, and Ram Das complied. The guru took more LSD than Ram Das had ever seen a human being take, but the guru seemed completely unaffected! He didn't have an "acid trip" at all. There was no change in his current state of consciousness; he didn't experience an altered state of consciousness when he took the LSD. Does that mean that the guru was already on some sort of "reality trip" or "spiritual LSD"?

Falling into hypnosis

Close your eyes and relax. You are *soooooo* relaxed. Your breathing is slow. You're beginning to feel sleepy. You are *soooooo* relaxed.

Well, did it work? Hello? Are you under my hypnotic spell? Probably not. I'm not even trained in hypnosis. It's a special skill, and not all therapists or psychologists are trained in it. *Hypnosis* is a procedure in which a person called a *hypnotist* suggests changes in sensations, feelings, thoughts, or behaviors to a subject. Some psychologists think hypnosis is simply an increase in suggestibility that allows the hypnotist to "control" a subject's behavior. Other psychologists propose that hypnosis is actually an altered state of consciousness in which a person *dissociates* (separates) from her normal or regular state of consciousness.

The key to understanding the mechanism of hypnosis is *suggestion.* A *suggestion* is a directive given to the subject to act, feel, or think in a particular way. A hypnotist begins the process with some pleasant suggestions and progresses to more sophisticated requests. This process is called *hypnotic induction,* and it's considered a light hypnotic trance.

Hypnosis has been used for many different purposes ranging from entertainment to helping people stop smoking. The more controversial applications of hypnosis involve past-life regression and the recovery of repressed memories. There is little scientific evidence supporting the legitimacy of past-life regression through hypnosis. It's virtually impossible to prove. Why? Anything that someone reports can only be verified through historical records, and if I can look it up for verification, the individual in question could have looked it up to fake a regression.

Chapter 5

Getting Sensitive

· ·

In This Chapter

▶ Sensing the world

▶ Seeing things a bit more clearly

▶ Feeling the heat

▶ Constructing your perceptions

· ·

Seeing is believing! I have no idea where that phrase came from, but it says something important about people. That is, people have an easier time understanding or comprehending things if they can see them, touch them, hear them, and so on. Why doesn't everyone believe in ghosts, UFOs, or any number of things that most people have not experienced firsthand? Precisely the point. Most people haven't experienced these phenomena with their own senses, so they don't believe in them. How do you know if something is part of the world you live in or not — and whether it's real?

The subject of psychology is made up of a bunch of different areas of study that all point to the ultimate questions of why and how humans do what they do. This chapter focuses on the why and how of sensing and perceiving the world. They're as obvious as the nose on your face, but it's easy to overlook the impact of senses to everyday thoughts, moods, and actions. Psychology as the study of behavior and mental processes includes taking a look at how our senses — the ability to see, hear, taste, touch, feel, and so on — actually work.

Humans aren't just little brains floating around inside a body with no contact with the outside world. Quite the contrary; most people are typically in full contact with the world around them, taking in information, processing it, and using what they perceive to navigate a wide range of possibilities. So why is understanding materialism important? Because the way people actually maintain contact with the information that's processed is through the physical materials that create it.

In this chapter, I take a closer look at the ways people sense and perceive the world.

Building Blocks: Our Senses

Physicists and chemists have, for a long time, been pointing out that the world is made up of material stuff: particles, atoms, molecules, and various forms of energy. Basically, the universe is one big ball of energy. Everything consists of a particular configuration of energy. A working definition of *sensation* is the process by which we receive raw energy/information from the environment. If you want a definition in a suit and tie, then *sensation* is the process of mentally acquiring information about the world through the reception of its various forms of energy.

Here are the forms of energy that humans most commonly experience:

- Light (electromagnetic energy)
- Sound (acoustic energy, or sound waves)
- Heat (thermal energy)
- Pressure (mechanical or physical energy)
- Chemical energy

Some organisms experience the same kinds of energy as humans do, but other forms of life are sensitive to different ranges of the energy forms. Sharks can smell chemical particles (of blood, for example) in far smaller quantities than people can, and dogs can hear much higher frequencies of sounds.

For each form of energy that humans sense, a specific organ system or "device" is used to receive it. Aristotle, an ancient Greek philosopher (around 350 BCE, who some say was the last man to know everything there was to know) claimed that humans have five basic senses. Each of the five basic human senses are receptive to a specific form of energy. Psychologists now know that humans have at least 10 different senses, but Aristotle recognized the major ones:

- **Sight** receives light energy.
- **Hearing** receives sound energy or sound waves.
- **Touch** receives mechanical energy.
- **Smell** receives airborne chemical energy.
- **Taste** receives chemical energy.

The sensing process

When light travels from a light bulb or sound waves travel from a radio speaker, sensing devices, or *accessory structures,* intercept them. The eyes, ears, skin, nose, and mouth are called *accessory structures* because they provide access to the environment. After the energy reaches a sensory structure, it has to get inside the brain somehow. Light, sound waves, and heat waves don't bounce around inside a person's head — not in mine, at least. So, how do they get inside?

First, keep in mind that the brain uses its own form of energy. In Chapter 3, I describe a specific type of energy in the brain; it's called *electrochemical energy.* Electrochemical energy involves the creation of an electrical signal from chemical reactions. Electrochemical processes occur in many areas of nature. For example, some sea creatures such as eels can generate electric charges by using the electrochemical process. In the brain, this energy is how neurons communicate with each other and operate. So, in order for the brain to process the various forms of energy that a person's sense organs receive, each form of energy has to undergo a transformation process, called *transduction,* that turns the raw energy into electrochemical, or *neural,* energy. Transduction is a fairly common process encountered often in today's digital world as sounds and images are transduced or transformed into digital "bits" or code and transmitted via the Internet and cellular phone networks across the world.

The presence of specific types of cells, *receptors,* in each of the sensory systems makes transduction possible. Each sensory system has its own type of receptor cell. After the receptor cells *transduce,* or convert, the environmental energy, a neural signal travels along a *sensory nerve,* taking the information to the parts of the brain that are involved in processing and analyzing the information.

Does the music you listen to or human voices have only one tone? Does the light you see come in only one color? Of course not! Each of these sensory experiences, or *stimuli,* is made up of a complex array of wavelengths of light, frequencies of sound, intensities of smells and tastes, and so on. And your sensory systems are on the job to sort it out for you. Through the process of *coding and representation,* your brain captures the complexity of the environmental stimuli you encounter.

Humans experience the complexity of a stimulus after the brain translates its different features into a specific pattern of neural activity. The theory of *specific nerve energies* states that each sensory system provides information for only one sense, no matter how nerves are stimulated. In other words, specific parts of the brain always label the stimulation they receive as light or sound.

Synesthesia

Some people claim to hear light and see sounds. Other people report that certain sounds have a color. *Synesthesia* is the name of an ability that certain people have to sense one (or more) forms of energy with a sensory system other than the one typically used for the stimulus. This phenomenon is estimated to affect about one in every 2,000 people. Scientists suspect that this experience is a result of some "wires" or neural connections in the brain being crossed. Simon Baron-Cohen, a world-famous autism researcher and psychologist, hypothesized that synesthesia is possible when extra connections in the brain allow for otherwise separate sensory systems there to interact. Whatever the cause, I think it sounds kind of cool. I'd love to be able to see the music when I dance because I sure can't feel it!

Psychologists have worked with neurosurgeons to conduct experiments with patients who, for various medical reasons, need a portion of their skulls removed, which exposes their brains. The neurosurgeons took an electrode and zapped specific parts of the exposed brains with a little jolt of electricity. When they applied this shock, a weird thing happened. The people in the experiment said, "I can hear chickens squawking." If they zapped the part of the brain that processes taste, a person may have said, "I can taste tomato soup. Mmm, that's good."

How is this possible? When a particular part of the brain is stimulated, the brain thinks that it's receiving a specific kind of information from the sense organ it processes, even if it's not. So, specific sensory systems are wired into specific brain regions, permitting the brain to know the difference between hearing a sound and seeing a light.

Different aspects of a stimulus are coded in the brain depending on which neurons are activated and the pattern of neuron activation. If neurons in the visual system are activated, for example, the brain senses light. If the pattern of neural activation differs, the brain senses different wavelengths or intensities of light so it can distinguish between sunlight and candlelight. The end of the sensory trail leads to a neural *representation* of the sensation in a specific region of the brain where you finally hear the music or see the colors.

Seeing

Sight is arguably one of the most important human senses. Although the other senses are also important, being able to see is critical for getting along in the modern world. In this section, I chronicle a little journey — the journey light takes through the eye and into the brain, completing our sensation of light.

The journey begins with *electromagnetic radiation,* more commonly known as light. Visible light occupies wavelengths between 400 and 750 nanometers. I remember from physics class that light travels in waves. The intensity of light is calculated by measuring the size of the waves, and its frequency is measured by how many peaks of a wave pass a particular point within a specific period of time. Wavelength is important to the topic of how people sense light because different wavelengths make it possible to experience colors.

Here's the process:

1. Light enters the eye through the *cornea.*

2. Light passes through the *pupil.*

3. The *lens* of the eye focuses the light onto the *retina.*

4. Light energy is converted into neural energy — an action known as light *transduction.*

Grasping the process of light transduction requires a closer look at the retina, a part of the eye that's located on the back lining of the eyeball. The retina contains some special cells called *photoreceptors* that are responsible for transduction. These cells contain chemicals called *photopigments* that are broken apart when the photons of light traveling in the light wave make contact with them. This event starts a chemical reaction that tells the cell to fire a signal to the *optic nerve.* The signal then travels to the *visual cortex* of the brain, the part of the brain responsible for analyzing visual stimuli. So, light is transformed into neural energy by literally breaking up chemicals in the retina, which triggers a neural signal. These chemicals are stored in two different cells (called photoreceptors) in the retina, *rods and cones.*

Rods contain a chemical called *rhodopsin,* which is very light-sensitive. This chemical reacts to very low-intensity light and helps with peripheral vision. That is why we see mostly in black and white when it is dark; it's also why we can sees stars at night better if we don't look right at them.

Cones contain chemicals known as the iodopsins, which are closely related to rhodopsin. Each of three types of cone contains a different form of iodopsin. The three types of cone respond to different wavelengths of light and are involved in seeing color.

Seeing colors

Some people are colorblind to particular shades of blues, greens, and reds. This condition means that these people have a hard time sensing the specific wavelengths of light associated with those specific colors. They lack a photo pigment that is sensitive to the wavelengths. Typically, they only have two types of cones, not three. Fortunately, most people get to see the world in all its rainbow-hued glory.

There are two basic theories of color vision, the *trichromatic theory* and the *opponent-process theory*.

- **The trichromatic theory** is really basic. The idea is that the retina contains three different types of cones (photoreceptors) that each responds to different wavelengths of light, and these provide our experience of different colors.

  - *Short-wavelength* cones respond to light around 440 nanometers, or blue light.

  - *Medium-wavelength* cones respond to light around 530 nanometers, or green light.

  - *Long-wavelength* cones respond to light around 560 nanometers, or greenish-yellow light.

  When each cone system is partially activated, combinations of these three basic colors are visible as colors like aquamarine and orange. But the point here is that the human experience of all colors originates from these three basic cone inputs.

- **The opponent-process theory** of color vision states that the brain contains different types of neurons that respond differently to different colors. The idea is that these cells fire more — when compared to their baseline, or background, level of firing — when stimulated by one type of light, and they fire less when stimulated by another. So, if you're looking at red, your specialized red cells increase their firing rate. When you're looking at green, your red cells chill out with the firing rate and your green cells increase their firing rate. "Cell sets" exist for yellow and blue as well.

  This theory explains something called the *negative-afterimage effect* images in your mind's eye that are different colors than the actual image you're seeing. The most popular example uses a US flag that has black instead of white stars, green stripes replacing the red ones, and yellow instead of a blue background. After looking at the image for a while, a person can close her eyes and see the flag in its real colors because the cells being stimulated by black, green, and yellow light are recovering from the stimulation and begin "seeing" white, red, and blue light instead. Try it. Stare at a 1×1-inch yellow square for about 30 seconds and then look at a white sheet of paper. You should see a blue square instead of the white paper.

So which theory is correct? As is the case frequently in psychology, and in science more generally, an either/or question ends up being answered "both!" Psychologists now know that the trichromatic theory describes what happens in the retina of the eye, whereas the opponent-process theory describes what happens in the brain.

Figuring distances

How can you tell how far away something is from you just by looking at it? Well, maybe you can't, but some people are really good at eyeballing distances. Personally, I need a tape measure, ruler, land-surveyor, and a global positioning satellite to figure distances, but depth and distance are calculated by the body's visual systems, using two inputs: *monocular cues* and *binocular cues*.

✔ **Monocular cues** are simple; you know that some things are bigger than other things. Dogs are bigger than mice. Cars are bigger than dogs. Houses are bigger than cars. Because you know these things from experience, whenever you see a mouse's image on your retina that's bigger than an image of a dog in the same scene, you know that the mouse is closer to you than the dog. Similarly, if you see a dog that's bigger than a car, you figure the dog is closer.

The rule is that things that cast bigger images on our retinas are assumed to be closer. Artists use this rule all the time when they want to depict a three-dimensional scene on a two-dimensional canvas.

✔ **Binocular cues** are interesting and a little weird. Remember the Cyclops from the *Sinbad* movies? He only had one eye. According to binocular vision rules, he would have had a hard time figuring out distances because binocular distance cues depend on two eyes providing information to the brain.

• *Convergence* is a binocular cue and refers to information provided by the muscles of the eyes to the brain in order to calculate distances. When your eyes are pointing inward, toward the nose, the brain knows that you're looking at something close to you. When your eyes are pointing outward, the brain knows that you're looking at an object farther away.

• *Stereoscopic* vision is the other, and more important, type of binocular cue. Try this real quickly. Make a square, a viewing frame, with your hands by connecting your thumbs and index fingers at the tips while keeping the rest of your fingers folded. Then, close one eye and focus on an object around you. Frame the object in the middle of the box. Now, close that eye and open the other. What happened? The object should have moved. This happens because of stereoscopic vision. Each of your eyes gives you a slightly different angle on the same image because they are set apart. Your brain judges distance by using these different angles by calculating the difference between the two images.

Hearing

Sound travels in waves and is measured by its *amplitude* or *wave size* and *frequency* or *number of waves per unit time*. Each of these translates into a psychological experience: Amplitude determines loudness (my neighbor's rock band), and frequency provides pitch or tone (the screeching lead singer of said neighbor's rock band). The structures of the ear are specifically designed to *transduce,* or convert, sound-wave energy into neural energy.

A sound first enters the ear as it is funneled in by the *pinna.* A human's crumpled-up outer ear is designed as a "sound scoop." As the wave passes through the ear canal, it eventually reaches the eardrum, or the *tympanic membrane.* The vibrating eardrum shakes three little bones *(malleus, incus,* and *stapes,* Latin words for *hammer, anvil,* and *stirrup),* which amplifies the vibration.

After the sound wave reaches the inner ear, the *cochlea,* auditory transduction occurs. The cochlea contains the hardware for the transduction process. The cochlea is filled with fluid, and its floor is lined with the *basilar membrane. Hair cells* (they actually look like hairs) are attached to the basilar membrane. The sound waves coming into the inner ear change the pressure of the fluid inside the cochlea and create fluid waves that move the basilar membrane. Movement of the basilar membrane causes the hair cells to bend, which starts the transduction ball rolling. When the hair cells bend, their chemical properties are altered, thus changing their electrical polarity and positioning them to fire and send a neural signal. The sound waves, now turned into neural electrochemical energy, travel to the *auditory cortex* (the part of the brain responsible for hearing) for perceptual processing.

Touching and feeling pain

The sense of touch includes sensing pressure, temperature, and pain. Specialized cells in the skin sense touch by sending a signal to the spinal cord and then on to the brain. Transduction in touch is a physical or mechanical process; it's much more straightforward than the chemical transduction in the eye for vision. When heat, cold, or weight stimulates touch receptors in the skin, a neural signal travels to the brain, much the same way that the hair cells of the inner ear operate.

Pain is a special case for the sense of touch because it would be difficult to avoid harm and survive in this world without a sense of pain. Because it hurts when you touch fire, you're motivated to avoid getting too close to it, which helps you avoid damaging your flesh and possibly dying. Pain is an important signal that something is harming, damaging, or destroying the body.

Two specific nerve fibers located throughout the skin signal pain to the brain: the *A-delta fibers* and the *C fibers*. A-delta fibers carry sharp sensations and work rapidly. C fibers communicate chronic and dull pain and burning sensations.

Some people seem to have a really high threshold for pain. The *gate-control theory of pain* states that pain signals must pass through a gate in the spinal cord that "decides" which signals get through to the brain and which ones don't. If another sense is using the pain pathways at a given time, the pain signal may not reach the brain. For example, rubbing your thigh when your ankle aches seems to help dull the pain in the ankle. That's because the rubbing signal (pressure) from the thigh is competing with the pain signal from the ankle for access through the gate. Amazing, right? I'm always blown away by the complexity of the human body.

Smelling and tasting

The sense of smell is called *olfaction*. Sometimes I can smell my neighbor's barbecue on the weekend. I have that experience because little particles from the cooking food, *volatile chemical particles,* become airborne and travel over to the smell receptors in my nose. Inside my nose are thousands of olfactory receptors that can sense tens of thousands of different odors.

The molecules from the volatile chemicals cause a chemical change in the receptors in my nose, which sets the transduction process in motion. The chemical energy is then converted into neural energy by the receptor cells, and a signal hits the *olfactory bulb* in my brain where the signal is processed. The olfactory bulb also connects with the part of my brain that involves emotion. Some researchers think that this physical connection in the brain is why smells can activate emotional memories from time to time.

Perhaps you've heard talk about the impact of *pheromones,* which are scents that animals send out as signals to other animals during mating season. Some companies market pheromone products for humans, especially for men out there who are desperate to find a date. Do humans really produce pheromones? The research jury is still out, but a few recent findings seem to suggest that the answer is yes. The pheromone system depends on a second organ of smell, the vomeronasal organ, or Jacobsen's organ. This system is prominent in animals as small as moths and as big as elephants.

Gustation refers to the sense of taste. Taste is a chemical sense made possible by chemical receptors on the tongue known as *taste buds.* All tastes are variations on five themes: sweet, sour, bitter, salty, and umami. Umami has generally been accepted as a fifth taste dimension. The receptors are activated by monosodium glutamate (MSG), often added to processed food Approximately 10,000 taste buds are on every tongue, reacting to the molecules of food and converting chemical energy into neural energy that sends information to the area of the brain involved in analyzing taste information.

Balancing and moving

Smart as he was, Aristotle missed some important sensory systems. Ballerinas and ice skaters can appear to float through space, their movements balanced and defying gravity. These marvelous abilities are possible in part due to the *body senses,* the sensory processes of the body's orientation (in space) and movement — oftentimes referred to as the *kinesthetic sense.* Without the senses of balance and movement, it would not be possible to walk in a straight line or even stand up.

Structures known as the *vestibular organ,* located in the inner ear, and receptors located throughout the body are involved in balance and the kinesthetic sense. The vestibular organ consists of a set of "canals" that are filled with fluid that contain hair-like receptor cells. As the head moves around, the fluid inside the canals moves or flows, bending the receptor cells and causing these cells to fire, telling the brain that the head is in motion. Movement of the fluid triggers the sensation of movement.

The kinesthetic sense results from the firing of receptors located throughout the body in the skin, muscles, and joints. The firing of these receptors provides sensory information to the brain about the particular body part in motion, pressure, and the orientation of the body parts to each other. When the sense of movement, balance, orientation, body part in motion, and the body parts in relation to each other are all working together in a well-coordinated manner, graceful and fluid movement is possible.

Finishing the Product: Perception

The world is much more complex than a bunch of singular sounds, smells, tastes, and other sensations may indicate. You hear symphonies, not just notes. You see fireworks, not just single photons of light. You indulge your taste buds with flavorful foods, not individual salty, sour, bitter, umami, and sweet tastes. So take a moment to thank your ability of perception for these pleasures. I'll wait.

Perception is the process of organizing, analyzing, and providing meaning to the various sensations that you're bombarded with on a daily basis. If sensation provides the raw material, perception is the final product.

Here are two popular views of the complex process related to perception:

- **Ecological:** This idea states that the environment provides all the information you need to sense the world; very little interpretation or construction is required. For example, when I perceive a tree, it's not because I've constructed a perception of it in my mind. I perceive the tree because the tree has provided me with all the necessary information to perceive it as it is.

- **Constructionist:** In this view, the process of perception relies on previous knowledge and information to construct reality from fragments of sensation. You are not just a passive recipient of sensory information. Instead, you are actively constructing what you see, hear, taste, and feel.

Regardless of whether you're an ecologist or a constructionist, the process of perceiving has some basic tenets. If sensation is the process of detecting specific types of energy in the environment, how do you know what information is worth detecting and what's just background noise? After all, you can't possibly respond to every bit of sensory energy you encounter. All the roaring traffic, howling wind, bustling pedestrians, and other stuff would easily overwhelm a person. That's why the perceptual systems have a built-in mechanism for determining what information should be detectable.

Threshold theory

The concept of an *absolute threshold* refers to the minimum amount of energy in the environment that a sensory system can detect. Each sensory system has an absolute threshold below which energy does not warrant or garner perceptual attention. A stimulus must be higher than your absolute threshold for you to notice it's there.

Another type of threshold, the *difference threshold,* is described by *Weber's law,* which introduces the *just-noticeable difference (JND).* The JND is the smallest difference between two stimuli that lets you know they are different. Each sensory system determines a constant fraction of intensity for each form of energy that represents the smallest detectable difference between energy intensities. The idea is that the difference between two stimuli has to exceed the JND in order for it to be detectable; otherwise, an observer will think the two stimuli are the same. For example, the just-noticeable difference for brightness is about 1/60th: I can barely tell the difference in brightness between a 60-watt and a 61-watt bulb, if they made 61-watt bulbs.

Signal-detection theory

Another theory known as *signal-detection theory* takes a slightly more complicated look at the problem. An overwhelming amount of environmental energy is considered background noise (think traffic sounds when you are in your automobile). When you encounter a stimulus, called the *signal* (think your car radio), you need to distinguish between the signal (car radio and traffic noise) and the background noise (just the traffic sounds). That's why you have to turn up the car radio when there is heavy traffic at rush-hour; there's more noise, so you need to increase the strength of the signal. Signal- detection theory says that your ability to perceive stimuli is based on your individual *sensitivity* and *response criterion.* Sensitivity refers to a basic characteristic of each perceptual system: what it is able to distinguish. The response criterion is determined by situational factors, like emotions and motivations. Based on your sensitivity and response criterion, you can either correctly detect a stimulus *(hit),* fail to detect a signal when one is available *(miss),* detect a signal when there isn't one *(false alarm),* or report no signal when there isn't one *(correct rejection).*

To understand response criterion, imagine that your task is to tell whether I turned a light on. Compare two situations: In one, you earn $100 every time you see the light when it occurs (a *hit*), but you lose $1 every time you say the light was on when it actually wasn't (a *false alarm*). In the other situation, you earn $1 for each *hit* and lose $100 for each *false alarm.* Would you behave the same way in each situation? I wouldn't — in the first case I would say "light" every time I even suspected it had come on; in the second case I would not say "light" unless I was really sure.

Individual biases and motivations determine response criterion and affect whether a person makes an accurate detection or not. This means when people think I'm not listening to them, it's not my fault. I'm not detecting their signal because my response criterion is set too high. See? I'm an innocent victim of my perceptual processes.

Organizing by Principles

The perceptual system is not made up of a bunch of arbitrary rules and random processes. Psychologists and other researchers over the years have discovered principles that guide the way human perceptual systems organize all the information they receive from the sensory systems:

- ✔ **Figure-Ground:** Information is automatically divided into two categories: either figure or ground, or foreground and background. Figural information is obvious and immediate; ground information is not very meaningful.

- ✔ **Grouping:** This large category contains principles that people use to determine whether information belongs in a specific group with similar stimuli. These characteristics of the information or stimuli help with the grouping process:

- **Proximity:** Stimuli that are close together in space are perceived to belong together.

- **Common fate:** Stimuli that move in the same direction and at the same rate are grouped together.

- **Continuity:** Stimuli that create a continuous form are grouped together.

- **Similarity:** Similar things are grouped together.

✔ **Closure:** This principle is the tendency to fill in missing information to complete a stimulus. There is a smart-phone game app that demonstrates this nicely in which only a portion of a popular company's or corporation's logo is presented and you have to guess the correct the company by completing or "closing" the rest of the logo.

Most psychologists today are in the *constructionist* camp. (See the "Finishing the Product: Perception" section earlier in this chapter.) They view perception as a process of building your sense of reality out of fragments of information. People are born with some of the rules for organizing information, but a few other factors can influence the way you perceive things.

Personal experiences have a powerful impact on how you analyze sensory information. The concept of a *perceptual set*, defined as an expectation of what you will perceive, attempts to capture this. You use cues from context and experience to help you understand what you're seeing, tasting, feeling, and so forth. For example, if I'm driving down the street and see someone in a police uniform standing next to someone's car window, I assume that an officer is making a traffic stop. I could actually be seeing a person in a police uniform asking for directions, but my past experience suggests otherwise.

A person's culture is another powerful influence on how stimuli is perceived. A good example of the impact of cultural influences on perceptions involves figuring out a story line based on a series of pictures. If I have four pictures, each containing a different piece of a puzzle that, when viewed in sequence, can tell a story, I'm likely to imagine a story that's different from the one my Spanish colleague imagines. For example, say I'm looking at a series of pictures that show these images:

✔ A woman is carrying a bag.

✔ A woman is crying.

✔ A man is approaching a woman.

✔ A woman is standing with no bag.

Tricking the eye

The organizing principles of the perceptual systems make perceptual illusions possible. You may see things that aren't really in front of you or see things moving when they're motionless. Illusionists, including magicians, use your perceptual organizing rules against you. They have a keen understanding of how the perceptual systems work, and they take advantage of this knowledge to perform their tricks.

What's going on here? I may see a woman who is upset because she dropped her bag and a man who is coming to help her. Or, I may see a woman crying out of fear because a man is coming to steal her bag. Depending upon my culture or subculture, not to mention my personal experience, I may see two very different stories.

Part III
Thinking and Feeling and Acting

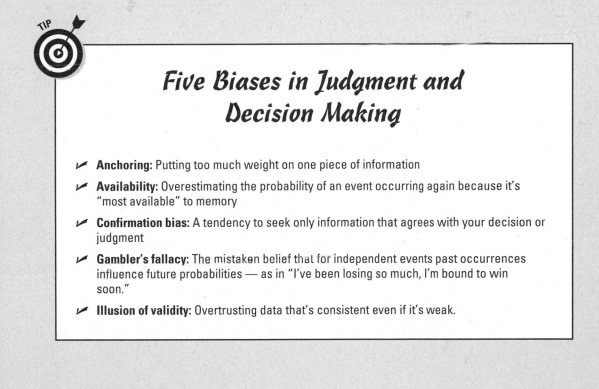

Five Biases in Judgment and Decision Making

- **Anchoring:** Putting too much weight on one piece of information
- **Availability:** Overestimating the probability of an event occurring again because it's "most available" to memory
- **Confirmation bias:** A tendency to seek only information that agrees with your decision or judgment
- **Gambler's fallacy:** The mistaken belief that for independent events past occurrences influence future probabilities — as in "I've been losing so much, I'm bound to win soon."
- **Illusion of validity:** Overtrusting data that's consistent even if it's weak.

Take a mock intelligence test at www.dummies.com/extras/psychology.

In this part...

- Get exposed to the thinking on human thought, which psychologists call cognition, including both the contents of thoughts and the thought process.

- Realize what being smart is all about via a discussion about communication, language, intelligence, and the different theories of "being smart."

- Get in touch with your feelings in a chapter on emotion and motivation — whether you're more interested in the roots of love or anger.

- Check out the psychological understanding of learning with a refresher on Ivan Pavlov and his famous dogs and the theory of operant conditioning that followed.

Chapter 6

Thinking and Speaking

*B*efore I get into the complex psychological concept of thinking, here's a little mental experiment. Imagine yourself lying in your bed having just awakened from a good night's sleep. You reach over to shut off your annoying alarm, toss the blankets to the side, and head for the bathroom. Now, here's the experimental part. When you get to the bathroom, you forget why you're in there. The answer may seem obvious because you just got out of bed and walked straight to the bathroom, but you've forgotten. You look around and can't figure out where you are. Nothing seems familiar, and you're surrounded by a strange world of shapes, figures, objects, sounds, and lights. You look into an object that reflects an image of some other thing back at you, but you don't know what it is. You're confused, disoriented, and basically lost. Your mind is completely blank. You can't even think of anything to say in order to cry out for help. You're stuck there. What are you going to do?

If the example seems a little strange, or at least a bit abstract, it's because the situation *would* be strange. Without the ability to think, life would be similar to the bathroom situation I just described. Thinking enables you to recognize objects, solve problems, and communicate. You'd really be in trouble if you couldn't think. You wouldn't even be able to figure out how to get out of the bathroom.

In this chapter, I describe the concepts of thinking (cognition) and language and their component processes such as attention, memory, decision making, intelligence, language (including speech and nonverbal language such as American Sign Language), and comprehension.

Finding Out What's On Your Mind

What exactly is thinking? A bit later in this chapter, I ask you to analyze your own thought processes, so it would help if you knew what you're analyzing. In psychology, the term, *cognition* refers to the mental processing of information including memorizing, reasoning, problem solving, conceptualizing, and imagining.

Studying thinking (or, more strictly, cognition) is pretty difficult. Why? It's hard to see! If I opened up your skull and looked inside, would I see thinking? No, I'd see a wrinkly, grayish-pink thing (your brain). In the early years of psychological research on thinking, psychologists asked people participating in studies on thinking to engage in something called introspection. *Introspection* is the observation and reporting of one's own inner experience. Psychologists gave participants a simple math problem to solve and asked them to talk out loud as they performed the calculations. These exercises were intended to capture the steps involved in the thinking process. It is important to keep in mind that a great deal of thinking or cognition occurs outside of conscious awareness. In that sense, introspection would not be very helpful now would it?

Try it! Get a piece of blank paper and a pencil. Your instructions are to solve the following math problem and write down each step that you take, one by one:

$$47,876 + 23,989$$

The answer is 71,865. If you didn't get this right, don't worry about it; everyone has weaknesses. Actually, if you got the wrong answer, the introspection technique may be able to reveal what you did wrong. Take a second to go over each of the steps you went through to solve the problem.

You just participated in a psychological experiment, and it didn't hurt a bit, did it?

Now, imagine how hard it would be to use introspection to analyze all of your thinking. It would be pretty difficult — impossible, in fact. Part of the reason psychologists don't rely on introspection anymore is that people are blind to most of what our minds (or brains) are doing. Introspection can't capture sophisticated thought processes. These days, psychologists use computer modeling, formal experiments, and other complex means for researching thinking. Psychologists try to build model systems that think the way people do.

Thinking Like a PC

Finding out how thinking works has been a pursuit of inquiry since Aristotle, through the Renaissance with Descartes, and into the modern era. A useful tool that thinking thinkers use to explain the workings of the mind is metaphor. Numerous metaphors have been developed through the ages, including the mind as a steam engine, a clock, and even a computer. In this section, I introduce you to the concept of the mind and thinking as computational processes, in which representations of information are manipulated as the actual process of thought.

Computing

Upon the advent of the modern computer, psychologists and related investigators began to look at the operations performed by computers, called *computing* or *computation,* as potential models for human thought processes. This was a significant breakthrough. Using the computer as a model for how thinking occurs is called the *computational-representational model of mind* (and thinking). The idea is both profound and simplistic: The mind and all of its complex processes, such as perceiving, thinking, problem solving, and so forth, make up an information-processing machine that performs computations.

What is a "computation"? A computation is a manipulation of symbols according to a preset rule that transforms one set of symbols into another. For example, assume that there is the following rule for representing the letters W, S, D, O, and R:

W = 1

S = 2

D = 3

O = 4

R = 5

So the word "words" would be represented as "14532," and the word "sword" would be represented as "21453." That transformation is a computation. So, the brain, as a computational "device," transforms one type of information, such as light waves (or the letters in the "words" example), into another type of information, neural patterns (or the numbers in the "words" example.

Representing

Computations are performed on mental representations. A *mental representation* is a symbol of a particular stimulus (like a tree) in the mind. The term "symbol" is used here in a very loose sense to refer to something standing in for something else. So the stimulus "tree," for example, may come to be symbolized by the activation of a specific set of neurons in the brain.

Sit back for a second, get comfortable, and conjure up an image of a pink rose in your mind. Concentrate so that the image is clear; see the green stem and leaves, the pink petals, the thorns. Try to imagine the rose in detail. If someone comes into the room as you're doing this and asks if there is a rose in the room, what would you say? If there isn't actually a rose in the room, then you'd say "no." But consider the idea that there is actually a rose in the room, or at least it's in the room because there's one inside your mind, the rose that you're imagining. So, if I cut open your skull and looked into your head, I'd see a pink rose, right? Of course not! The rose only exists in symbolic or representational form inside of your mind.

Remember, thinking consists of symbols that represent information about the world, the objects within it, and the manipulation of those symbols. The mental manipulation of symbols is based on combining, breaking down, and recombining symbols into more complex strings or systems of symbols that have meaning. Take the word "rose" again. It consists of simpler parts called letters, and the specific combination of those letters gives rise to the specific word and image of the object called "rose." The letters can be rearranged to spell the word "sore," which is an entirely different thing and thus an entirely different thought. This reveals that even a simple system like the alphabet can give rise to an almost infinite set of larger and more meaningful symbols or representations.

Where do all these symbols come from? Symbols are generated by sensing things in the world. When I see a rose, there's a corresponding symbolic representation of that rose in my mind as I think about it. From this point on, the *Psychology for Dummies* definition of thinking is the mental processing of information as computations performed on representations and the various operations involved in that process.

Processing

Your mind goes through four basic steps when processing information:

1. Stimulus information from your senses reaches the brain. (You see Lebron James slam dunk for the first time.)

Turing's challenge

Alan Turing came up with something called the Turing test. Turing (1912–1954) was a British mathematician and computer scientist who was instrumental in helping crack secret German submarine codes during World War II. In his time, a popular parlor game involved placing a man and a woman behind two different doors; guests had to communicate with them by typewritten notes. The point was to guess correctly if it was the man or the woman behind a particular door based only on their answers to the guests' questions. Turing proposed that the comparison be changed from a man and a woman to a computer and a human being to find out if guests could determine whether the computer or a human was answering their questions. If guests couldn't tell the difference, then the computer would have to be considered to be a suitable "stand in" for the human. That is, such a test result would mean that a computer could "represent" human thought in its own way — in a symbolic architecture, or computer language. The Turing test is a demonstration of how computation can be performed on symbols or representations and is an analogy for how the human mind can perform computations on symbols and represent the real world in mental terms.

2. The information is analyzed. (Your brain thinks, "Wow. Those are impressive moves.")

3. Different possible responses are generated. (Your brain tries to figure out how he's doing it.)

4. A response is executed and monitored for feedback. (You throw on your basketball shoes and head for the court.)

These basic mechanisms of information processing are sometimes called the *architecture* of thought. These are the *rules of thought* and require all the following basic components:

- ✔ **Input:** Sensory information that comes in from your world or from within your own mind and is considered.

- ✔ **Memory:** System necessary for storing knowledge. Information about people and other elements in the world is stored in the mind and memory.

- ✔ **Operations:** Rules that determine how information in the memory system is utilized (reasoning, problem solving, and logical analysis). Take math as an example: If I have 100 numbers stored in my memory and am confronted with a mathematical problem, operations determine how I solve that problem.

- ✔ **Output:** Action "programs" that involve telling the rest of the mind and body what to do after the thinking operations have been carried out.

Exploring Operations of the Mind

Jerry Fodor (born 1935), is an American philosopher (What? Seriously consider the advice of someone who's not a psychologist? Blasphemy!), who proposed that the mind's complicated information-processing system can be divided into specific operations, or modules, that perform specific thinking tasks — an attention module, a problem-solving module, and so forth. In the sections that follow, I introduce some of the more significant mental operations or procedures, including attention, memory, concept formation, and problem solving.

Focusing your attention

There's a great scene from one of my favorite movies, *Dumb and Dumber* (1994), starring Jim Carey (Lloyd) and Jeff Daniels (Harry) in which Harry tells Lloyd a story about how a girlfriend broke up with him in high school.

Harry tells Lloyd that he didn't know why she ended the relationship — something about him not listening to her — but he wasn't paying attention when she told him the reason.

Harry didn't pay *attention,* one of the most critical and primary thinking processes. The world and your own mind are full of information and stimulation. It's extremely noisy, buzzy, fuzzy, colorful, blurry, and chock-full of stuff. How can you select and focus on what is important and ignore all the rest?

As part of information processing, attention is defined as the cognitive process of selecting stimuli and information from the environment for further processing while excluding or inhibiting other stimuli and information. There's simply too much information buzzing around in people's minds and in the environment to attend to it all. Efficient and effective information processing requires selection.

Psychologists Daniel Simons and Christopher Chabris conducted an experiment that illustrates this selective feature of attention. In short, experimental subjects were asked to watch a video of people innocently passing a basketball to each other. Partway through the video, a person in a gorilla suit enters the frame, pounds on his chest, and then leaves the frame. Subjects were asked if they remember seeing the gorilla; about half of them reported never noticing a gorilla. This is known as *inattentional blindness;* when a person is focusing on something, he misses unrelated information. This is an active principle in magic shows and sleight-of-hand tricks. Sorry, I don't think David Copperfield is a wizard, but he sure knows how to harness inattentional blindness!

Different types of attention processes exist:

- ✔ **Focused attention:** Concentration on one source of input to the exclusion of everything else

- ✔ **Divided attention:** Focus on two or more inputs simultaneously

Psychologist Donald Broadbent developed a cognitive model of attention in which attention is characterized as a channel with limited capacity for input to pass through. Sensory information is processed first, and then semantic (or meaning) information is processed. The key to Broadbent's model is that inputs need to be attended to in order to be further processed.

Broadbent's model does not explain all the data being collected through research so other models have been developed. One research finding known as the *cocktail party effect* presented a challenge to Broadbent's model. Ever been at a noisy party and suddenly you hear your name mentioned from across the room? Well, you weren't particularly attending to or waiting to hear your name, but you did anyway because it's important. Your mind attends to *important* information.

Experiments have lead cognitive psychologists to characterize attention as a dynamic process in which both selection for attention and selection for "non-attention" are made at the same time. Guided search theory is a dynamic model of attention that proposes that attention is guided by salient information from previous searches or episodes of attending. It is considered a top-down model of attention in that people are considered to be actively searching rather than passively receiving inputs as is more the case in Broadbent's model.

Packing it away in the ol' memory box

Thinking involves the manipulation of mental symbols that you store as concepts — representations of the objects you encounter in the world. How are these mental symbols stored? Memory!

To conceptualize memory, envision a bank. Think about your checking account and your savings account. Each of these accounts does something a little different with your money because they have different purposes. Checking accounts typically function for everyday and short-term use. Savings are intended to be for longer-term storage. Your memories store information in different ways as well.

Three separate storage systems are involved with memory: *sensory memory, short-term memory,* and *long-term memory.*

Sensory storage

Sensory memory is a split-second memory system that stores information coming in through your senses. Have you ever looked at the sun and then closed your eyes and looked away? What happens? You can still see a type of sun in your mind. This afterimage is a visual sensory memory known as an *iconic* memory. For auditory stimuli, it is called *echoic* memory. This process happens so fast that it is sometimes considered a part of the perceptual process (for more on perception, see Chapter 5), but is, in fact, part of the overall memory system.

Short-term memory

Short-term memory (STM), also known as working memory, consists of the information that is active in your consciousness right now, the things you're aware of. The light on the book page, these words being read, the grumbling in your stomach, and the sound of traffic outside your window are all parts of your conscious awareness, and they're all being stored in your STM. Things you are not aware of can simply be forgotten in many cases.

How much information can your STM store? The general consensus is that it can store seven items of information, plus or minus two items. This is sometimes called the "magical number seven" of STM capacity.

Does that mean that I can only store seven words, seven numbers, or seven other simple items in my STM? No. Thanks to a process called *chunking,* I can store a lot more information than that. A classic example of chunking is the use of *mnemonics,* which enables you to take a big chunk of information and break it down into a little phrase, so it's easier to remember.

Here's an easy way to form a mnemonic. If you have a list of things you want to memorize, take the first letter of each word on the list and make a catchy phrase out of it. I learned this one in eighth grade and never forgot it: "Kings play chess on fine green silk." Do you know what that stands for? It stands for the way biologists classify different organisms on the earth: Kingdom, Phylum, Class, Order, Family, Genus, and Species.

The duration of memory for the STM system is approximately 18 seconds. You can extend the length of time that you store information in STM only by engaging in something called rehearsal. *Rehearsal* is the process of actively thinking about something. Rote rehearsal is repeating something over and over again in your mind or out loud so that you don't forget it. Rote rehearsal will work, but not as effectively as a more effortful type of rehearsal, such as building a mnemonic like "Kings play chess on fine green silk."

Long-term memory

If the information in STM is rehearsed long enough, it eventually ends up in your memory's savings account, the *long-term memory* (LTM). You basically have two ways to deposit information into your long-term memory bank:

- ✔ **Maintenance rehearsal:** You transfer the information from your STM through repetition until it's committed to long-term storage.

- ✔ **Elaborative rehearsal:** Your mind elaborates on the information, integrating it with your existing memories. When information is meaningful and references something that you already know, remembering is easier and forgetting becomes harder.

The more you process the information, linking it to what you already know, the better you will remember it!

You can break down the LTM into three basic divisions:

- ✔ **Episodic memory:** Events and situations unique to your experiences (marriages, birthdays, graduations, car accidents, what happened yesterday, and so on)

- ✔ **Semantic memory:** Factual information such as important holidays, the name of the first president of the United States, and your Social Security number

- ✔ **Procedural memory:** Information on how to do things like riding a bike, solving a math problem, or tying your shoes

Theoretically, the size and time capacity of LTM is infinite because researchers haven't found a way to test its capacity. It has enough capacity to get the job done. This may sound kind of strange when you consider how much information you seem to forget. If the information is in there somewhere, why do you forget it?

Fahgetaboudit!

Have you ever been told to forget about something? Try this: Forget about cheese. Did it work? Did you forget about cheese or did you actually think more about cheese? The irony of someone telling you to forget something is that it's impossible to forget about something you're actively thinking about, making "forget about it" bogus advice. If someone really wants you to forget about something, then she shouldn't mention it to you at all.

Forgetting information stored in LTM is more of an issue of not being able to access it rather than the information not being there. Two forms of access failure occur, and both involve other information getting in the way:

- **Retroactive interference:** Having a hard time remembering older information because newer information is getting in the way

- **Proactive interference:** Having a hard time remembering newer information because older information is getting in the way

The next time you watch a sitcom on television, try to remember the details of the first 10 to 12 minutes, the middle 10 to 12 minutes, and the last 10 to 12 minutes of the program. Or, listen to a lecture and try to remember what was said during the beginning, middle, and end of the presentation. You may notice something psychologists call the *serial position effect*. Information from the beginning and end of the show or lecture is easier to remember than the middle. Why is that?

The serial position effect occurs because the information at the beginning of the show or lecture is usually committed to long-term memory due to the amount of time that elapses. The information at the end of the show is being kept in your short-term memory because it's fresh in your mind. The middle stuff? It's just gone.

Conceptualizing

When was the last time you went out with a friend just to talk? Did you go to a coffeehouse? Did you talk about recent romances and frustrating relationships in your life? Did you talk about politics or the weather? It doesn't matter; you were talking about a concept.

A *concept* is a thought or idea that represents a set of related ideas. *Romance* is a concept. *Relationship* is a concept. *Politics* is a concept. *Weather* is a concept. All these concepts are represented as symbols in your information-processing system of thought, and they get into this system through learning. In other words, concepts are derived and generated; they are formed. When objects share characteristics, they represent the same concept. Some concepts are well-defined, others are not.

Consider the following words:

Tail, Fur, Teeth, Four Legs

What do these words describe? It could be a cat, a dog, a lion, or a bear. The fact is, you really can't tell just from those words. Some crucial detail is missing, some piece of information that clearly defines the concept and separates it from others.

Now, consider this list of words:

> Tail, Fur, Teeth, Four Legs, Bark

What is being described now? This has to be a dog. Why? Cats, lions, and bears don't bark. The feature "bark" uniquely defines the concept of "dog." "Bark" is the concept's *defining feature*. It is an attribute that must be present in order for the object to be classified as an example of a particular concept. Consider the following words:

> Feathers, Beak, Eggs, Fly

These words describe a bird. Hold on a minute. Aren't there at least two birds that don't fly? Penguins and ostriches don't fly, but they're still birds. So, flying is not a defining feature of a bird because animals don't have to have that attribute in order to be considered a bird. However, most birds do fly, so "flying" is what is called a *characteristic feature* or attribute. It is an attribute that most, but not all, members of a concept group possess.

Think about a chair. Try to imagine and picture a chair. Now, describe it. (Describe it to someone else or you'll look funny describing an imaginary chair to yourself.) Your imagined chair probably consists of wood, four legs, a rectangular or square seat, and a back constructed of two vertical supports on each side of the seat connected by a couple of horizontal slats. This is a typical chair. It's common. In fact, it may be considered as a prototypical chair. A *prototype* is the most typical example of an object or event within a particular category. It is the quintessential example of the concept being represented.

Thinking is much more complex than simple one-word descriptions. When developing a thought, single word concepts are combined into sentence-long concepts, sentence-long concepts into paragraph-long concepts, and so on. In other words, attributes are combined into concepts. Concepts are combined into propositions. Multiple propositions are combined into mental models. Finally, mental models are combined into schemas, which are used to represent the world in a language of thought.

For example, check out this process, which continuously builds upon itself:

- ✔ **Proposition:** "War is hell" is a combination of two related concepts, war and hell being related.

- ✔ **Mental model:** Clustering thoughts help you understand how things relate to each other:
  - War is hell.
  - World War II was a war.
  - World War II was hell.

✔ **Schemas:** Organizing mental models into larger groups form basic units of understanding that represent the world. An example here is "Some of the soldiers who fought in WWII experienced psychological trauma. Some people believe that this was due to the extreme nature of war. Some people have even said that war is hell."

Another example may be to consider the concept "book." Combine the concept of book with another concept, like reading. Then connect those concepts to another concept, like library. Now you have three related concepts: book, reading, and library. This set of concepts may form the proposition of studying (as opposed to reading for pleasure). You can then embed studying into larger divisions, or schema, of school or a certification process.

Concepts are formed from co-occurring features encountered in experience. They represent ideas in relation to each other. That is, in order to understand, comprehend, or grasp the meaning of a concept, the representational mind relates concepts to other concepts.

For example, anyone who regularly interacts with kids will tell you how difficult it is to explain certain concepts to a curious toddler because it's tough to find words she already knows and can use as a reference.

Child: "What's a computer?"

Parent: "A computer is like a . . . a . . . um . . . TV . . . um . . . but . . . um . . . you can type on it."

Child: What's type mean?

See where this is going?

Some cognitive scientists and psychologists have found their way out of this concept trap by suggesting that all concepts are innate and inborn. One of the more interesting and fruitful approaches to this problem comes from the theories of *embodied cognition (EC)* and *embodied simulation (ES)*.

The core idea behind EC and ES is that the mind comprehends or grasps concepts through a process of simulation that uses the motor and perceptual parts of the thinker's brain to represent the experience. This simulation allows for comprehension because people understand concepts through reference to the bodily experiences they associated with them.

"In over your head"

"Slap in the face"

"Eye-opening experience"

All capture the essence of EC and ES. You understand the meaning of these phrases in terms of bodily experience. Bodily, sensory, and motor experiences are the meaning; they are the experience, the concept. If I want to understand a new concept, I use my body, sensory, and motor experiences to come to an understanding. I understand "eye-opening experience" because I have opened my eyes and know (because I've experienced it) what that means.

Interestingly, EC/ES proponents say that the parts of the brain that you use to actually open your eyes, or move your arm, or see the sunrise are the same parts of that you use when you conceptualize the meaning of "eye-opening" and other such phrases. Ultimately EC/ES are relative newcomers to the cognitive psychology arena, but they hold a lot of promise and are being hotly researched.

Making decisions

Go left and get there five minutes late. Go right and *maybe* get there on time; it's a risk because sometimes there's major traffic that way. It may mean you'll be 20 minutes late. For many people, the morning commute is a daily problem. How can you get to work on time with the least amount of travel time, encountering the least amount of traffic, and experiencing the least amount of stress? You have to solve this problem, and part of solving this problem requires you to make some decisions. Perhaps you'll use reasoning to choose your course; maybe you won't.

People solve problems all day long and make hundreds, if not thousands, of decisions every day. In fact, a condition related to mental exhaustion is called "decision fatigue" — simply having too many problems and making too many decisions in a given day. Some choices are life or death, some less so; but it all adds up.

Decision making is the act of choosing an option or action from a set of options based on criteria and a strategy. The study of decision making is really a complex cross-discipline science in and of itself, spanning economics, political science, computer science, management and business, and marketing. And I don't know about you, but sometimes I just flip a coin.

I once worked at a job in which the most important decision made all day long (at least as perceived by my co-workers) was where to go for lunch. We had a "Wheel-O-Lunch" we'd spin; where it stopped was where we'd go — theoretically. Usually we ended up discussing and ultimately overriding the wheel's "choice" due to recollections of bloating, large bills, or "I had that for dinner last night" qualifiers and caveats. This illustrates a point well discussed in decision-making research: There is more than one way to make a decision, and most people use a variety of approaches.

Choosing

Flipping a coin is one way to make a decision, but that's not really a cognitive process, is it? It's simply a way of letting chance choose for you — it's not really choosing at all. But people do make choices by using processes such as *intuitive decision making* which refers to choices based on what is most easy, familiar, or preferred. I'm sure you can see how this may work some of the time, but sometimes a decision to do what is preferred is the wrong choice. Just think about the last time you ended up eating that fourth piece of cake only to regret it later.

Decisions can also come from a more scientific approach based on *empirical* evidence through trial and error, experiment, estimation, experience, or consultation with an expert. *Consumer Reports* provides experimental evidence to tell you which blender to buy or which brand of deodorant to use.

If you are pressed for time or need to make a lot of decisions with limited resources, then your choice for choosing may be to use a *heuristic,* which is a mental short cut based on principles, rules, maxims, and so forth. Ethical decision making can be considered heuristic, choosing based on a code of ethics. My religious beliefs may be factored in to my decision making.

Amos Tversky and Daniel Kahneman studied heuristic decision making and identified different types of this model. Here are two commonly used heuristics:

- **Representative heuristic:** Making a choice based on the situation in question being similar to another situation. If you were lost in the forest while on a horse-riding outing you may try to retrace your tracks to find your way out. You start looking for your tracks and by using the representative heuristic, decide that the tracks you find are, in fact, horse tracks because you are familiar with and know what horse tracks look like. Too bad you don't know what bear tracks look like!

- **Availability heuristic:** Making a decision based on how easily or readily available information is. This is the "first thing that comes to mind" approach to choosing. News agencies are guilty of spreading the use of this heuristic. Oftentimes they all report on the same story or similar stories so the most recent story of the latest fad diet is fresh on your mind. The next time you choose a diet, let the heuristic choose for you, fad all the way!

Reasoning

Reasoning is a thinking process that involves two basic components:

- **Premises:** These are statements about some object or event that support a conclusion. Premises declare some state of affairs such as, "All fire trucks are red." Another premise may be, "My dad drives a fire truck at work."

> ✔ **Conclusions:** The points derived from the premises. They are only valid if they can be logically or reasonably drawn from the premises. A logical conclusion for the premises stated here may be, "My dad drives a red truck at work."

Reasoning is the act of drawing conclusions based on the truth of the premises that precede the conclusion. Reasoning can help people figure out if their conclusions are valid or if they make logical sense. When arguments make logical sense, reasoning is good. It makes logical sense that my dad drives a red fire truck at work because this follows from the premises.

But what if it went like this: All fire trucks are red. My dad's truck is red. Therefore, my dad's truck is a fire truck. This is not logical because the first premise doesn't state that all trucks are red, only that fire trucks are red. So, other trucks can be red, including fire trucks. My dad may drive a red Toyota. Logic is like a measuring stick for verifying our reasoning.

There are two basic types of reasoning:

> ✔ **Inductive:** In inductive reasoning, you begin with making observations (the premises) in order to collect facts to support or disconfirm (validate) some hypothetically stated outcome or situation (the conclusion).
>
> Consider the following:
>
> Monday it rained.
>
> Tuesday it rained.
>
> Therefore, I conclude that Wednesday it is going to rain.
>
> This is an example of inductive reasoning. Two observations or premises are used to predict a third outcome. I think my local weather person uses inductive logic to make his forecasts, not the million-dollar computer technology that the TV station advertises.

> ✔ **Deductive:** Deductive reasoning uses premises that claim to provide conclusive proof of truth for the conclusion. A conclusion based on deductive logic is by necessity true provided that it begins with true premises. Deduction often begins with generalizations and reasons to particulars.
>
> Consider the following example of deductive reasoning:
>
> All men should be free.
>
> I am a man.
>
> Therefore, I should be free.
>
> The conclusion follows logically from the two premises. It has to be that way based on what is stated in the premises. Here's an example of a false conclusion:

> All chickens lay eggs.
>
> My bird laid an egg.
>
> Therefore, my bird must be a chicken.
>
> This is false because the first premise refers to a subset of the larger category, birds. The second premise includes this larger category, and therefore refers to some events not covered by the first premise. If you turn the two premises around, you can create a logically valid argument:
>
> All birds lay eggs.
>
> My chicken laid an egg.
>
> Therefore, my chicken must be a bird.

People make decisions in some pretty haphazard ways. What happened to deliberation, to thinking things through, to being rational? *Rational* decision-making models are all based on the assumption that people make decisions after weighing the costs and benefits of options and ultimately choosing the option in which the benefits outweigh the costs. These costs may include factors such as utility, risks, functionality, and quality.

The famous psychologist Herbert Simon proposed that although humans can be rational decision makers, this rationality has *bounds,* or limits. In his theory of *bounded rationality,* Simon proposes that because the environment is so complex, a prospective decision maker cannot possibly rationally weigh out *all* the options in order to come to the optimal decision. So, rational decisions are bound; therefore, decisions must be based on limited information, short cuts, and reasonable estimation. Simon does not lament this situation; he states that bounded rationality is a fact of cognition and the human mind, and it usually results in relatively solid and good decisions.

Dan Ariely in his well-known book *Predictably Irrational: The Hidden Forces that Shape Our Decisions* (2008), further addressed the concept of limited rationality. He experimentally identified many situations in which decisions are not only based on incomplete information but also are sometimes downright irrational and based on nonoptimal information. Bottom line, people make irrational decisions. What's interesting is that Ariely shows that people make irrational decisions in predictable ways:

✔ **Relativity:** Sometimes a choice between two options is based on the relation between them, not on the absolute quality of each choice. For example, in US presidential elections, many people say they dislike both candidates, but end up picking the one they determine is "less bad."

✔ **It's Free:** Free things are good right? Well, not always; but sometimes a less good choice is made (irrational) because of its free status. Waiting in line for three hours to get a free gift with purchase isn't always worth the three hours of waiting.

> ✔ **Hot and Cold:** Decisions made when you're emotionally aroused are different from the choices you make when you're calm. This is an oldie but goodie when it comes to common sense and decision making; yet people violate it all the time. Decisions made when emotions run strong can be predictably irrational.

Supposedly, reasoning and the ability to solve problems logically are two of the primary abilities that set humans apart from animals. In case you're wondering, humans can reason, animals can't. I know that this fact may be up for debate, especially if you consider all the human behavior and decisions that are clearly not based on reason, but bear with me. I'm talking about capability, not performance.

Solving problems

Problem solving sounds pretty straightforward. You have a problem, and you solve it. Did you ever watch that television show *MacGyver* from the 1980s? MacGyver could solve just about any problem that came his way. He could turn a toothpick into a Jet Ski or a rocket launcher. I'd sit back and watch in amazement, and then I'd get out my trusty toolbox and dismantle the toaster, trying to turn it into a satellite receiver — four hours later, I'd just have a pile of parts and no way to make toast. MacGyver clearly had better problem-solving skills than me.

Newell and Simon (1972) are pretty much the godfathers of problem-solving psychology. Nearly every research study on the topic cites their study. They defined these basic steps of the problem-solving process:

1. Recognizing that a problem exists
2. Constructing a representation of the situation that includes the initial state of the problem and the eventual goal (a solution)
3. Generating and evaluating possible solutions
4. Selecting a solution to attempt
5. Executing the solution and determining if it actually works

These steps are sometimes identified by the acronym IDEAL, which Bransford and Stein formulated in 1993:

I — Identify the problem

D — Define and represent the problem

E — Explore possible strategies

A — Action

L — Look back and evaluate the effects

The world has as many problem-solving strategies as there are problems, but most people tend to use the same ones over and over again. For instance, *trial and error* is a popular way to solve a problem. I've seen young children use trial and error when trying to put shapes into their respective holes in a bucket. A child will pick up the circle block and try putting it in every cut-out until it fits, and then move on to the next block.

The trial-and-error strategy is pretty inefficient, but sometimes it's the only strategy available, particularly for situations that have no clear definition for the problem, when part of the process is figuring out what the problem is.

Here are a couple more common problem-solving techniques:

- **Means-ends analysis:** This strategy involves breaking the problem down into smaller sub-problems to solve to get to the end result.

- **Working backwards:** This way to solve a problem is like taking something apart and putting it back together again in order to figure out how the object (or problem) is built.

- **Brainstorming:** A technique that involves coming up with as many possible solutions to the problem without editing them in any way. It doesn't matter how implausible, unfeasible, idiotic, or ridiculous the solutions are; you just put them all out there and eliminate them after you can't think of any more possible solutions. Even my idea to have Superman use his super-cool breath to stop global warming is included in this technique.

- **Analogies and metaphors:** These strategies involve using a parallel or similar problem that has already been solved to solve a previously unrelated problem. The Cuban Missile Crisis was like a nuclear-powered game of chicken, and whoever flinched, blinked, or chickened out first was the loser. I guess President Kennedy was pretty good at playing chicken.

Thinking You're Pretty Smart

Acting intelligently is perhaps the pinnacle and most grand cognitive process of the human mind. After all, the cognitive processes of managing information and the various components of attention, remembering things, and so forth ought to produce something useful, right? Indeed, you can view intelligence as the collective output of human cognition that results in an ability to achieve goals, adapt, and function in the world. This is *intelligent behavior.*

Psychologists have been trying to figure out what intelligence is for a long time. Plenty of examples exist to support the theory that humans lack intelligence. Just take a look at those goofy home-video shows. A guy forgets to turn off the electricity before rewiring a room, or a hiker tries to feed a bear and almost becomes dinner. Maybe I'm entertained by these misfortunes of others caught on videotape because these people couldn't have been any less intelligent. Or perhaps I feel giddy because I did not suffer their fate.

People differ in their abilities to solve problems, learn, think logically, use language well, understand and acquire concepts, deal with abstractions, integrate ideas, attain goals, and so on. This impressive list of human abilities represents some of the ideas of what intelligence actually is; these abilities *are* the stuff of intelligence. For a more concrete definition, *intelligence* can be understood as a collection of cognitive abilities that allows a person to learn from experience, adapt successfully to the world, and go beyond the information presented in the environment.

Considering the factors of Intelligence

Sure, intelligence is a collection of cognitive abilities, but a unifying construct called "intelligence" that can be measured and quantified must exist, right? Psychologists think so, and they've been working tirelessly to test and measure intelligence for a long time. As part of this work, psychologists have developed intelligence tests and worked with militaries, schools, and corporations, trying to sort individual differences in intelligence in the service of job selection, academic honors, and promotions. From all this testing has emerged the concept of "g" as a general and measurable intelligence factor.

The g-factor is comprised of subcomponents known as *s-factors*. Together, the g- and s-factors comprise what is called the *two-factor theory of intelligence*:

- **g-factor:** Some psychologist comes up with a test of mental abilities and gives it to a lot of people. When a score is calculated and averaged across abilities, a general intelligence factor is established. This is factor one of the two-factor theory, commonly referred to as the *g-factor,* or the general intelligence factor. It is meant to represent how generally intelligent you are based on your performance on this type of intelligence test.

- **s-factor:** The individual scores on each of the specific ability tests represent the s-factors. An s-factor score represents a person's ability within one particular area. Put all the s-factors together, and you get the g-factor. Commonly measured s-factors of intelligence include memory, attention and concentration, verbal comprehension, vocabulary, spatial skills, and abstract reasoning.

So, intelligence according to the psychometric theory is a score on an intelligence test. How can this be? Each test is made up of subtests, and typically, people who score high on one test do well on the other tests, too. This reveals a relationship among the individual abilities as measured by the subtests; the general intelligence concept underlies that relationship.

In a related theory, psychologist and intelligence research pioneer Louis Thurston (1887–1955) came up with a theory of intelligence called *primary mental abilities*. It's basically the same concept as the s-factor part of the two-factor theory, with a little more detail. For Thurston, intelligence is represented by an individual's different levels of performance in seven areas: verbal comprehension, word fluency, number, memory, space, perceptual speed, and reasoning. Thurston's work, however, has received very little research support.

Getting a closer look

Psychologists continue to divide general intelligence into specific factors. The *Cattell-Horn-Carroll Theory of Cognitive Abilities* (CHC Theory) proposes that "g" is comprised of multiple cognitive abilities that when taken as a whole produce "g." Early work by the individual contributors to CHC theory, Raymond Cattell, John Horn, and John Carroll, converged to produce a model of general intelligence consisting of ten strata with numerous individual abilities within those strata. They are as follows:

- **Crystallized intelligence (Gc):** comprehensive and acquired knowledge
- **Fluid intelligence:** reason and problem-solving abilities
- **Quantitative reasoning:** quantitative and numerical ability
- **Reading and writing ability:** reading and writing
- **Short-term memory:** immediate memory
- **Long-term storage and retrieval:** long-term memory
- **Visual processing:** analysis and use of visual information
- **Auditory processing:** analysis and use of auditory information
- **Processing speed:** thinking fast and automatically
- **Decision and reaction speed:** coming to a decision and reacting swiftly

Researchers continue to work with the CHC model and have developed research programs looking into adding to the 10 strata. Many professionals believe that sensory and motor abilities need to be more fully included in this theory, and researchers are looking at "tentative" factors such as tactile abilities (touch), kinesthetic ability (movement), olfactory ability (sense of smell), and psychomotor ability and speed. Wait a minute, you mean I can be a smart smeller?

Many intelligence researchers and practitioners have accepted CHC as a triumph of psychological science and the consensus model of psychometric conceptions of intelligence. It is, however, a working model, and many intelligence investigators and theorists consider CHC theory as a strong beginning or second act but not the final word on intelligence.

Adding in street smarts

Robert Sternberg developed the *triarchic theory* of intelligence in part to address the street smarts controversy, which holds that many intelligent people may be smart when it comes to academics or in the classroom but lack common sense in real life or practical matters. An urban myth claims that Albert Einstein, unquestionably gifted in mathematics and physics, couldn't tie his own shoes. I don't know if this is true or not, but Sternberg seems to agree that an important aspect of being intelligent is possessing a good level of common sense or practical intelligence. The three intelligence components of his theory are as follows:

- **Componential:** *Componential intelligence* depends on the same factors measured by traditional intelligence tests (memory, verbal fluency, and so on). This is the book smarts aspect of intelligence. Sternberg emphasized that these abilities are often disconnected from ordinary life, issues, and problems. Einstein seemed to have possessed this component.

- **Experiential:** *Experiential intelligence* encompasses the ability to deal with two different types of problems: new problems and routine problems. It requires the ability to recognize new problems, as opposed to everyday problems; search for and generate solutions; and implement solutions.

- **Contextual:** *Contextual intelligence* is a type of practical intelligence that allows people to go about their daily lives without walking in front of cars, telling police officers to get lost, or letting the trash pile up to the ceiling. This is the street smarts aspect of intelligence that psychologists sometimes seem to lack in the eyes of their clients.

Excelling with multiple intelligences

Have you ever wondered what makes Michael Jordan such a good basketball player? What about Mozart? He wrote entire operas in one sitting without editing. That's pretty impressive! According to Howard Gardener (1983), each of these men display a specific type of intelligence.

Gardener generated a theory known as *multiple intelligences* from observing extremely talented and gifted people. He came up with seven types of intelligence that are typically left out of conventional theories about intelligence:

- **Bodily kinesthetic ability:** Michael Jordan seems to possess a lot of this ability. People high in bodily kinesthetic ability have superior hand-eye coordination, a great sense of balance, and a keen understanding of and control over their bodies while engaged in physical activities.

- ✔ **Musical ability:** If you can tap your foot and clap your hands in unison, then you've got a little musical intelligence — a little. People high in musical intelligence possess the natural ability to read, write, and play music exceptionally well.

- ✔ **Spatial ability:** Have you ever gotten lost in your own backyard? If so, you probably don't have a very high level of spatial intelligence. This intelligence involves the ability to navigate and move around in space and the ability to picture three-dimensional scenes in your mind.

- ✔ **Linguistic ability:** This is the traditional ability to read, write, and speak well. Poets, writers, and articulate speakers are high in this ability.

- ✔ **Logical-mathematical ability:** This intelligence includes basic and complex mathematical problem-solving ability.

- ✔ **Interpersonal ability:** The gift of gab and the used-car salesman act are good examples of interpersonal intelligence. A "people person" who has good conversational skills and knows how to interact and relate well with others is high in interpersonal ability.

- ✔ **Intrapersonal ability:** How well do you know yourself? Intrapersonal intelligence involves the ability to understand your motives, emotions, and other aspects of your personality.

Any one of us can have varying degrees of Gardener's intelligences. I may be one heck of a baseball player and a singing math whiz, but I may be unable to carry a conversation, get lost walking home from the grocery, and have no idea how I feel about all that.

Making the grade — on a curve

Psychologists like to measure stuff, especially stuff related to human behavior and thought processes, like cognitive abilities. Measuring and documenting individual differences is at the core of applied psychological science (find more on applied psychology in my free online article "Applying Psychology For a Better World" at www.dummies.com/extras/psychology).

Whether you ascribe to CHC, Sternberg's model, or the concept of multiple intelligences, don't forget the concept of average. Intelligence is considered to exist in the human population along what is called a *normal distribution*. A normal distribution is essentially a statistical concept that relates to the ultimate range of any particular trait or psychological phenomenon across a population.

Individuals vary in how intelligent they are. A normal distribution (see Figure 6-1) is established by assuming that if the full population took an intelligence test, most people would center around average scores with some variation — from slightly less than average to slightly higher than average. A normal distribution is also referred to as a *Bell Curve* because it looks like a bell with a bulky center and flattening right and left ends. Most people are somewhere in the range of average intelligence. Increasingly fewer people are at intelligence levels that are closer to the highest and lowest ends of the spectrum.

Figure 6-1:
Normal
distribution.

At the high end of the intelligence curve are people considered *intellectually gifted*; at the low end are those considered *intellectually disabled* (see Chapter 13 for more on intellectual disability).

Shining bright

Einstein was a genius right? So what exactly is a genius?

Psychologists typically refer to super-smart people as intellectually gifted rather than use the term genius. But there is no uniform cutoff score on an intelligence test to determine giftedness. An average standard intelligence score is 100 and, generally speaking, any score above 120 is considered superior. Giftedness is granted to people in the top 1 to 3 percent of the population. That is, out of 100 people, only one, two, or three are considered gifted.

Many psychologists are wary of defining giftedness in such numerical and statistical terms and warn that cultural and societal context must be factored in. One culture's genius is another culture's madman? I'm not sure it's that dramatic, but it is important to consider that giftedness is multifaceted and not so easily tied to a cutoff score.

Numerous attempts have been made to pin down a definition of intellectual giftedness. Eminent American psychologist Robert Sternberg proposed that giftedness is more than superior skills related to information processing and analysis; it also includes superior ability to capitalize on and learn from one's experiences to quickly solve future problems and automatize problem solving. He proposed that gifted people are especially skilled at adapting to and selecting optimal environments in a way that goes beyond basic information processing and what is considered general intelligence or "g."

Researchers continue to examine the concept of intellectual giftedness, and one consistent finding is that gifted individuals have stronger *metacognitive skills*, or knowledge of their own mental processes and how to regulate them. These three specific metacognitive strategies are often used by gifted individuals:

- ✔ **Selective Encoding:** Distinguishing between relevant and irrelevant information

- ✔ **Selective Combination:** Pulling together seemingly disparate elements of a problem for a novel solution

- ✔ **Selective Comparison**: Discovering new and nonobvious connections between new and old information

Figuring Out Language

Intelligence is definitely a crowning achievement of cognition, bringing together component processes to produce learning and adapting beings, you and me! But stopping with intelligence sells human cognition short because another amazing and sophisticated set of processes accomplishes the unified goal of language.

The human mind produces, utilizes, and comprehends language. It is one of the most sophisticated and unique cognitive abilities that humans possess. Yes, other species communicate with sounds and have "language" of sorts — think whales and birds — but when was the last time a dolphin told a story or wrote the *sus scrofa domesticus* (pigs) equivalent to *Romeo and Juliet* (would that be *Ham*let?)

Language as a cognitive process has been extensively studied and hotly debated, and continues to be a central focus of cognitive psychology. The study of language in general is called *linguistics,* and the psychological study of language is called *psycholinguistics.*

Babel-On

Perhaps one of the most amazing things about language is that you and I ever learn how to do it. Babies don't come out talking. They take their time, absorbing and learning. Eventually sounds, words, sentences, paragraphs, stories, and treatises all come out.

In Chapter 12, I introduce language developmental milestones to give you a sense of what kinds of language should be happening when. This section describes the underlying cognitive models of how language develops in the first place.

Numerous models of language development exist in the fields of linguistics and psycholinguistics, but the three most prominent are *Nativist, Behaviorist,* and *Interactionist.*

Nativist

Noam Chomsky, a philosopher, linguist, and political thinker, is the foremost proponent of nativist theory. The core of the nativist argument is that language is innate, essentially inborn, and wired into your DNA and brain development. In many ways it simply unfolds as does the development of the brain, liver, pancreas, and that weird-shaped birthmark on your back.

The rules of language are inborn in what Chomsky calls *Universal Grammar.* All speakers in the world, regardless of individual language differences possess this universal grammar as part of their human genetic endowment. Children can even create their own languages or various forms of slang with its own grammatical rules and structure because of something Chomksy calls the *language acquisition device* — an inborn cognitive module or mechanism that is triggered by language in the environment. Note that, according to his view, the module is only triggered; there is no learning from the environment going on.

Behaviorist

The behaviorist model says language is learned. People learn it by observing speakers in the world and through classical and operant conditioning processes (see Chapter 8 for more on classical and operant conditioning). Evidence in support of the behaviorist perspective includes the fact that it can take months and sometimes years for a person to develop proper language skills. Behaviorists believe this illustrates the learning process.

Interactionist

Nature or nurture? Both! Language is innate *and* learned according to this model. A prominent version of interactionist theory is the *social interactionist* approach, which holds that parents and mature language speakers model and provide a learning scaffold for language learners, guiding them toward mature and correct language use through social interaction.

Sounds, bites, pieces, and pieces

To understand how the mind does language, researchers have broken the it into different parts. Language, it seems, can be understood in terms of the rules of its use, known as *grammar.* Grammar is divided into three parts:

- ✔ **Phonology:** the smallest units of speech (phonemes) that determine how sounds are used to make words

- ✔ **Syntax:** ways in which words and phrases are combined to make sentences

- ✔ **Semantics:** meaning

An estimated 800 or so different phonemes exist in the human language family. English speakers use 52; some languages use well over 100. Think about how various languages sound. Some seem faster. Some use guttural sounds; other seem smooth and airy. Different languages have different sounds and phoneme (the smallest distinct unit of sound in a language) use.

Consider this sentence: Store the to Jon went. Does that sound right to you? Probably not, because the rules of syntax determine how words are put together in a way that makes sense in a given language. Also, subtle changes in positions of words within a sentence can change the meaning of a particular phrase and convey a very different thought. Take the following words, for example, and see how rearranging them changes the meaning of each phrase drastically: robbed, Louis, bank, the.

> Louis robbed the bank.

> The bank robbed Louis.

These mean two very different things. Same words, different meanings depending on syntax. Either way, poor Louis.

I've noticed an interesting phenomenon when conducting cognitive testing and administering vocabulary tests. Certain wrong definitions occur over and over again. I ask a person the meaning of the word "yesterday," and she answers, "The things I did yesterday." Now, I'm not sure what that means per se, but the fact that this definition, albeit not really the right one, occurs again and again is fascinating. To these people, "yesterday" refers to the set of actions he or she engaged in on the previous day. The word means something different to them than it does to me.

Because I don't really know what they are talking about, we are not really communicating or understanding each other. The other person is not responding to the semantic rule of grammar that determines the shared and agreed upon definition of the word "yesterday." Semantic rules determine that the meanings of words are universal or widely understood and agreed upon, which makes it possible to communicate. When you say "elephant," I know you're talking about a large animal with a long nose because of semantics. This all applies to signed languages, too, which have their own grammar and which will develop in the same way as spoken languages provided there is a rich signing environment around a deaf child.

Chapter 7

How Does That Make You Feel?

*W*hy do people get up and go to work every day? Why did my teenage cousin get her bellybutton pierced? Why do people go to the gym? Honestly, I think the best part of psychology is getting to ask all these interesting questions!

But there isn't always a lot of mystery behind why people do what they do. Most of us work to pay the bills and earn money for vacations, comfort, and entertainment. You eat to stay alive. You tolerate irritating neighbors to avoid going to jail. These things make sense and don't usually require much thought. But when someone does something extraordinary, extremely difficult, or horrific, the "Why?" question comes up.

Trauma, especially when caused by someone else, often leaves a person feeling confused and in need of answers. Why would someone do such a thing to me? Answers can help people come to terms with the way they feel.

But the quest for answers isn't always focused on the negative. Take Mother Teresa, for example. She dedicated the greater part of her life to working with the sick and the poor in India. She lived in abject poverty, sacrificing all comfort in order to help the poor and seemingly forgotten. Why would she do such a thing? Mother Teresa's dedication to her religious calling and duty was remarkable. She endured harsh conditions and stayed the course; her motivation was strong and unyielding. Were her actions a result of love for the people she helped?

In this chapter, I introduce the psychological approach to motivation. Simply knowing the nuts and bolts of an action leaves a gaping hole in what you know about behavior if you don't know why someone chooses a certain course of action — or at least why he thinks he does something.

In addition to exploring the various theories of motivation, I also take a look at emotions, which some psychologists tag as the primary motivating factors for all of us. Psychologists make a big deal about emotions because of the central role emotions play in human behavior and mental processes. "Why we do what we do" has a lot to do with the way we feel.

A popular retort about seeing a psychologist is that she'll always ask, "How does that make you feel?" So what's the big deal about feelings and emotions? Most people agree that being hungry or tired can be important. But wait a minute. Is hunger a feeling? What about feeling tired? It seems like some people wouldn't know an emotion if it crash-landed on their doorstep. Yet other people seem to be a little too "in touch" with their emotions. For the record: Hunger and fatigue are not considered emotions. But, like food and sleep, emotions are important to psychological survival.

Calling on Tony for Some Motivation

Tony Robbins, an American motivational speaker, has built a multimillion-dollar empire by helping people find their proverbial kick in the pants. I'm not familiar with the specifics of his technique, and I'm not even sure his approach to motivation really works, but he's got an army of celebrities endorsing him. And from a business standpoint, it doesn't really matter whether or not his technique really works. The point is that people want to be motivated. People need to be motivated. People are spending a lot of money to find out how to motivate themselves the Tony Robbins way.

It's hard to imagine life without motivation. Without incentive to get things done, I may decide to just sit on the couch all day, eating chips and watching television. Not everyone wants to save the world or cure cancer! Whatever I choose to do, psychologists who study motivation believe that some psychological process is responsible for my behavior.

In the following sections I describe the various theories related to the sources and structures of motivation — ranging from basic biological needs to a striving for independence and freedom.

Would you like some adrenaline with that bear?

Over the course of human evolution, certain behaviors were naturally selected (put in the "to keep" pile) because they contribute to the survival of particular individuals in a species. Imagine a group of people that lives in a forest with wolves, bears, and various other dangerous beasts. Now, imagine that a group of three men and three women from this community encounters a bear. One man and one woman take off running the instant they see the bear, and they get away. Another man and woman stand there, frozen in their tracks. They become the bear's lunch. The final couple tries to fight the bear with sticks and rocks. They lose.

If the man and woman who ran away decide to have a child, there's a good chance that their child will be a runner when it comes to encounters with bears. The other couples (the freezers and the fighters) died, so they can't have children. This is a crude illustration of how evolution selects for traits that help us survive. Those who survive reproduce. It is safe to assume that the couple that ran away had better instincts than the other two couples. Their instincts were better in the sense that they were able to stay alive. Instincts that help keep us alive stay in the gene pool.

Trusting your instincts

Does a plant grow toward sunlight because it wants to? Would a little rebellious plant, the black sheep of ferns, grow toward the shade just to be different? No, a plant couldn't perform this feat even if it wanted to. Plants grow toward the sunlight because they can't help themselves. They need sunlight in order to survive. That's an instinct.

An *instinct* is an automatic, involuntary, and unlearned behavior that occurs in response to a specific trigger, or *stimulus*. Numerous examples of what are considered human instincts can be found in phrases that people use every day: the maternal instinct, the survival instinct, the killer instinct, the gut instinct, and so on. Instincts motivate in the sense that you do what you do because you have to do it. You take certain actions automatically and involuntarily.

James McDougall came up with a way to classify some of our basic instincts. He believed that an instinct can be identified by pinpointing its intended goal. He identified numerous instincts, including parenting, seeking food, and mating. If you're looking to relieve your guilt about eating so many cheeseburgers, you can use the nonscientific and flimsy excuse: It's just your food-seeking curiosity instinct driving you!

A lot of instinct research has been done with animals. Instincts are also called "modal action patterns" by animal researchers. Geese fly south for the winter. Why? Maybe they like the poolside bars in Florida, or maybe it's instinct. Konrad Lorenz conducted extensive research exploring the instinctive behaviors of animals. Lorenz's specific approach is known as the *ethological* approach to motivation; and according to Petri, an ethologist, instinctive behaviors have *action specific energy* — the idea that a specific trigger sets an instinct into action. All instinctive behaviors have a specific trigger or triggers, called *key stimuli.* Driving by a nice coffee shop is a key stimulus for my coffee instinct. Maybe caffeine helped my ancestors survive. Were there Starbucks in Neolithic Europe, I wonder? Key stimuli come from the environment. Key stimuli that come from other members of an animal group are called *releasers*.

Key stimuli produce behaviors that are fixed and automatic. These behaviors are called *fixed action patterns.* One of the popular examples of a fixed action pattern is something that Lorenz called *imprinting.* Imprinting is a kind of bonding instinct between a young animal and its parents. Remember that cartoon where the baby duck hatches from its egg and starts following around the first animal that it sees, even though it's not a duck? That's imprinting.

Feeling needy

Many people can relate to being worried about money and finances. I'm sure that even the billionaires of the world have spent one or two sleepless nights of their lives mentally counting their Benjamins. Some have learned to live on a budget, setting aside money for the mortgage, car payments, medical insurance, and household costs — even keeping a little money for entertainment if there's any left over. When I started living on a budget, something weird began to happen. When I went to a store and saw something I liked, such as a pair of shoes or fancy power tool, I asked myself if I really needed it. Part of developing a budget involves figuring out what you truly need and what your financial priorities are.

I first spend my money on what I need. My needs are a powerful determinant in what I do with my money. I may even say that I'm *driven* (or pushed) by my prioritized needs. Satisfying my needs is one of my top, if not the top, drives in my life. Needs drive my behavior; they motivate me.

Clark Hull came up with a theory of motivation that emphasized need satisfaction. Needs are generated from two things: *homeostasis* and *equilibrium restoration.* I experience homeostasis when my needs are met and I feel balanced — not in need of anything. When my needs aren't being met, I find myself out of balance, and I'm then motivated to restore the equilibrium through the satisfaction of my needs.

Hull's theory is called *drive reduction theory* because people are driven to satisfy their needs. *Drives* are motivations toward satisfaction and homeostasis. There are two kinds of drives:

✔ Biological needs that are necessary for survival are called *primary drives.* Hunger, fatigue, and thirst are all examples of primary drives. If you think about it, primary drives play a pretty big role in everyday life. A large part of the day revolves around satisfying hunger and obtaining shelter.

✔ Any need other than a primary drive is called a *secondary drive.* A lot of these are learned from families, social groups, and the larger culture. The importance of secondary drives is determined by how they become associated with primary drives. People are driven to go to school and get good grades in order to have a better life and provide for themselves and their families. Secondary drives have no inherent worth; they only matter as they relate to primary drives.

One of the limitations of drive reduction theory is that it leaves no room for needs that seem only peripherally related to our biological survival. Does a day of surfing restore my homeostatic balance? What basic need does surfing satisfy? I may be able to stretch it a little and say that I make it a point to go surfing because if I don't, I'll get depressed and then I won't be able to go to work and then I won't be able to eat. That would make surfing a secondary drive at the bottom of a long chain of other secondary drives. But most people probably don't reduce, consciously anyway, their every activity to the lowest common denominator of biological survival.

Although it's not technically an instinct theory, Abraham Maslow's motivational theory states that motivations stem from a basic set of needs that you naturally strive to satisfy. Maslow believed that some needs are more basic than others. Eating is more basic than getting an A on your English final. They're both needs (for some people anyway), but one is more fundamental than the other.

Maslow created a priority list of needs that he arranged into a triangle called the *hierarchy of needs:*

- At the lowest and most foundational level are *basic physical needs* for food, water, and sleep. These needs direct behavior until they are satisfied.

- The next level of the triangle contains needs for *safety and security* such as proper shelter and protection.

- *Love and belonging* is the next level of need.

- The fourth level of need is *self-esteem*, striving toward situations that enhance self-worth.

- *Self-actualization* — the need to fulfill our top potential and to live at a high level of awareness of ourselves and our desires — is the top level. When someone has reached the highest part of the triangle/hierarchy, he has a *peak experience,* or a feeling that signals arrival at the highest level of motivation. It is important to point out though that even for one who self-actualizes, these peak experiences are brief and infrequent. A person does not settle in at the level of peak experiences.

Arousing interest in prime rib

Optimal level of arousal theory is considered a more refined version of drive reduction theory. Instead of just being driven to satisfy basic biological needs at a minimum level, this theory states that people are motivated to reach the highest level of satisfaction possible.

What do I mean by "highest level of satisfaction?" Think of this as the "prime rib theory" of arousal. When my body needs energy, I get hungry, and I develop a primary drive or motivation to eat something. Now, if this theory was the "hamburger theory" of arousal or the "minimal level of arousal theory," then I'd just get a greasy drive-through cheeseburger and be done with it. But why would I eat hamburger if I can eat steak? I can satisfy the primary need and also enjoy great flavor at the same time.

Another component of the optimal level of arousal theory involves being driven to seek the best (optimal) level of arousal in order to maximize performance. In an example of how optimal level of arousal theory may work, in 1908 psychologists Yerkes and Dodson found that people perform activities best when moderately aroused — not too relaxed, not too uptight. This is called the *Yerkes-Dodson law.*

Have you ever had to make a presentation in front of a large group or class? Were you nervous? If so, how nervous? Throwing-up, passing-out nervous? Being that nervous constitutes an extreme level of arousal; and if you've been there, you know it doesn't contribute to a top-notch performance. Similarly, if someone is too relaxed, he may not put out enough effort to properly prepare for the presentation, and he may end up giving a terrible performance. The best place to be is right in the middle.

Getting cheaper long distance is rewarding

When I come home and find the red light on my answering machine flashing, I wonder who called. Was it a friend I haven't talked to in a while? A long-lost relative? No, it was one of those annoying long-distance phone companies trying to get me to change my provider.

A lot of marketing efforts are based on a motivational theory called *expectancy theory.* Expectancy theory holds that motivations are the product of an individual's analysis of the potential rewards associated with a particular behavior and the likelihood of achieving those rewards. Long-distance carriers count on me associating a switch with an expectation of a reward. This is a straightforward but powerful means of motivating people, especially if you can get them thinking that the rewards are likely to come rolling in!

Incentive theory, which is closely related to expectancy theory, simply states that we are motivated to seek rewards and avoid negative experiences such as pain. My experience with spam e-mail ads has led me to expect pain in my inbox from unsolicited purveyors of stuff I don't need every day, which over-powers the expected reward of saving a few bucks from their "great deals." What I expect, whether it's really the case or not, ultimately has a powerful effect on my behavior. When I see these e-mails I don't even open them, I just delete them.

Facing your opponent-process theory

Sometimes I am motivated to do things that aren't much fun, like going to the gym — at least I don't think that's much fun. Some people may like it. But the point is that people can engage in behaviors that seem more painful than pleasurable on the surface. This doesn't mean that they have some masoch-istic need or instinct. Motivations that may appear outwardly painful and not so pleasurable can sometimes be explained with the *opponent-process theory*, which states that people are motivated not by the initial response or incen-tive, like the pain of a tough workout, but by the reaction that occurs after the initial response, like the reflection of a toned, fit, and healthy body in the mirror looking back at me.

For every response that occurs, there's an opposite reaction called the *opponent process.* After being exposed to a particular stimulus for a while, the initial response diminishes, and the opposite response grows stronger.

A lot of people like to eat hot and spicy foods. Personally, I like to taste my food, not feel it for 20 minutes after I take a bite, but to each his own. What's the opposite response, the opponent process, of hot foods? It's the endorphins — those natural painkillers released by the body to combat pain.

Spicy foods actually chemically burn the tongue, and the body combats those burns with these natural painkillers. It feels good when the endorphin painkillers kick in to soothe the burning. People who enjoy hot foods think that they eat spicy foods for the spice, but according to opponent-process theory, they're just a bunch of endorphin junkies. Yep, they're burning their tongues in order to benefit from the opposite or *opponent* reaction of endorphin release!

The opponent-process theory has been used to explain the sometimes baffling affliction of drug addiction. Of course, when a substance or drug is used there is a high, euphoria, and an experience of pleasant feelings. Once the effects of the drug wear off, however, there is an unpleasant experience from the aftereffects of the drug. According to the opponent-process theory, the addicted person then uses the drugs again to get relief from those unpleasant experiences. They don't use for the initial high necessarily — they use to alleviate the negative aftereffects.

Knowing who's the boss

Freedom may be the best motivator of all. Throughout history, societies and large groups have sacrificed their lives for the right to determine their own fates, make their own decisions, and be masters of their own lives. The US Declaration of Independence, authored by Thomas Jefferson, is perhaps the quintessential document of such self-determination, the right to determine one's actions without compulsion from others or outside influence.

Edward Deci and Richard Ryan proposed a psychological theory of motivation known as *self-determination theory (SDT);* it states that the human motives for competence, autonomy, and relatedness are at the center of what drives behavior. These fellows may even be considered the "Thomas Jeffersons" of motivational psychology. They propose and cite research to support the concept that the needs to feel competent, autonomous, and related are universal human needs and found in all cultures. These needs are considered necessary for people to feel a sense of well-being and to perform or achieve at an optimal level at life's tasks such as work, school, and relationships. SDT acknowledges two different kinds of motivation:

- ✔ **Autonomous motivation** is *intrinsic,* or internal, to a person; it comes from within and reflects a sense of non-coercion and freedom of choice.

- ✔ **Controlled motivation** is a function of external contingencies and rewards or punishments such as shame, pay, or public recognition.

Controlled motivation is associated with feelings of being pressured to think, feel, or act according to some external standard as opposed to an individual's internal standard. A wonderful historical example of autonomous motivation is the great American Rosa Parks, an African American woman who challenged racial segregation in the United States by sitting in the "white only" seats on a public bus. She was brave enough to sit on a bus seat of her own choosing. Despite the pressure to conform and concede and have her motivation "controlled," *she chose* where to sit, was autonomously motivated, and changed history. According to SDT, it is best to be in control of one's self, to be one's own boss, to have the freedom to make choices; this satisfies a basic human need and drives motivation.

Deci and Ryan consider autonomy to be synonymous with being in control of oneself, to regulate oneself, to engage in *self-regulation*. Whereas SDT refers to the human need and motive to be autonomous and in control of oneself, *self-regulation* is a set of psychological controls over emotions, behavior, and thoughts in a manner that is consistent with meeting personal goals. SDT can be considered the "why" of human behavior but self-regulation is the "how."

Psychologist Andrea Burger defines self-regulation as an individual's ability to monitor and modulate cognition, emotion, and behavior to accomplish goals, and/or to adapt to the demands of specific situations. Self-regulated behavior involves controlled, focused, and attentive thought and action as opposed to impulsive and reactive action. Self-determination, it would seem, is not possible without adequate self-regulation.

Being autonomous and in control of yourselves is all well and good, but many people have had the experience of letting themselves down after a resolution to diet, exercise, quit smoking, or change some other undesirable aspect of their behavior. They "want" to diet but they overeat. They want to exercise, but end up watching that movie they rented instead.

This is where the concept of willpower comes in. There is a struggle for self-control going on, a struggle of the will. Roy Baumeister defines *willpower* as the ability to resist short-term temptations in order to meet long-term goals. Some psychologists consider willpower a logical component of self-regulation, to be in control of oneself in the face of competing or contradictory motives or impulses. You can diet and lose weight or enjoy eating that entire plate of Kung Pao chicken and bloat.

Psychologist Walter Mischel in the 1960s conducted a very simple but powerful set of experiments popularly known as the "marshmallow studies." Basically, the experimental subject, a child, is offered a small reward such as a marshmallow but is told by the researcher that he or she could get a bigger reward if they don't eat the marshmallow while the researcher steps out of the room for a short time. If they delay their gratification for a short time, they will get a bigger reward. Well, some children could do it and some could not. Those who could were considered to have stronger abilities to delay gratification. Follow-up research on those same children many years later showed that children who could delay had better academic outcomes and were less likely to be overweight.

Research suggests that willpower is a psychological ability that exists in all people to a greater or lesser extent. Willpower has been likened to a "mental muscle" that can grow, get stronger, weaken, fatigue, and even atrophy. Strong willpower has been associated with success at behavioral change such as quitting smoking or sticking to an exercise regime. Stress and needing to resist too much temptation have been found to weaken willpower. This is why it's probably a good idea to avoid going to a donut shop when all you want is a cup of coffee. Unless of course you've already "chosen" to eat an apple fritter or a chocolate twist.

Launching Countless Bad Poems: Emotions

At this point, none of the theories on motivation address the power of emotion to spur action or initiate behavior. Yet emotion and motivation are intimately related. When I need something, I am motivated to satisfy that need. When my stomach growls, I know I'm hungry. But how do I know when other, more psychological needs aren't being met, like the need for self-esteem? When certain personal needs aren't being met, emotions send out a signal. Emotions can indicate that you are not reaching your motivational goals (in the form of disappointment, for example) or that you are meeting your motivational goals (perhaps in the form of happiness).

In the following sections I define emotion, explore its functions, and discuss how emotions can be "used" to improve functioning.

An *emotion* is a complex phenomenon with three interrelated components:

- ✔ **Subjective experience:** When I have a particular emotion, I call this a *feeling.* My experience of sadness may consist of wanting to cry and lacking energy or motivation. This is my experience of sadness; it's subjective.

- ✔ **Physiological response:** All emotions are comprised of responses that involve brain and nervous system activity. When I'm angry, my heart beats quickly and my breathing rates increases. When I'm sad I may feel tired.

- ✔ **Expressive component:** Each emotion is expressed and communicated in a unique way. Facial expressions, body language, posture, words, phrases, gestures, and numerous other means of expression accompany and communicate the experience of an emotion.

Another theory of emotions that has gained more support over the last few years comes from evolutionary psychology. Psychologists subscribing to this perspective view specific behaviors and mental processes as adaptive responses developed through natural selection. Emotions are assumed to be part of this adaptation process.

TIP

Feelings save lives

In addition to signaling whether someone has achieved his or her goals or not, emotions have a couple of other functions. Emotions prepare people for and alert them to potentially dangerous situations. Gavin De Becker sings high praises for this function of emotions in his book, *The Gift of Fear* (Dell Publishing). In a sentence, fear saves our lives. Have you ever been in a situation where you got that feeling that something just wasn't right? That "feeling" was your emotions alerting you to the possible presence of danger that you may have not consciously observed or been aware of. De Becker advocates listening to that voice more often and being more attuned to it as a powerful survival tool.

Positive emotions can provide relief from the trials and tribulations of life. Happiness feels good. What would life be like if you never felt happy? Pretty miserable, obviously! It's easier to have a good relationship with someone who is happy. Happiness also leads to socializing, which may lead to romance, which may lead to children, which may lead to passing on whatever genes worked to produce that happy procreator in the first place. Positive emotions have the potential to make people more attractive and allow for social connection.

Cosmides and Tooby propose an extensive set of behavioral and mental programs (think computer programs) that help people address the challenges of survival. Each program functions independently, which creates a logistical nightmare. If you think getting ready for a camping trip is logistically difficult, try coordinating all the behaviors and mental processes that humans possess! This is where emotions come into play. Cosmides and Tooby view emotions as "master programs" of sorts, working to organize and integrate all those behaviors and thoughts. From this perspective, emotions serve a regulatory function. They help people figure out what they need to do in a particular situation and whether or not they've accomplished a desired goal.

Finding out which comes first, the body or the mind?

If emotions consist of three components — subjective experience, physiological reactions, and the expressive component — which comes first? Do I think and feel angry before my muscles tense up? Do I say I'm angry before I know I'm angry? Figuring out this process can get confusing; it's like the chicken or the egg argument for emotions. But don't worry; Farmer Cash — that's me! — is here for you to put all the eggs in the right basket. Three main theories address the birth order of emotion components.

James-Lange theory

The *James-Lange theory* attempts to make sense of this mess. When a person encounters a situation or stimulus that leads to an emotional reaction, his body reacts first. There is a set of automatic physical reactions to emotional stimuli. The sensory systems respond by sending signals to the emotional centers of the brain, creating a state of arousal. After this physiological reaction, the brain analyzes what is occurring. Finally, after arousal and appraisal, the subjective experience of the emotion occurs. The brain then recognizes fear, for example, after interpreting this long chain of physiological reactions. Emotional expression comes after recognition of an experience of emotion.

First you see the bear. Then your heart starts pounding, and other fear-related physiological reactions occur. You think to yourself that your heart is pounding, and you are running away from the bear and must be scared. Only after the analysis are you able to communicate that you are "scared."

Cannon-Bard theory

The *Cannon-Bard theory* of emotion is a variation on the James-Lange theory. This theory also proposes that the physiological reaction to stimuli occurs before the subjective experience of an emotion, but there's a little twist. Cannon-Bard doesn't agree that the complex activities of muscle activation and the subsequent actions (like running from a bear) are the first physiological processes to get involved.

Specific parts of the brain that are considered less sophisticated are activated first, according to Cannon-Bard. These "lower" parts of the brain then simultaneously send signals to three "higher-level" brain areas: the appraisal area, the arousal area, and the experience area. When compared to James-Lange, the main difference here is that arousal, analysis, experience, and expression all occur at the same time, but only after more basic areas of the brain are cued or activated.

So I encounter the bear, my lower brain areas activate, and then I run, analyze my running, realize I'm scared, and yell out, "Help, I'm going to die" all at the same time. If this fascinates you, check out Chapter 3 to read more about the brain.

Two-factor theory

Stanley Schacter of Columbia University and Jermone Singer of Penn State University are psychologists who came up with a third variation on the emotional process. Their *two-factor theory* takes elements from James-Lange and Cannon-Bard but changes things around just a tiny bit. Instead of having an initial reaction from the body or lower brain areas followed by the evaluation process, the two-factor theory states that physiological reactions and cognitive appraisal occur together, creating a feedback loop and co-producing the subjective experience of an emotion. Information from the situation and the environment are used in the appraisal process. Emotional arousal is seen as *generic* (not specific to a particular emotion) until an evaluation is conducted.

According to this theory, I see the bear and experience physiological arousal and cognitive appraisal at the same time. "I'm aroused and there's a dangerous animal in front of me. I must be scared."

Expressing yourself

When someone is smiling, is she happy? What about someone who glares at you, puffs out his chest, and turns red in the face? Can you guess what emotion he's experiencing? Of course you can. All emotions have an expressive and communicative component that consists of verbal signals, facial expressions, eye contact, and other body movements and nonverbal expressions.

Some people believe that the expressive components of emotions are innate or inborn. The same goes for the ability to discern what someone is feeling by observing these expressions. Some emotional expressions seem to be universal, such as smiling when happy and frowning when sad.

Certain situations place constraints on these aspects of emotions as well. Although not always the case, people don't typically cheer and laugh at funerals and they don't usually scream angrily at people when given a compliment or a gift. In some cultures, funerals are somber, quiet affairs in which there is very little public display of emotion, although in other cultures there may be a great outpouring of emotion with people screaming, hitting themselves in the head, and grabbing at the casket of the deceased.

Injecting a little fun

Consider the following experiment: Research subjects are given a shot of epinephrine that activates their sympathetic nervous system. It engages their fight-or-flight response. Some subjects are told what the injection will do, and others are told either something misleading or nothing at all about the injection. Then the subjects are placed into one of two groups: an anger-situation group or a euphoria-situation group. The anger group is asked to fill out an insulting questionnaire that's designed to make them angry. The euphoria group is put in a room with a researcher who is laughing, smiling, and having a good ol' time!

Both groups received the same drug, so their bodies produced the same physiological reaction and the same type of arousal. But do you think they experienced arousal as the same emotions? The subjects in the anger group said they felt angry, and subjects in the euphoria group said they felt happy. Keep in mind that both groups had the same physiological arousal so their experienced emotion was all based on the information provided to them by environmental cues applied to the generic experience of autonomic nervous system arousal. Just as the two-factor theory predicted, subjects apparently labeled their physiological arousal by evaluating the situation, or the context.

Culture has a lot to do with how and when emotions are expressed, including what emotions are appropriate to feel and express.

Speech gives expression to feelings in several ways:

- **Rate of speech:** Rate of speech can increase or slow down depending on how a person is feeling.

- **Tone of voice:** A person's voice can be friendly or sharp, and this tone variation says a lot about the emotions being experienced.

- **Volume:** Volume of voice conveys information as well. When someone is angry or excited he may talk more loudly, for example.

If you want to appear calm when you're angry, make an effort to speak slowly, use soft tones, and keep the volume down. If you're looking to intimidate someone, speak fast, in harsh tones, and very loudly. This sends the signal that you're angry.

Human beings experience many different emotions: fear, sadness, elation, and disgust to name just a few. Take a second and think about your life: What emotions do you experience most often? As a therapist, I've seen the whole range, but love and anger are two feelings that come up time and time again — maybe more than any others. People want to talk about wanting love, not getting love, giving love, and so on. They also want to express their anger in a safe place where they know they won't experience retaliation.

Feeling the power of love

Love makes the world go 'round. Or is it money? Whether love makes the world go around or not doesn't diminish the power that it seems to hold over most people, who want love, even if they don't want to admit it at times. It feels good to be loved and to love someone else. I think most people would have a hard time arguing that there's just too much darn love in the world.

If you think love is magical, I hope I don't burst your bubble with a psychological analysis of it. Elaine Hatfield and Richard Rapson, psychologists at the University of Hawaii, identify two specific types of love:

- **Passionate love:** Intense love with a sexual or romantic quality. It's the kind of love Romeo and Juliet had for each other. It's the kind of love you don't have for your grandmother!

- **Companionate love:** This is the love between friends and family members. There isn't much passion here, but there are high levels of attachment, commitment, and intimacy.

Robert Sternberg created a theory that outlines six forms of love. Each form is distinguished by varying degrees of *passion,* a strong desire for another person and the expectation that sex with that person will be rewarding; *commitment,* the conviction that a person will stick around, no matter what happens; and *intimacy,* the ability to share our deepest and most secret feelings and thoughts with another person.

Here are Sternberg's six forms of love that are based on varying levels of passion, commitment, and intimacy:

- ✔ **Liking:** There's intimacy but no passion or commitment here. A relationship with a therapist is a good example of this form of love. I can tell my therapist my thoughts and feelings, but I don't necessarily feel passion for or commitment to her.

- ✔ **Infatuation:** Here, there's passion but no intimacy or commitment. This form of love is like lust. It's the one-night-stand or seventh-grade crush version of love.

- ✔ **Empty love:** This is what people have who are committed but share no passion or intimacy. Some married couples are committed to each other out of necessity or convenience and stay together despite the lack of passion or intimacy.

- ✔ **Fatuous love:** This is the highest level of commitment and passion but it offers low levels of intimacy. Romeo and Juliet seemed to be under the spell of fatuous love. I don't see how they could have become intimate when they never really got a chance to talk.

- ✔ **Companionate love:** This form of love is being committed and intimate but lacking in passion. It epitomizes a really good friendship.

- ✔ **Consummate love:** I guess Sternberg used *consummate* to describe this form of love because it's the total package: high passion, strong commitment, and deep intimacy. This has got to be "consuming."

Are the foundations of love formed in childhood? Some psychologists feel that our love relationships as adults are extensions of our childhood attachments. Children who have healthy attachments have more mature adult relationships with higher levels of intimacy and trust, and they're comfortable with higher levels of interdependency. Children who experience anxious or ambivalent attachments to their primary caregivers may "fall in love" too easily, seeking extreme closeness right off the bat and reacting intensely to any suggestion of abandonment. Glenn Close's character in the drama-filled movie *Fatal Attraction* must have had a hard time with attachments when she was a child. Children who avoid social interaction tend to be uncomfortable with closeness and have a tough time with being dependent upon others in their adult relationships.

Hatfield and Rappon proposed that people possess love templates in the form of mental schemas or scripts. Templates are formed early in life and are revised and solidified over the years as individuals experience various relationships with other people. These templates shape how a person thinks about relationships and determine what expectations he has upon entering into relationships. It seems that a lot of people on those TV dating shows have some pretty interesting love schemas because some of their expectations are, let's just say, interesting.

There are six basic love schemas that apply to romantic relationships. Each schema is differentiated by a person's comfort level with closeness and independence and how eager she is to be in a romantic relationship.

- ✔ **Casual:** No strings attached. Interested in a problem-free relationship. Dream on!

- ✔ **Clingy:** Seeks closeness (a little too much) and fears independence. Anybody got a spatula?

- ✔ **Fickle:** Uneasy with both closeness and independence. Can't make up your mind? Flip a coin already!

- ✔ **Secure:** Comfortable with both closeness and independence and doesn't rush things.

- ✔ **Skittish:** Fearful of too much closeness and perfectly comfortable with independence. Don't run!

- ✔ **Uninterested:** Just not into the whole relationship thing.

Everyone has an opinion on each of these love schemas. It's hard to judge people who may use one type of schema over another. Different schemas seem to apply to different periods of life, but many people strive toward the secure schema. If someone feels that her schema is causing problems in her life, therapy is a good place to work out these issues.

Acknowledging anger

Speaking of issues, anger is an issue that deserves a lot of attention. On the one hand, anger can be suppressed and not expressed enough. But on the other hand, anger is expressed in inappropriate and extreme ways every day. Either way, anger is a natural emotion and is as important to human relationships as love.

Have you ever seen that T-shirt that has "I'm not prejudiced, I hate everybody" printed on it? Wonderful message, right? That ranks right up there with the bumper stickers with the cartoon character Calvin, from the American cartoon *Calvin and Hobbes,* peeing on everything from the symbols of different car manufacturers to the Internal Revenue Service. Sometimes it seems like there's a heck of a lot of anger out there.

Where does anger come from? Lots of theories exist. One is that anger is a consequence of experiencing negative or painful feelings. All kinds of things can lead to negative feelings: unpleasant physical conditions, physical pain, limits on our movement, and even loud noises. I like to refer to this theory as the "grouch factor." Psychologists theorize that the following things trigger anger:

- **Feeling depressed:** People who are depressed are more at risk for feeling angry. Even sadness and grief can generate angry feelings. It is not uncommon for people to become extremely angry when someone they are close to dies.

- **Being separated from desires:** When people are unable to engage in a desired activity or carry out a desired action, they tend to become angry. Sroufe proposed the existence of an *anger* system, which works like a pressure cooker. A person gets increasingly frustrated as his desires and activities are blocked time and time again, which eventually leads to the experience of anger with the blockade. There are no guidelines in this theory about where the breaking points are.

- **Separation from attachment figure(s):** An *attachment figure* is someone we have attached to or formed a strong emotional bond with. When someone you are attached to leaves you, you may react with anger. These types of anger reactions were determined by researchers observing young children's reactions to being separated from their mothers. This seems to happen as adults as well. Have you ever seen someone fly into a rage when their romantic partner wants to break things off? This has been the story in many horrific romantic related crimes, unfortunately.

Although it can be quite destructive, anger is a valid and important emotion, and there are some positives to it. Anger can be pretty adaptive. It can aid in self-defense, fuel ambition, and sometimes prevent someone from acting aggressively toward another person. If someone is going to hurt you, sometimes a display of anger can make her think twice.

Keep in mind that some people react to anger with even more anger, so be careful with this tactic. Anger can mobilize a lot of physical energy in a short period of time. If two angry people meet up, who is going to be the one back down first? Maybe neither. When I worked in the prison system, I witnessed this often. Tough guys with a lot to prove would meet anger with anger and the result was not pretty; usually both people got hurt and put other inmates and correctional staff at risk as well.

Anger need not be destructive, as long as it is expressed appropriately and constructively. Research shows that children who appropriately express their anger have fewer emotional and social problems growing up. Infants and toddlers sometimes use anger as a signal that they're frustrated and may need help with something, like eating.

Checking out happy

The other day, in the middle of my workday, I caught myself feeling good and particularly positive and I stopped to think about what I was doing, what was going on around me, and what may be producing this positive experience. Was I happy?

Philosophers, poets, and many a middle-ager in midlife crisis would agree: Happiness is an elusive concept. Psychologists do not disagree. The exact definition of happiness and how to study and research it has been controversial, in part because research consistently shows that happiness is more than having the experience of positive emotions. Happiness can be understood as a multifaceted experience consisting of many things, including a person's self-view of life satisfaction, positive beliefs about life, and having more positive emotions than negative ones on average. Happiness is considered synonymous with well-being in psychological research.

Was my positive experience the other day the product of my exceptional cup of coffee, the unexpectedly delicious breakfast burrito, the warm welcome I got from the clinic staff, or my sense of being helpful to my first few clients? What were the ingredients of my happiness that day? What are the ingredients of my well-being?

Take two people: One has a good job, friends, a loving spouse, and well-behaved children; the other has unpredictable work, few friends, and no spouse. Which person is happier? This question gets to the heart of the approach to happiness known as *subjective well-being (SWB)*.

University of Illinois psychologist Ed Diener has done some important work on subjective well-being and the self-evaluation process involved. The SWB approach to happiness posits that well-being is essentially the strong positive emotions a person may experience as she reflects on and evaluates her life. SWB is the "whatever floats your boat" approach to happiness. The answer to the initial question is whoever evaluates her life more positively — the friendly person with a good job or the single guy with unstable work. Maybe neither; maybe both; the answer does not come from some objective list of "happiness ingredients." The happiest person of the two is the one who individually and subjectively judges himself or herself to be happy. That's it!

Perhaps this approach seems rather simplistic; to some people it is wholly profound. Whichever position a person may take, the subjective well-being theory of happiness leaves one's judgment of happiness up to individuals to judge for themselves.

Some think the SWB approach to happiness is too limited because it does not address why or how someone has high SWB or what she bases her SWB evaluations on. It doesn't address what "leads" to SWB and therefore is not prescriptive, not helpful, cannot be learned from, and cannot be taught.

Psychologist C. D. Ryff presents a more "list like" approach to happiness known as the *Psychological Well-Being Approach*. Ryff's model proposes

- **Self-acceptance:** Feeling positive about yourself
- **Positive relations with others:** Good relationships
- **Autonomy:** Being independent with self-control and self-determination
- **Environmental mastery:** Being able to choose and create environments that fit your needs and wants
- **Purpose in life:** Having beliefs that give meaning to your life
- **Personal growth:** Developing your potential and growing as a person

Martin Seligman is another psychologist who approaches happiness from a broader perspective than the "whatever floats your boat" approach of SWB. Seligman's ingredients to happiness and the good life are captured in the acronym *PERMA*:

- **Positive emotions:** Feeling good more often than feeling bad
- **Engagement:** Feeling absorbed and highly focused on what you are doing — akin to being "in the zone" during a sports performance or composing a piece of music
- **(Positive) relationships:** Having good relationships with good people in your life
- **Meaning:** A sense that your efforts and talents are serving a purpose greater than oneself
- **Accomplishment:** Mastery and success at the highest level or a particular pursuit, be it work, sports, or school

Taking the SWB, Psychological Well-Being Approach, and PERMA model all together, it would seem that some degree of positive subjective evaluation, good relationships, mastery, and meaning are core components to the good life, to happiness. So, the next time I'm feeling happy, it just may be a result of that good cup of coffee and breakfast burrito (SWB), warm staff (good relationships), and knowing I'm helping somebody (mastery and meaning)!

Discovering your smart heart: Emotional intelligence and styles

In 1996, psychologist Daniel Goleman introduced the public at large to the concept of *Emotional Intelligence* in his book, *Emotional Intelligence: Why It Can Matter More than IQ*. In the years since, there has been a great deal of research on Emotional Intelligence (EQ) — a person's ability to perceive, control, and utilize his emotions in a productive manner. EQ has been likened to a form of intelligence because it is seen as a particular mental skill or ability and has been found to be associated with some positive outcomes in a person's life, just as being traditionally (cognitively) intelligent has, as in success at work.

Psychologists Mayer, Salovey, and Caruso define EQ as the ability to accurately reason about emotions and use that knowledge to enhance thinking. Dr. Reuvan Bar-On considers EQ to be a set of emotional skills that help a person cope and succeed in the world and environment. Perhaps an example of "emotionally unintelligent" behavior or skill can illustrate the point best. During a staff meeting I once saw a well-respected colleague scream and berate a graduate student for making a menial clerical error on some documentation. This caused quite an uproar, but it was later revealed that the colleague had received very distressing news about his personal health just a few minutes before the meeting. The poor student was the target of a lot of emotion he did not deserve. The colleague was clearly not aware of how his emotions were playing out in this interaction. Not so smart, not an example of high EQ.

Richard Davidson, in his book *The Emotional Life of Your Brain: How Its Unique Patterns Affect the Way You Think, Feel, and Live and How You Can Change Them,* takes the concept of emotion perhaps a little further than the concept of a "skill" or "ability" in his model of *emotional style.* For Davidson, it's less about EQ and more about a person's predominant and consistent responses to his or her life's experiences. Davidson proposes the following six dimensions for determining a person's emotional style:

- ✔ **Resilience:** How quickly you recover from stress and challenge
- ✔ **Outlook:** How long you can maintain a positive perspective
- ✔ **Social intuition:** How good you are at picking up social signals
- ✔ **Self-awareness:** How well you perceive body sensations related to emotions
- ✔ **Sensitivity to context:** How good you are at using your surroundings in regulating your emotions
- ✔ **Attention:** How focused you are

Both emotional intelligence and emotional style approaches look at emotion from a broader perspective that put emotional "skillfulness" and ability at the heart of coping and success. It's not enough to be "book smart"; you need to be "heart smart" — to know how you feel, what do to about it, and how to use it to your advantage.

Chapter 8

Barking up the Learning Tree: Dogs, Cats, and Rats

*A*thletes are some of the most superstitious people around — only gamblers can outdo them in this category. When I played college baseball, I had one teammate, a pitcher, who wore the same undershirt without washing it for as long as he kept winning. Some of us kind of hoped we'd lose so he'd wash his shirt. Other athletes carry lucky charms, perform rituals, or engage in elaborate routines to keep a winning streak alive.

I had a couple of superstitions of my own during my college baseball years. For starters, I couldn't knock the dirt off just one of my cleats (shoes) with my bat. I had to do both, even if the other one was clean. And when running in from the field, I never stepped on the chalk line. The other players never questioned me about my superstitions; they had their own weird habits.

When I started studying psychology, I began to wonder where this stuff comes from. What convinced me that I'd have a bad game if I stepped on the chalk line? At some point in time, I must have stepped on the line and then had a bad game. I saw a connection between what I did (stepped on the line) and what happened to me (had a bad game). I drew a connection between my behavior and a consequence, in this case, a negative consequence. Psychologists call this *superstitious learning*.

When an actual connection exists between what you do and a particular event that follows, be it positive or negative, a specific type of learning takes place. You learn that when you do something, the action is followed by consequence. Behaviorists use the acronym A-B-C: Antecedent (what happens before)→Behavior (the action performed)→Consequence (what happens after the action). All learning is a process of *conditioning*, a type of learning in which an association between events is made.

In this chapter, I describe the learning process and point out how learned behaviors apply to *classical conditioning*, a type of learning in which in which two events become associated with each other, as well as *operant conditioning*, learning in which an important consequence follows a specific response, leading to that response being more or less likely to happen again.

Both classical and operant conditioning lead to learning. What is "learned" in classical conditioning is that two previously unassociated stimuli are now "related" or *associated*. A good example is something called *taste aversion learning*. I once ate a shrimp cocktail and got ill and vomited. From that point on, just the thought of shrimp cocktail has made me nauseated. I *learned* that shrimp cocktail and illness are related, at least for me. I *learned* that the *taste* of shrimp was *aversive* because it was associated with nausea.

In operant conditioning, the learned association is between a particular behavior and what happens after it, the consequence. If you've ever caught a fish in a particular spot on a lake or river, you know from that point on you will continue to try that spot first every time you go fishing. What you learn is that your behavior of fishing (behavior) in spot X (context) resulted in a *positive consequence*, or a reward. The receipt of that reward increases the likelihood that you will repeat the behavior that triggered the reward when you are next in the same situation.

Classical conditioning is about two stimuli becoming related to each other. Operant conditioning is about the relation of two stimuli increasing the likelihood that a behavior will occur again (or not).

Learning to Behave

You've been there or at least you've seen it, and I'm not judging — too much. It's the public tantrum with all the key ingredients: parent shame, onlooker disdain, child out of control. And only the coveted toy, piece of candy, or permission has the power to end it. Desperate, you give in and appease the hostile creature.

Most people seem to agree that throwing a public tantrum to fulfill an emotional or physical goal is a *learned behavior*, a response that is taught or acquired through experience. So when a tantrum erupts, parents tend to bear blame for teaching the child that tantrums work. Because work they do! A screaming and flailing child often does get what he wants; children see it work for others (observational learning), and they experience results when they do it (operant conditioning). So why not create a spectacle?

More than a hundred years ago, a group of British philosophers asked this very same question and tried to figure out the nature of learning. They observed that when two experiences occur together in time (temporal contiguity) and space (spatial contiguity), they become associated with each other. In other words, people learn that when event or object A occurs, so does event or object B. It sounds gossipy — "A and B are always together!" The freeway and traffic stay together; hamburgers and French fries don't make individual plans; and tantrums go hand-in-hand with new toys. They go together. They're associated!

Public tantrums capitalize on associations. The child realizes, "Every time I'm in the store, my terrible behavior leads to a new toy in my hands." And unfortunately for the tired, stressed out, and impatient parent, frequency is at play as well. The parent learns that buying a toy stops the tantrum — quick relief for the weary! As this scene continues to play out over and over again, an ever-stronger association forms.

The good news is that learned behavior can be unlearned through the same learning processes, which is also known as conditioning.

Drooling like Pavlov's Dogs

Kind of a gross visual, huh?

Personally, I would rather go to the dentist than conduct research on the salivation patterns of dogs. That's just me. But one brave man, Russian physiologist Ivan Pavlov, was up for the job. Pavlov was actually studying digestion with dogs when he became interested in how the presentation of food automatically activated the salivation response in the dogs that he was studying. He found that the formation of saliva was automatic.

Try it. Think about something really tasty and see if your mouth waters automatically. Did it work? It should have because salivation is a reflexive response to food. It's the body's way of preparing to receive food. Saliva helps break down food into digestible bits.

In this section, I describe how Pavlov figured out why certain associations trigger certain natural responses and thereby discovered classical conditioning. I also point out how associations can change to alter certain learned responses.

Conditioning responses and stimuli

Pavlov constructed a device to collect the saliva directly from the dogs' salivary glands as the glands went to work. He could then measure how much saliva the dogs reflexively produced. Picture a dog strapped into a cage with a tube attached to its salivary glands and this wacky scientist counting each drop. Not even Hollywood could have imagined a more eccentric scene.

At this point, Pavlov was probably happy with his canine digestion research; but one day, he noticed something strange — the dogs salivated sometimes even when the food wasn't presented. What was going on? Was something else causing the salivation?

Pavlov came up with an *associationist* explanation. That is, the dogs had learned to associate other stimuli with the food. But what was triggering this response?

Pavlov conducted a whole series of experiments to figure out how the dogs had learned to automatically associate non-food stimuli with food in a way that produced salivation. A typical experiment went something like this:

1. Pavlov placed his dogs in their harness with the saliva tubes attached to the dogs' salivary glands.

2. He rang a bell and observed whether the dogs salivated or not. He found that they didn't.

3. Then he rang the bell, waited a few seconds, and then presented food to the dogs. The dogs salivated.

4. He repeated the bell plus food presentation several times. These pairings, by the way, are called *trials*.

5. After Pavlov was satisfied with the number of trials, he presented the bell alone, without the food.

6. He found that the bell by itself produced salivation!

Conditioning refers to learning through the associative process, learning through experience. Pavlov's discovery became known as *classical conditioning*.

After conducting his experiments, he identified four necessary components of classical conditioning:

- **Unconditioned stimuli (US):** The food that Pavlov presented to his dogs, the *unconditioned stimulus*, is the thing that triggers the unconditioned response. Food prompts salivation.

- **Unconditioned responses (UR):** Pavlov's dogs automatically, or reflexively, salivated when presented with food. They didn't need to learn or be conditioned to salivate in the presence of food. Pavlov called this response the *unconditioned*, or not-learned, *response*. It happened without learning. It was a reflex.

- **Conditioned stimuli (CS):** The bell that Pavlov rang in a typical experiment, called the *conditioned stimulus*, is the item that the dogs learned to associate with the food through the process of pairing trials. After enough trials, a conditioned stimulus produces a response on its own.

- **Conditioned responses (CR):** After the CS begins producing the UR without the US, the response is called the *conditioned response*. In symbolic form, this system looks something like Table 8-1.

Table 8-1	Classical Conditioning
Trial Number	*Result*
	US→UR (food automatically produces salivation)
1	CS + US→UR (bell + food produces salivation)
2	(bell + food produces salivation)
3	(boll + food produces salivation)
4–9	(bell + food a few more times produces salivation)
10	CS→CR (bell alone produces salivation)

Becoming extinct

The power of classical conditioning is pretty impressive. Just think — if you appropriately pair two stimuli, the CS alone will eventually get the job done. But when the pairing stops, and the CS is producing the response by itself, the power of the CS eventually fades. If a CS is presented enough times without the US, the CS eventually will cease to elicit the CR.

This phenomenon is called *extinction,* and it is a way to reverse the process of classical conditioning. For example, Pavlov's dogs learned to salivate at the sound of a bell. But if the bell continued to be presented without the delivery of food, the dogs would eventually stop slobbering to the bell.

But wait, there's more!

Something even more interesting happens if the US is reintroduced sometime after extinction — *spontaneous recovery.* At this point, the CS's ability to elicit the response comes bouncing back, and once again the CS triggers the CR. This means that you can use classical conditioning techniques to teach an old dog new tricks, and you can reverse the process through extinction. With this skill, you'll never be the boring guy at the party sitting in the corner. You can dazzle your newfound friends with classical conditioning tricks and come to the rescue of parents of a toy-hungry tantrum king by teaching them to just stop giving in and let extinction take over.

Here's a fun party trick if you're thinking about testing your own classical conditioning prowess.

1. Gather a few people together — family, friends, coworkers, whomever. Get some packets of powdered, lemonade drink mix. This stuff is really sour without sugar. Give one packet to each participant.

2. Ask each person in the crowd to dip a finger in the lemonade and take a lick. (This is the US.) Ask them to observe if their mouths watered. They should have. If not, get yourself some better droolers.

3. Now choose a CS (a bell, a light, a whistle, whatever). Go through the process of pairing the CS with tasting the lemonade (CS→US→UR over and over again).

4. After 10 to 20 trials, go through a couple of trials where you present just the CS and ask the participants to observe if their mouths watered. They should have! That's classical conditioning.

5. If your crew is really into spending this kind of time with you, you can now start playing around with extinction and spontaneous recovery!

One more way to reverse the effects of classical conditioning is worth mentioning. You've conducted the lemonade test, and you've successfully taught your Pavlovian subjects to drool on command. If you want to change the effect, choose another US that produces some other response (UR) and classically condition your subjects with the new US. This process is called *counterconditioning.*

Counterconditioning works especially well if the new US produces a response that is incompatible with the old CR. If the old CR was a watering mouth, maybe you pick a new US that produces a dry mouth. I don't know what that may be — maybe eating sand.

I guarantee that if you classically condition the bell with the eating of sand, the bell will have a very hard time triggering a watering mouth ever again . . . unless, of course, you reverse the process all over again. Just be sure to give your subjects a break from time to time, and don't actually try the sand-eating thing as a parlor game; it's just an example!

Classic generalizing and discriminating

You may be thinking, "Big deal. Dogs learn to salivate to a bell; so what?"

Well, if you're going to be so tough to impress, you should know that classical conditioning is actually a very important phenomenon in terms of human survival. It helps people learn things simply by association, without effort; and this can be very beneficial. In other words, after a CS becomes associated with a US to the point where the CS produces the CR by itself, that learning can expand automatically through a process known as *generalization*.

Generalization happens when something similar to the CS — I'll call it CS-2 — elicits the CR, even if CS-2 has never before been associated with the original US. For instance, if you learn to associate certain facial gestures, like a snarl or a sneer, with eventual violence, then the snarl or sneer (CS) produces fear (CR), whereas only a flying fist or a verbal threat (US) elicited fear (UR) in the past. You may then generalize the snarl and experience fear in connection with direct and non-averted eye contact (CS-2). This generalization can save your tail. Generalization helps people adapt, because learned responses are applied to new situations.

Generalization can backfire, though. If, for example, I am attacked by a gray-colored pit bull, I may get scared every time I see a gray dog of any type, even a Chihuahua. This "over-learning" can limit my behavior and cause unnecessary suffering because I become afraid of dogs that pose no actual danger to me, so instead of just avoiding gray pit bulls I avoid all dogs.

Another example of generalization backfiring comes from the traumatic experiences of war veterans who suffer from post-traumatic stress. If they've experienced loud explosions and heavy gunfire and developed a strong fear reaction to these events, these veterans may respond to hearing a car backfire or some other loud noise in the same way they responded to gunfire in a war zone. This can make life pretty difficult, especially for people living in an urban area with a lot of loud noises.

When people begin to overgeneralize learned behaviors, a process known as *discrimination* is absent. You know how to *discriminate,* or tell the difference, between stimuli such as the sound of a potentially fatal gunshot and the merely annoying sound of a car backfiring. Discrimination is learned when a CS-2 (or 3 or 8 or 25) is presented enough times without eliciting a response. It becomes apparent that only the CS, and not the CS-2, is necessarily going to produce the CR.

Conditioning rules!

If all it takes to trigger a natural response to an unnatural stimulus is pairing a natural stimulus with an unnatural stimulus and presenting them together for a while, it can't get much easier.

But not so fast! The process sounds as straightforward as it gets, but some specific rules must be followed in order to achieve conditioning.

In order for associations to form, they must conform to the following two very important rules:

- ✔ **Contiguity:** Associations are only formed when events occur together. For example, I feel depressed when I wake up every Monday morning and think about going back to work. Therefore, for me, work and waking up are associated.

- ✔ **Frequency:** The more often that two (or more) events occur together, the stronger the association becomes.

Contiguity, when one event follows another in time, is absolutely required for classical conditioning to occur. Think about it: What if Pavlov had presented the bell (CS) after he presented the food (US)? Or what if he had presented the bell 15 minutes before the food? The CS must come immediately before the US in order for the association to form.

Each of these sequence and timing scenarios represents conditioning techniques that aren't very effective. If Pavlov presented the US before the CS, which is a process known as *backward conditioning,* the dogs would have either made no association at all or an extremely weak one. If he presented the bell well in advance of the food, a process known as *trace conditioning,* the dogs may have formed a weak association, if any.

The best way to ensure that a strong or more quickly formed association is formed during the conditioning process is to follow these guidelines:

- ✔ Present the CS just before the US and keep the CS on or around until the US appears. This way, the CS is perceived to be contiguous with the US.

- ✔ Conduct a lot of trials with the CS and US paired frequently. The strength of the association is a direct product of the frequency of the pairing.

- ✔ Use a strong or intense CS to condition faster. A bright light conditions faster than a dim one. A loud bell conditions faster than a faint one.

But I don't want to mislead you into thinking that all you have to do is frequently present an intense CS before a US to achieve classical conditioning. Even though the rule of contiguity states that if two stimuli are contiguous, an association will form, it's actually not that simple.

Blame it on a pesky graduate student named Robert Rescorla who questioned whether contiguity was enough. Maybe he thought it all seemed too simple.

Rescorla proposed that another rule — the rule of *contingency* — be added to the list of conditioning requirements. His idea was that a CS not only has to be contiguous with a US; it also has to be an accurate predictor of the US. In other words, if the CS is presented at random times (at 1 minute, 7 minutes, 2 minutes, or 12 minutes, for example) with the US, then the CS isn't a credible predictor of the US. The learner (animal or human) gains no predictive power from experiencing the CS, so the CS fails to trigger the CR. Therefore, the CS must be presented with the US in a way that the learner can anticipate, with a fair degree of certainty, that the US is soon to come.

Adding another rule to the requirements of Pavlov's classical conditioning is quite the accomplishment for a graduate student. But Rescorla wasn't finished. Later, he and another psychologist, Allan Wagner, made another huge contribution to learning theory. Ready?

The Rescorla-Wagner model (1972) simply states that in order for a CS to be maximally effective, the US must be unexpected. The learning process is dependent on the element of surprise. If a learner expects the US every time she sees the CS, then she learns to associate it properly; but eventually, the strength of the association reaches a maximum. The strength increases dramatically at first and then levels off as the novelty of the CS wears off and it becomes more "expectable." Therefore, the power of an association to elicit a CR is a function of surprise. The more novel the CS, the stronger the association.

Battling theories: Why does conditioning work?

Knowing how to perform classical conditioning is useful (check out the "Conditioning responses and stimuli" earlier for the how-to on this trick), and the conditioning response enables people to learn about their environment in ways that improve adaptability and a little something called survival. But why does conditioning work? Why do previously unrelated stimuli become associated with each other?

Pavlov believed that the simultaneous activation of two distinct areas in the brain form associations between a CS and a US. This activation results in the formation of a new pathway between the two areas. It's like sitting next to a stranger on the bus and, through some polite chitchat, realizing you both know the same person. These two previously unrelated people become associated through this common association and a new connection is born.

Clark Hull presented an alternative account. He believed that the association formed is actually between the CS and the UR, which then becomes the CR. Scientists are at their most creative when they figure out how to make two different theories compete with each other in predicting the outcome of an experiment. This creativity makes it possible for them to dream up a critical experimental test. Holland and Staub set out to test Hull's theory. They conditioned rats by using noise and food pellets.

According to Pavlov, the rats learned to associate the noise with the food. But Holland and Staub pitted Pavlov's idea against Hull's by trying to make the food an unattractive US. First, they taught the rats to associate noise (CS) with food (US). Then they put the rats on a turntable and spun them around to make them nauseous. Here, they taught the rats to associate food with nausea. Then, after spinning them for a while, they presented the noise again, and the rats didn't respond to it. This "devalued" the food by associating it with nausea.

Pavlov thought that the original connection was between the noise and the food. But Hull predicted that devaluing the US would not make a difference in the rats' response; he suggested that the critical association forms between the noise (CS) and eating (UR). Devaluing the US did make a difference, though. Spinning the rats on the turntable and making the food less attractive to them as a result should not have made a difference, according to Hull, but he was wrong. A connection must exist between the CS and the US; the CS can't be left out of the loop for conditioning to occur.

So, Pavlov rules the day!

This isn't just rigid tradition. It actually has predictive value. Learning doesn't stop here, however. Check out Chapter 9 for new adventures in learning about learning.

Studying Thorndike's Cats

Operant conditioning takes place in all facets of everyday living — in homes, the workplace, and public spaces. Parents use rewards, or operant conditioning, to get their children to do their homework or follow through on chores. Here's how operant conditioning works.

Every month I get paid at my job. Am I paid just to sit around and take up space? No, I'm paid for performing the duties of my job, for working. I do something, and something happens. I work, and I get paid. Would I work if I didn't get paid? Probably not, for two reasons.

First, I have better things to do with my time than to work for free. (My credit card debtors wouldn't be too happy with me either.) Second, according to operant conditioning theory, I work *because* I get paid. The "something" that follows my working behavior is a reward, a positive consequence.

When I do something like work at my job, something happens; I get paid. Then what happens? I keep going to work every month, so that paycheck I get must be having an effect on me. Way back in early 1900s, Edward Thorndike created a theory, known as the *law of effect,* that addressed this idea of a consequence having an effect on behavior.

Thorndike decided to look into this phenomenon by doing research with cats. He constructed the *puzzle box* made from a wooden crate with spaced slats and a door that could be opened by a special mechanism. Thorndike placed a hungry cat inside the box and closed the door. He then placed some food on a dish outside of the box that the cat could see through the slats in the crate. Sounds kind of cruel, doesn't it? The cat would reach for the food through the slats, but the food was out of reach. The only way for the cat to get the food was for Thorndike or the cat to open the door.

Obviously, Thorndike wasn't going to open the door; he was conducting an experiment. The cat had to figure out how to open the door himself. You don't see a lot of cats going around opening doors. So what did he do? It's suspenseful, isn't it? What will the little hungry cat do there in the puzzle box? Will he open the door and feed voraciously on the prized food that was just beyond his reach only moments before? Or will he meet his demise and starve at the hands of a fiendish psychologist?

The cat had to figure out how to open the door, and Thorndike was a patient man. He waited and watched, waited and watched. The cat wandered around the box, stuck his little paw out, meowed, bounced off the walls, and acted in any number of random ways inside of the box. But then, something remarkable happened. The cat accidentally hit the latch that was holding the door shut, and the door miraculously opened! Hurray! The cat got to eat, and everyone lived happily ever after.

What did Thorndike learn from his little experiment?

Nothing. He wasn't done yet.

So he put that poor cat back inside the box to go at it again. No problem, right? The cat knew what to do; just hit the latch, little kitty! But when it got back into the box, the cat acted like he didn't know that he had to hit the latch to open the door. He started acting in the same random ways all over again.

Never fear, eventually the cat triggered the latch by accident again and was again rewarded by gaining access to the food. Thorndike kept performing this experiment over and over again, and he made a remarkable observation. The amount of time that it took for the cat to figure out that the latch was the key to freedom — well, food! — got shorter and shorter with each subsequent trial. Why was the cat getting faster? Thorndike proposed that the food helped the cat learn the association between the triggering the latch and the escape.

Thorndike's law of effect states that a response that results in stronger satisfaction to an organism (for example, animal or human) will be more likely to be associated with the situation that preceded it. The greater the satisfaction, the greater the bond between the situation and response.

Basically, the consequence of getting the food served as a reward for learning how to open the box. The cat's opening-the-box behavior is like my job, and his food is like my paycheck.

So getting back to my original question of whether my paycheck has an effect on me or not — the fact is, I keep working, just like Thorndike's cat kept opening the box to get the food. Therefore, the consequence of my action does appear to lead me to perform that action again.

Reinforcing the Rat Case

When a consequence of an action or event increases the probability that the event or action will happen again, that consequence is called a *reinforcer*. It's like a reward, and rewards often motivate a repeat of actions that earned the reward. Operant conditioning is all about the effects of reinforcers on behavior.

B. F. Skinner, one of the most famous psychologists of all time, followed in Thorndike's footsteps in using animals to investigate operant conditioning. He constructed a box with a lever inside and called it a *Skinner box*. When an animal pressed the lever, a food pellet fell out of a feeder and into the box. Skinner wanted to see if rats placed in the box could learn to press the lever in order to receive the food.

This task was a lot harder than one may think. Rats aren't used to pressing levers to get food. Skinner had to facilitate the process a little bit with a procedure known as *shaping*, a technique of rewarding successful approximations to the goal. Skinner rewarded the rats with food for performing a behavior that was close to, but not exactly, the required response. Shaping was done gradually so that the rats eventually got to the point where they pressed the bar and received their reinforcers of food.

After the rats got the hang of it, they learned to press the bar for food the same way Thorndike's cats learned to open the door. The rats learned because the reward of the food taught them how to press the bar.

Finding the right reinforcer

In the cases of both Thorndike's cats and Skinner's rats, the subjects learned because they were rewarded with food. Food is a powerful reward for animals, but it's just one type of reinforcer. Anything that increases the likelihood that a behavior will occur again can be used as a reward or reinforcer. It can be food, money, recess, or vacations. It can also be something intangible like approval, praise, or attention from another person.

There are two basic types of reinforcement:

- **Positive reinforcement** is the use of any reinforcer that increases the likelihood that a behavior will occur again.

- **Negative reinforcement** occurs when the removal of negative stimuli leads to an increased likelihood that a behavior will occur again. A good example of this is when a student gets disruptive in class during an assignment he is trying to avoid or escape. The teacher sends him out of the room and negatively reinforces the disruptive behavior. The teacher thinks she is punishing the student but he is actually getting out of an aversive demand.

The basic idea of operant conditioning is that behaviors that are reinforced (either positively or negatively) are more likely to occur again. But is this true for all reinforcers? Are all reinforcers created equal? If Skinner had given the rats five dollars each time they pressed the lever, would they still have learned the response?

Probably not. Differences between reinforcers exist and affect the impact that the reinforcers have on responses. Not all consequences are rewarding or reinforcing as they vary from person to person (or animal to person).

Two types of positive reinforcers are effective:

- **Primary reinforcers** are rewards that don't require shaping or prior training to be effective. Examples may be food or pleasurable physical sensations.

David Premack in 1971 came up with the interesting idea that primary reinforcers can be identified by looking at what people spend most of their time doing. If they spend a lot of time watching television, riding bikes, or sleeping, then these activities may be considered primary reinforcers. His *Premack principle* states that high probability responses can be used to reinforce lower probability responses. This is like using ice cream to get your child to eat his or her vegetables. If they want the ice cream (high probability response), they'll eat their vegetables (low probability response).

✔ **Secondary reinforcers** are things that become reinforcing through experience and learning. This result happens by associating the secondary reinforcer with a primary reinforcer by using classical conditioning techniques (see the section "Conditioning responses and stimuli" earlier in this chapter).

The best example of a secondary reinforcer is money. We aren't born knowing the value of money (and some of us never get it). But, eventually we learn the value of money as we experience its association with the things we like such as food, clothing, shelter, and expensive cars. So, money "acquires" its value to us as it becomes associated with primary reinforcers. In some institutions, like schools and hospitals, caretakers reward appropriate behaviors with *tokens*, which may be cashed in for specific rewards later. This type of system is called a token economy, like local money.

After identifying what a subject considers to be reinforcing, it becomes possible to influence behavior by providing rewards for performing the appropriate responses.

For example, consider an office manager who is having a difficult time getting her employees to come back from lunch on time. What can she do? First, she needs to figure out what is reinforcing for the group or each individual. Not all rewards are the reinforcing to all people. Then, she has to start rewarding anyone who performs the desired behavior, coming back from lunch on time. She could give them little gifts, money, or smiley-face stickers.

Or, the office manager could use negative reinforcement. For instance, she could send a really whiny employee out to lunch (who complains profusely and gets everyone's anxiety up at the thought of being late) with the latecomers. The latecomers hate hearing the whiny employee complain so much that they start returning on time just to avoid hearing him go on and on.

This concept of negative reinforcement confuses a lot of people. How can taking something away or removing a noxious stimulus increase the probability of a behavior? You may have some experience with this tactic if you've ever had a new puppy in your home that wouldn't stop whining while you tried to sleep. If you kept the puppy in another room or in the garage, you probably responded to the whining by getting up and checking on the cute little creature. What happened when you went to the puppy? It probably stopped crying. If you then went back to bed, I bet the crying woke you again less than ten minutes later.

The problem in this situation is that *your* behavior was under the control of negative reinforcement. The puppy's whining was a noxious (and annoying) stimulus. When you went to the garage, the whining stopped, increasing the likelihood that you kept going to the puppy every time he cried. You were negatively reinforced for going to the puppy — and that puppy got positively reinforced for whining! Oops.

Using punishment

Both positive and negative reinforcements are consequences that are likely to increase certain behaviors. But what about that other consequence, *punishment?* Punishment is any consequence that decreases the likelihood of a response and not necessarily something typically thought of as a punishment. For example, if every time you call a certain friend he seems distracted, like he's not listening to what you're saying, you may experience negative feelings of not being valued; this "punishment" is likely to lead to you calling at person less often.

One type of punishment is straightforward — the introduction of something noxious or aversive.

Another type of punishment, *negative punishment*, involves removing a reinforcer, such as taking away a child's bicycle. Again, as for reinforcement, punishment can be a very individual matter; what one person experiences as aversive or punishing may not apply to the next person.

Punishment is used to influence people's behavior all the time. Parents punish children. Courts punish convicted criminals. Credit card companies punish people for late payments. But does punishment work?

Punishment can be a very potent and effective means for decreasing the frequency of a behavior, but keep a few things in mind:

- ✔ Punishment should be the least intense form necessary to produce the desired response. Recipients may acclimate to each subsequent increase in punishment, however, and overly intense punishment is problematic as well. In order for punishment to be effective over a long period of time, you have to adjust its intensity in a meaningful way.

✔ To be effective, punishment must occur as close in time as possible to the response being punished. If a parent waits three weeks to punish a child for breaking a lamp, the kid's likely to be completely clueless about why she's being punished; therefore, the punishment has no effect on deterring future behavior.

✔ Punishment should be firm, consistent, and accompanied with a clear explanation of why the punishment is being administered.

There are ethical issues associate with punishment which mean it has to be considered very carefully in all circumstances.

WARNING!

Of course, a lot of people are uncomfortable with the idea of inflicting pain or suffering on another person in order to alter behavior. The use of punishment can have some negative consequences:

✔ **Fear:** When people are effectively punished, they may learn to anticipate future punishment and develop severe anxiety while waiting for the next shoe to drop. This can have a disruptive effect on the life of a punished person, which can lead to avoidance and apathy.

✔ **Aggression:** I've worked in both jails and prisons, and I've seen men become angrier and more aggressive as a result of the harsh conditions that they face while incarcerated. When the time comes for these people to be released and face the world in a reformed manner, they are dysfunctional and institutionalized, often unable to make the transition to the outside world as a result of their punishment.

The person delivering the punishment may become an aversive CS through conditioning. For example, a child may avoid a parent who punishes the child frequently. Contiguity does its thing — that person is there every time I get scolded ("Just wait until your father gets home." Thanks, Ma).

Scheduling and timing reinforcement

Have you ever wondered why people keep going back to places like Las Vegas and Atlantic City time and time again to donate their money to the casino expansion fund? The bottom line with gambling is that the big winner is always the house, the casino. Everyone knows this, but some people can't stay away.

People keep going back because of something called a *schedule of reinforcement,* a schedule or determination for what responses to reinforce and when to reinforce them. There are four basic schedules of reinforcement, each with different effects on the response in question:

✔ Fixed ratio (continuous and partial types)

✔ Variable ratio

✔ Fixed interval

✔ Variable interval

Ongoing rewards

Perhaps the most common form of reinforcement is called *continuous reinforcement,* in which the ratio is one-to-one. One behavior, one reward. It involves reinforcing a behavior every time it occurs. Every time I pull the slot machine handle, I win! Yeah right, I wish.

Continuous reinforcement is good for the shaping phase of learning (see "Reinforcing the Rat Case" earlier for a discussion of shaping) or for what is called the *acquisition phase.* Learning a new behavior takes time. Continuous reinforcement speeds up the learning process.

The problem with continuous reinforcement, however, is that it extinguishes quickly. If I'm reinforced every time I return to work on time from lunch, then I'm likely to stop returning on time as soon as my boss stops reinforcing me for this behavior.

Patting heads sporadically

Often, reinforcement in our world is intermittent and sporadic. Of course we don't win every time we pull the lever on the slot machine. B. F. Skinner didn't design slots.

B. A. Loser, the casino behavioral psychologist, did. Reinforcement on a less frequent basis (for example, requiring more than one response) is called *partial reinforcement.* There are two types of partial reinforcement schedules, and each is further divided by how predictably or randomly the reinforcers come.

✔ The first type of partial reinforcement is called a *ratio schedule that involves more than one response being required to gain a reward.* With a ratio schedule, reinforcement is only given after a specific number of responses have been given. If a parent is using this schedule with his children, he may only give a reward for some number of A's his child gets on her report card or after a certain number of times the child cleans her room. Ratio schedules can then vary based on whether a fixed number of responses or a variable number of responses are required to receive the reinforcement.

- A *fixed ratio* reinforcement schedule involves always reinforcing for the same number of given responses. If I'm going to reward my child for every two A's she earns, that never changes; reinforcement follows every two A's.

- A *variable ratio* reinforcement schedule involves giving reinforcement for a varied number of responses provided. I may reinforce my child for two As now, but then I may reinforce her for one A, three A's, or ten A's down the line. The key to this approach is to keep the recipient guessing. Doing so has a powerful effect on the persistence of a response because people keep doing the requisite behavior because they don't know when the reinforcement will come. A variable ratio is much more resistant to extinction than continuous reinforcement.

✔ The other type of partial reinforcement schedule, an *interval schedule,* is based on the amount of time that has passed between reinforcements. You still have to respond to get a reward, but you have to wait a certain time before your response "works."

- I get paid once a month. Time determines when I get paid. My pay schedule is an example of a *fixed interval* reinforcement schedule. The time frame never varies.

- The other type of interval schedule is *variable interval.* Here, responses are reinforced per a varied amount of time passed since the last reinforcement. This approach would be like getting paid at the end of one month, and then getting paid two days later, and again three weeks later, and so on. Variable interval schedules are also very resistant to extinction for the same reason as variable ratio schedules; the responder never knows when he is going to get reinforced, so he has to keep responding to find out.

Gambling is motivated by a variable interval schedule so that people keep pumping the money in, waiting for the big payoff.

I'm sure you've heard "You can't win if you don't play." The next time you think you're "due" or bound to win because you've been sitting at the same machine for three days without a shower, sleep, or anything to eat, remember that it's variable. You never know when the machine is going to hit. So try to manage your rage if you finally give up and the next person who sits down wins it all!

That's why they call it gambling.

The timing of the reinforcement is also critical. Research has shown that reinforcement must occur immediately, or as quickly as possible, following the desired response. If you wait too long, the connection between the response and the reinforcing consequence is lost. Skinner's rats would have never figured out how to press that lever if they were given a food voucher redeemable only after five visits to the Rat Food Deluxe shop — instead of instant gratification for their achievement.

Becoming Aware of Stimulus Control and Operant Generalization

Have you ever noticed how people slow down on the highway when they see a traffic cop? That's probably because they've all gotten tickets from them at one time or another. What happens when a good old city (non-traffic) cop is on the road? Nobody slows down. They just ignore him. Is this an example of a blatant disrespect for the law? No. It's an example of *stimulus control*, the idea that a response can vary as a function of the stimulus present at the time of reinforcement or punishment. Although both law enforcement authorities can give tickets for speeding, most of us know that city cops don't typically give tickets on the highway. The stimuli have different effects on our behavior because they have led to different consequences. Punishment only comes from the traffic cop.

Sometimes, when we learn a response due to reinforcement, we may automatically *generalize* that response to other similar stimuli. If I generalized my traffic cop ticket experience to city cops, I would slow down for city cops, too. Or, if I'm reinforced for coming back from lunch on time, I may also generalize that behavior to coming to work in the morning on time. Generalization helps speed up the learning process because we don't have time to receive reinforcement for every single response we elicit.

Discovering Operant Discrimination

Sometimes people can over-learn a response or behavior. They then engage in the response when they shouldn't because they've generalized a little too much.

I think this happens to psychotherapists sometimes. We may be in a social situation, not working, when someone starts talking about how hard his or her day was. "Tell me how that makes you feel," may slip out. Everyone looks at the psychotherapist in question like a quack. Maybe it's time for a vacation.

I've also seen this phenomenon in movies. An ex-cop overreacts to seeing his grandson point a water pistol at him, and he takes the kid down to "remove the threat." These are problems of *discrimination,* responding to only one of two or more particular stimuli. The problem is remedied by presenting someone with both stimuli and only reinforcing the response to the correct one. Put grandpa in the middle of a hold-up and throw his grandson with a water pistol into the mix. Only reinforce the Detective Grandpa when he successfully neutralizes the threat of the robber (stimulus 1) and not for taking grandson out (stimulus 2). He's learned to discriminate between a real threat and a benign one.

Part IV

Me, You, and Everything in Between

The Five Personality Traits of Humanity

- ✔ **Openness to Experience:** Curious and open to new ideas and novelty
- ✔ **Conscientiousness:** Organized, thoughtful, dependable
- ✔ **Extroversion:** Outgoing, sociable, and stimulation seeking
- ✔ **Agreeableness:** Tolerant, sensitive, warm
- ✔ **Neuroticism:** Anxious, temperamental, moody

Take a mock personality test at www.dummies.com/extras/psychology.

In this part...

- ✔ Discover personality theory, the most common personality types, and topics such as knowing yourself, developing identities, forming relationships, and communicating.

- ✔ Get connected to those around you and find out the influence that others have on your behavior and the different ways people behave in groups.

- ✔ Take a look at developmental psychology and trace development from conception to adolescence.

- ✔ Get out your cigar and cozy up with Sigmund Freud's work on the structure of the psyche and his famous theory of psychosexual development, including defense mechanisms, denial, and repression (plus discover other theorists who came after him).

- ✔ Get hip to contemporary approaches to abnormal psychology, including neuropsychological and cognitive explanations for psychological problems like anxiety disorders, depression, schizophrenia, and posttraumatic stress disorder.

Chapter 9

Developing an Award-Winning Personality

• •

In This Chapter

▶ Realizing that the song remains the same

▶ Recognizing the power of the ego

▶ Greeting the people and objects around us

▶ Learning behavior from others

▶ Being a good representative

▶ Discovering the personality traits you're born with

• •

Your old friend Mary contacts you out of the blue. You're excited to hear from her so you decide to meet up for coffee and catch up. While waiting for her to arrive at the coffee shop, someone taps you on the shoulder.

You turn around to face a stranger and ask, "Can I help you?"

"It's me, Mary!"

You realize it's your friend, but you didn't recognize her. She's older; she's put on some weight and has a different hairstyle. She looks really different. It seems that so much has changed, but has it?

After sitting and talking for a while you see that "old friend" again. She's got that same smile, the same twinkle in her eye, same laugh, same sense of humor, same warm heart, and same passion for life. If you closed your eyes and only listened to her words and her voice, ignoring the physical person you didn't recognize at first, you'd know her in an instant.

Mary changed in some dramatic ways. But you recognize how she hasn't changed as well. You realize that she's the same person you befriended all those years ago. Her body, appearance, address, clothing, and relationships changed, but her "self," her "Mary-ness," the essence of who she was continues to be the same.

These stable characteristics are what famous psychologist Philip Zimbardo describes as a complex set of unique psychological qualities that influence behavior, thinking, and emotions across situations and time — which is an excellent working definition of personality.

A *personality* is a stable system of tendencies to act, think, and feel a particular way.

Describing someone's personality is, in essence, developing a whole person picture out of the various bits of information available about them that hold true through the passing of time and changes in circumstance.

Personality theories assume that a particular set of general characteristics can serve as a summary for what a person is like. The qualities that first come to mind when you think about a person are usually the qualities that are most central to him. The more central that quality is, the more useful that aspect is in predicting the individual's behavior and distinguishing him from other people.

Mary's "Mary-ness" is her personality. It's what makes her unique in the world. Personality is what makes you unique. Tens or hundreds of people around the world may have the same name as you or may look like you, but nobody has your identical personality.

If you go to a party after work, are you the same person as you are at work? Of course, you may act a little different, but most likely you're still the same basic person. This is because of your personality, your unique set of psychological and physical components that determine who you are.

In this chapter, I describe the field of personality psychology and cover various grand theories of personality, including psychoanalytic approaches, social learning approaches, and trait-based approaches.

As you read about these personality theories, keep in mind that nobody fits perfectly into these categories. An important concept in psychology is the principle of *individual differences.* No one *is* a personality theory: The theories are *tools* for understanding the complexity of human behavior, thoughts, and emotions.

Knowing Who's a Nerd

Whether you realize it or not, you have a theory of personality that you use to classify people and tell them apart.

When I was in high school, common classifications were nerds, jocks, and partiers. A simple-minded scheme, indeed, but it came in handy from time to time as a shortcut of sorts to getting to know people. I wouldn't know them individually, of course, but I may know a little something about them to get the relationship ball rolling.

Each person is a personality theorist with varying degrees of sophistication, and specific groups of personality theorists are out there. Astrologers, psychics, theologians, poets, and others have been trying to classify people for centuries, each using a different kind of insight into personality to develop theories.

Consider the following personality description:

> You have a great deal of unused capacity that you have not turned to your advantage.
>
> Sometimes you have doubts as to whether you have made the right decision or done the right thing.
>
> At times you are sociable; at other times you keep to yourself.
>
> Security is one of your goals in life.

Do these characteristics describe you? If so, are you thinking that a secret personality-analyzing computer chip is imbedded in the binding of this book? Or are the above descriptions so vague and general that they apply to pretty much anyone?

I vote for the latter.

The *Barnum effect* refers to personality theories that are so general that they can apply to most everyone; these theories provide very little specific information about a particular individual. It was named after P. T. Barnum, the famous circus owner who allegedly perfected a personality-description technique in his sideshow fortunetelling acts.

After learning about the Barnum effect, I hope you never again see another fortune cookie or horoscope in the same way.

Personality theories can be classified into the following broad categories:

- ✔ Psychoanalytic and psychosocial theories
- ✔ Social learning theory
- ✔ Cognitive theory
- ✔ Trait theories

Getting into the Mood with Freud

Sigmund Freud, a 19th-century neurologist from Austria, formulated one of the most comprehensive theories of human personality ever created. The depths of his analysis and range of ideas are yet to be rivaled.

This section explores Freud's theories on memory, instincts, and the famous defense mechanisms (actually much of the work was done by his daughter, Anna Freud) and how these concepts contribute to a one-of-a-kind personality.

And of course, no discussion of Freud would ever be complete without mentioning his theory of psychosexual development and the ideas about Oedipus and sex.

Having unique memories

What kind of personality would you have if someone erased all of your memories? Your 16th birthday? Your high school prom? Moving into your first apartment? Would you just be a blank blob of eating, sleeping, and wandering flesh?

Freud believed that memories and how they are arranged in the mind are vital parts of personality. He proposed three basic divisions of memory that are differentiated by how aware or conscious each person is of the context of those divisions:

- ✔ **Conscious:** Your active awareness constitutes your conscious level of awareness. Here, you're aware of those things that are current and in the moment, like the book on your lap, its yellow cover, the typeface in horizontal rows, and your stomach growling because you haven't eaten in six hours. Your *conscious* awareness is dominated by the things you're hearing, seeing, and feeling.

- ✔ **Preconscious:** The preconscious is made up of ordinary memories, such as birthdays, anniversaries, and how to ride a bike. People are rarely actively aware of memories in the preconscious, unless deliberately conjured up or activated. But preconscious memories still play a powerful role in shaping personality.

- ✔ **Unconscious:** The memories and experiences that you're not aware of are part of your unconscious collection. These memories are deep inside your mind and difficult to access. So the next time you can't answer a tough question, just simply tell the inquirer that the answer is locked away deep inside your unconscious. Thousands or even millions of things go on inside your mind that you're not aware of; you're unconscious or unaware of them.

Actually, Freud thought that the unconscious mind is filled with all the memories, thoughts, and ideas that are too troubling, disturbing, and horrible to keep in conscious awareness. This is where you harbor your most basic desires and conflicts and your truest feelings, unfiltered and unedited by the niceties of everyday life. Your unconscious does not lie!

Your conscious, preconscious, and unconscious memories help make you a unique individual, giving you all the special personality quirks that your friends love so much.

Getting down with id, ego, and superego

Freud would have been a great Hollywood screenwriter. His "story" of personality is one of desire, power, control, and freedom. The plot is complex and the characters compete. Personality is a drama of sorts, acted out in the mind. According to Freud, "you" are a product of how competing mental forces and structures interact.

The ancient Greeks thought that all people were actors in the drama of the gods above. Freud proposed that you and I act out the drama of our minds, pushed by desire, pulled by conscience. Under the surface, a person's personality represents the deeply internal power struggles.

Three main players carry this show:

- **Id:** Controls drives and impulses
- **Ego:** Negotiates with the id, pleases the superego
- **Superego:** Keeps individuals on the straight and narrow

Each of these characters — or parts of a person — has its own idea of how the story should unfold. Each has powerful motives and is out for itself.

Wanting it for the id

The initial structural component and first character in Freud's drama of personality is the *id*. Has an urge, impulse, or desire so strong that it just had to be satisfied ever overpowered you? A new car, sexual desire, a dream job? The answer is probably a resounding "yes!"

Where does such desire come from?

According to Freud, desire comes from the part of your personality called the *id*, located in the deep seat of the mind. The id contains all of the most basic animal and primitive impulses that demand satisfaction. It's the Mr. Hyde emerging from the restrained Dr. Jekyll. It's that little devil that sits on your shoulder, whispering temptations and spurring you on.

The id is a container of sorts that holds desires. Relentlessly driven by a force Freud called the *libido,* the collective energy of life's instincts and will to survive, the id must be satisfied! You are born with the id in full force. It's unregulated and untouched by the constraints of the real world.

When a baby gets hungry — I mean really hungry — does she sit quietly, understanding the adults are busy at the moment, and wait until someone can feed her? Anyone who's ever gotten out of bed in the middle of the night to feed a baby knows the answer to that.

But I don't want to give the id a bad rap. Where would you be without desire? Desire pushes you through life; it leads you to seek the stuff you need to survive. Without your id, you'd die — or be really boring until that happens. A large part of your personality consists of your desires and your attempts to satisfy them.

Feeling okay with ego

Wouldn't it be nice if you could get everything you wanted, whenever and however you wanted it? The id wants what the id wants, after all.

Unfortunately most of us know otherwise. It can be frustrating when a desire goes unmet or gets stifled. Blame your ego for that.

The *ego* is the second mental apparatus of personality. The ego's main function is to mediate between the id's demands and the external world — reality. (Cue the Rolling Stones' song "You Can't Always Get What You Want.")

The ego is like a sports agent for a really talented athlete. Even though the athlete may demand a multimillion-dollar contract, the agent reminds him that he could price himself out of a job. So the ego negotiates with the id in order to get what it wants without costing too much in the long run. The ego accomplishes this important task by converting, diverting, and transforming the powerful forces of the id into more useful and realistic modes of satisfaction. It attempts to harness the id's power, regulating it in order to achieve satisfaction despite the limits of reality.

The final judgment

The ego's job of mediating the near-constant bickering between the id and reality is relentlessly micromanaged and judged by the superego. *Superego* is another name for your conscience. It expects your ego to be strong and effective in its struggles against the libido's force.

Usually, a person's conscience comes from his parents or a parental figure. As he grows, he internalizes their standards, those same standards that make him feel so guilty when he tells a lie or cheats on his taxes. But does everyone have a conscience? Conscience can vary by degree, some people have less and some have more. Certain people throughout history have committed such horrible acts of violence that it seems they are void of conscience. A strong bet is that such people lack the basic capacity to feel guilt, so nothing stops them from acting out violent fantasies.

This is a key feature to the psychopathic personality (for more about personality disorders, see Chapter 13).

Thinking about sex

It can read like a newspaper headline: "Sexual Satisfaction Fuels Personality Development!"

Well not really, but Freud's psychosexual component of personality development was definitely about pleasure. Freud's search for the answer to the question of what makes one person's personality different from others led him to theorize that the clues to understanding the uniqueness of an individual's personality are found in infancy and childhood. Eureka, childhood is destiny!

The personality that you live with today — the one that charms in order to get dates, makes lists and never gets anything done, ensures that the bathroom is always sparkling clean — was forged and molded in the fires of infancy and struggles of your childhood. In fact, according to Freud, you were a unique final product by the time you hit puberty.

Freud's model of personality development proposes a series of stages in which people grow and mature. Within each stage, a person is particularly focused on a part of the body known as an *erogenous zone*. It's kind of like focusing on your washboard stomach when you're 18 years old and your love handles when you're 40; each stands out at a different time in your life. The pleasure sought by your inborn instincts is focused on sexual desire and gratification, through proper stimulation of each erogenous zone. If properly stimulated, you progress to the top of Freud's psychosexual peak, sexual and psychological maturity. If not, you're fixated on that particular zone and stuck in that particular stage of personality development.

Here are the stages by ages:

- **Oral:** Birth to 18 months
- **Anal:** 18 months to 3 years
- **Phallic:** 3 years to 7–8 years
- **Latency:** 7–8 years to puberty
- **Genital:** Puberty to adulthood

Freud's personality development model is like having five miniature person-alities that each lasts a couple of years until you reach maturity. The model is reminiscent of a typical high school freshman who begins school with one personality only to have an entirely new persona by the end of the year, complete with wardrobe and a secret language. It's Geek Von Bookworm one minute and Joe Slick the next.

Each personality stage presents you with a unique challenge, and the theory says that if you successfully overcome that challenge, you acquire a fully mature personality. (That's *Mr.* Joe Slick to you!) But, if you somehow fail to overcome the challenge of a stage, you'll be stuck, or *fixated,* there. This is where a lot of your personal uniqueness comes from, your "stuckness" or fixation at a particular stage of personality development.

Opening your big mouth

The *oral stage* is Freud's first stage of personality development. From birth until about 18 months of age, an infant's life centers on his mouth. The main task of this stage is to satisfy oral desire by stimulating the erogenous zone of the mouth. Notice the infant's reflexive sucking and the way his head and mouth turn toward his cheek as it's gently brushed. Infants are born with a very well-developed sense of taste, and their mouths are the most sophisticated tools they have to explore their world. Their mouths far outperform their hands and fingers in grasping the world around them.

One of the first objects out there in the world that provides an infant with oral satisfaction is his mother's breast, which is his main source of connec-tion and satisfaction. But eventually, all infants must be weaned from their mother's breast. I mean, when was the last time you saw a 10-year-old breast feeding? But the weaning process presents the infant with his first conflict between desire and reality.

If an infant fails to wean or is weaned harshly or incompletely, he may become fixated at the oral stage. He will develop an *oral character* in which he's dominated by feelings of dependency and helplessness. Infants are not able to provide themselves with autonomous satisfaction; as long as they are in the oral stage, they depend entirely on (m)others.

(M)other

For a lot of people, the first human they ever meet is their mother. With the exception of the nurses and obstetrician in the delivery room, mom's face is the first face you see. You're dependent on her for everything — she's the center of your world — for a pretty long time. Throughout most of the world, moms are held in pretty high regard. I once heard that the most common tattoo in the United States is "Mom" inside a heart.

Ultimately, as an infant successfully overcomes the challenge of weaning and gains control over the ability to satisfy oral desires, he moves on to the next stage of personality development.

Take a minute to reflect on your childhood. It may be difficult to remember infancy, but most of people can conjure something up from the ages of 2 to 3 years. Did you have a pacifier? How long? Did you suck your thumb? Just how oral were you? Do you chew your pens now? Are you bitingly sarcastic? Freud may be tempted to say, "You are fixated!"

Taking control of your poop

Freud's second stage of personality development is all about the erogenous focus of the *anal stage*. Think about pleasure and your relentless libido striving for satisfaction. Think about defecation. Say what?

That's right, Freud emphasized a person's control over defecating as the pleasure center from 18 months to 3 years old. The central conflict for toddlers is control! Kids in this stage want the ability to poop whenever they want and wherever they want. Like in their pants! But the reality that they have to hold it sometimes creeps in, conjuring images of long trips in the family car, "Are we there yet? I have to go!"

Who and what withholds the pleasure of pooping at will? Our parents and the constraints of reality do. (Find information about reality constraints in the section "Getting down with id, ego, and superego" earlier in this chapter.) In fact, some of your adult characteristics may be the consequence of how your parents handled your toilet training. According to Freud, your creativity and productivity are indicators of how well you've successfully navigated the anal stage.

If you're stuck in the anal stage, you're dominated by anal satisfaction. This satisfaction can come in one of two ways:

- If you're messy, sloppy, or careless, it indicates an expulsive rebellion against parental control.
- If you're withholding, obstinate, and obsessed with neatness, you've learned control in reaction to your toilet-training experience.

Either way, you're in control. Maturity and success in the anal stage result in your ability to control yourself. So let go, but make sure you do it in the right place and at the right time.

Marrying your mom

Just when you thought that all of your personality traits had been described, Freud comes up with his third stage: the *phallic stage*. I promised you sex, and it's time to deliver — well, sort of. The 3- to 5-year-old child is focused on the erogenous stimulation of the genital area, the penis and vagina specifically.

King Oedipus

Freud found ancient support for his ideas about a child's sexual desire for his or her parents in the famous (or maybe not) Greek play, *Oedipus Rex*. The basic story is about a king who has a male child who, prophets predict, one day will kill the king and marry the queen. To prevent this, the king takes the child to the woods and leaves him to die. The child is discovered by some peasants in the woods, however, and is raised to be a healthy adult. One day, the child returns to the city to make his fortune. On the road to the city, he encounters the king; neither of them is aware of his relation to the other. There is a scuffle, and the king is killed. As the son arrives in the city, he soon makes his fortune, rising to the top of civic society. He attracts the eye of the mourning queen and eventually marries her, thus fulfilling the prophecy.

In the phallic stage, gratification begins with autoeroticism. That means *masturbation* to the rest of you. But the need for satisfaction soon turns toward our parents, typically the parent of the opposite sex. As sexual satisfaction expands, a child finds himself within the realm of one of Freud's most controversial and strange contributions to the study of personality, the Oedipus complex, which essentially states that a male child sees his own mother as a sexual object of desire, causing inevitable conflict with his own father of course.

As adults, many people cringe at the idea of marrying someone like their mothers or fathers; the idea of having sex with someone who reminds you of a parent probably seems gross, but you've all known a little boy or girl who wants to grow up one day and marry his or her parent.

There's just one problem: Nearly every culture on the planet has a taboo against sex between parents and their children.

Freud observed that children in the phallic stage of personality development shift from self-gratification to seeking gratification from their opposite-sex parent. But the taboo is not the only thing that stands in the child's way; the other parent seems precariously in the way, an obstacle. How would your father feel, you think, if you tried to make a move on your mom? However, the libido knows no bounds and must have satisfaction. It figures that the opposite-sex parent is its rightful object of desire.

Why?

This is where Freud gets a little complex. Basically, all children are initially attracted to their mothers because she's often their primary caregiver. She's their primary source of pleasure and satisfaction. She's the end all and be all of satisfaction. From there, kids split by sex (or gender, as most people refer to it).

✔ **Boys:** For the male child, the attraction to the mother continues to develop into what Freud called the *Oedipus complex*. The male child's father blocks him from his mother. This gets to be really frustrating for the male child. It's so bad that the frustration eventually blossoms into full-blown hatred for the father.

This complex is riddled with conflict as boys find themselves afraid of their fathers because they want their mothers all to themselves. Freud called this fear *castration anxiety*. The male child is afraid that his father will cut off his genitals. Because of this fear, the male child takes an alternative route: If you can't beat 'em, join 'em. Junior learns to identify with his father, adopting his masculinity and seeking his own "mother" of sorts. He can't have sex with his mother, but he can live vicariously through his father. This supplies him with symbolic access to his mother and satisfies his libidinal desire at this stage of personality development.

✔ **Girls.** Freud was thoroughly criticized for his neglect of female sexuality. So he consulted the Greeks again, finding a similar Oedipal tale about a woman named Electra. Electra gets someone to kill her mother to avenge the death of her father.

For girls, attraction shifts from the mother to their fathers because female children come to resent their mothers for a very strange reason, *penis envy*. According to Freud, little girls stop desiring their mothers because they realize that they lack a penis. How can they have sex with their mothers without a penis? So what about that "can't beat 'em, join 'em" philosophy? Unlike little boys, little girls can't identify with their fathers because they lack a penis. So what are they supposed to do? They spend the rest of their lives looking for a penis. Essentially, they spend the rest of their lives looking for a man to make them complete.

You may be sitting there right now saying to yourself, "Come on, this is too much!"

That's a common response to Freud's ideas. To benefit from Freud's ideas and get past the preposterous nature of such a thing as wishing to have sex with your mother and murder your father, think metaphor; think analogy. Freud's ideas are best understood when processed symbolically. For example, try to picture Oedipus as a frustrated little kid who needs to share his mother's attention with his father. Daddy stands in the way; he needs to get lost. Don't get caught up in the theatrics.

That's a lot to take in, I know, and it all seems a little weird. Did I say a little? Okay, it seems really weird! How does it relate to personality?

Freud believed that if a boy or man successfully aligns himself with his father, he turns his conflict into a deep striving for success and superiority in society. At one point in history this may have meant conquering women, conquering the business world, and becoming the captain of the football team. This superiority may mean something different in today's culture context, perhaps mastering one's own limitations or overcoming some significant personal challenge. This, he considered to be a successful response to the male castration anxiety of the phallic stage.

But not all men get to this point. If a male child fails to join forces with Dad and finds himself fixated, he's emasculated, according to Freud. He becomes a "failure at life," unable to strive for achievement because of the disabling guilt generated from competing with his father for his mother's attention.

With successful resolution of the Electra complex, a girl finds herself equipped to deal with her adult sexual and intimate relationships. She turns her penis envy into a healthy search for a good "fatherly" husband. But if she fails, she becomes fixated and possibly overly seductive and flirtatious. I know, I know . . . but women's liberation happened a long time after Freud!

Taking a time out

With successful resolution of the conflicts of each previous stage, children enter into a more quiet time of psychosexual development called *latency*. The libido loosens its grip on the personality, and sexual impulses cease to dominate. Kids find more freedom to explore and expand on the skills they've gained from each subsequent stage.

Latency lasts from about six years old until puberty. Things cool down, so to speak. There's no rivalry with the opposite-sex parent. There's no battle for control over satisfaction. It's a time for basic social exploration like making friends and forming social cliques. I think this time period matches everyone's basic notion of childhood a little better than Freud's previous stages. It's less perverse and conflict ridden for sure.

Peaking sexually

With the onset of puberty, the smooth ride of latency turns turbulent again. The flames of earlier conflicts are rekindled. Desire begins to dominate the picture again in the *genital stage,* but this time it's different. The self-centered pleasure-seeking child of earlier stages gives way to a more mature form of satisfaction. A concern for the pleasure of others begins to shape the direction of psychosexual development, and the child is now open to learning how to engage in mutually satisfying love relationships.

Freud never proposed that all people reach this point of full maturity. It's more like an ideal, something to strive for, a lifelong project. But if somebody doesn't make it (at least some of the way), he can easily drift back into selfish phallicism, which seems to conjure images of the selfish lover who doesn't care about the pleasure of his partner: As long as he gets what he wants, he's just fine. But if you make it, eat your heart out, Don Juan! You'll be attentive and actually care if the other person in the interaction is enjoying his or herself.

Freud's little girl

Anna Freud was Sigmund Freud's daughter. She followed in her father's footsteps and made some substantial additions to his theory of personality. For some reason, the Freuds emphasized anxiety and protection in their work on personality. Kind of makes you wonder what kind of home Anna grew up in.

I can see it now. She brings home a C- on her psychology final. How could she have missed that question on the id, ego, and superego?

Maybe she was too busy thinking about defense mechanisms!

Anna took much of what her father created and applied it to children's problems and helping them in therapy. Her additions to Sigmund's theories supported and expanded his earlier work. Many people have never heard of her, but make no mistake about it — Anna seemed to inherit her father's gift for understanding the human personality.

Being defensive? I'm not defensive!

So you're walking along your favorite hiking trail in the mountains and a bear jumps out, rises up on its hind legs, and looks really hungry. What do you do? Stand and fight or take off running?

If this situation poses a real threat to your survival, then you may have to defend yourself. But is defending your body from physical harm the only time you go on the defensive? Sometimes a person's reputation or standing in the community can be challenged. No question, sometimes you have to defend or protect yourself psychologically. This is an important aspect of personality.

Anna Freud (Sigmund's daughter) developed the concept of defense mechanisms. You can be afraid of anything: bears, bullies, or gossip. Some people even scare themselves. You can fear the wrath of your own conscience — or its tool, guilt.

"Stop being so defensive!" is something you've probably heard, but don't worry; everyone is defensive. Freud believed that your characteristic ways of defending yourself against your anxieties are strong determinants of your overall personality. How do you cope? How do you psychologically defend yourself? How do you protect yourself from painful thoughts, impulses, or urges?

The Freuds proposed several important defense mechanisms. Keep in mind however that defense mechanisms are not used consciously. A person does not decide to engage in one; rather these happen on an unconscious level:

- ✔ **Repression:** Keeping a thought, feeling, or memory of an experience out of consciousness. It's the "forget about it!" approach. Many things may be the objects of repression, including forbidden desires or a painful, emotionally difficult situation.

- ✔ **Denial:** Refusing to accept that something exists or happened. Denial can also involve altering the meaning of an event so that its impact is diverted. If something important to you goes wrong, you may just say to yourself, "That's not so important after all." This is the common "sour grapes" response.

- ✔ **Projection:** Attributing a threatening urge, impulse, or aspect of oneself to someone else. If you think that the best offense is a good defense, you may use projection a lot. Instead of acknowledging that you're mad at someone, you may accuse him or her of being mad at you.

- ✔ **Rationalization:** Creating an acceptable but incorrect explanation of a situation. I once knew a habitual thief who only stole from big businesses. He would never think of robbing the Smiths, but super-megastores look out! He explained that big business makes money from "ripping people off," so he's just trying to even the score. A modern day Robin Hood, I guess. Unfortunately for him, the judge he faced for his crimes was not a fan of fairy tales.

- ✔ **Intellectualization:** Thinking about something logically or coldly and without emotion. For example:

    Therapist: "Mr. Jones, your wife has left you, and you've recently lost your job. How does that make you feel?"

    Patient: "I've found that the organization in my home has been much improved, less clutter now; her things took up so much room. As for the job, the economy had been slowing down for some time, I could sense that it was coming."

- ✔ **Reaction formation:** Doing the opposite of what you would really like to do. Ever gone out of your way to be nice to someone you really disliked? That's an example of reaction formation.

- ✔ **Regression:** Returning to an earlier or more childlike form of defense. Physical and psychological stress may sometimes lead people to abandon their more mature defense mechanisms. If you've resorted to whining when asking your boss for a raise, consider it a display of regression.

The Freuds made unparalleled contributions to understanding how people's characteristic ways of coping comprise basic personality. It would be a mistake to assume that psychologically defending oneself is a negative behavior; it is basic to survival. Defenses protect and keep you from becoming overwhelmed. Without them, you're on a fast track to a nervous breakdown.

Going Beyond Freud

Do you know ego? That symbol of American freedom and the US Postal Service? No, that's an eagle. The ego is Freud's master negotiator between desire and morality.

Feeling phrenological?

In the 18th and 19th centuries, a scientist named Franz Joseph Gall tried to classify people's personalities based on the shapes of their skulls and the unique patterns of lumps on their heads. Don't worry, though, no one is using that technique anymore — apparently lumps tell us very little. Actually, many thinkers who made legitimate contributions in other areas came up with relatively useless theories for personality. Bad personality theories are often guilty of something called the *Barnum effect* (described in the section "Knowing Who's a Nerd" earlier in this chapter). Although a good personality theory is tough to come by, it leads to accurate descriptions of individuals and makes it possible to distinguish people from one another.

Even though a lot of people were and still are pretty impressed with Sigmund's ideas, many of Freud's colleagues and contemporaries decided to go their own way and develop other personality theories. Many of these individuals felt that Freud did not give the ego enough credit in shaping personality. Most of these people believed that ego was more than just a mediator. For some, the ego became synonymous with personality itself.

Heinz Hartmann

Heinz Hartmann was a follower of Freud who led the dissent and march toward emphasizing the ego in personality. For Hartmann, the ego played two key roles in shaping personality:

- Reducing conflict
- Promoting adaptation

Sigmund Freud talked a lot about conflict among the id, the ego, and the superego. He basically proposed that a lot of tension exists between a person's desires and the reality of satisfying those desires in a socially acceptable and appropriate manner.

Hartmann's idea of ego is similar to Freud's in that it helps to satisfy the id's desire and appease the superego's rules. But Hartmann's ego was out for itself in a way that Freud never mentioned.

According to Hartmann, the ego is a central part of the personality that has its own desire or need for satisfaction; Freud's ego is more like a referee with no real agenda of its own. What satisfies the ego according to Hartmann? Thinking, planning, imagining, and integrating are all the sexy stuff of Hartmann's ego. Built-in satisfaction occurs when humans engage in these processes, and this accomplishment pushes people toward greater independence and autonomy. Being independent and self-sufficient is a satisfying feeling. Children get pretty happy at the prospect of being seen as as big kids instead of babies. Little do they know what's waiting for them when they are actually grown up . . . poor things.

Robert White

In the 1950s, Robert W. White, another psychoanalyst, added to Hartmann's ideas about the ego. This strive for self-sufficiency and the satisfaction that comes with it stem from a drive White called *effectance motivation* — the motive or need to feel like you can make an impact or have an effect on your surroundings. It's like having a little community activist inside all of us, pushing us to make a difference but in a personal and individual way.

White added another need to this idea, the *competence motive* — the need to make an effective impact on the world. So, having an impact is not good enough; it's more satisfying to have an effective impact. And this is more than the effectance motivation; you need to have a competent effect. It makes me wonder if teenagers who paint graffiti aren't just out to satisfy their effectance motive without much regard for the competence motive. Call me crazy, but scrawling your name on a wall is not very artistic. Don't get me wrong, though; I've seen some pretty impressive graffiti art. I'm just wondering about those "taggers."

The need for effectance and competence push people toward mastery, a desire to be an effective person. Children's games such as King of the Hill and Follow the Leader seem to reflect a need to be in charge. But Hartmann and White weren't saying that everyone has a need to be a leader, just a need to be leaders of themselves — to have self-control. People actively seek information and stimulation in order to master their world and themselves — the Manifest Destiny of personality.

Domination is not the issue either. Healthy satisfaction of these motives is adaptation acquired through proper impulse control and flexibility when faced with necessary adjustments and challenges. I can feel like a master if I subject other people to my will, but this would not be a healthy satisfaction of mastery need.

Balancing act

The ability to control your impulses and to adapt to the demands of a situation is called *ego control*. But don't get carried away with too much ego control; it can turn into over-control. And all work and no play make Johnny a very dull boy. (I always wondered where that saying came from. I don't think it came from psychologists.) Balance between complete lack of control and being too rigid is important. Flexibility is the key!

Erik Erikson

Erik Erikson had close ties to the psychoanalytic/Freudian theory of personality but he's typically not considered a psychoanalyst per se. Nevertheless, Erikson had some very influential ideas that are rooted in psychoanalytic personality theory. He didn't spend much time talking about the lustful id or the judgmental superego though; Erikson was focused on the ego — in a very different way from Freud.

Erikson viewed personality as a product of social interactions and the choices a person makes in life. He presented the ego "in development" as personal identity, shaped and molded by an individual's experiences. In other words, as you relate to other people, you go through a series of eight stages in which the goal is to develop a coherent sense of self, a firm recognition of who you are.

Each stage presents a challenge or a crisis in which you go in one direction or another. When you reach a personality fork in the road, your choices have a strong impact on who you are.

Here are Erikson's stages of psychosocial development:

- **Basic trust versus mistrust:** In the first year of life (unless someone is fixated or stuck in a particular stage), the basic experience of interacting with an attentive, consistent, predictable, and trustworthy caregiver turns into a basic trust of the world. This basic trust includes trusting yourself and knowing that, when caregivers are not available, you can take care of yourself.

    But what if mom and dad drop the ball? If a child experiences a consistent lack of responsive care giving and her needs are not adequately met, she may never learn to trust her environment. Inconsistent or intermittent care can also lead to a lack of trust. Either way, when a child's sense of basic trust is undermined, it can lead to withdrawal and sometimes even to a full walling-off from relationships.

- **Autonomy versus shame and doubt:** When a child is 13 to 36 months old, her rapidly expanding abilities can develop into a sense of independence from caregivers or a sense of shame or self-doubt and insecurity. If mom and dad are too overbearing, constantly telling kids in this age range not to touch things, not to talk, and not to try on their newfound confidence, children may develop a sense of shame and doubt in themselves.

- **Initiative versus guilt:** This stage is characterized by continued expansion of a person's sense of independence through channeled, purposeful, and responsible behavior. Actions contain less of a sense of rebellion and more of a sense of self-initiative. During this period, which occurs when a person is 3 to 6 years old, the unique desires of a child emerge and really start to give definition to their little personalities.

I've got to admit, I have issues. I hate being called irresponsible. Maybe I'm stuck in this stage, but no matter; I feel really guilty when I fail to act responsibly. This is what can happen when a preschooler fails to develop a sense of initiative. Guilt can arise from feeling too anxious or misguided in your actions. It's the feeling of letting yourself down. You're not cutting it! You're lazy! You're irresponsible! Help, I need therapy!

✔ **Industry versus inferiority:** "Time to shape up!" — that's what Erikson says people hear most between the age of 6 and adolescence. Playing around and experimenting with the environment is no longer tolerated. Parents expect a child to achieve something when he or she engages in an activity. Color inside the lines.

If a child views playtime as a chance to unwind and relax from the pressures of the school day, is he heading toward inferiority? No, using playtime to relax is purposeful and important. But if an apparent lack of goal-directedness in a child's overall most-of-the-time behavior exists, then a sense of being a slacker or being without purpose can lead to feeling inferior.

✔ **Identity versus identity confusion:** During adolescence, teenagers experiment with new identities and views of themselves. There's a push at this age to find out who you really are and what you're all about. Erikson called this an *identity crisis.* If a teen successfully navigates the abysmal waters of teenage identity confusion, she emerges with a more solid sense of self and a clearer identity. If not . . . well, *identify confusion* is the state of unresolved identity crisis. Sometimes teenagers get lost in the confusing search for a genuine identity; some of these kids withdraw and never really feel a true sense of self.

✔ **Intimacy versus isolation:** According to Erikson, the wild single days must come to an end, and one's ability to find and develop intimacy becomes the primary task of personality development. After somebody knows who she is, she turns to developing close relationships with other people who know who they are. The goal of this stage is intimacy.

✔ **Generativity versus stagnation:** At some point, a person needs to be needed and to feel like she's guiding the next generation. A desire to leave a legacy and impact younger people develops during middle adulthood. When people feel that they've done nothing or can do nothing for the next generation, they develop a sense of *stagnation* instead of generativity.

✔ **Integrity versus despair:** As life winds down and old age creeps in, people often sit back and reflect on things they've accomplished. They think about whether their life was well spent or wasted. If someone feels a sense of satisfaction with the way she lived her life, she feels *integrity,* a basic sense of wholeness or of being complete. If not, *despair* is likely to follow. Ever wonder why elder adults like to tell stories from their lives?

Relating to Object (s)

Still other expansions of Freud's theory emerged among the most dominant forces in personality theory during the last half of the 20th century and into the 21st. The works of contemporary theorists are considered more "interpersonal"; two of the most popular are the *Self Psychology* of Heinz Kohut and *Object Relations* theory.

In both Self Psychology and Object Relations theory, personalities are the product of how the mental representations of a person's self and relationships with other people, and the interactions of these concepts in a social setting, are stored and play out. That is, the focus is on an idea of self in terms of the actual people and our relationships with them.

Self Psychology

Heinz Kohut proposed that a person's subjective experience of self is a core feature of personality. Kohut's self is essentially synonymous with personality. And he proposed that in order for a person to develop and maintain an experience of a cohesive self, two needs must be met: a need to be "mirrored" (have one's actions and desires reflected by caregivers) and a need to experience an "other" as idealized.

Mirroring happens when a caregiver bonds with, reflects back, and accepts the person. This satisfies the need to feel ultimately valued and leads to a healthy version of self worth (not overblown). This is referred to as *healthy grandiosity*. I once witnessed a father encouraging his son during psychological testing. Every time the boy answered a question, right or wrong, he would say, "You are my champion!" The boy beamed! One need met, one to go.

Even though the self is feeling grandiose, a need to experience the caregiver as idealized, larger, and stronger remains. For healthy personality to develop there should be a balance between the grandiose self and the idealized other. A person can be both confident and secure with others at the same time, and these two poles form the core of the personality, according to Kohut.

Object Relations

Object Relations theory is not really one theory but rather a collection of theories from a variety of thinkers. Four well-known contributors to this body of thought are Melanie Klein, Ronald Fairbairn, D. W. Winnicott, and Margaret Mahler. Mahler developed a nice synthesis of much of the others' works, so she is the main focus for this discussion.

All of the object relations contributors basically share two broad emphases:

✔ The idea that a person's pattern of relating to others is established during the interactions of early childhood

✔ The assumption that whatever pattern is formed, it tends to recur over and over again throughout a person's life

Mahler stated that babies are born without the ability to distinguish themselves from things that are "not self." This proposes that infants are in a virtual state of psychological fusion with the objects in their environment.

For those of you who are mothers and have carried a baby, you may know a little about this. In reality, a mother and her fetus are biologically intertwined. They're not joined at the hip, just seemingly everywhere else. They are physically connected; when one thing happens to the mother, it also happens to the fetus and vice versa.

Mahler extended the idea to a more psychological sense. When an infant is born, she is in a state of personality fusion with her mother or primary caregiver. Is this because of the beautiful, harmonious love that they share for each other? Not exactly. This fusion is more a function of the dependency of the infant and her undeveloped survival skills.

As a person grows and personality develops, this fusion breaks down, and an infant gradually develops a more differentiated personality that is separate and distinct from her mother's personality — and others' as well.

With the goal of a completely differentiated personality in mind, here are the stages of personality development presented by Mahler:

✔ **Autistic stage (birth to 2 months):** The infant is in a sleeplike state of psychological isolation that's similar to being in the womb. This is a time of total union; the baby can't tell the difference between himself and his mother. In the infant's mind, the mother is an extension of himself. The autistic stage is a closed system, and all emotional energy remains referenced to the baby's own body, not directed outward to external objects.

✔ **Symbiosis (2 to 6 months):** Now, a dim awareness of an "other" begins to emerge. This other is experienced as something that satisfies hunger, thirst, and other discomforts. The relationship is as if the other exists only to serve the baby's needs. (Sometimes I think old-fashioned husbands think this about their wives!) There is still no distinction made between "I" and "you," though. We are one and the same.

✔ **Hatching (6 to 10 months):** At this point, the infant's world begins to open up a little bit and expand. "Hatching" is a sense of difference between the infant and the objects in her environment. However, this can be a scary thing, and the comfort of symbiosis is not long forgotten.

As infants begin to psychologically open up to the big, bad world, they often require something to take with them on their journey. This comforting thing is called a *transitional object.* Remember Linus from *Peanuts?* He took his blanket, his transitional object, everywhere. It comforted him. Linus seemed a little older than 10 months, so he clearly had some issues.

Infants also develop stranger anxiety during hatching. *Stranger anxiety* is the feeling of being wary and sometimes even fearful of people you've never seen or met before.

✔ **Practicing (10 to 16 months):** This is the stage in which little Johnny gets carried away with his independence. Children are fully aware of their separateness here, and they try out their independence. Some psychologists think that kids go through this stage again when they hit their teens. Ever hear a child at this age use the word *no?* I bet you have! Repeated use of *no* is a great example of "practicing" independence. So the next time some bratty 15-month-old kid yells, "No!" at you, just be patient. They'll soon realize that they're in this big scary world all by themselves. Sounds a little cruel, huh?

✔ **Rapprochement (16 to 24 months):** Just when Junior thinks he's running the show, something starts to happen to his confidence — he realizes he's all alone. That can be pretty scary for anyone, but especially for a 1½-year-old child. The solution? Reengage with mommy! This is like running back home after not being able to make rent in your first apartment, although I'm not sure how embarrassed the 20-month-old is.

✔ **Object constancy (24 to 36 months):** After a child returns home so to speak, he is eventually able to develop a strong enough sense of self and security to go out on his psychological own again. This stable sense of self is developed in part by the child realizing that some consistency exists between his fluctuating moods and his mental states. It may sound kind of strange to think that just because there's a change in mood, a pre-object constancy child would experience a less stable sense of himself, but he does. Before this stage, with each passing mood and thought, children experience uncertainty about their identity. But as this stage begins, children develop a more sure sense of themselves.

Learning from Others

The subject of television and violence has caused a lot of controversy over the last few years. Many people believe that the constant barrage of violent images is creating a more violent character for our society. There's little argument that violence in US schools is higher today than ever before, but why?

Violence is a complex issue, and many causes and explanations for it have been put on the table. Some theories suggest that there are simply more violent personalities in the world. After all of the personality theories discussed so far, what do you think about the concept of a violent personality?

In 1977, Albert Bandura conducted a now-famous study that looked into the possibility of a violent personality and turned his theory into a broader theory of personality. The experiment is now called the *Bobo Doll study*. Bobo dolls are those plastic blow-up figures with a weighted bottom that bounce back when you hit or kick them. The experiment consisted of an adult punching and kicking a Bobo doll while a young child watches. Then, the child is put into the room with the Bobo doll by himself. Can you guess what happens? Little Johnny turns into Little Rocky. He punches and kicks that Bobo doll just like he saw the adult do it.

Bandura's *social-learning theory* explains this phenomenon. Basically, people can learn something just by watching or observing it. This is one of those "no duh!" theories in psychology. But hey, no one else put the theory out there the way Bandura did. Social-learning theory has become a powerful theory of personality and its development. Our personalities are a product of our observational learning experiences from those around us. We're all just a bunch of copycats. If you see your parents being obnoxious, you probably act obnoxious, too.

Bandura continued to add to his copycat theory of personality by addressing the question of why people do what they do. In other words, what motivates people to act in certain ways?

He introduced two very important concepts to address this:

- ✔ **Self-efficacy** is a personal belief in one's ability to successfully perform a behavior. This belief is based on what Bandura called the *self-appraisal process,* which is simply an analysis of one's actions — an evaluation of successes and failures. A sense of one's capabilities arises from this process, and a person is motivated by her beliefs about her ability to succeed and inhibited by expected failures. You do what you think you can do and vice versa.

- ✔ **Self-reinforcement** is as simple as giving yourself rewards for doing things. Some parents give their children rewards or reinforcement for doing their homework or cleaning their room. Bandura believed that everyone does this for themselves to some extent and that most people would benefit from doing more of it. So the next time you do something, give yourself a little reward. It will help your self-efficacy.

Representing Ourselves

Some psychologists emphasize the way people represent themselves and their experiences of the world as core aspects of personality and behavior. You've probably been to an office party or holiday party at school where some genius tries to be helpful by giving everyone a nametag. I'm always tempted to put something goofy on mine or to use someone else's name.

The tag is a crude form of representation, or presentation, of yourself to other people. Sometimes I put a nickname on mine — I've had a few. Nicknames are good examples of a "tag" that tells you a little more about a person than her everyday name. When you meet someone nicknamed "Stinky" or "Psycho," you get a different impression than you would from "Lefty" or "Slim."

Nametags, nicknames, and common names are all examples of representations of who you are. They are convenient and shortened ways to organize a whole lot of information about someone. Ever have a conversation about a movie and forget the name of the main actor? "You know, that guy who was in that one movie with that one woman?" Just saying "Brad Pitt" is so much easier than explaining the person's characteristics every time you want to talk about him. This way of organizing information about people and the world is the product of the human mind's tendency to impose order and structure on our experiences.

Schemas

The structured representation of experience is based on recurrences of similar qualities of a person or experience across repeated events. This order takes the form of *schemas,* or mental constructs for "Joe," "Brad Pitt," or "me." Joe is my neighbor who plays his music too loud. Brad Pitt is a famous actor that every man envies. Me? I'm that guy who envies Brad Pitt. After these structured representations of the self and others are developed, people can use them to recognize and understand newly encountered information; the representations influence how a person interacts with the world.

Unhelpful schemas are emphasized in schema-focused therapy developed by Dr. Jeffery Young.

 Cognitive personality psychologists emphasize the schema-based representation of experience as the central organizing construct in human personality. Two basic types of schemas play a role in establishing regularities and patterns of personality: self-schemas and socially relevant schemas.

✔ **Self-schemas** are the organized units of information about yourself; sometimes these are called *self-concepts*. What is the concept of "you" or "me"? An in-depth discussion of how a person's identity is developed is beyond the scope of this section, but, exact details aside, your identity is represented in the form of schemas.

✔ **Social-schemas** are integrated conceptual networks that incorporate your own sense of identity and others' opinions of you. These schemas provide detailed information about someone, ranging from demographics (such as how old someone is) to his values, and this information can be updated automatically through experience or revised through conscious attention and effort.

Scripts

S*ocially relevant schemas* involve the representation of categories of other people, environments, social behavior, and stereotyped expectations. These are sometimes called *scripts,* organized sequences of actions typically expected in various situations. Is an actor in a movie presenting his off-screen personality or simply acting out a script that tells him how to act, when to speak, when to cry, and so on? It's a script, of course.

Imagine, now, that everyone you see in a day is acting out a "personality" script of his or her own, written by the author of experience and development. These scripts determine the how they act out — what they say and do. This is the gist of the scripts theory of personality. Pretty simple, right?

Not so fast! A sense that personalities are actually quite complex holds water. Walter Mischel (1980) attempted to add some flavor to the rather dry basic version of personality scripts. He introduced five ways that an individual person's personality is more than just scripted by a situation: *competencies, encoding strategies, expectancies, subjective values,* and *self-regulatory mechanisms.*

✔ There is so much more to personality than meets the eye, and one important aspect of personality is an individual's unique collection of skills and abilities for solving problems and analyzing the world. Mischel called these *competencies.*

How you engage and overcome the challenges in your life, in part, defines your personality. Are you a "go-getter" or an "analyzer"? Have you ever built something like an extra room, a playhouse, or maybe a doghouse? How did you go about doing it? Some people sit down and figure everything out in advance, drawing out a blueprint with precise measurements and specifications. Others just get what supplies they think they may need and figure it out as they go along. A good way to test yourself is with something I call the "Directions Test." When you buy something that needs to be assembled, do you look at the instructions, or do you toss them to the side?

✔ Because cognitive personality theory puts so much emphasis on information and how it is stored and interpreted, an important aspect of personality involves the strategies and constructs used to organize information. This is the process of building those complex schemas and scripts that eventually guide your behavior. *Encoding strategies* are a person's unique way of managing and interpreting the world. It is pretty easy for two people to witness the exact same event and come up with two entirely different interpretations of it. Anyone who's ever had an argument with a wife, husband, or significant other can vouch for that!

✔ You're only as special as your expectations of a situation. Are you an eternal optimist or a pessimist? *Expectancies* consist of expectations or predictions that one event will necessarily follow another. These expectations set up the rules for what to do and how to manage specific situations. If the rules match the reality of a situation, then the behavior will be effective, and a feeling of mastery will develop. If not, I guess the only option is to keep on trying.

✔ Do you work for free? Not many of us do. Most of us work for the incentive of getting paid. Incentives act as motivators toward a certain behavior. People are not all tempted by the same things, though. *Subjective values* represent what things are important to individuals and determine what they are willing to do to earn them. Hey, if you like getting little golden stars on your paycheck instead of a raise for a job well done, knock yourself out. That's what makes you so unique.

✔ What are your goals in life? Do you have a master plan or a blueprint? You may not realize it, but according to Mischel, all of us have what he called *self-regulatory systems and plans.* You set a goal, you go for it, you analyze whether you meet that goal or not, and you make the necessary adjustments. Each of us has a unique way of doing this that characterizes our personal style.

Ultimately, according to this representational view of personality, how a person sees themselves and views the world, and the ways that these views get planned out in the form of behavioral blueprints represent personality.

Getting the Magic Number 5

Aren't people just born with their personality? Maybe instead of all those psychodynamics of Freud and the relating objects of Kohut and Klein, there are just fixed qualities of "personhood" present from the beginning. This is essentially the position of *Trait theories* of personality. Trait theories are derived from directly describing and measuring characteristics found in the general population and are not tied to any particular theory such as psychoanalytic or cognitive theory. A *trait* is a stable feature of someone's personality that leads him or her to behave or think in a particular way. Traits don't vary from situation to situation. They travel with a person *across* situations and circumstances.

Trait theories propose that there are a core set of personality traits that exist to varying degrees in all people as a common and universal feature of being human. Humans walk upright and have one heart, large brains, and personality traits. Dogs, on the other hand, walk on four legs, have one heart, medium brains, and no personality traits. Wait a minute; I know some dog-lovers out there just stopped reading. Relax, I'm sure Rover has some traits, but that's another subject.

Gordon Allport (1897–1967) approached personality from a different perspective than other psychologists. He studied language as a means to determine what traits constituted the core of personality. Allport examined words used to describe people and pared them down into three essential categories of traits:

- ✔ **Cardinal traits:** A single characteristic that guides the majority of a person's actions. Think of one personality feature that best describes someone you know: cool, kind, hotheaded, or arrogant.

- ✔ **Central traits:** The 5 to 10 main traits that make up a person's major personality features. For example, when describing your sweetheart, you may refer to these characteristics: funny, considerate, intellectual, passive, and genuine.

- ✔ **Secondary traits:** Less influential characteristics that affect fewer situations than the more predominant traits.

Allport essentially started the method of trying to filter personality from a large list of descriptors to a core short list of traits. Another psychologist, Raymond Cattell, continued this method and developed a personality test (for details on personality testing, see Chapter 14) that measured 16 (core) traits, called the *16pf* (16 personality factors).

Still another psychologist (Hans Eysenck) went even further using the same method and concluded that all personality consists of varying degrees of three traits:

- ✔ **Extraversion:** Sociable, outgoing, active

- ✔ **Neuroticism:** Tense, anxious, guilty

- ✔ **Psychoticism:** Aggressive, cold, egocentric

The culmination of the trait approach over years and years of personality research resulted in an empirically acceptable and generally well-regarded trait model of personality known as the *Big Five*. This model establishes a set of five traits that are considered the most core features of personality. Think of each factor as a continuum of high and low levels of these featured traits:

- ✔ **Openness to Experience:** An "open" person is independent rather than conforming, more imaginative than practical, and prefers variety over routine.

- ✔ **Conscientiousness:** A conscientious person is careful rather than careless, disciplined and not impulsive, and well-organized.

- ✔ **Extraversion:** Extraverts are talkative, fun loving, and sociable.

- ✔ **Agreeability:** Agreeable folks are more sympathetic than critical, kind and not cold, and appreciative.

- ✔ **Neuroticism.** Neurotics are characteristically tense, anxious, and insecure.

What's your "Magic 5" formula? With a list of five factors, there is a wide range of possible combinations. That leaves a fair amount of room for individuality and considering that these are dimensions, it may just cover the billions of people on the planet.

What's your personality like? You can take a free mock personality test online at www.dummies.com/extras/psychology.

Chapter 10

Catching the First Boat off Isolation Island

*O*ne of the things that distinguishes psychology from other social sciences is the focus of its investigations and applications. Although psychologists do focus on groups at times, they focus a majority of their work on individuals. Therapy, for example, is typically an individual affair, even if it's group therapy.

Americans love the classic individual. John Wayne walked tall and independently for years. Rambo single-handedly took on entire divisions of enemy soldiers. These guys stood on their own. They were individuals who resisted pressures to go along with the crowd. They seemed to know who they were, and they were never willing to compromise their self-identity. Sometimes that's called integrity — which fits because one of the meanings of the word integrity is wholeness or completeness, and these guys were complete individuals. They had strong character and dominant personas. They knew who they were, and no one could tell them otherwise.

In case you haven't noticed, however, psychologists take nothing for granted. If I had John Wayne in therapy and he came in with his macho, "I know who I am, and I'm not going to change" attitude, I'd take the bait. I'd say, "Okay, who are you?" It's easy to take knowing who you are for granted. Until someone asks, most of us go around assuming we know who we are. This is the age-old question of *self.* What is a self, and how do I know if I have one? What is my identity? Who am I?

Feeling Self-Conscious

Have you ever seen a dog stand in front of a mirror? Sometimes they bark at themselves or stand there with a puzzled look. Believe it or not, the ability to recognize oneself in the mirror is pretty advanced, and dogs have yet to demonstrate that they can do it. Some psychologists argue that it is a uniquely human ability, although some research has shown that teenage chimpanzees, magpies (a type of bird), elephants, and orangutans can recognize themselves in a mirror.

When we've developed a sense of self-awareness, we've achieved a state of self-consciousness. Why do I say "developed?" Aren't we aware of ourselves at birth? Actually, it may take up to five or six months for an infant to develop anything even remotely resembling self-consciousness.

The mirror technique is one of the tools that psychologists have used to test infants' and toddlers' levels of self-consciousness. The simplest form of this test involves just setting an infant down in front of a mirror and watching her response. Some researchers have shown that 5- to 6-month-olds will reach out and touch the mirror image, suggesting they think it's another baby, or at least different from them.

In 1979, Michael Lewis and Jeanne Brooks-Gunn conducted a sophisticated version of the mirror test. They applied some blush to the noses of two sets of children — 15- to 17-month-olds and 18- to 24-month-olds. The idea: If the kids look in the mirror and see the blush on their nose, they'll touch it or try to remove it in some way. But this requires the child to realize that the person in the mirror is himself. So what happened? Just a few of the 15- to 17-month-olds actually reached up and touched their noses, but the vast majority of the 18- to 24-month-old children did it. So, the older children were more likely to recognize themselves in the mirror.

Showing up in the buff

I used to have this recurring dream where I would find myself naked in some public place. In one of the dreams, I was back in elementary school, and the only thing I was wearing was a fur coat, with nothing underneath. I was pretty worried about what these dreams meant. Did I have a fur-coat fetish or was I an exhibitionist?

I was glad to find out that these dreams were probably about self-consciousness. Each of us has different situations that exemplify feeling extremely self-conscious and exposed. For some people, the situation is public speaking; for others, it's dancing in a nightclub or wearing nothing but a fur coat.

Self-consciousness and self-awareness are the same thing. Being self-conscious just means being aware of oneself. But too much of anything can be bad. Usually when someone says she is "self-conscious" she means that she is aware of some flaw. This is not the type of self-consciousness I am talking about in this section.

Here, I'm talking about these specific types of awareness:

- ✔ Body awareness
- ✔ Private self-consciousness
- ✔ Public self-consciousness

Becoming aware of your body

Body-awareness begins with a simple question: Where do I physically begin, and where do I physically stop? Remember the movie *Malice* with Bill Pullman, Nicole Kidman, and Alec Baldwin? In one scene, Bill and Alec are sitting in bar, and Alec asks Bill to name the part of his body that is most expendable. In other words, Alec wants Bill to choose the part of his body that he could lose without taking a severe blow to his sense of self. If you've seen the movie, you know why he asks this creepy question; it's foreshadowing.

What part of your body is most important to your sense of self? It may sound strange, but being able to tell the difference between your body and some-one else's body is crucial to self-consciousness. Think about newborns. The physical connection between a child and a breast-feeding mother is undeni-able, and a child's realization of a sense of difference, or separateness, from the mother develops slowly over a period of several months.

Keeping it private

How well do you know yourself? Are you always trying to figure yourself out? The internal focus on your thoughts, feelings, motivations, and overall sense of self is called your *private self-consciousness*. When you "look within," you're privately self-conscious. But if you "look within" a little too much, you can be privately "spaced-out."

Showing it off

I was leaving for work one morning and realized, when I got outside to my car, that I'd forgotten something. I did the big finger snap and the one-eye squint, made an about-face, and went back inside. What are these things? They sound like something from a *Seinfeld* episode, but you know these actions, I bet — those behaviors you do when you forget something. Why did I make these gestures? If I didn't, I'd look like an idiot for walking to my car and then walking back again for no apparent reason. Why did I need a reason? Someone was watching me!

This is the *invisible audience* phenomenon — a sense that you're on display when you're in public and that people are watching you. Teenagers always seem to be on stage. If they trip over a crack in the sidewalk, they turn bright red and run off giggling. This is an example of *public self-consciousness,* a sense of being in the presence of others, our public image — whether others are actually watching or not.

The most noticeable aspect of public self-consciousness is awareness and focus on appearances. People don't spend billions of dollars a year on nice clothes, gym memberships, and diets for nothing. Public self-consciousness is a big part of who you are and how you see yourself.

Identifying Yourself

An easy way to find out who you are is to ask other people. Your identity is often deeply tied to the way other people see you. When you look into the mirror, what do you see? Have you ever wondered how you look to other people? Do they see the same person you see in the mirror? The part of your self-concept that is based on other people's reactions to and views of you is called your *looking-glass self,* one of the most basic concepts of self. People are, after all, social creatures, and it would be hard to argue against the idea that at least part of a person's self-concept depends on the views of others.

Daniel Stern (a notable psychoanalyst specializing in infant development) proposed a theory of self-concept that gives us a good look into how people develop a unique "self." From his studies on infants, he proposed that all people are born with an innate ability to become aware of themselves through a series of experiences.

People are born with the *emergent self,* which basically consists of subjective experiences of joy, distress, anger, and surprise. Feelings! The *core self* begins to arise between the ages of 2 and 4 months, when memories start to form and people develop a sense of their physical capabilities. Next comes the *subjective self,* which emerges when an infant realizes that she can share her experiences with other people. A good example of this is when a baby tries to give you a drink off her bottle before she drinks it. And finally, the *verbal self* develops as we use language to organize a sense of self.

Arnold Buss, an American researcher and psychologist, provides a good look at the meaning of *identity*. Two aspects comprise a person's identity:

- ✔ Personal identity
- ✔ Social identity

Forging a personal identity

My *personal identity* consists of the things that make me stand out in a crowd — like my massive biceps and athletic prowess. Actually, I'm thinking of something a little more psychological, even though physical appearance does make up part of a person's identity. According to Buss, the personal identity is comprised of a *public self* and a *private self*, each with its own components.

Three important aspects make up the *public self:*

- ✔ **Appearance:** As I mention earlier in the "Showing it off" section, being aware of your appearance is very much a part of your identity. This is not a uniquely western perspective. Cultures all over the world engage in elaborate and sophisticated attempts to improve appearances and enhance personal beauty, as defined by each particular culture. Some philosophers state that a sense of aesthetics is essential for the good life — central to a person's self-concept.

- ✔ **Style:** George Clooney, Johnny Depp, and Jay Z have style. The way they talk, their body language, and their facial expressions are undeniably "them." Everyone has a peculiar way of speaking and moving. Even a person's handwriting is unique. These things make up a person's style. Don't get confused by the Clooney, Depp, or Z examples though; style isn't about being "cool." My style is unique to me, whether it's cool or not. It's the "Dr. Cash" style, and no matter what others may say, I think it's very cool.

✔ **Personality:** Personality theories attempt to account for individuality based on differences among personalities. If someone put my personality inside another person's body, would my friends recognize me? Maybe not at first, but they may eventually start to notice that something is up because personalities make people unique; they make a person identifiable. Personalities are enduring, and they don't change easily. Because of their consistency and stability, personalities are good representations of who a person is, even if he acts differently from time to time. Chapter 9 is about personality.

The *private self* consists of characteristics that are difficult for others to see and observe. When a patient comes in for psychotherapy, a psychologist has a difficult time helping him if he refuses to talk about his private self — his thoughts, feelings, and daydreams and fantasies.

✔ **Thoughts:** Knowing what someone is thinking is hard, unless he tells you. Some people are better than others at figuring out what people are thinking, but it's really nothing more than a sophisticated guessing process. My thoughts are unique to me.

✔ **Feelings:** Mental health professionals often evaluate new patients at psychiatric hospitals with something called the *mental status examination.* The professional observes the patient, partly to figure out how the patient feels. This observable aspect of how someone feels is the *affect.* But what about what the person says? I've often not seen someone's depression even when she tells me that she is extremely sad. This is called *mood,* a person's own private experience of feeling. When patients tell me how they feel, I have to take their word for it. It's pretty hard to tell someone that he's not sad when he tells you he is.

✔ **Daydreams/Fantasies:** Who would you be without your daydreams and fantasies? Again, fantasies are typically private, especially the sexual ones. Yours are unique to you, and they define you.

You are what you do

The most interesting aspect about identity is that, as people grow older, the way they define themselves changes. Elementary school children often define who they are by the things that they do. Very young children may identify themselves by saying, "I run. I play. I ride my bike." When these children become teenagers, this shifts to psychological concepts such as beliefs, motivations, desires, and feelings. "I want to go to the dance" or "I feel very sad today." How do adults define themselves? Probably by combining both types of self-definition: activity and psychological concepts, "I'm a sad psychologist who can't golf."

Carving out a social identity

What's your name? Where are you from? What's your religion? Each of these questions is a component of one aspect of your *social identity* — those things that identify you with a particular societal category.

Group affiliation refers to things such as your vocations and social clubs. Many people identify themselves by the type of work they do for a living. "I'm a fireman!" "I'm a cop!" I'm a psychologist. But another important dimension of the social identity is the kinds of social clubs and cliques a person affiliates with. One would be hard pressed to deny the strong identification that many college men have with their fraternities. Other people see themselves as "cowboys" because they strap on boots, jeans, and a cowboy hat and go line dancing at a local Western club. No matter what you're into, it often gives you a sense of uniqueness that goes beyond the other aspects of personal identity. Your social identity is comprised of certain identity factors that, when taken all together, equal the social "you." These factors include kinship, race and ethnicity, and religious beliefs.

Kinship

Most people realize that *kinship* is central to social identity. Your relatives are your "kin," and most people get their last name from their family of origin. In the United States, last names are legal names and a fairly reliable way to identify people. Although many people have the same name, many more do not.

In Arabic culture, a last name is not the primary way to identify someone's kin. Legally, last names are often used for identification, but a person is socially identified by who his father is, and a father is identified by who his oldest son is. Instead of being "Mr. Nasser Khoury," an individual in this culture would be "Father of Josef" or "Abu Josef." The son, "Josef Khoury," would be "Son of Nasser," or "Bin Nasser," or "Josef Nasser." For more on family, see "Cavorting with Family and Friends" later in the chapter.

Ethnicity and nationality

Ethnicity is another important aspect of social identity and is defined as a classification of belonging to a particular group based on a similar cultural tradition. Often, you can find these common categories on job and school applications. The categories are rather arbitrary in name, but they do include a lot of information. Some people are more comfortable not identifying ethnic differences between people because they fear discrimination. But ethnicity is very much a part of who people are and the culture that guides their lives.

Nationality is not the same as ethnicity. I can be a born-and-raised Canadian citizen with Japanese ethnicity. Both ethnicity and nationality are important pieces of information about a person because a Peruvian citizen of Japanese descent is likely very different from a Canadian citizen of Japanese descent.

Religious and group affiliations

Religious affiliation affects a person's social identity to varying degrees. In Israel, for example, most of the inhabitants of the city of Nazareth are of Arabic ethnicity, but there are two distinct religious groups: Muslims and Christians. An individual's religious identity is a core aspect in determining who she is. Some Americans strongly identify themselves by religious denomination: Roman Catholic, Presbyterian, Lutheran, Muslim, Jewish, Hindu, and so on.

Mustering up some self-esteem

Unfortunately, sometimes having a *looking-glass self* can be a bad thing. (See "Identifying Yourself" earlier in this chapter.) As long as other people see you in a good light, all is well. But this is often not the case. Children, for example, are sometimes belittled, put down, or verbally abused by their own parents. Even adults know that others don't always hold them in the highest esteem, so many people don't have very high regard for themselves.

Sorry for the depressing introduction, but many people have come to understand the concept of *self-esteem,* an individual's evaluation of her self-worth, through its absence. Most of the people I know are pretty quick to point out if someone they know has low self-esteem. These folks are a dime a dozen. I mean, have you ever seen the "Self Improvement" section of a bookstore? It's usually pretty big, and I've yet to come across the "You're Already a Great Person!" section in the bookstores and libraries I visit.

Buss provides a good review of six main sources of self-esteem:

- ✔ **Appearance:** People usually feel better about themselves when they feel attractive. A lot of social psychology research has demonstrated that people judged to be attractive are granted more favors and preferred for social interaction than those who are not. Looking good means feeling good!

- ✔ **Ability and performance:** People feel better about themselves when they get good grades, perform well at work, and otherwise do things successfully. The more a person is able to accomplish for himself, the more likely he is going to feel good about himself.

✔ **Power:** When a person feels like she's in control of her life, she's more likely to feel good about herself. There are at least three sub-sources of a sense of power: dominance, status, and money. Domination can be achieved by coercion, competition, or leadership. Status and money pretty much speak for themselves. I'm not saying that unknown, poor people feel bad about themselves, but they'd probably feel better if they had some status and a bigger bank account.

✔ **Social rewards:** Three types of social rewards tend to make people feel good about who they are.

- *Affection:* People like you.

- *Praise:* Someone tells you that you're doing a good job.

- *Respect:* Others value your opinions, thoughts, and actions.

✔ **Vicarious elements:** This source of self-esteem is all about feeling good about yourself because of things "outside" rather than "inside." *Reflected glory* makes you feel good because you get a boost from being around or associated with successful, powerful, or popular people. It's the I-know-famous-people form of self-esteem. Having nice material possessions can also make some people feel better about themselves.

✔ **Morality:** Morality involves being a good person and living according to the standards and rules of social conduct that you admire. Being a good person never hurts self-esteem. For the most part, morality is a relative term. But, when someone feels that he's taken the moral high ground (however he defines it) in a situation, he is likely to have positive self-esteem.

In addition to these sources of self-esteem, some research also suggests that certain aspects of personality can make an impact on self-esteem. Shyness and social loneliness have been found to be associated with a sense of low self-worth. On the flip side, people who are optimistic and sociable typically report feeling better about themselves. It seems, then, that being social and having good relationships are important to feeling good about oneself. That brings me to the topic of relationships, as I leave the realm of the isolated self behind.

Getting Attached

Humans are unarguably social creatures. Some are very social, and others are less so; but most people have a desire to socialize at least a little bit. In fact, if a person has an extreme disinterest in social interactions, he may have a form of mental illness called *schizoid personality disorder.* Personality disorders are tackled in depth in Chapter 13.

The most basic human relationships are between two people — husband and wife, brother and sister, friend and friend. How do you cross the divide between your isolated self and the people in the world around you? Psychologists have approached this problem by looking at what is typically a person's first relationship: mother and child. I realize that this is not the first relationship for everyone. Some people are raised by their grandparents or by foster parents. So in actuality, the earliest relationships that people have are with primary caregivers, who may or may not be their mothers.

Realizing even monkeys get the blues

Researchers often analyze the primary relationship between a caregiver and a child by using a concept called *attachment*. John Bowlby is considered the dominant figure in attachment research. (Does that mean he has high self-esteem, you think?) Bowlby's theory stated that infants are essentially dependent on their caregivers for providing the necessities of life (food, shelter, stimulation, love, and so forth). For the most part, infants are helpless, except for their ability to "attach" to and form a relationship with their primary caregiver(s). This connection or attachment ensures that the infant's needs are met.

When an infant finds himself in a threatening situation, he attempts to reconnect to his primary caregiver. This is called *attachment behavior* — anything an infant does to attain or maintain closeness to someone perceived as better able to cope with the world. A primary caregiver is viewed as an *attachment figure*. If you know that your attachment figures are available when you need them, you feel more secure.

Bowlby viewed attachment as an essential aspect of leading a productive and psychologically healthy life. In fact, when attachment is lacking, infants often suffer from depression, anxiety, and a generally poor psychological well-being. In the 1950s for example, mental health professionals began to investigate the effects of long-term hospitalization and institutionalization on infants, and they documented severe problems. The adverse effects of inadequate or absent care during infancy and early childhood were undeniable. Children need access to caregivers whom they know and are connected to.

In 1959, University of Wisconsin-Madison psychologist Harry Harlow conducted an interesting experiment with monkeys. He put baby monkeys in a cage with two different dummy versions of mother monkeys. One of the dummies was made of soft cloth and had no food; the other was made of wire but had food for the babies to eat. The babies preferred contact with the soft dummy over the wire dummy in spite of the presence of food. Harlow conducted another experiment in which he deprived baby rhesus monkeys of social contact with other monkeys for as long as six months. When these monkeys were released to be with others, their behavior resembled that of a depressed and anxious human with severe levels of withdrawal, self-harming behavior (such as biting themselves), and nervousness.

Attaching with style

It should be undeniable that attachment represents an essential relationship for all people, but I'm sure you well know that the gap between ideal and reality can be vast; the concept of human attachment is no exception. Some people are in therapy today because of the less-than-ideal relationships they had with their primary caregivers. So if Bowlby presented us with the ideal, what else is there?

Various *attachment styles* theories address the variations on Bowlby's ideal relationship. They used the *strange situation* technique to determine the nature and extent of children's attachment. In the strange situation, a child and her primary caregiver are put in a room with some toys to play with. Then, the primary caregiver gets up and leaves the room. Researchers observe and record the child's reaction. After a while, a stranger comes into the room, and the child's reaction is recorded again. Finally, the primary caregiver comes back into the room, and the child's behavior is recorded one last time.

Researchers designed the strange situation to determine if a child uses the caregiver as a secure base from which to explore the environment. A child sees a caregiver as a *secure base* — a safe place to launch explorations into the world from but someone to safely return to if there is a need. The strange situation observed the following in order to answer these questions:

- When the caregiver leaves, does the child fuss or react with protest?
- If there is a protest, is it because the child prefers to be with the caregiver, or is it because the child fears that the caregiver won't return?
- When the caregiver returns, does the child welcome him or her back, or does the child react in some other, more resentful or distant manner?

The answers to these questions lead to a description of three basic attachment styles:

- **Secure:** Securely attached children exhibit the following behavior:
  - They use their primary caregiver as a secure base from which to explore their environments.
  - They protest a little when their caregiver leaves but eventually calm down, seeming to trust that he will return.
  - While with strangers or other adults, they're friendly but not overly so.
  - Upon reunion, they go to the primary caregiver and seek connection.
- **Anxious/ambivalent:** Anxious/ambivalently attached children act in the following ways:
  - They do not use their caregivers as secure bases to explore from.

- They sometimes resist initial contact with the caregiver but staunchly resist any attempt to break it off after it has been established.

- They are avoidant or sometimes aggressive in the presence of strangers.

- They cry excessively upon separation and are difficult to console.

✔ **Avoidant:** Avoidant attached children act as follows:

- They seem to need less contact from the caregiver.

- They are indifferent when left alone or cry only because they are alone and not because they seem to miss the caregiver.

- Upon the return of the caregiver, they either avoid or ignore her.

Before anybody designs his own little "strange situation" at home to see how much his children love him or not, let me tell you about *goodness-of-fit*. Goodness-of-fit refers to how well the primary caregiver and the child are matched in terms of temperament and personality. This fit can have an effect on attachment style and should be considered before anyone writes himself off as a horrible parent or "unlovable child."

Caregivers and infants sometimes can look like they're engaged in a harmonious dance, perfectly synchronized with each other. Other times, they look like they both have two left feet. If a mother is high-strung and energetic, she may not do well with a mellow baby — and vice versa. The style of interaction and how smoothly it happens is a powerful factor in establishing a secure attachment. So if you're having trouble and you think that your child is poorly attached, take a look at the style of interaction and see whether there's anything you can do differently to improve it.

Cavorting with Family and Friends

Ever wonder why so many people get depressed during the holidays? Maybe they're not looking forward to going into debt to finance all those gifts. Or maybe the holidays remind them how lonely they are. I'm not buying it. Here's my explanation: The holidays mean getting together with family, and families are pretty good at embarrassing and belittling each other by pointing out weight problems and receding hairlines or pitiful salaries. That can be pretty depressing! Fortunately, families are good for some positive things, too.

A *family* consists of at least two people related by blood, marriage, or adoption. It seems like families have changed quite a bit over the last 20 years, including increasing numbers of single-parent families, gay marriages, and blended families of divorce. A lot of marriages end in divorce, so children are learning to manage two sets of parents, half-siblings, and split holidays. Even though the modern face of the family has changed, many of the basic functions of a family have not.

The *McMaster model of family functioning* breaks down seven major components of, you guessed it, family functioning:

- ✔ **Problem solving:** The family's ability to resolve issues and maintain family functioning.

- ✔ **Communication:** The clarity and directness of information exchange in a family. You knew this one was coming.

- ✔ **Roles:** The different behaviors and responsibilities of each family member in terms of meeting basic needs, performing household tasks, and providing emotional support and nurturance.

- ✔ **Affective responsiveness:** Each family member's ability to express and experience a range, intensity, and quality of emotions.

- ✔ **Affective involvement:** The family as a whole's interest in the values, activities, and interests of others.

- ✔ **Behavior control:** The rules and standards of conduct. Belching at the dinner table was never a laughing matter in my family — even if we were supping on soda and cauliflower!

- ✔ **Overall family functioning:** A family's ability to accomplish its daily tasks across the other six areas. If you had to give your family a grade, what would it be?

Children of divorce

The effects of divorce on children have been a matter of controversy since the first pen scrawled across the dotted line of those famed papers. And many parents stay together "for the sake of the kids." Yet most research tends to show that children are not necessarily adversely affected by the divorce of their parents. Boys seem to do a little worse than girls in the long run, but research indicates that the most important predictor of how children will cope with a divorce is the nature of the marriage. If the parents always fight and have a tumultuous relationship while married, then the divorce is also likely to go poorly and have a negative impact on the children's adjustment. Researchers often advise couples to not argue or discuss divorce-related issues in front of children and to keep overall conflict to an absolute minimum in order to avoid undue stress and strain and coping difficulties for the children.

Parenting with panache

A good friend of mine recently had a baby. Just when I was about to offer him some psychological advice on parenting, he started talking about all the advice people had been giving him and how it bothered him. I kept my opinion to myself. "Crying opens up their lungs." "Don't give babies a pacifier." There are almost as many opinions on how to raise children as there are people on the planet. Fortunately, psychologists have been trying to simplify things.

Diana Baumrind, a clinical and developmental psychologist, took on the task of trying to boil down parenting into something a little more manageable. She came up with three main parenting styles: *authoritarian, authoritative,* and *permissive:*

✔ **Authoritarian:** These parents are rigid and dictatorial. Some kids feel like prisoners in their own families; parents are overly strict and don't listen to what the children have to say. They're like the drill sergeants of parenting. What they say goes, and there's no discussion about it. Unfortunately, all that toughness tends to backfire. Authoritarian parents tend to have children that are either overly passive or excessively rebellious and sometimes hostile. These parents can learn a lot from the next style of parenting.

✔ **Authoritative:** These folks tend to approach parenting with a more democratic style. Parents from previous generations often criticize how "today's" parents try to reason with their children too much. "What that kid needs is a good spanking!" Authoritative parents listen to their children and allow them to have input, while maintaining parental authority and control. Children seem to thrive in this environment, and they tend to act more sociable, feel more capable, and be more well-adjusted in general as they grow up.

✔ **Permissive:** There are two types of permissive parents:

 • **Indulgent:** Ever go to one of those backyard beer parties in high school? Me neither, but I hear they can get pretty wild. I've always wondered where those kids' parents are. Oh, I get it; they've got the "cool parents." Indulgent parents are involved with their children but shy away from control, authority, and discipline. They sometimes even enable their children to engage in questionable behavior because they don't want to alienate their kids.

 • **Indifferent:** These parents are neglectful due to a range of possible factors, including career obsession, drug abuse, or self-centeredness. Whatever the reason some people adopt this style, permissive parents tend to have children who report feeling ill-equipped to deal with the demands of growing up.

Embracing your rival: Siblings

Ever wonder what siblings are good for? Those of you who are only children may have fantasized about having a brother or a sister. Those with siblings may think those creatures are pretty much only good for fighting and stealing your crush, but psychologists have found that there's actually more to it.

Siblings have a powerful effect on a person's development. They create a family environment that would be very different without them. Siblings are also good sources of friendship, companionship, and affection. Sometimes they can even be role models. Here are three other distinct functions that siblings provide for each other:

✔ **Mutual regulation:** Acting as sounding boards and testing grounds for new behavior, like practicing a break-up speech before delivering it to an unsuspecting sweetheart

✔ **Direct services:** Easing household burdens and sometimes providing practical support, such as rides, help with homework, or fashion advice

✔ **Support:** Helping each other in times of need by forming alliances and sticking together

Many people are familiar with sibling rivalry and discord. Research shows that the most common negative qualities associated with siblings are antagonism and quarreling. Some people think that the fighting goes away as people grow older, but the truth is that the basic emotional character of sibling relationships remains pretty stable over time. Interactions can change, but the feelings remain much the same.

Getting chummy

How does that old saying go? "Friends are forever?" Or is it "Diamonds are forever?" I never can remember. I don't have many diamonds, so it doesn't really matter much anyway. But I do have friends, and friendship is an important element in life. Why do we remember Tonto's name? Because he's the Lone Ranger's friend.

Psychologists Willard Hartup and Nan Stevens provide a nice review of research related to friendship. They basically define *friendship* as a relationship between mutually attracted people engaged in a reciprocal relationship of exchange. Friends are different from non-friends in that our relationships are typically mutual. There's a lot of giving and taking and giving again in most friendships.

Good friends provide support and help people cope with life's problems. But making friends isn't necessarily easy; it requires a fair amount of social skill. It doesn't hurt if you're socially well-adjusted. Being equal and fair also helps. And knowing how to manage conflicts when they arise helps maintain the friendships you develop.

Who are your friends? I'm guessing they're people much like you. Friends are typically similar in age, gender, ethnicity, and ability. A lot of times friends also have a similar lifestyle. Generally speaking, as people get older, friends tend to be people you work with, which means that they're probably of the same socioeconomic class as well. This still remains relatively true despite the popularity of social media and the use of the Internet as a social tool. Shoot, guess that means no rich friends for me!

Friendship tends to have a positive effect on psychological well-being. People who have good friendships tend to be more sociable, helpful, and confident. Friends are good for your health. So go out there and make a few!

Understanding Person Perception

Humans are social beings, and no small part of survival depends on a person's ability to understand the human environment. Social understanding — including alliances, enemies, allocations of resources, division of labor, relationships, communication, and self-awareness — is vital. Each person must possess a basic level of *social skill* to get along within the human environment. Researcher and psychologist Ewing Phillips offers a good working definition of social skill: the ability to communicate and interact with others in a way that allows for one's needs and goals to be met without interfering with others' goals.

In this section, I describe three very important social skills: understanding other people's behavior, understanding your own behavior, and communicating.

Explaining others

People are always watching other people. When you go to a public place like a park or a busy shopping mall, how often do you just watch people? You may notice people's clothes, the bags they're carrying, or the conversations they're having. You're noticing all kinds of things about them and using your observations to draw conclusions.

Don't believe me? How many times have you decided that the teenager with purple hair and a pierced nose is just looking for attention? When's the last time you figured that the woman driving a brand-new SUV with kids in the back is a stay-at-home soccer mom with a successful husband paying the bills? Where do people come up with these ideas? Maybe, the purpled-headed kid is conducting a psychology experiment. Perhaps the woman is a CEO and single mom. How do you know? If you're like most people, you almost instinctively begin drawing conclusions about other people based on what you see, hear, and experience.

The area of psychology that's devoted to understanding how people go about thinking about people, including themselves, is known as *social cognition;* it tries to break down the mental processes involved when people observe, think about, and make inferences about other's behavior.

Assuming

Trying to explain other people's behavior can be difficult. You can't look inside their minds, so you can only guess what's going on in there. But this doesn't stop people from trying to explain others' actions. In fact, it's so common that there's a word for it. The complex process of drawing conclusions about other people's intentions and characteristics, based on a person's observations of them, is the social cognitive process known as *person perception*. Almost everyone uses some assumptions in the person-perception process, including these:

- ✔ People are *causal agents;* they play an active and intentional part in producing their own behavior. Nobody or nothing else causes them to behave in a particular way.

- ✔ People are like me, thinking and feeling in the same ways I do. Thinking like this allows people to use themselves as a baseline when trying to understand other people.

Snapping to judgment

Have you ever experienced love at first sight? I've always wondered how that works. How can you fall in love with somebody based on just looking at him or her? Maybe research in the area of *snap judgments* can help answer that question. Snap judgments of people are instantaneous, automatic, and unconscious evaluations.

Snap judgments follow two types of cues:

- ✔ **Static cues:** Things that are relatively unchanging about a person like appearance, gender, and body type (not including clothing). People use this information to make *evaluative judgments* about other people, and these judgments can be right or wrong. I may evaluate a person with a particular hairstyle as laid-back and easygoing (long and hippie-esque), or I may see him as nerdy and uptight (high and tight around the ears). Either way, I'm using an aspect of someone's physical appearance to make a judgment about what kind of person he is.

> ✔ **Dynamic cues:** Things that tend to change depending on the situation, such as facial expressions, clothing, and mannerisms. When I see a person smile, I may evaluate him as generally happy, or I may assume that he just heard a funny joke. Either way, I'm using relatively basic information to make snappy evaluations of a person's personality or life.

Making an impression

Snap judgments are really just the beginning of attempts to figure out other people. We all make snap judgments and usually are unaware it's happening. In the process of *impression formation,* people go beyond snap judgments and make in-depth inferences about the kind of person someone is.

Solomon Asch, at Swarthmore College, came up with a popular theory of impression formation that focuses on the existence of *central traits* that color interpretations and perceived meanings of observed traits. It's like people have an internal sense that certain traits go together. For example, an attractive person may have an easier time getting someone to help him change a flat tire than an unattractive person. This may be related to an assumption that the attribute of attractiveness is automatically connected to the attribute of gratefulness. I'm not going to help an unattractive, ungrateful person change his tire.

Implicit personality theory

Jerome Bruner and Renato Tagiuri in the 1950s considered the internal sense of traits that belong together as part of an *implicit personality theory.* People learn that certain traits go together because they've either been told that they go together or observed them going together. I was told a thousand times that polite people don't interrupt, so I guess I'm pretty rude because I interrupt all the time. Interrupting and rudeness "belong" together in my implicit personality theory.

Basically, implicit personality theories are stereotypes. Stereotypes are an inevitable consequence of attempts to make sense of the social world. Stereotypes are thinking shortcuts. No one can possibly store independent evaluations of every single person he ever meets. This would take up way too much space in the human memory. Instead, people categorize other people, and sometimes this categorization results in the formation of stereotypes. Unfortunately, in an attempt to simplify the world, people often over-generalize negative aspects of others, which too often leads to prejudice and racism.

Figuring out the causes of others' behavior

Snappy judgments based on limited information aren't the only thinking shortcut; most people also attempt to determine why a person did what she did or what caused a particular behavior. This is known as *attribution,* a process by which a person's behavior is linked to either internal or external causes.

When making an attribution, a person typically considers three important pieces of information:

- ✔ **Consistency:** People generally behave in the same way every time a particular situation occurs.

- ✔ **Distinctiveness:** When a person behaves differently with different people and/or in different situations, his behaviors are considered "distinct."

- ✔ **Consensus:** There's agreement that all people act in a particular way when engaged in particular activities or within specific contexts.

Numerous possible combinations of these three pieces of information exist in varying degrees, and these variations provide clues to whether a behavior is internally or externally motivated. For example, the combination of high consistency, low distinctiveness, and low consensus leads to a *personal attribution* (internal cause or explanation for a person's behavior). When I act consistently across situations, respond to the same stimuli the same way every time, and act differently than other people in that same situation, it's probably me. High consistency, high distinctiveness, and high consensus lead to an external attribution. When I act the same across situations, but I respond differently — but the same as other people in the situation — to the same stimuli, it's probably the situation or the external environment. So what would you attribute my passion for polka music to? Doesn't everyone love polka?

All of this judging begs the question of whether or not people are accurate in their attributions. A consistent mistake is called the *fundamental attribution error.* Most of the time folks underestimate the role of external causes as determinants of other people's behavior. There's a tendency to see what people do as inherent to them, as actor-caused, because you lack significant information about a person's behavior across situations. When in doubt, attribute it to the actor. The more information you have, the better judge you become.

Conversely, people also have a tendency to see their own behavior as a result of external causes more so than other people's behavior (Jones and Nisbett). This is called the *actor-observer effect/bias.* Again, this tendency is probably due to the fact that people have access to more information about themselves.

Similarly, when it comes to success and failure, people tend to attribute their successes to internal causes and their failures to external causes. This reverses for other people's successes and failures.

Explaining yourself

Do the famous people who endorse products on television commercials actually use the products they promote? Does Beyoncé really drink Pepsi? Does Lebron James really use a Samsung smartphone? Does Shaq drive a Buick? Maybe so, and maybe no. I don't know Beyoncé, Lebron, or Shaq, so all I can do is guess. But let's just say for the sake of discussion that they do use the products they endorse. If I asked them why they endorse those products, what would they say, and what would these responses tell you about how well these people know themselves?

Researchers Leon Festinger and James Carlsmith performed a classic experiment that offers some insight into the "Lebron James question." They asked research subjects to perform a dull and boring task and then offered the subjects money to tell other people that the task was really interesting. There were two groups. One group was paid $1 each, and the other was paid $20 each. The subjects that received only $1 reported that the task was more interesting than the $20 subjects did when asked about their true feelings as opposed to their "endorsement" feelings. The $20 created a larger gap between the subjects' actions and what they thought they felt. This experiment demonstrates *cognitive dissonance,* the process of changing one's beliefs to match one's actions. If I do something that contradicts my beliefs and I can't think of a another plausible explanation (like they paid me big bucks to lie — $20 then would be worth about $150 now), I will alter my beliefs to match my behavior.

The subjects who were paid $1 must have figured that, if they were only getting bribed with one measly dollar, they must not have been so bored after all. The bigger the bribe, the more we perceive the task as being contrary to our true beliefs. In this case, the extra money represents an easy explanation for our behavior.

What does this tell us about our famous product endorsers? If they do use the products they endorse, they may do so because they don't want to admit that they only endorse the products for the money. Lebron may not want to admit to himself that he really wants an iPhone but endorses Samsung because he loves the money he gets to say that's the phone he prefers. So he may change his attitude to match his behavior.

Cognitive dissonance says a lot about how people know things about themselves and engage in the process of *self-attribution.* Daryl Bem of Cornell University developed a theory of self-perception that states that people know their own attitudes by drawing inferences based on observing their own behavior in the same way that they observe others. You know yourself in the same way you know others — by observing behavior.

When trying to figure out yourself and judging your own behavior, you may be guilty of some pretty interesting distortions. Here are three common distortions:

- **False consensus effect:** This is a tendency to overestimate how common your opinions and behaviors are, especially the undesirable ones. "Everyone's doing it!" People tend to see a consensus that is consistent with their opinions, whether or not one exists.

- **False uniqueness effect (FUE):** There's a saying in Alcoholics Anonymous, "You're terminally unique!" The phrase is used for people who think that their problems are so different from everyone else's that no one can possibly understand them. The FUE is the tendency to underestimate how common one's beliefs are, especially the desirable ones.

- **Self-handicapping:** When I was in college and I knew I had a tough test coming up — one I was pretty sure I was going to fail no matter how much I studied — I wouldn't study for it at all. That way, when I failed it, I could blame it on not studying instead of my lack of ability or intelligence. When people create excuses for failure in order to protect their self-esteem or self-image, they're engaging in self-handicapping.

Communicating Is Easier Said Than Done

One of Ronald Reagan's nicknames was "The Great Communicator." Supposedly, he could really get his point across, and people responded well to his speeches. I personally haven't taken the time to analyze Reagan's communication skills. But whether you're negotiating with nations as the president of the United States or trying to order a hamburger at a drive-thru, communication skills are vital to being a socially skilled person.

Owen Hargie, Christine Saunders, and David Dickson at the University of Ulster developed a model of *interpersonal communication* that identified several important components of the communication process. All episodes of communication are goal-directed, and several goals may be pursued simultaneously. A conversation varies as a function of the intended goal. If my goal is to visit with an old friend, I may talk about different things than if I'm conducting a psychological evaluation.

There are also several *mediating processes* that shape the communication process. Any psychological process that affects the meeting of a communicative goal or the outcome of communication can be a mediating process. One important process is called *focusing* (what one pays attention to), which can have a major impact. How you connect current conversational information with previous knowledge is also important, and *inference* — going beyond the surface information being communicated — is also important.

Another core aspect of the communication process is *feedback*, which is information provided to me by the other person about how effectively I am communicating, and how I use it. If you use feedback to change the way you communicate, then you can better meet the conversation goals. But some people seem to just ramble on, oblivious to signals from other people in a conversation that they're not making any sense. These ramblers are not picking up on the feedback. Here's a hint: When someone falls asleep while you're talking to her, that's important feedback.

Being a great communicator involves being good at three specific communication skills: asking questions, explaining, and listening.

Asking questions

An important feature of all effective communication is the process of *questioning*. Questions are a good way to open a conversation, gather information, and express to another person that you're interested in what he's saying. There are several different types of questions, such as:

- ✔ **Recall:** A question like "Where were you on the night of November 12 at 10 p.m.?" asks you to remember basic information. Just a little advice if the police ask you this question: Call a lawyer.

- ✔ **Hypothetical:** Questions designed to engender some creative thought such as "If you could have any job in the world, what would it be?"

Other questions that ask the responder to analyze, evaluate, or problem solve often have different formats that solicit different types of answers:

- ✔ **Closed-end** questions require just a yes or no or identification response.
- ✔ **Open-end** questions require description and elaboration.

There's an art to being a good questioner. Giving the responder a context and structure often helps the responder form answers that meet your actual information needs. You may start out by saying, "I have three main questions." The point is to clue the person in to what you are trying to learn.

Explaining

In addition to being good at questioning, the gift of gab often requires a certain level of skill at explaining oneself. Explanations provide information and clarify messages, and they're often used to demonstrate a point.

When making a point in a conversation, an individual can often bolster her argument by providing a solid explanation for the position being taken. Good explanations are clear, focused, and linked to the listener's knowledge base. Being brief and avoiding a lot fillers like "um," "uh," and "ya know" also helps. These terms interrupt the fluency of communication and can lead to loss of interest.

Sometimes it helps to pause and review so the listener can organize and absorb what has already been explained. It's also very important to use language that is appropriate to the audience or listener. If you're too technical, too gross, or too basic, you may lose their interest.

Listening

A third critical aspect of effective communication is listening. One-way conversations are poor excuses for communication. If no one is listening, there's no "co" in communication.

Here are some good listener guidelines:

- ✔ **Focus:** Turn off the TV, put away your phone, reduce extraneous noise, and don't fidget or fool with stuff around you. Doing your taxes or looking at your mobile phone while someone is talking is a dead giveaway that you're not really listening.

- ✔ **Clear your head:** Be aware of your biases and preconceived ideas and mentally prepare yourself to pay attention and absorb the information being offered by the other person.

- ✔ **Mentally engage:** Keep yourself focused by asking questions to clarify what the speaker is saying.

- ✔ **Wait:** Don't interrupt if you can help it. Respond when the other person finishes making a point.

- ✔ **Process:** Mentally identify the main point of the speaker's communication and organize what he is telling you into categories such as who, what, when, why, and how.

- ✔ **Remain open and attentive:** Don't use *blocking techniques,* such as denying someone's feelings or changing the topic. Take in what the person is saying.

- ✔ **Demonstrate attention:** Maintain eye contact, nod, and orient your body toward the speaker and keep an open posture. Don't cross your arms or turn away.

Asserting yourself

One of the most common problems I see in my clinical practice is that people don't know how to stand up for themselves and communicate their needs in a direct and confident manner. Complaints about pushy coworkers, jerky bosses, and grouchy spouses are commonly the result of a person's lack of assertiveness. For some people, assertiveness seems to come naturally; they're just good at telling people what they think in a way that doesn't put anybody off.

I'm not talking about being aggressive; that often involves a certain level of hostility and a denial of the other person's rights in the interaction. I am talking about something a little milder than aggression, *assertiveness.*

Assertiveness can be defined as standing up for one's rights and expressing one's thoughts, feelings, and beliefs in a direct, honest, and appropriate manner that respects others. Ever have someone cut in line when you're at the grocery store? Did you tell them to go to the end of the line, or did you keep your thoughts to yourself only to get increasingly resentful about it later? What about ordering food at a restaurant and getting something you didn't order? Did you eat it anyway or did you send it back? It sounds easy, but a lot of people won't say anything because they fear being seen as a jerk, being disliked, or hurting another person's feelings.

Assertiveness is a social skill that you can learn. Typically, when people get better at being assertive, the overall quality of their relationships improves. They no longer feel that they can't say what they really think or that they have to keep quiet for the sake of friendships. When people learn how to communicate assertively, they awaken to a whole new realm of possibilities in communication.

Want to be more assertive? *Basic assertions* are expressions such as "No, I don't like that movie" or "Thank you, but I've had enough fruitcake." *Empathic assertions* are statements used to convey that you understand the other person's position even if you're not going along with it. "I understand that you prefer fast food over Italian, but I'm really craving spaghetti."

When someone begins with a basic assertion and then progresses into more straightforward statements with little ambiguity, she engages in *escalating assertiveness.* This is a good skill to use with pushy salespeople, as this example demonstrates:

> **Salesperson:** Can I help you find something?
>
> **Customer:** No thanks.
>
> **Salesperson:** Well, we've got these great deals in women's apparel today.
>
> **Customer:** Really, I'm not interested.
>
> **Salesperson:** How about. . . .
>
> **Customer:** For the third time, can you please leave me alone? I don't want your help.

A particularly useful tool in assertive language is the "I statement" — using a personal position rather than pointing out the other person's behavior and using the "you" word. Instead of telling my boss that he's been hounding me and he's starting to tick me off, I may say, "I get the sense that you're putting unfair pressure on me, and I'm feeling frustrated." Easier said than done, I know, but it works pretty well. Try it!

The following is a quick list of verbal defense strategies that you can use against manipulative and rude people:

- **Broken record:** Simply repeating oneself over and over again. "I said no! What part of *no* don't you understand? I'll say it again. No! No!"

- **Fogging:** Agreeing with what someone is saying but not changing one's position. "You're right, I should watch what I eat. I have gained a few pounds." All the while thinking to yourself, "I'm going to eat whatever I feel like eating. When can I get away from this jerk?"

- **Meta-level:** Taking a conversation to a more abstract level than the original conversation. "I think this is a good example of how hard it can be to get one's point across. I've often wondered how we can get past this." I like to call this the old therapist switch-a-roo! "What is the ideal weight anyway? Being heavy used to be a sign of beauty and prosperity. I'm beautiful and prosperous, not fat."

Chapter 11

Conforming Like a Contortionist: Social Psychology

I'll never forget the time I saw news video of two groups of Buddhist monks fist-fighting for control over a monastery. I was shocked to see people whom I stereotypically perceived as peaceful acting so violently — toward each other! The image was disturbing, but it was also a potent demonstration of how a situation, or the influence of a group, can fuel individual behavior. These typically peaceful individuals seemingly were overcome by a situation that triggered them to engage in behavior that they themselves probably could not explain if asked.

It may be true that an individual is pushed and pulled by the dynamics of his personality and acts instinctively based on genetic makeup. Behavior also seems to vary as a function of thinking. However, psychology would be incomplete without considering the social influences on behavior and mental processes.

Social psychology is the study of the social causes of and influences on behavior.

Social psychologists have long suggested that many of the answers to questions about human behavior lie in understanding social influences such as group norms, conformity, and group pressure. This chapter explores these and other social influences on behavior and highlights the powerful impact of being around other people. The influence of social forces on individual behavior cannot be underestimated.

The study of social influences completes the biopsychosocial model of human behavior. (See Chapter 2 for more on the biopsychosocial model.)

Playing Your Part

Unless you're a hermit and you live by yourself in a shack in the middle of the desert, you exist within a *social matrix* — a multilayered configuration of social relationships that range from the parent-child bond to your co-worker–co-worker interactions. Picture yourself in the middle of a huge multi-ringed circle with each ring representing a level of social organization.

Each of these circles carries a set of expected behaviors — rules that dictate what each individual is supposed to do. Each social group's rules or behavioral expectations are called *norms.* Cultures have norms, families have norms, and even subcultures have norms.

A subculture may consist of a small social group, often organized around a recreational activity. A gang may be considered a subgroup within its own subculture. Gangs have their own language, clothing styles, and rituals that delineate clear rules for the behavior of each individual member. That social structure is what I'm talking about when I use the term *norm.*

Americans typically like to see themselves as rugged individualists, wincing at the idea of blindly following norms. But norms are not all that bad. They simplify complex social situations, allowing people to think about things other than how to act and what to say in a particular situation. Norms serve as "mental shortcuts," and social situations operate more smoothly when norms are clear.

Some norms seem to be universal. Psychologist Roger Brown in 1965 found that people almost universally speak more respectfully to others of higher status and more casually to those of lower status. This manner of addressing others is built into the very structure of some languages, including Spanish and French. The appropriate way to conjugate a verb depends on how well you know the person you're speaking to.

Certainly, universal norms exist, but some variations exist as well. If you're a Palestinian Christian, it is customary and normative to firmly resist any food offered to you while visiting someone's home and only to accept after much counter-insistence by the host. Americans on the other hand may even ask for something to eat or drink when visiting someone's home without thinking twice. Another common variation in cultural norms relates to waiting in line. Some cultures don't seem to appreciate the orderliness of waiting in a single-file line when ordering food at a fast-food establishment, but others do. The norm of *personal space* (the physical space or area around us) too can vary by culture. Some cultures seem to value personal space more than others.

Getting carried away

Role definitions are a powerful determinant of behavior, and the definitions sometimes overpower individual personalities and preferences. In 1972, Phil Zimbardo, psychologist and professor emeritus of psychology at Stanford University, conducted a famous experiment known as the *Stanford prison experiment* that illustrated the power of roles. College students were recruited to participate in a mock-prison situation in which they were randomly assigned to be either guards or inmates. The experiment took place in a makeshift prison in the basement of the psychology building at Stanford University.

The experiment revealed that people seem to naturally know what the roles of both inmate and guard entail, and Zimbardo had to discontinue the experiment within a week because of what he saw happening. The otherwise normal and healthy college students began to take their roles far too seriously. The guards treated the inmates inhumanely and with harsh disdain, and the inmates began to truly hate the guards and focus only on the circumvention of the "prison" system and survival.

In other words, the students got caught up in their roles and forgot about the reality of the situation.

A *role* is a specific type of norm that defines how a person should act in a specific situation. Each individual has certain roles to play (student, employee, brother, sister, parent, and so on) that dictate different behaviors for different situations. Typically, individuals have clear roles to play in specific situations.

Ganging Up in a Group

In a classic episode of the *Twilight Zone,* everyone gets plastic surgery when they reach adolescence, and everyone picks the same transformation so that everyone looks the same — a sort of Ken Doll for the men and a Barbie face for the women. In the episode, one girl decides to keep her natural-born look and is subsequently tormented and ridiculed for wanting to do so. She was under enormous pressure to conform, to give into group pressure, and to go along.

This dynamic is a very real part of everyday life in a community. Groups exert all kinds of pressure on their individual members. Sometimes groups have very clear and explicit rules that keep people in line; in other cases, the rules or pressures are more subtle.

In this section, I point out the group and social influences and determinants of an individual's behavior. This includes a discussion of how individuals conform and react to group pressure and influence an effort on tasks, as well as how people treat each other and "police" each other's thinking.

Conforming

Conformity is a change in behavior that results from real or perceived group pressure. Most people are surprised to realize how much individuals conform. I mean, how many purple houses are on your block? Not many I bet.

In a study from 1937, Muzafer Sherif, one of the founders of social psychology, looked at how people would change their judgments based on knowing how other people answered certain questions. Subjects were asked to estimate how far a light moved across a dark room. Sherif found that when other people were present and offered a different estimate, the subject would change his or her answer to be more in-line with what the others' answers were. Knowledge of the other people's answers influenced the subjects' answers.

In 1955, Solomon Asch, another pioneer in social psychology, found the same thing when he put people in a group and asked them to estimate the lengths of lines. Subjects changed their answers to go along with the group consensus. Both of these experiments are good examples of how an individual may conform under group pressure, even if the pressure is subtle.

Shocking, no?

Harvard University psychologist Stanley Milgram in 1965 conducted an obedience experiment that bordered on the extreme. In fact, it was so extreme that the same experiment would not be allowed today, because it would not pass the required ethics review. Subjects were seated at a control panel with a switch for delivering electrical shocks to a "subject" on the other side of a partition. The subjects were actually experimenters pretending to be participating as real subjects.

The premise: The subject is to be shocked each time that he or she gets a question wrong. With each subsequent wrong answer, the shock gets stronger and stronger. The shocks start at 75 volts and go up to 450 volts.

At some point, the subject is yelling and pleading with the real subject to stop administering the shock. An experimenter stands next to the real subject with a clipboard and a white lab-coat insisting that the real subject continue with the experiment and continue to administer shocks, despite the pretend subject's protests and obvious pain.

In reality, the fake subjects did not receive any shock at all; they only pretended to get shocked. But ask yourself, "When would I have stopped giving the shocks?" Maybe you think that you would have stopped the second the subject started yelling and asking you to stop. I'm sure the subjects in Milgram's study thought the same thing.

However, the shocking outcome (sorry about that one; couldn't resist) was that 63 percent of the real subjects went all the way to 450 volts in compliance (or obedience) with the experimenter! That's enough voltage to potentially cause death.

Obedience is an extreme form of conformity and often involves going against one's better judgment or truest intentions. When I think of obedience, visions of dog-obedience school pop into my head — me standing there with a collar and leash around my neck, jumping up to get my treat for performing the requested trick. Sounds extreme, doesn't it?

I would like to think that I'd walk out of an experiment in which I had to torture someone with electric shocks, but the majority of subjects in one famous study followed orders and didn't stop applying shocks (see the nearby "Shocking, no?" sidebar). Why?

There are eight factors that seem to increase conformity and obedience:

- **Emotional distance:** The more personal contact someone has with an individual, the less likely he is to act without compassion against that person. It's harder to be cruel to another person when the victim has a face.

- **Proximity and legitimacy of authority:** When an authority figure is close by, obedience is more likely. The authority's legitimacy also matters. You are more likely to be obedient to an individual that you think has genuine authority than someone you perceive to be a poser.

- **Institutional authority:** When an authority figure is part of an accepted institution, obedience is more likely. In other words, I'm more likely to comply with the suggestions of a court-appointed judge than some guy sitting next to me at the bus stop (assuming he's not a judge). Recognized institutional authority has a powerful effect on obedience.

- **Group size:** Groups of three to five people have a maximum effect on conformity pressure; groups containing fewer than three and more than five people have a less powerful effect.

- **Unanimity:** When groups are in complete agreement, it's more difficult for a single individual to resist conforming.

- **Cohesiveness:** The more a group feels that it is bound together and tightly organized, the more power the group has over its members. As an example, I used to play softball on a team without uniforms, and it just didn't feel right. We needed uniforms to be a *real* team. Uniforms are one way to increase cohesiveness because looking the same as others in a group strengthens a sense of unity.

- **Status:** People with a higher status than you tend to have more influence over your obedience/compliance.

- **Public response:** People conform more when their behaviors are made public. It's easier to disagree privately or anonymously.

Although conformity and obedience are not necessarily bad things, learning how to resist both may be important — just in case. One needs only to think of Nazi Germany, perhaps the most horrific example of the dangers of conformity, to understand why maintaining a certain degree of individual diversity is important in any social group.

The best way to prevent conformity may be to maintain a sense of and respect for human uniqueness. Freedom of speech and religious tolerance are also good protections against conformity. As long as people feel comfortable being themselves and can freely speak their minds, conformity is a little more difficult (see the "Birds of a Feather . . . Or Not" section later in this chapter for more on prejudice and stereotypes).

Doing better with help

"There's no I in TEAM!" A lot of coaches use this line in their pep talks, trying to convey the idea that the better a team plays together, the better their results will be. And social psychologists have found that this idea is true to a certain extent. When we're in the presence of others, people are more physiologically aroused and energized, and dominant behaviors are strengthened. This phenomenon is called *social facilitation*.

Robert Zajonc, professor emeritus at Stanford University, found that when a person does something relatively simple and routine, being in the presence of others improves her performance. But when a task is complex, having others around can hinder performance. So it may be a good idea to conduct that calculus contest somewhere other than Madison Square Garden. Although, folding laundry in the Garden is probably okay.

Kicking back

When I was in junior high school, teachers often asked me to participate in group projects. It usually went something like this: Four less-motivated students would pair up with the "smart" kid and let the "smart" kid do all the work. The motivationally challenged pupils would then ascribe their names to the project in order to get the credit.

This is an example of *social loafing* — the tendency for people to exert less energy and effort when engaged in a group task that ignores individual accountability.

In 1979, psychologists Latane, Kipling, Williams, and Harkins found, for example, that when people were put in groups of six and instructed to clap as loudly as they possibly could, the amount of noise produced was less than that of one person clapping alone. People loaf when engaged in activities as groups. Loafers are *free riders,* people who rest on the efforts of other people in the group, like those kids who just mouth the words in the school choir.

Hey, if nobody can tell if I'm singing or not, then why should I exert myself? I'm not getting credit for my individual effort anyway.

Remaining anonymous

Ever wonder why groups of people who do really awful things often wear uniforms? Take the Ku Klux Klan, for example. What's with the pointy hats? Researchers have found that diminishing individual identity and diffusing individual responsibility reduces people's inhibitions. Uniforms reduce the individual member's uniqueness as well as inhibitions. This dynamic can result in people doing things that they may not do if they were alone or more easily identifiable. When this happens, people become *deindividuated*.

A certain amount of freedom seems to accompany blending into a crowd or being anonymous. Maybe people are less afraid of getting caught doing something bad in this situation. Children, for example, have been found to steal more when they are deindividuated.

It seems that anonymity and a lack of unique identification can facilitate antisocial behavior — something to think about when you consider how anonymous American society can be. Some people don't even know their next-door neighbors. Then again, with social media and the Internet becoming ever more pervasive, living anonymously is getting harder and harder. (For more about the impact of the Internet on behavior and mental processes, check out the free online article "Ten Ways Psychology and the Internet are Intersecting" at www.dummies.com/extras/psychology.)

Thinking as one

Groups can have both positive and negative effects on individual behavior. You may perform some tasks better when working within a group and get lazier while performing others.

In 1971, Irving L. Janis, a research psychologist at Yale University and professor emeritus at the University of California, Berkeley, introduced a concept related to a potentially adverse effect of group participation: a phenomenon known as *groupthink*. When groups work to suppress disagreement and dissent in order to maintain group harmony, they are engaged in groupthink.

Dissent can sometimes threaten the cohesiveness of a group. When people start expressing ideas that are contrary to the group's views, the group sometimes reacts negatively. Galileo was one of the most famous victims of groupthink in history. He discovered evidence related to the solar system that challenged the prevailing thought of the day. Did he receive high praise and honors? Hardly! He was locked away in prison for being a heretic, a dissenter.

Groups work hard, both consciously and unconsciously, to prevent dissent. Janis identified eight symptoms of groupthink that can exist in a group:

- **Illusion of invulnerability:** When groups think they are untouchable, they're more likely to squash dissent.

- **Belief in the group's moral superiority:** When a group thinks it is ultimately moral, it ignores its own immorality.

- **Rationalization:** A group becomes more closed-minded as it collectively justifies its actions.

- **Stereotypes regarding the opposition:** When an opponent is viewed in biased or prejudiced terms, his statements that contradict the group's views are easier to ignore.

- **Conformity pressure:** Strong pressure on individuals to go along with the group's will and to not disagree minimizes dissent; non-conformers are cast out.

- **Self-censorship:** Group members keep their dissenting opinions to themselves rather than rock the boat in some cases.

- **Illusion of unanimity:** Internal dissent can sometimes be kept out of sight and away from the full group's view; therefore, dissent appears not to exist.

- **Mindguards:** Some group members take an active role in protecting the group from dissent or contrary information. They're like the "thought police" in George Orwell's book *1984*.

Groupthink can cause a lot of problems. Alternatives to the status quo may go unexamined, thus preventing a complete survey of any problem that the group faces. Risks may be ignored. And ultimately, the group makes decisions that can be compromised.

Here are some ways to avoid groupthink:

- Encourage everyone in a group to express his own opinions and viewpoints.

- Invite external people into the group to provide alternative viewpoints.

- Ask individual group members to play the devil's advocate role to work through conflicting ideas.

Persuading

I often wish I had a bit more power of persuasion. The greatest example of this power comes from the movie franchise, *Star Wars*. Jedi warriors have the ability to influence the thoughts of others by using "The Force" for what's called the "Jedi mind trick." In fact, I'm pretty sure that the guy who sold me my last car used the Jedi mind trick on me — the dark side of The Force, I think. But I digress.

Persuasion is a powerful force in all social interactions and arrangements. People don't just use it to sell products. There are two paths to persuasion:

- **Central route:** The central route occurs when the "persuadee" actively processes the potentially persuasive information. In 1991, Bas Verplanken, a professor of social psychology at the University of Bath, found that when people think deeply about something, any associated change in attitude or opinion is more likely to stay changed.

- **Peripheral route:** This approach involves getting someone to associate an intended message with certain images, sometimes positive and sometimes negative. It relies on the mind's natural ability to associate things. Remember classical conditioning? (If not, check out Chapter 8.) Examples of persuasion via the peripheral route include using showing hard-bodied models to sell gym memberships.

Psychologists Petty and Cacioppo warn that if you're going to try to persuade people, don't warn them that it's coming. Distracting the people you hope to persuade helps because they won't be able to mount a strong counterargument to your claims.

In addition, four key components make up any persuasive argument:

- **Credibility of communicator:** A message is more likely to be persuasive if someone perceived as credible delivers it.

  - Expertise is often a powerful indicator of credibility. People listen to experts. One thing to keep in mind, though: Just because someone says that she's an expert doesn't mean she necessarily is. When in doubt, always check credentials, including education, training, and experience.

  - People are more likely to be persuaded by someone seen as trustworthy. Such as an actor in a white doctor's coat pitching an herbal supplement for example.

- Attractive people's messages are more persuasive. The term *attractive* can relate to a person's physical appeal or personality and charisma.

- Similarity plays a role. The more someone is like you, the easier it is for her to persuade you.

✔ **Delivery approach:** Should a persuader appeal to someone's emotion or to reason and critical thinking? Here's a breakdown of these and other message-delivery options:

- *Reasoned approach:* In 1983, John Cacioppo and others found that when trying to persuade highly educated or analytical people, a reasoned approach is best. These individuals seem to like to think things over, analyzing information before making a decision. They're not necessarily smarter, but they are typically more aware of recent information.

- *Emotional approach:* Those who don't have the time or inclination to read every consumer review when going to buy a new car are more likely to trust other people and get swayed by emotional appeals. The thought process is "My sister said she loved her new car. I think I'll get one."

- *Fear factor:* A lot of persuasive messages use fear to scare people away from harmful or unhealthy behaviors (find examples in Chapter 18). These messages work. Fear-evoking ads are all around — telling you to stop smoking, to avoid abusing drugs, to vote for so-and-so and definitely not the other option, for example. There's only one catch. If you're going to scare people in order to persuade them, you need to provide concrete information on how to deal with or change their behavior; otherwise, the audience may freeze up or fail to act at all in the face of the fear.

- *Two-sided argument:* A two-sided argument is one that acknowledges the other position, giving the impression of fairness and objectivity. Advertisers have been using this technique for years, conducting "taste tests" and other comparative challenges with their rivals. You know what they're up to!

✔ **Audience engagement:** The best way to present persuasive information is to get your audience to play an active part in processing your argument. Active engagement captures the other person's attention and carries an expectation that he will comprehend the message, remember it, and then take action. As the amount of energy that a person invests in mentally processing a message increases, so does the likelihood that it will stick. Passive reception of a message, like listening to a lecture, is less likely to have an impact.

Easy as pie

There's a great rock video out by a band named Cake that demonstrates the influence of persuadee participation perfectly. In the video, a man walks around a beach, asking real people to put headphones on and listen to the new song. They're encouraged to comment on the song. This is a much more powerful advertising technique than if the man just walked up with a sign that read, "Check out Cake's new song. In stores now!" The persuadees are participating in their own manipulation. It's beautiful. I don't know whether the video makers were thinking this way, but if they were, they hit on a great persuasion technique!

✔ **Age of audience:** Research has found that older people are less likely to change their attitudes and opinions than people who are younger. The early twenties are years in which people are particularly vulnerable to persuasion. This is a time in many people's lives when choices abound and information is exchanged at a rapid rate. Many people in their early twenties are in college, entering the work force, and expanding their social networks. They're exposed to a whole new world of information, and this can make resisting persuasion more difficult.

Want to know how to resist persuasion? With the daily barrage of persuasive messaging that you may encounter, it helps to know how to stay committed to your own beliefs and attitudes. Psychologist William McGuire proposed that a good way to resist persuasion is through the process of *attitude inoculation,* which involves exposing yourself to weak, or weaker, arguments against your position in order to inoculate, or firm up, your resistance to counter-arguments. This process gives you practice and confidence in refutation. It's like warming up before a big game. And if you need to inoculate someone else's attitude or position on an issue, try presenting him with weak opposing arguments.

Being Mean

Most people probably think of themselves as civilized, but it's hard to ignore all the violence and rage that seems so prevalent in today's world. Some of the most horrific acts of human brutality have been committed in recent years — not in some savage society of the remote past. And, unfortunately, most people have experienced some form of violence and aggression. Mass atrocities affecting whole nations as well as smaller-scale heinous acts among individuals indicate that aggression and violence are unfortunate facts of human life.

Why do people act in a way that harms other people? What triggers a person's violence? Psychologists have searched for answers to these questions by studying *aggression,* a form of violence. *Aggression* can be defined as any behavior that is directed at and intended to hurt another person or persons.

Two types of aggression exist:

✔ **Hostile aggression** is driven by anger and is an end in itself.

✔ **Instrumental aggression** is used to serve some other purpose, such as intimidation or extortion.

Most of the theories about aggression focus on determining why hostile aggression is committed.

Acting naturally

One idea is that some people are born with a violent instinct and a genetic predisposition to act aggressively. It does seem that some children are naturally more aggressive than others, and research supports the natural-born killer theory:

✔ Freud proposed that people are born with aggressive instincts, and genetic studies show that identical twins are more likely to be more equally aggressive than fraternal twins (Rushton and others, 1986).

✔ Some research also shows higher levels of the hormone testosterone in both men and women who've been convicted of violent crimes when compared to those convicted on nonviolent crimes (Dabbs, 1988).

The brain may have something to do with it as well. Specific centers in the brain seem to be implicated in producing and inhibiting aggressive behaviors. Individuals with severe damage to the frontal lobes of the brain have long been observed as having more difficulty controlling their aggressive impulses than people without this damage because this inhibition is seen as one of the functions of the frontal lobe. This difficulty with controlling aggression is a disinhibition process.

Being frustrated

Or maybe violent and aggressive people are just frustrated. I'm one of those drivers who gets angry when I'm stuck in traffic and other drivers are rude. Now, I don't curse out my window at people or get into fistfights, but I sure do get frustrated.

In 1989, social psychologist Leonard Berkowitz, known for his research on human aggression, found that sometimes frustration leads to aggression, and sometimes it doesn't. When someone does get frustrated, she can get angry, and when a person feels angry, she's predisposed to act aggressively. It's like the body and the mind are poised, on alert, to act with aggression. This trigger comes from a cognitive evaluation of a situation and usually a conclusion that the person who is ticking you off did so on purpose. This scenario is likely to produce an aggressive response. So if you step on someone's toes, you'd better hope she realizes it was an accident.

Doing what's learned

Maybe the violence comes down to people being a product of their environment. An aggressive person may have learned to act aggressively by watching other people do it.

Albert Bandura, professor emeritus at Stanford University, would agree. *Social learning theory* holds that aggressive behavior is learned by observing others and by seeing aggressive people rewarded for such behavior. Little boys are often rewarded for being "tough." Boxers and MMA (Mixed Martial Arts) fighters are paid big money to beat people up. Some may say that aggressive acts are rewarded on a regular basis in our society, too. What child wouldn't see the benefits of aggression in such an environment?

Violence on television and in video games has come under fire in recent years because of its perceived connection to the dramatic increase in youth violence. Americans watch a lot of TV. American kids, in particular, spend a ton of time in front of different kinds of screens.

Even as far back as 1972, Gallup polls reported that Americans were watching an average of seven hours of TV a day. In 2012, that number was about the same, 6–7 hours per day. Regardless of your opinion on the connection between violence and television, the fact is that there's a lot of violence on the tube.

In 1990, George Gerbner found that seven out of ten programs contain violent scenes, with primetime programming containing five violent acts per hour. No doubt about it, TV doles out a heavy dose of violent images. A United States Senate Committee in 2006 found that an average American child sees 200,000 violent acts and 16,000 murders on TV by age 18.

Blaming media

I've watched violent television all my life, and I don't consider myself a violent person. Most research concludes that there is a modest positive correlation between exposure to violence in the media (film, television, music, Internet, and video games). That is, the more violent a child's media viewing is, the higher chance a child will engage in aggressive behavior.

The American Academy of Pediatrics states, "Extensive research evidence indicates that media violence can contribute to aggressive behavior, desensitization to violence, nightmares, and fear of being harmed" in children.

My question is, why is there so much violence in our media anyway? Does it offer viewers something valuable? Is it an emotionally arousing persuasion technique used by corporations to sell their goods? I don't know, but it may be worthwhile to examine the reasons behind the inclusion of so much violence in the entertainment industry.

Lending a Helping Hand

I've always marveled at people like Mother Teresa who devote their entire lives to helping others. Mother Teresa's sacrifice was unquestionable. What drives people to help in this way? It certainly wasn't money for the saint. I never saw Mother Teresa driving around in a Rolls-Royce.

A favorite topic among social psychologists is *altruism,* having concern for and helping other people without asking for anything in return. Maybe these psychologists study altruism with such zeal because it's an integral part of everyday life. People are constantly presented with situations in which someone needs help, even if it's a sad, late-night commercials showing starving children in other nations.

I think most people like to see themselves as helpful people. Or, if not particularly helpful, then at least willing to help in certain situations or when the need is severe.

The comedian Louis C. K. has a routine about sitting in first-class on a flight and seeing a war veteran and soldier sitting in coach. He thinks about giving his seat to the soldier but doesn't actually give up his seat. He feels really good about himself for thinking about it, though. In Mr. C. K.'s fantasy, he was a very helpful person. He was proud about being willing to help, even if he did nothing in reality. A great deal of research by social psychologists investigates why, when, and who people actually help. Some of the findings are surprising, even shocking.

In New York City in 1964, a woman named Kitty Genovese was brutally murdered outside of her apartment by a man with a knife. She struggled with the attacker and screamed for help for nearly 35 minutes. No one came to her aid. Later reports by 38 of her neighbors stated that they had witnessed the crime and heard her screams, but they did nothing to help her.

What happened here? Why didn't anyone help? As you're reading this, you may be telling yourself that you would have helped. When I first heard this story, I thought, "What was wrong with those people?" Think about it, though. It's not likely that all 38 people were cold, callous individuals who didn't care about a woman being murdered within earshot. Instead, they were influenced by social psychological principle in which social situations have a powerful influence on individual behavior. The Kitty Genovese story illustrates the main point of social psychology — the power of a situation is a major factor in determining an individual's behavior.

Why help?

Before I introduce you to some of the main theories of why people perform altruistic acts, I want to conduct a little test.

The next time you're in a public place, try one of these experiments:

- ✔ **Experiment #1:** Drop five coins on the floor near a group of people and act like you don't notice. Time how long it takes for someone to help you. Try to remember as much about them as you can.

- ✔ **Experiment #2:** Pretend to trip and fall in the public place. Make the same observations. (This may make an interesting YouTube video, but it is not recommended for safety reasons).

If you performed these experiments, what happened? Who helped you? How long did it take to receive help? Do you know why a person decided to help you? I know — it was probably because of your stunning good looks! Actually, believe it or not, attractiveness does make a difference. I cover this later in the chapter.

Theories about why people actually help others are all over the map. Here are some of the popular ones:

- ✔ **Social exchange theory:** Helping is a type of trading process.
- ✔ **Selfishness theory:** Helping someone may lead to rewards.
- ✔ **Genetic theory:** Helping is a genetic impulse.

Exchanging social goods

Researchers E. B. Foa and U. G. Foa introduced *social-exchange theory,* the idea that helping is part of a reciprocal process of giving and receiving social "goods" such as love, support, and services. Individuals try to minimize personal costs and maximize benefits, just like any good businessperson does. In helping situations, if the benefit of helping is higher than the cost of not helping, a person is more likely to help. This kind of makes sense if you consider that sometimes helping people involves putting ourselves at physical risk or serious inconvenience.

Also supporting this theory is A. W. Gouldner's *reciprocity norm,* which holds that a cultural norm tells people they should return help to those who help them. You scratch my back, and I'll scratch yours. In turn, people don't hurt those who help them out. Never bite the hand that feeds you! There's only one catch to this theory: Sometimes, people can get offended if you offer them help. If they can't return the favor, they may feel demeaned by the offer. Reciprocity works best when it's between equals.

Looking out for number one

In the 1950s, Ayn Rand wrote *Atlas Shrugged,* a famous philosophical novel that promoted the "virtue of selfishness." If each person looks out for "numero uno," all will be well, the theory goes.

Rand was not alone in thinking that selfishness isn't all that bad. Similar to social-exchange theory, the selfishness theory argues that helping behavior is driven by a person's *own* best interests. Do you give in order to receive? Some rewards are external, like praise and notoriety, and others are internal, like reducing negative feelings such as guilt.

Motivated by the love inside

In 1991, social psychologist Daniel Batson came to the rescue of humanity's sense of goodness with his theory that people help others because individuals have a natural *empathy* for other people, especially those they are attached to.

Empathizing about sympathy

Some people get confused between empathy and sympathy. *Empathy* involves a personal understanding of someone's suffering, and *sympathy* is distant and impersonal concern about another person's suffering. Imagining being in someone else's shoes is a type of empathy, and feeling sorry for a person who's actually wearing uncomfortable shoes is the gig with sympathy.

Psychologist and professor emeritus at New York University Martin Hoffman found that even infants seem to possess a natural ability to "feel for" others. They cry when they hear another baby cry. Are they just crying because the sound of the other baby's crying is hurting their ears? Probably not; it's more likely that they cry because they are in touch with the other baby's pain. People can relate to feeling upset at the sight of another person's misfortune. This natural empathy may encourage helping behavior.

How often do you help those people who stand on the side of the street holding the "Will work for food" signs? Do you feel a responsibility to help them? They're hoping you do. The *norm of social responsibility* holds that people should help others who need it. Bernard Weiner at UCLA in 1980, however, found that people typically apply this norm only in situations in which we perceive the person needing help as not having caused the situation due to her own negligence or fault. If I think that the person only needs help because she "did it to herself," I am less likely to adhere to the norm of social responsibility.

Do you think that the guy standing with the sign on the side of the street made some bad choices or somehow screwed up? Ask him; you never know until you ask. You may be eschewing your social responsibility if you don't offer some help.

Richard Dawkins also supports the genetic theory in his book *The Selfish Gene* (1976), in which he proposed that people are altruistic because their genes compel them to be. The idea of *kin protection* states that genes promote altruistic behavior toward kin or family in order to ensure the survival of the group's genetic makeup. Following this line of reasoning, I'm much less likely to help someone I don't know. Why would I? They don't share my genes.

The more genetic material I share with someone, the more likely I am to help him or her. That's it. Nothing fancy.

When to help?

One of the most remarkable findings in altruism research is the idea that people are less likely to help when they're in the presence of others than when they're alone. This sounds strange, doesn't it? I may think that the fear of appearing cold and uncaring in front of others may encourage people to help more.

But research shows otherwise. When someone is in a crowd, he is actually less likely to notice that other people need help. In New York City, for example, people are always surrounded by other people. It's a crowded place, and most people can't take the time to notice everything and everyone around them simply because of the sheer volume of information; it's easier to fade into a crowd.

Strangely enough, when others are around, people are also less likely to interpret someone's behavior as indicative of needing help. Bystanders look to others for a sign as to how they should respond in a situation. If the other people don't act alarmed, then an individual typically won't be alarmed (or react) either. If the situation is ambiguous, not a clear-cut helping situation, a person's interpretation of the event in the presence of others is likely to be that intervention is not required. This is especially true if the other people are strangers.

A final problem with helping in the presence of others is called *diffusion of responsibility.* People usually just assume someone else will take care of whatever needs doing. If no one else is around, then I'm the only one left; I've got to help. But if others are around, it's easy to assume they'll do it. What happens when everyone assumes that everyone else is going to offer assistance? Help doesn't happen.

That's exactly what two researchers, psychologists Latane and Darley, found in a 1968 study in which experiment subjects were witness to a victim of a feigned seizure. Persons who were led to believe they were alone reported the emergency to authorities more quickly than those who believed they were just one among other witnesses.

It's not all bad news when it comes to groups, though. Research has found that when someone in a group takes action, others are more likely to jump in. Helpful people in this scenario serve as *prosocial models* and are a strong influence on altruistic behavior. The problem is getting someone to make the first move. Until someone does, the negative forces of the bystander effect are active. The *bystander effect* or *bystander apathy* is the dynamic of not getting involved in a situation when there are too many people standing around; you're likely to just stand there, too. So go ahead and be a hero. Make the first move — someone has to.

Who gives and receives help?

In my personal life sometimes I feel like helping people and sometimes I don't. Sometimes I would rather watch television than help my friend move that new couch. Still others seem to always have help available when they need it (unlike my couch-purchasing friend). Are certain people more helpful or "help-able" than others?

What about how helping affects feelings? I've always wondered about the origins of the tradition of buying cigars for friends when a baby is born. I still don't know where it comes from, but altruism research shows that happy people tend to be more helpful or giving (happy dad, cigar as gift). Does that mean that sad people aren't helpful at all? It actually depends on how rewarding helping others is to the person experiencing sadness. If sad people aren't too self-absorbed and self-focused, altruistic acts can be very rewarding for them. Feeling good, doing good! Feeling bad, doing good! Sounds good, especially if I'm feeling bad.

Pious people are often viewed as helpful. Many nonprofit organizations are operated by religious denominations. But are religious people really more helpful than their non-religious neighbors? Here's what research shows: When people indicate that religion is very important in their lives, they have been found to give 2.5 times as much money to charity as those who indicate that religion is not very important. The verdict — religious individuals are definitely generous, and, in some research findings, they're more generous than non-religious individuals.

Researchers Eagly and Crowley in 1986 found that women get helped more often than men, and attractive women get helped more often than unattractive women. I guess the ugly men out there are out of luck. Luckily for them, similarity to the helper seems to be a factor. The more someone looks like or dresses like me (or you), the more likely I am to help them out. So, you better cross your fingers and hope that the next time you're in of need help, someone thinks you're looking good.

Birds of a Feather . . . or Not

Airports, particularly international airports, are amazing places, I think. The diversity in these places is amazing. People of all colors, shapes, sizes, cultures, and nationalities all under one roof. But this diversity provides fertile soil for discrimination. Whenever people with differences are together, there is the potential for prejudice.

In this section, I introduce you to prejudice, stereotypes, and discrimination and describe how you can respond to these social dynamics.

Finding out about isms

Prejudice is a negative and disrespectful attitude, thought, or belief about a person based on his membership in a particular group. Some law enforcement agencies have been accused of using a prejudicial and controversial practice that's known as *racial profiling* in which officers can assume that certain individuals are potentially involved in criminal activity simply because they belong to a particular "race" or ethnic group.

A well-known example of potential racial profiling has been in play at airport security checkpoints following the terrorist attacks in New York, Washington, and over Pennsylvania on September 11, 2001. As a result of that attack, airport security may be more inclined to stop and more thoroughly and intensely question individuals of perceived Middle Eastern descent. If that's indeed happening, then airport security is guilty of racial profiling.

Psychologist Lynne Jackson proposes that prejudice is, in part, based on *stereotypes,* beliefs that most members of a group possess the same characteristics, traits, and behavioral tendencies. White men can't jump or dance. Arabs are terrorists. Asians can't drive. These blanket statements are offensive, right? That's the point of prejudice based on stereotypes; these conclusions about individuals based on their affiliation to a certain group are disrespectful.

Moreover, people often see what they expect to see. So if a person in the target group happens to perform the behavior our stereotype predicts — boom! Stereotype strengthened. The other people in that same group who don't behave according to our stereotype are often not noticed.

Some common forms of prejudice include the following:

- **Racism** centers on a person's perceived "race" or ethnicity.
- **Sexism** is based on a person's gender.
- **Ageism** focuses on a person's age.
- **Ableism** is based on a person's disability.
- **Nationalism** centers on a person's national origin.
- **Sanism/Mentalism** relates to a person's mental abilities or mental illness.

Religious intolerance (negative attitudes about a person based on his spiritual beliefs) and homophobia (fear of people with a homosexual orientation) are also common forms of prejudice.

What about *psycholigistophobia*? That irrational fear of a person's occupation being a psychologist and the belief that all psychologists are crazy, have a beard (if they're male), and love to offer free advice at cocktail parties. Okay, I made this one up and I shaved my beard. But psychologists have a rep!

Stereotypes can be conscious or unconscious. I can be aware of my stereotyped beliefs or not. But where do stereotypes and subsequent prejudice come from? From a social learning theory perspective, prejudices may be learned. People can certainly be taught specific beliefs by parents, the community, peer groups, and culture.

Some theorists propose that prejudice is a consequence of human evolution, that the mental process is an inherent part of the human mind that evolved to help humans identify who's part of "their" group and who's not, who poses a danger or is a potential competitor for resources.

Yet many psychologists propose that, ultimately, prejudice is a cognitive evaluation process that's essentially a consequence of the mind's tendency to "chunk" information together for the purpose of making vast amounts of information more manageable. Prejudice is a mental shortcut. Research shows that in situations in which people are distracted, tired, or unmotivated, they are more vulnerable to prejudicial and stereotypical thinking. Lynne Jackson likens this dynamic to a sort of "lazy process" that emerges when people lack the resources to carefully process social information.

Understanding discrimination

The human mind may have a tendency to group people in the form of prejudice, and this is often not an innocuous process. Prejudice can lead to *discrimination* — differential treatment of a person or group based on prejudicial attitudes and beliefs. Prejudice, although perhaps seemingly natural, is often deployed by advantaged groups and individuals against groups and individuals who enjoy lower levels of social advantage.

Here are two common forms of discrimination:

- ✔ **Interpersonal:** Individual acts of discrimination such as not picking the short-statured kid for the basketball team (He may be quite good!)

- ✔ **Institutional:** Policies, procedures, rules, laws — voter ID laws that prohibit the poor or elderly from voting because they don't have proper identification, for example — or a culture within an organization that systematically disadvantages one group in comparison with others

Making contact

The seemingly automatic bias in human thinking, fortunately, can be addressed through an approach known as *contact*, which was formally studied by the psychologist Gordon Allport. Contact holds that when a group of diverse people get together to collaborate on reaching a common goal or project, positive attitudes toward each other increase and negative attitudes decrease. This does not mean that you can just throw a block party and invite all your diverse and prejudiced friends, and they'll learn to get along. To work, contact encounters must be structured to support equality, cooperation, and safety.

Psychologists Pettigrew and Tropp analyzed hundreds of studies and proposed the following key ingredients of a successful "contact" encounter:

- **Reduction in anxiety** occurs through exposure to others without threat or harm.
- **Increased empathy** is a result of learning from and about others.
- **Increased knowledge** about others decreases stereotypes.

A person can also reduce his stereotypic and prejudicial attitudes simply by having friends and associates who are friends with or associated with people of the other group. This is a vicarious contact situation and works to reduce prejudice and stereotypes because a person you already trust is showing trust in another person, which means you can in turn trust that person as well.

For example, if your best childhood buddy befriends a colleague who belongs to a group you have a prejudice against, you're more likely to become less biased toward that person and group after learning your trusted friend enjoys their company.

Research also suggests that clear, well-communicated cultural and group norms *against* prejudice can have a big impact. Often, prejudice in individuals is the result of group pressure to conform and adopt prejudicial attitudes. Flipping that around, the same pressure to conform can be a powerful influence as well.

Chapter 12

Growing Up with Psychology

• •

In This Chapter

▶ Getting started

▶ Exploring and mastering

▶ Experimenting

▶ Building and connecting

▶ Aging

• •

Have you ever wondered what it would be like to have a psychologist as a parent? What if both parents were psychologists? Would that be a good thing or a bad thing? You may imagine that the typical dinner-table conversation would sound something like this:

> **Parent:** How was your day today?
>
> **Child:** Fine.
>
> **Parent:** Fine, huh? That's funny; somebody doesn't look like he had an all right day. What about it honey? How was your day, really?
>
> **Child:** I got into a fight with that big, stupid bully at school again. Well, I didn't really get into a fight. He just took my lunch pail and threw it into the trash can.
>
> **Parent:** How did that make you feel? Frustrated? Angry? What role did you play in the situation?
>
> **Child:** You know, just once I'd like to hear you say that you'll do something about it or protect me somehow. Maybe you could teach me how to defend myself. I'm tired of being in therapy at the dinner table. I'm going to my room.
>
> **Parent:** Well, I guess I messed that one up. How does that make me feel?

I don't know if having a psychologist as a parent is necessarily a good thing or a bad thing. Some people seem to think that it would scar a kid because everything she does would be overanalyzed. But that's not really fair. If a parent is a pediatrician, would people expect her to leave her medical knowledge at the door and not treat her own children if they became ill? Of course not. But anything can be overdone.

One of the largest areas of psychological study is psychological development. Although many people think of children when they hear the term, developmental psychology covers the entire span of human life. *Lifespan psychology* is the study of human psychological development from conception until death.

I describe some of the areas traditionally covered in lifespan psychology in other chapters in this book. Personality development, for example, is the focus of Chapter 11. Self-development and the development of relationships are explored in Chapter 10. Therefore, this chapter focuses on physical and motor development, cognitive development, and social development.

Beginning with Conception and Birth

The process of psychological development begins with conception. Genetic processes, which play a big part in the future development of behaviors and mental processes, originate with the union of a woman's egg and a man's sperm. Each coupling creates a new genetic combination called a *genotype* — the genetic makeup of an individual.

Through a complex process that's best understood by geneticists and biologists, genes express themselves in what's called the *phenotype* — the actual manifestation of genetic codes in observable biological and psychological processes as shaped and impacted by our environment. So, this means that I may have the genotype for being tall and muscular, but if I suffer from malnutrition and never exercise, I may be letting myself fall short of my genotype potential.

In this section, I introduce you to pregnancy and the process of fetal development.

X's and Y's get together . . .

Sperm and eggs are specialized cells in the body that contain half of the genetic material necessary to make a whole person; they're called *sex cells* because they are involved in sexual reproduction.

Human beings contain 46 chromosomes. You get 23 chromosomes from your mother and 23 from your father. Non-sex-related cells contain a full set of genetic material with 46 chromosomes. A person's chromosomes determine the unique aspects of his biological and psychological makeup. They are the genetic building blocks of cellular construction.

The 23rd pair of chromosomes, the sex chromosomes, determines the sex of the child. Sex chromosomes can be either the X or Y variety. Sperm cells can carry either an X or a Y chromosome, but an egg can only carry an X. When the sperm and the egg get together, their unique combination determines the sex of the child.

Boys have a 23rd chromosome pair that contains one X and one Y (XY) chromosome. Girls have two Xs (XX). Because the mother can only give an X chromosome and the father can give either an X or a Y, the father's sex-chromosome contribution plays the deciding role.

The role of genetics in human behavior and mental processes has been part of the decades-long dispute known as the *nature versus nurture* debate. Proponents of the nature argument believe that behavior is genetically determined. Biology is destiny, so to speak. The nurture advocates believe that the environments in which a person grows up determine his psychological makeup. This debate has been basically squashed in the last 25 years by the middle-ground position that both biological and environmental factors are involved, with different weight being given to one or the other depending on the psychological process in question.

Uniting and dividing all in one night

Biological development begins with the process of sexual reproduction. So it goes that psychological development begins as well as behavior; mental processes are intrinsically tied to biological development. For more on the relationship between psychology and biology, flip to Chapter 3.

The development process begins after a man and woman have sexual intercourse:

Germinal stage (conception to 2 weeks)

1. **The sperm and egg meet, combining their half-sets of chromosomes.**

   This is *fertilization,* and it occurs in the *fallopian tubes.*

2. **Twenty-four to thirty hours pass as a one-celled *zygote* (the fertilized egg) begins to divide itself.**

   This occurs in the fallopian tube as well. Through a process called *mitosis,* each chromosome makes a copy of itself and contributes the copy to the formation of a second cell. Cells continue to divide and multiply, repeating this process throughout fetal development. Fetal development is underway!

3. **Three to four days pass while the fertilized egg travels to the uterus.**

   Upon reaching the uterus, *implantation* occurs. During implantation, the fertilized egg rests against the wall of the uterus and eventually merges with and becomes implanted in the lining of the uterus.

4. **The *embryonic period* begins.**

   This period occurs about 14 days after the *pre-embryonic stage,* or the *germinal period* starts. The *embryonic period* lasts until the end of the eighth week of pregnancy.

Embryonic stage (3rd week through 8th week)

5. **Cells continue to divide.**

   The beginnings of a recognizable human take shape. The rudiments of the nervous system and other bodily systems are beginning to take shape.

Fetal stage (9th week through birth)

6. **The *fetal period* begins and lasts until birth.**

   This begins in the third month of pregnancy. This final stage is an extremely delicate process. Psychological difficulties can sometimes be traced to problems in fetal brain and nervous system development. Intellectual disability, learning disabilities, and other cognitive disorders are sometimes linked to fetal difficulties.

It's extremely important for expecting mothers to maintain proper nutrition, avoid infectious diseases, and eliminate drug, alcohol, and tobacco use. These behavioral changes won't guarantee the birth of a healthy child, but they certainly increase the odds.

The biological developments of each period are highlighted in Table 13-1.

Table 13-1	Fetal Development by Stage of Pregnancy
Germinal (Weeks 0–2): What's There?	
Amniotic sac	Placenta
Embryo	Umbilical cord
Embryonic (Weeks 3–8): What's There?	
Buds (arms and legs)	Heartbeat
Eyes and ears	Nervous system
Fingers and toes	Spinal cord
Fetal (Weeks 9–36): What's There?	
Organ systems working	Sex organs
Red blood cells	White blood cells
Fetus is very active	Fetus is sleeping like a newborn

Going from Diapers to Drool

About 36 weeks after conception, some lucky woman has just given birth to a healthy child. Infancy is an exciting time in which both physical and psychological developments occur at an unprecedented rate. One minute, children do nothing but sleep, and the next minute they're playing peek-a-boo.

In this section, I describe early child development including motor and cognitive development and language development.

Survival instincts

For approximately nine months as a fetus, a child relies almost exclusively on his mother for survival. This dependence doesn't end with birth. Although the infant's basic biological systems are functioning on their own, the maintenance of those systems requires the attentive care of a parent or primary caregiver. Sometimes, new parents can get overwhelmed with the responsibility of caring for an infant. The good news is that infants are born with a pretty impressive set of basic skills to help them survive.

In fact, nearly all of the most basic human survival skills are present at birth. When I say *basic,* I mean really basic — breathing, sucking, swallowing, and eliminating. Babies need to breathe to get oxygen. They need to swallow and suck to eat. They need to eliminate in order to cleanse their systems. You nervous parents-to-be out there can rest assured that you won't have to teach your infant how to suck on a bottle or a breast. It's natural and automatic. It's reflexive.

These skills are part of a broader list of innate reflexes infants are born with that aid in their survival. Here are a few more:

- **Rooting reflex:** Turning their heads in the direction of a touched cheek in an attempt to suck

- **Moro (startle) reflex:** Stretching out their arms and legs and crying in response to a loud noise or a sudden dropping motion

- **Grasping reflex:** Grabbing on to things, such as someone's finger

Motoring about

One of the most anticipated areas of infant development for a lot of parents is a child's motor development. Parents can't wait to watch their child gain more and more prowess in her physical abilities. Infants have very little control over their limbs and head when they're born. It takes time for the central nervous system (brain and spinal cord) and the peripheral nervous system (nerves outside the brain and spinal cord) to get things coordinated.

The progression of control begins with control of head movements and then turns to control of the limbs and torso, which usually begins around the age of 6 months. Eventually, greater fine motor control kicks in around the 8- to 12-month mark. For example, children may begin to grab things with just two fingers when they are 9 months old. Table 13-2 shows this progression.

Table 13-2	Synopsis of Motor Development in Infancy
Age in Months	**Abilities Present**
1–3	Lifting head and sitting up with support
4–8	Holding head still and balancing it; looking around; using thumb to grasp; sitting up briefly without support
8–12	Coordinating hand activities; controlling trunk and sitting without support; crawling; beginning to favor the use of one hand over the other; sitting to standing position while holding on to something; walking with help, taking simple steps
14	Standing alone and walking alone without difficulty
18	Running and tumbling

As infants turn into toddlers, their motor behavior becomes more sophisticated. They can run, kick, throw, ride tricycles, and perform a variety of other complex motor-behavior sequences. *Fine motor skills,* increased dexterity, and control over the use of their fingers and hands continue to develop as children figure out how to manipulate small objects like cups, crayons, and little toys.

Finding out about full development

Table 13-2 is not a comprehensive list of the development of motor abilities in infancy. For more complete coverage of these abilities and most of the other aspects of development that I mention in this chapter, I highly recommend T. Berry Brazelton's book, *Touchpoints: Your Child's Emotional and Behavioral Development* (Perseus Press). Dr. Brazelton is a well-respected pediatrician with a lot of great ideas and observations pertaining to children.

Thinking things through

Cognitive developmental theory is the study of the development and maturation of thinking. A Swiss psychologist named Jean Piaget is the father and reigning king of cognitive developmental theory. Piaget began thinking about thinking as he watched his own children grow up, analyzing their behavior and theorizing about the thoughts running through their little heads. I guess having a psychologist for a parent really can be kinda scary.

Piaget is considered to be a *mentalist:* because his theory holds that a person's overt behavior is due in a large part to how she thinks about

the world. Piaget emphasized how you think, instead of what you know. After all, a dictionary contains a lot of information, but can it solve the equation 2 + 2? Piaget defined intelligence as the collection of mental abilities that help an organism adapt. He also suggested that intelligence involves seeking *cognitive equilibrium* — a harmonious balance between an individual's thinking and the environment. You constantly encounter novel situations and stimuli from your environment. These new experiences challenge the human mind, which leads to an imbalance. Thinking is the process that restores the balance.

Flexing their muscles

While infants are beginning to rely on their reflexes and developing more control over their muscle movements, their brains are developing at an extremely rapid rate. Actually, brain development begins during pregnancy and continues throughout childhood and adolescence. The progression of brain development begins with the motor areas of the brain. Without the necessary brain development in these areas, infants would not be able to respond reflexively and gain control over their bodies.

The next stop on the brain-development express is the *somatosensory* areas of the brain, the areas involved in sensation and perception (the olfactory, taste, pain, auditory, and visual areas). Infants are born with a good sense of hearing. They can discriminate between their mothers' voices and strangers' voices, for example, which may be a result of hearing their mothers' voices throughout pregnancy. Their senses of smell and taste are also keen. Visual acuity is less developed at birth and gradually develops over the course of the first year of life.

Scheduling time for schemata

Like a road map or template, children use what Swiss psychologist Jean Piaget called *schemata,* or mental modes of thinking, to represent, organize, and integrate experience. *Schemata* are basic ways of thinking about the world. Rather than sit passively by as the world presents them with information, children actively construct an understanding and mental representation of the world. There are three basic schemata:

- **Sensorimotor schemata:** These organized patterns of thought are generated from a child's direct interaction with and manipulation of the objects in their environment.

  For example, when a 1-year-old takes everything off her plate and drops it on the floor, she's not just trying to annoy her mommy and daddy. According to Piaget, she's developing a sensorimotor schema to understand the relationship between cause and effect. It's a simple representation of a basic mechanical relationship: "I drop food. Then, mommy and daddy turn red. This is fun!"

- **Symbolic schemata:** With the development of these schemata, a child begins to symbolically represent earlier sensorimotor relationships. He can think about the objects in his world without having to directly interact with them.

- **Operational schemata:** These internal, mental activities involve the manipulation of the symbolic representations of objects. Operational schemata involve the ability to think abstractly and to solve problems without actually having to physically attempt a solution. So, instead of jumping in front of a car to see if it hurts, the child can imagine jumping in front of a car and decide whether it would hurt.

Basically, the three schemata begin with concrete interactions with the world and progress to a more symbolic and abstract thinking process. This is a hallmark of Piaget's work; remember that you start out with the concrete and then graduate to the abstract. Now that I think about it, maybe that's why I never did well in Sunday school. I couldn't get past the idea that clouds didn't seem strong enough to support heaven. Wouldn't everything fall right through? I still haven't figured that one out.

People are born with two processes that help further develop thinking:

- **Organization:** Organization involves combining the different schemata already developed with new and more complex schemata. You're basically constantly shifting your understanding of the world to create a better and more complete picture.

- **Adaptation:** Adaptation is a process of getting adjusted to the demands of the environment. Adaptation is accomplished by two distinct subprocesses:

- **Assimilation:** Little kids use assimilation all the time. When little Jimmy calls a horse a "doggy," that's assimilation in progress. Children attempt to understand novel objects in their environment by drawing upon what they already know and applying that to new objects and situations. It's kind of like using a template; the child tries to fit everything into that one template If the child only knows one type of four-legged animal with a tail, then even a horse is a "doggy."

- **Accommodation:** Accommodation is essentially the opposite process of assimilation; instead of adding new experiences to old *schemata*, existing schemata are altered to fit the new information. The child may split a current category in half ("doggy" turns into "big dog" and "little dog") or create a new category (doggy becomes "dogs" and "horses") for remembering experiences. Cognitive growth, then, is the ongoing and persistent process of children applying (assimilating) their understanding to the world and making accommodations for new information. This is the overall process of adaptation, which allows for the maintenance of cognitive equilibrium between thinking and the environment.

Getting your sensorimotor running

The *sensorimotor stage* is the first stage of cognitive development, and it lasts from birth to 2 years of age. During the sensorimotor stage, the problem-solving abilities of an infant grow beyond simple reflexes. Infants extend reflexive behaviors to novel objects in their environment. An infant may suck on a little toy in addition to his mother's nipple or the nipple of a bottle. It can take some babies a few tries to get used to sucking on a pacifier until he is able apply his natural sucking knowledge and ability to other objects.

Almost accidentally, babies discover that they can have a physical effect on the objects in the world. They gradually build on these accidental discoveries and develop intentional and coordinated responses on a simple scale. Eventually, babies progress to a type of experimentation or trial-and-error learning in which they do things to the objects around them just to see what kind of impact they can have on these objects.

The ability to imitate people also develops during the sensorimotor stage. Babies often smile when you smile at them. One of the most common forms of imitation is cooing. When an infant develops the ability to imitate, she often coos back at people who coo at her. That's so cute!

A final key development in this stage is the development of a skill called *object permanence*. If you hide something from a baby who has not yet developed object permanence, he forgets about it. But, when babies achieve object permanence, they remember that the object is still around even if it's not in plain sight — they try to look for the object when you conceal it. So, if you're going to hide things from your children, do it before object permanence develops.

Learning within the lines

Sometimes, when I'm playing with toddlers, I catch myself quizzing them and testing the limits of their knowledge. I may read them a book and ask them to point things out on each page, "Where's the ball?" This sort of toddler homework is perfectly okay, as long as I don't overdo it, which I have a tendency to do.

A lot of parents begin to teach their children some of the rudiments of knowledge that serve as a foundation for future school learning. Recognizing objects and categories of objects such as shapes, colors, animals, numbers, and letters are basic skills that all children need to possess. Although some level of preexisting skill is present, a child's ability to recognize objects increases around the ages of 18 months or 2 years. Children love to learn stories, songs, and nursery rhymes at this time in their lives.

Play is a very important part of a toddler's discovery experience. By the age of 2½, most children can play alongside their peers in both cooperative and independent activities for a sustained period of time. Prior to this age, children may engage in short sessions of independent play or interactive physical play (like patty-cake) with adults or older children. Toddlers and preschoolers prefer more natural toys such as sand, mud, and water. They invent their own games but still don't do too well with rules and regulations.

Some parents expect their children to learn how to recognize and write letters before they get to kindergarten. But, for most toddlers and preschool-aged children, these skills are too advanced, and very little retention can be expected prior to kindergarten. By the age of 5, children do begin to form letters.

Drawing, however, is a related skill that toddlers and preschoolers do demonstrate some ability in. Most 2- and 3-year-olds can scribble, and by the end of this period, they can easily create straight lines, curves, and loops. Four- and five-year-olds begin to draw representations and pictures with simple designs. They can easily color within the lines.

Saying what you think

A lot of parents remember their child's first words. When their little one utters the words *momma* or *dada,* their hearts usually melt. *Ball* usually doesn't get the same reaction.

The dominant position in psychology on the development of language is that language is innate and gradually unfolds as the child's brain develops. This doesn't mean that children are born with a language, but that they're born with the innate mental capacity to learn and grasp the rules of the language community they're born into. Parents can facilitate language development by providing a supportive and stimulating environment and prompting children to use their words to communicate their needs and desires.

Children aren't born speaking in sentences or giving speeches. Well, at least none of the children I've ever met. Children learn to talk little by little. Language develops in stages over the course of the first two to three years of life. Here's a quick overview of language accomplishments that make parents so darn proud:

- ✓ **0–4 months:** Infant speech begins with *cooing*. For the first few months, infants make sounds that come naturally from the movements of the mouth (feeding, breathing, and sucking) and from crying. Making a "raspberry" sound or humming are good examples of sounds that come from natural mouth movements.

  The vocal behaviors associated with crying are experimented with and the use of voice begins. These sounds occur both spontaneously and in response to interaction with others. A baby may coo in response to a mother's cooing, for example. These interactions often serve as a basis for future social development as well as parent and child engaging in sound-making games, taking turns, and getting a feel for each other's interaction style.

- ✓ **5–8 months:** Infants slightly refine their basic sounds. Around the seventh or eighth month, infants begin to form sounds that resemble syllables. In English, some syllable sounds are easier to utter than others, such as *ma* or *ba*. It's pretty hard to get a 6-month-old to utter a *th* or *l* sound. This stage of experimenting with sounds is called "babbling."

- ✓ **12–18 months:** Around the one-year mark, infants begin to use simple monosyllabic words. Early consonant and vowel sounds are then combined to produce early polysyllabic words like *momma* or *boo-boo* or *bye-bye*. This process continues for the next few months, as new words occasionally emerge and mastered words serve as a foundation from which to generalize.

- ✓ **18 months:** Language development explodes around the time infants reach the 18-month mark. Building upon their ability to generalize, children begin to form simple two-word sentences (called "telegraphic speech"), and then three-word sentences, and on and on. The next thing you know, you're answering more "why" questions than you ever thought possible.

> Children learn new words at the approximate rate of one word every two hours. That's staggering! I've taken Spanish at different points throughout my life, and I felt super productive if I could learn one word every two weeks. Pretty sad, I know.
>
> This explosion in language development continues until children are about 3 years old. Their language skills expand beyond using one word for many things — *ball* is no longer every round object, *doggy* is no longer anything with four legs, and so on.

Most children have learned the greatest portion (the structures, rules, and a great deal of vocabulary) of their native language by the age of 4. By the time they're ready to enter kindergarten, kids have acquired approximately 8,000 words and learned to use language in a variety of social situations. They can also ask questions and make negative statements. At this point, the rudiments of language are solidly in place, and it's simply a matter of continued learning and increased sophistication, building upon the existing foundation.

Blooming social butterflies

The earliest relationships infants have are with their primary caregivers. A parent and a baby often engage in simple visual and touching games with each other. Infants also make facial gestures at strangers. The interactions between an infant and her primary caregiver have been likened to a dance in which each partner takes cues from the other in a scene that almost seems choreographed. This process of using feedback from each other to gauge social interaction has been called *reciprocal interaction,* and it often depends on the primary caregiver's ability to respond to the cues given by the child.

A good connection between an infant and primary caregiver is often the result of something called the *goodness of fit* — the fit between a child's and a caregiver's temperaments and styles. I've often heard parents say that each of their children had a different temperament and that learning to respond differently to each child was a challenge at times. Some children may be very outgoing and seek social stimulation, but others can be shy and may require a lower-key style of interaction. I think part of the art of parenting is knowing how to match up with a child's temperament; this often represents a significant challenge in therapy with children.

An infant's social circle gradually expands to include siblings, and she begins to show signs of *separation anxiety* (fear of being left by a primary caregiver) between the ages of 7 and 9 months. From 16 to 24 months, infants are able to spend time playing and interacting with others without too much significant involvement from their primary caregivers. From the beginning of 3 to 4 years of age, children's social worlds continue to expand. Sometimes quarreling occurs as they encounter the limitations of dealing with other children. Sharing and taking turns become more important, and simple friendships and fondness for specific children also begin to emerge.

Getting on the Big Yellow Bus

Most children enter kindergarten around the age of 5. This marks a significant turning point in child development — learning, cognitive, and social skills become increasingly important. Children leave their parents and the protective and facilitative environment of the home to begin interacting with a larger and more complex world. School-related skills, such as writing, reading, spelling, and simple mathematics, begin to occupy a great deal of their mental energy and time.

Mastering the crayon

During kindergarten, children learn to use tools and writing-related materials with greater skill. Some children may be exposed to such things as scissors, glue, or paint for the first time in kindergarten. They're also expected to learn how to write letters, their names, and a few simple words during this year in school as well as acquire the basics of reading, including letter recognition and beginning phonics. As children progress through school, these skills are expected to expand with the ability to read and write larger pieces of information.

Mathematical skills begin with counting. By the age of 4 or 5, most children can count with one-to-one correspondence. *One-to-one correspondence* is when a child can count each object she is presented with. So, if I put five apples out, children at this age will count ("One, two, three," and so on) for each apple. As children progress from kindergarten through the school system, they develop concepts of addition and subtraction, and eventually they develop more sophisticated operations that extend to advanced multiplication, division, and sometimes, even fractions.

Being preoperational doesn't mean you're having surgery

The sensorimotor stage of cognitive development is followed by the preoperational and operational stages. Thinking continues to become more sophisticated, using the gains from earlier stages and applying these to more difficult problems.

The *preoperational stage* (ages 2 to 7) marks the development of symbolic thought. A child now possesses the ability to allow one object, a symbol, to represent another object. A hallmark of this is pretend play. How can a stick become a sword, or a bathroom towel be a superhero's cape? Symbolic representation!

The most striking features of preoperational children's thought processes, however, are the abilities that they don't possess. Kids at this age have a hard time classifying objects into two or more categories. For instance, if you ask them if there are more total balls or more red balls in a collection of four red balls and three green balls, they usually answer "red balls." They've locked onto one prominent feature of the collection of balls and cannot think abstractly to solve the problem. How much does 50 pounds of feathers weigh? A preoperational child may give some figure less than fifty pounds as his or her answer.

A classic development that sharply marks the difference between a preoperational child and a concrete operational child is called *conservation* — the ability to understand that something remains the same even though its appearance or surface properties may change.

Get a tall glass of water and an empty short glass. With the child present, pour the water from the tall glass into the smaller short glass. Now, ask the child which glass had more water in it. The child will always say the tall one; it's bigger. However, after the child gets older and progresses to the concrete operational stage, she can solve this problem.

The *concrete operational stage* marks the development of a child's ability to mentally represent a complex series of actions and perform relational logic. At this stage, children use a skill called *seriation,* which allows a child to arrange objects in a series on some dimension, like bigger to smaller, smaller to bigger, taller to shorter, and so on. Believe it or not, most children can't do this until they're about 7 years old.

A concrete operational child still gets hung up on more abstract problems, or problems that are hypothetical. If a problem has no basis in reality, the concrete operational child has a very hard time answering the question. They balk at "what if" questions because these questions require them to abstract concrete knowledge to situations that have never happened. Luckily, they get there in the formal operations stage, which comes in adolescence.

In the zone

Cognitive development does not occur in a social vacuum. At least that is what the famous Russian psychologist L. S. Vygotsky emphasized. Vygotsky proposed that a child's social and cultural environment determined the types of and extent of the cognitive skills and abilities that get developed. The demands of the social and cultural environment emphasize what is necessary and important cognitively.

For Vygotsky, cognitive development is particularly shaped by the "teachers" a child encounters during development. A child will adjust to the expectations of those teachers and cognitive mentors, learning from and internalizing their cognitive processes. These "teachers" are referred to as the *more-knowledgeable-other (MKO),* the person in a learning situation that has more knowledge, cognitive skill, and understanding. Keep in mind that these "teachers" don't have to be actual teachers or even adults — they can simply be other people who are MKO's such as other children.

When a child is developing cognitively, there will be gaps between what he can do and what is expected. For instance, a child may be expected to know his times tables up to five but only knows them for 1 and 2. But, with guidance and help, a child may be able to perform above the level achievable independently. The gap between what can be done and what cannot but can be facilitated by a MKO is what Vygotsky called the *zone of proximal development*. He believed that the zone of proximal development is where instruction should be most focused and intense, to push cognitive development along.

Becoming even more social

The primary social-development issues for school-aged children are peer relationships and social functioning outside the home. By the time children enter school, their relationships with their parents are pretty well solidified. These relationships continue to develop, but relationships outside of the home are the primary focus between the ages of 5 and 12.

During these years, expectations of a child's social ability grow dramatically. Parents no longer tolerate tantrums and less sophisticated social problem-solving techniques, such as hitting other children. Children are expected to follow rules and instructions, especially in the classroom. Their affiliations with other children increase, and they start to develop a small, core group of friends.

If a child has social difficulties, these problems show up when she enters school. Problems related to getting along with the other children, joining in games, and cooperating with the routines expected of them when they're away from their parents can sometimes lead to peer rejection, emotional difficulties, or school failure.

Agonizing over Adolescence

Perhaps one of the most significant events in a child's life is his or her experience with puberty. Puberty is marked by an increase in the sexual hormones of progesterone, testosterone, and androgens. Development of secondary sexual characteristics, such as pubic hair, maturation of the genitalia, menstruation and breast development for girls, accompanies puberty. Interest in sex is markedly increased as boys begin to take interest in girls, and vice versa. Adolescents no longer think that members of the opposite sex have cooties or are gross.

Along with these wonderful physical changes come some pretty profound changes in thinking. By the time children reach the ages of 11- or 12- years-old, they can solve the "what if" problems they are faced with because they reach the cognitive-developmental peak of formal operations. This period is called *formal operations* because the concrete thought processes of childhood are combined into more advanced concepts such as abstractions.

Children can now reason based on hypothetical questions. They don't need concrete examples or demonstrations like they did during the earlier stages of cognitive development. They've become little scientists, able to conduct mental mini-experiments instead of having to tackle problems by using trial and error.

Keep in mind that just because kids and adolescents can ask and answer these questions doesn't mean they actually do. When I was a teenager, I repeatedly failed to ask myself, "What if I get caught lying to my parents?" I should have used my formal operational thinking a little more.

Pining over puberty

Exactly when puberty begins is a questionable matter. It can come at different times for different children. But researchers have noticed that the age of onset for puberty has been gradually decreasing. On average, kids are entering puberty at younger ages. This development has been dubbed the *secular trend,* and researchers believe that it's due to better childhood nutrition.

The average age of onset for puberty in Western countries is showing a decline of three months per decade.

The timing of puberty can have serious repercussions, depending on when it comes. Boys who develop later than others sometimes suffer from peer ridicule and social setbacks related to popularity and dating. Girls who develop too early sometimes find themselves in situations that they're mentally and emotionally not prepared for because their bodies make them look older than they really are.

What about sex? A great deal of variation in sexual norms exists across societies, but whether or not a society puts strict limits on adolescent sexual behavior, sexual desire is a primary issue for members of this age group. Most of the time, teenagers learn about sex from their friends and from the media. The old birds and the bees talk doesn't come up as often as people may think.

Moving away from parents

One striking difference between childhood and adolescence is the diminished importance of parents in a teenager's life. Prior to adolescence, parents and the home occupy center stage in a child's life. During the teen years, adolescents begin to express their independence and autonomy by making friendships their top priority.

Social functions that involve parents take a back seat to teen-exclusive functions, such as dances, parties (without chaperones), and outings at this stage in a child's development. Hanging out, texting, going on Facebook, and staying overnight at friends' houses are commonplace.

Peers are a major source of self-esteem, and fitting in is often more important than parental acceptance. Teenagers experiment with identity and social roles. Relationship skills and patterns laid down in childhood grow in sophistication at this stage. Romantic relationships become extremely important. Being the star of the household gives way to desires for being popular or well-liked among friends.

Existing as a Grown-Up

Although many teenagers beg to differ, there is life after adolescence. In fact, the majority of a person's years on this planet take place in what is referred to as *adulthood,* defined as the years between 18 and death. Adulthood is often divided into three periods:

- ✔ **Young adulthood:** ages 18–39
- ✔ **Middle adulthood:** ages 40–64
- ✔ **Late adulthood:** ages 65+

In adulthood people keep growing, changing, and developing. These years are just as packed with life as the previous 18, simply in different ways. In this section you will be introduced to the developmental tasks of adulthood including marriage, work, and retirement.

Looking at you

Young adulthood covers a wide range of ages; a great many of the impactful experiences of a person's life happen during these years, including starting and finishing college, beginning a career, getting married, and starting a family. All in all, these can be very busy and productive years. A lot is going on.

Physically, people peak in strength, reflexes, and stamina in their mid-20's; upon entering middle adulthood they become more and more aware of the changes in their bodies and how their bodies are less resilient, more susceptible to disease, and overall less youthful than in young adulthood. Women enter *menopause* sometime in their late 40s early 50s, in which they stop menstruating, are no longer fertile, and experience hormonal changes that can sometimes lead to very unpleasant experiences such as hot flashes and even panic attacks.

Connecting and working

Relationships in adulthood continue to develop. Intimacy is typically sought, sometimes resulting in marriage. Although the divorce rate for first marriages in the United States is about half of all marriages, people still get married. However, people are getting married at later ages — not in their early 20s as much — and nearly half (47%) of the United States adult population is unmarried according to the US Census Bureau in 2012.

Having and raising children can be a large part of young adulthood, although not all adults choose to have children. This is another trend throughout the United States that suggests that cultural and societal mandates to "get married and have kids" is less prevalent than in previous decades.

A significant portion of modern adulthood involves working and achievement. Middle adulthood sparks questions that consider the wisdom of decisions made in young adulthood. If a person goes to college right after high school — or enters the workforce right away — she will likely reflect back and wonder if it was the right choice. Am I doing what I wanted to do? Does my daily life have meaning? Have I met my goals? Did I do what I wanted to do?

As late adulthood approaches, one begins to prioritize what is important in life and what is less important. As people transition to this final phase, they begin to see themselves as old.

Aging and Geropsychology

If old age is upon you, you're not alone. According to the National Council on Aging, the population of 65+ will grow by 74 percent between the years 1990 and 2020. By contrast, the under 65 set will grow 24 percent during this same period.

Perhaps most obviously, bodies have and continue to age, which means many physical changes occur at every stage of life, especially late adulthood. Hair and skin thin and may gray. Bones become more brittle, and muscle tone decreases. Energy and stamina decrease, and sensory capabilities decline with less acute vision, sight, hearing, and even taste.

Physical decline in aging has been looked at from at least two explanatory models:

- **Genetic programming theories of aging:** Aging is the result of genetic programming in which cells stop dividing and growing and begin a "self-destruct" course toward eventual death.

- **Wear and tear theories of aging:** With time, bodies break down from use, the buildup of waste and toxins take their toll, and the body wears out, like an old shoe.

Of course the body is not the only thing about a person that's aging. Cognitive changes in late adulthood include some minor changes such as slightly slower processing speeds and less effective and efficient memory. On the upside, people in this stage experience stable and, in some cases, improved problem-solving strategies and information.

Memory, however, remains one of the main concerns for the aging and aged population and their families. Am I inevitably going to lose my memory? The data and research in this area spell out a much more complex picture than one may expect. For some people, memory loss and impairment does not occur. For others, mild forms of memory loss may occur for specific domains such as episodic memory (memory for events) while other forms of memory, such as memory for general knowledge and facts, remains relatively untouched by age (for more about memory, see Chapter 6).

For some, aging comes with an increased risk for actual diseases that leads to cognitive decline and memory impairment generally referred to as the *dementias*. One of the most prevalent dementias is *Alzheimer's disease*. Although not fully understood, Alzheimer's is a progressive brain disease that results in gradual and irreversible cognitive decline. Prevalence is estimated to be about 20 percent of people 75 to 84 and almost 50 percent of people over the age of 85. Medication treatments have been shown to help with some cognitive improvement for some people, perhaps slowing the progression of the disease, but there is currently no known cure for Alzheimer's.

Socially, late adulthood can be filled with grandchildren and friendships and, despite the clichés, it does not have to include loneliness. Of course, the specter of death is there and seeing friends and peers die is an inevitable stressor. Some people age quite gracefully; some do not, but is there really a good way to age?

I live in a community that is considered a retirement and resort community for the most part. I see what I refer to as "positive models" of aging around me every day — people in late adulthood exercising (more than me, by the way), working, volunteering, socializing, and looking pretty darn good doing it all. I can only hope to follow their model.

Older adults being social and active is known as the *activity model of aging*; psychologists postulate that people who age best are those who maintain their interests, activities, and social interaction, and continue to live their lives in line with middle adulthood in most respects.

Chapter 13

Modern Abnormal Psychology

A fictional Mr. Smith is a 30-year-old married man with two children who lives in a quiet suburban neighborhood. He works as a shipping manager for a local trucking company. Mr. Smith has been in relatively good health and is considered by most people to be a pretty average guy. About three months ago, Mr. Smith approached his wife with the idea of getting a home security system. She agreed, and they installed an alarm system. Mr. Smith then told her that he wanted to install cameras around the perimeter of their home. She reluctantly agreed and soon after began waking up in the middle of the night to find Mr. Smith peeking out of their bedroom curtains with binoculars. He became very agitated when she questioned him about his behavior.

Mr. Smith's actions continued for several weeks, and he wouldn't tell his wife what was going on. Then one day she found a gun as she was cleaning out their closet. She'd never known her husband to own a gun, so she confronted him about it out of concern for their children's safety. When she approached him, he told her that he bought the gun to protect them from the neighbor next door. Mr. Smith said that he had been watching the neighbor for a few months, and he was convinced that the neighbor was involved in a real-estate scheme to get their home. The plot involved the neighbor hiring some criminals to break into their home and rob them, in order to scare them into moving and selling their home at a really low price. The neighbor could then buy the house for next to nothing, tear it down, and expand his own home onto the property.

Do you think there's anything strange about Mr. Smith's behavior? Should his wife be worried, or is he being adequately protective? The answers to these and related questions are part of the field of *abnormal psychology* — the psychological study of abnormal behavior and mental processes. But what is abnormal about certain behaviors?

In this chapter, I introduce you to the concept of psychopathology and the various disorders that characterize modern abnormal psychology such as schizophrenia, bipolar disorder, depression, and anxiety.

Figuring Out What's Normal

By *abnormal* I mean not normal — something beyond the usual and customary. I've never taught a psychology course without at least one student raising a protest against the concept of abnormal behavior. "Who gets to decide what's normal and what's not?" he tends to ask. This is an excellent question. How is a standard of normalcy determined and who has the final say on this matter?

It's important to distinguish between abnormal behavior that's due to a mental illness and abnormal behavior that's not. A lot of abnormal behaviors are not associated with the presence of a mental illness. Take dancing in a mosh pit, for example. It's pretty abnormal to find enjoyment in running into people and bouncing around a pit of human pinballs. Yeah, I think that's abnormal; but do I think that this behavior is a result of mental illness? For the most part, no!

Every society in the world has standards of behavior and conduct that delineate what are acceptable and unacceptable behaviors. Individuals, families, and even groups have *norms,* or standards. When people act outside those norms, society labels either the behavior or the person himself as "abnormal." There are at least four different ways, or criteria, to define normal versus abnormal behavior:

✔ **Normative criterion:** People act abnormally when they do things contrary to what the majority of people do or act very differently than what is expected. Individuals are expected to live up to societal norms; when that doesn't happen, people suspect something is amiss. Sometimes statistics are used by professionals and researchers to figure out who's outside the norm. If nine out of ten people act a certain way, then the behavior of the one person who doesn't conform is statistically abnormal. The non-conforming behavior is considered rare.

✔ **Subjective criterion:** Sometimes a person senses his feelings may be different from those of most other people or that he may be doing things differently from how most others do it. In this very limited sense, the person is "abnormal." If I feel like something is wrong with me because of my awareness of my being different, then I may consider myself a suitable subject of abnormal psychology. This is a case of judging one's own behavior as abnormal.

✔ **Maladaptive criterion:** Does my behavior help me survive and successfully function in my society? If not, according to this criterion, maladaptive behavior is abnormal. If I have a difficult time adapting and adjusting to life's demands, my behavior is maladaptive. This may include my engagement in a pattern of risky or otherwise harmful or destructive behavior that would make it more likely I would not survive or function well in society.

✔ **Unjustifiable or unexplainable criterion:** Sometimes people act in ways and do things that can't be explained. People often assume that there must always be a reason why someone acts in a certain way. If a reasonable explanation for certain actions doesn't exist, people may label the behavior as abnormal.

No matter what definition for abnormality is used, it's pretty hard to argue that everything is normal. I realize that some people think that life for some people is a big free-for-all, but in reality, every society requires a degree of order. Whether it's a family, a tribe, or a nation, mores and laws enforce and maintain structure. I define *abnormal behavior* as maladaptive behavior and mental processes that are detrimental to an individual's physical and psychological well-being.

So, if someone acts abnormally, does that mean he has a mental illness or psychological disorder? No, not necessarily. A person can act abnormally for any number of reasons. In fact, at one point in history, people believed (and some still do) that abnormal behavior was caused by demonic possession or moral weakness. What about committing murder? Isn't that abnormal? Murder actually meets all four of the criteria established earlier to define abnormal behavior.

The concept of *mental illness* comes primarily from psychiatry. *Psychiatry* is a branch of medicine that deals with mental disorders. During the 19th century, people who acted abnormally became the province of physicians. These "crazy" people were seen as sick instead of morally inept or demonically possessed. This way of looking at abnormal behavior was actually a big advance in human healthcare. When physicians began to be responsible for the care of people behaving abnormally, abnormal behavior became a medical problem, an illness, to be diagnosed and treated like other illnesses and diseases. This approach to mental illness is known as the *medical model of mental illness*.

Compared to medical doctors, *psychologists* are relative newcomers to the field of mental illness as defined by psychiatry. As physicians tried to figure out ways to help people from a medical model perspective, psychologists eventually joined in, bringing their knowledge of human behavior and mental processes to the research, diagnosis, and treatment of abnormal behavior that was attributed to a mental illness.

Categorizing Symptoms and Disorders

Over the years, psychiatrists and psychologists have worked to delineate the abnormal behaviors that suggest the presence of a mental illness. This process is called *taxonomy* — the science of classification. Today, the most widely used classification system for determining the presence of a mental disorder is the *Diagnostic and Statistical Manual,* 5th Edition *(DSM-5)* published by the American Psychiatric Association in 2013. The first *DSM* was published in 1952.

The definition of a mental disorder presented in the *DSM-5* is that a mental disorder is essentially a significant behavioral or psychological "syndrome" in associated with "distress," or "disability" or with a risk of death, pain, or loss of freedom.

A couple of key words in this definition need extra attention:

- ✔ **Symptom:** A behavior or mental process that is a sign or signal of a potential disorder. Symptoms are usually found within the following categories:

  - Thinking or thought processes

  - Mood or *affect* (referring to how someone feels emotionally, such as depressed, angry, or fearful) and vegetative symptoms (concerning eating, sleeping, and energy level)

  - Behavior (such as violence, compulsive gambling, or drug use)

  - Physical signs (such as muscle or joint pain, headaches, excessive sweating)

- ✔ **Disorder:** A collection of symptoms that indicate the presence of a *syndrome* (co-occurring groups of symptoms). In developing a taxonomy of abnormal psychological disorders, psychiatrists, psychologists, and other researchers look for specific groups of symptoms that tend to occur together, distinguishing one set of co-occurring symptoms that are distinct from other sets of co-occurring symptoms.

I want to make a couple of final points before getting into the specific mental disorders most commonly observed by mental health professionals today. First, it's important to realize that psychologists view all behavior on a continuum of normal to abnormal. For example, crying is a normal behavior, but crying all day every day for more than two weeks is abnormal. Second, everyone has experienced a symptom of mental disorder at one time or another. But simply having a symptom does not mean a person has the actual disorder. Remember, disorders consist of specific groupings of symptoms that define a particular syndrome. The rules for determining what symptoms constitute a disorder are complex and include specific time frames and degrees of severity.

So don't get carried away and start diagnosing everyone you know just because you see a symptom or two. It's not that simple; a symptom does not a disorder make!

Grasping for Reality

One of the most well-known signs of mental disorder is losing touch with reality. When someone loses touch with objective reality and begins imagining things and acting on those imagined things, he may be suffering from a class of illness known as *psychotic disorders.*

Psychotic disorders are considered by mental health professionals but also by many a layperson (particularly family members of those who suffer from psychotic disorders) to be the most severe of all mental disorders. In addition to losing touch with reality, people who are suffering from a psychosis often have severe functional deficits related to basic self-care (eating, shelter, and personal hygiene), social and occupational functioning, and thinking.

Schizophrenia

The most common form of psychosis is *schizophrenia.* Psychiatrist Eugene Bleuler used the term schizophrenia in 1911 to describe people who exhibited signs of disorganized thought processes, a lack of coherence between thought and emotion, and a state of disconnection from reality. It may be easy to think that "schizophrenia" stands for "split-personality," but that's a mistake. In schizophrenia, the different components of personality (thoughts, emotions, behaviors) are inconsistent — for example, a mother laughing when her son breaks his arm because the bone poking through his skin looks funny.

Today, the *DSM-5* criteria for schizophrenia include:

- **Delusions:** A delusion is a firmly held belief that a person maintains in spite of evidence to the contrary. One common type of delusion is a *paranoid* or *persecutory delusion,* which involves intense fear that you're being followed, listened to, or otherwise threatened by someone or something. Check out the vignette in the introduction to this chapter. Mr. Smith appears to be experiencing a paranoid delusion. He "knew" that the neighbor was out to get his house!

  Another common form of delusion is the *grandiose delusion,* in which a person experiences an extremely exaggerated sense of worth, power, knowledge, identity, or relationship. Someone who is grandiose may believe he can speak to supernatural beings or that he is a supernatural being himself! Or, he may just think that he's the smartest, most attractive person alive.

✔ **Hallucinations:** A hallucination can be defined as a perception that occurs without external stimulation that is experienced as very real. Hallucinations can be auditory (hearing voices or sounds), visual (seeing people who are not there, demons, or dead people), olfactory (smells), gustatory (tastes), or somatic (experiencing physical sensations within the body). Most hallucinations are auditory and often involve someone hearing a voice or voices commenting on his or her behavior.

Command hallucinations are a potentially dangerous form of auditory hallucination because they involve a voice or voices telling the sufferer to do something, often involving violent or suicidal behavior.

✔ **Disorganized speech and thought:** If you've ever had a conversation with someone, and you had no idea what she was talking about, you may have witnessed disorganized speech and thought, which are characterized by extremely tangential (mostly irrelevant), circumstantial (beating around the bush), or loosely associated (jumping from one unrelated thought to another) speech. These abnormal styles of communicating may be evidence of a *thought disorder*. An extreme form of thought disorder is called *word salad* — when a person's speech is so incoherent that it sounds like another language or nonsense. Sometimes people even make up words that don't exist, called *neologisms*. For example, "I think the glerbage came by and sluppered the inequitised frames from me."

✔ **Grossly disorganized or catatonic behavior:** When a person behaves in a disorganized manner, she may act extremely silly or childlike, easily get lost or confused, stop caring for herself and her basic needs, do strange or bizarre things like talk to herself, or be extremely socially inappropriate. Catatonic behavior involves complete immobility, absolute lack of awareness of one's surroundings, and sometimes being mute.

✔ **Negative symptoms:** A negative symptom refers to the absence of some usual or expected behavior. The absence of the behavior is what is abnormal. Three negative symptoms are often associated with schizophrenia:

  • **Flat affect:** When a person exhibits no emotionality whatsoever

  • **Alogia:** Indication that a person's thought processes are dull, blocked, or generally impoverished

  • **Avolition:** When a person has no ability to persist in an activity; looks like an extreme lack of motivation

When a person experiences these symptoms, he may be suffering from schizophrenia. I say *may* because a person may exhibit these symptoms for different reasons: drug use, sleep deprivation, or a physical disease. Making the diagnosis of schizophrenia is a complex and very serious task. Specific time frames and *rule-outs* are involved. Rule-outs involve eliminating other possible or plausible explanations.

Schizophrenia is diagnosed in about 4 to 5 of every 1,000 people. Generally the condition is diagnosed in individuals between the ages of 18 to 35. Sometimes, but rarely, it's diagnosed in childhood. Schizophrenia typically begins in the late teens and early twenties and is fully present by the mid- to late twenties. It can develop rapidly or gradually, and there can be periods of less severe symptoms. Some sufferers are chronically and persistently ill. Periods of illness can be characterized by a marked inability or diminished capacity to function in everyday life, often leading to school failure, job loss, and relationship difficulties.

Don't be fooled by how easy it is to list the symptoms of schizophrenia and describe them; they are very serious. Individuals with schizophrenia often face enormous challenges in society and sometimes end up in jail, in hospitals or similar institutions, or living on the streets because of their illness.

Revealing schizophrenia's causes

Determining the causes of psychological disorders constituted part of the old nature-versus-nurture debate. Are the causes of schizophrenia organic (biochemical/physiological) or functional (resulting from experience)? At the moment, perhaps because of the wide array of newly developed brain-scanning techniques, the organic explanations are far more prominent. However, the best answer may lie in a synthesis of the two points of view. This is still a very difficult topic to tackle because numerous theories for the cause of schizophrenia exist, each with varying degrees of scientific support. The main theory in practice today is the *diathesis-stress model*, which merges two different areas of research.

First, some definitions. A *diathesis* is a predisposition to a particular disease. *Stress* can be defined as any number of psychological and social factors. So, the diathesis-stress model holds that schizophrenia is the consequence of a stress-activated diathesis or predisposition.

Proposed biological diathesis for schizophrenia includes problems with brain chemistry and/or development. Researchers have found malformed parts of the brain in people with schizophrenia. These biological abnormalities can lead to problems with thinking, speech, behavior, and staying in contact with reality.

For the stress component, psychological factors address the reality distortion associated with schizophrenia. Why do schizophrenics make a break from reality? Some experts propose that the world experienced by someone with schizophrenia is so harsh, and its conflicts so intense, that the person needs a vacation from it. Research supports that psychic trauma, such as child abuse, can be related to psychotic breakdowns, and it certainly constitutes a harsh reality that inspires an escape. The research, however, does not state that child abuse causes schizophrenia in all or even a majority of cases, but it's a potentially overwhelming stressor. Trauma is a form of extreme stress, regardless of the source. This stress may interact with the diathesis, the predisposition, and lead to psychotic symptoms.

A social factor related to schizophrenia that has shown promise in recent research is a phenomenon known as *expressed emotion.* Expressed emotion (EE) refers to negative communication by family members directed at the person suffering from schizophrenia. EE often consists of excessive criticism. Family members may comment on the patient's behavior, "You're crazy!" for example. EE also includes emotional over-involvement of family members that can overwhelm the patient. Let me be perfectly clear, though: I am not saying that criticism and over-involvement cause schizophrenia, but only that these factors may contribute to the stress component of the diathesis-stress model, as may many other stressors.

You may think that you've developed schizophrenia after reading about its causes. Don't get too caught up in the detail. The bottom line is that a lot of the research out there about schizophrenia is inconclusive. What's known is that brain abnormalities in schizophrenics may interact with certain kinds of stress in a way that triggers the disorder. The devastating effects of schizophrenia keep researchers working hard to figure out this disorder. Research has come a long way, but there's still an awful long way to go.

Treating schizophrenia

Schizophrenia is one of the most difficult mental disorders to treat. Its effects are often debilitating for both the individual with the disease and his family. Approaches to treating this illness range from medication to helping individuals develop important functional skills such as money management or social interaction methods.

- ✔ Antipsychotic medications such as Haldol and Zyprexa are typically the first line of treatment for people suffering from schizophrenia or related psychotic disorders. Although they are extremely beneficial, these medications are known as *palliatives* because they don't cure disease; they just lessen the intensity of symptoms.

- ✔ Psychosocial treatment and rehabilitation have also shown promise in managing schizophrenia. Patients learn social and self-care skills that can help reduce the number of stressors they face.

- ✔ Although seemingly out of fashion in recent years (too labor-intensive and therefore too expensive), psychotherapy, specifically cognitive therapy, has been used in recent years to teach patients to challenge their delusional belief systems and become better "consumers" of reality.

Most recent research agrees that a combination of medication and talking therapy is the most effective treatment intervention for schizophrenia. Early intervention and solid social support are also factors associated with a favorable prognosis. With medication, psychotherapy, and support from family and friends, many people suffering from schizophrenia can lead productive lives.

A core problem is that the symptoms of schizophrenia are often so severe that people with this condition often have a difficult time achieving levels of emotional and behavioral consistency necessary to maintain jobs and effective relationships. In addition, perhaps because of damaged self-esteem, poor self-image, and ambivalent attitudes about relating and succeeding, schizophrenics are notorious for inconsistent medication compliance, which only intensifies unpredictable behavior and well-being.

Struggling with other types of psychoses

In addition to schizophrenia, two other forms of psychosis are *delusional disorder* and *substance-induced psychotic disorder*.

- ✔ **Delusional disorder:** Characterized by the presence of fixed false beliefs, not particularly bizarre, that are held despite evidence to the contrary. Moreover, these beliefs are not particularly functional or helpful. For example, a husband may be obsessed with the idea that his wife is having an affair but unable to prove it or find any evidence. This belief would be classified as a delusion if it persisted for at least one month. In a different scenario, someone may think that the water in his home is poisoned, contrary to evidence that it is not. The key thing about a delusional disorder is that the delusional person has no other signs of psychosis, such as those found in schizophrenia.

- ✔ **Substance-induced psychotic disorder:** Exists when prominent hallucinations or delusions are present as a result of being under the influence of a substance or withdrawing from a substance. People under the influence of LSD or PCP often exhibit psychotic symptoms, and it's not unusual for people who have used cocaine or amphetamines to experience psychotic-like symptoms when they "come down" — an experience that mimics psychotic symptoms. This problem can be very serious, and anyone considering using drugs, including cannabis or alcohol, should know that they may experience psychotic symptoms as a consequence of this decision.

Feeling Funky

I wonder if blues music would be around if all those musicians were psychotherapy patients. Those songs don't seem particularly sad though; they just seem a bit pitiful to me. Nevertheless I sometimes ask new patients if they've ever been depressed; some of them reply, "Sure, doesn't everyone get depressed?" Not exactly.

Sadness is a normal human emotion typically felt during experiences of loss. The loss of one's job, lover, child, or car keys may trigger sadness. But that's just it — this is sadness, not depression. *Depression* is an extreme form of sadness that includes a number of specific symptoms. Being dumped by a boyfriend or a girlfriend at one time or another is a fairly universal experience. How does it feel? Sad. Most people feel fatigued, unmotivated, and sleepless when they get dumped. But all of these feelings eventually go away. People get over it and move on. The same kind of response is normal when a loved one dies. This is called *mourning* or *grief.* Again, grieving is not depression. Depression is something different.

In this section, I discuss major depressive disorder, how it manifests, and some of the theories and explanations behind it.

Staying in the rut of major depression

When someone is depressed to the degree of needing professional attention, she experiences a majority of the following symptoms of *major depressive disorder over a minimum of a two-week period* (because anybody may experience these on occasion or for a day or two, or hours):

- ✔ Depressed mood for most of the day and for most days
- ✔ *Anhedonia* (marked disinterest or lack of pleasure in all or most activities)
- ✔ Significant weight loss or weight gain, without trying, and decreased or increased appetite
- ✔ Difficulty sleeping or excessive sleeping
- ✔ Physical feelings of agitation or sluggishness
- ✔ Fatigue or lack of energy
- ✔ Feelings of worthlessness or excessive guilt
- ✔ Difficulty concentrating and focusing
- ✔ Repeated thoughts of death or suicide

Hopefully, most people who ask, "Don't we all get depressed?" won't have that same response after seeing all of these symptoms. If you are experiencing three or more of these symptoms or if you have any doubts, get thee to a doctor!

Sometimes, depression can become so severe that the sufferer may think about committing suicide. Many dangerous myths about suicide are floating around. One is that people who talk about suicide don't do it. This is false! In fact, talking about suicide is one of the most serious signals that someone may actually do it. All talk about suicide or self-harm should be taken very seriously. If you're worried about someone or having suicidal thoughts yourself, contact a mental health professional or call a local crisis or suicide hotline immediately.

Depression is one of the most common forms of mental disorder in the United States, occurring on average in about 15 percent of the population. Major depressive disorder can occur just one time in a person's life or over and over again, lasting for months, years, or even a lifetime. Most people who suffer from a recurring major depressive disorder have periods of recovery in which they don't experience symptoms, or they experience the symptoms in a less intense form. Depression can occur at any point in a person's life and doesn't discriminate against age, race, or gender.

Revealing depression's causes

Depending on whom you ask, the search for the causes of depression can be divided into two camps:

- **Biological:** Biological theories of depression place blame on the brain and the malfunctioning of some of the chemicals that comprise it.

- **Psychological:** The psychological theories of depression focus mostly on the experience of loss.

The *biogenic amine hypothesis* is the most popular theoretical explanation of the biological underpinnings of depression. According to this hypothesis, depression is a function of the dysregulation (impaired ability) of two neurotransmitters in the brain, norepinephrine and serotonin.

Neurotransmitters are chemical substances in the brain that allow one neuron to communicate with another neuron. The brain contains many different neurotransmitters, each with varying functions, in specific regions. Specific neurotransmitters help certain brain regions do the work of particular human activities. The parts of the brain seemingly most affected in depression are those involved with mood, cognition, sleep, sex, and appetite.

Psychological theories of depression come from several sources:

- **Object Relations Theory:** Melanie Klein in the early 20th century proposed that depression was the result of an unsuccessful child developmental process that may result in a difficult time coping with feelings of guilt, shame, and self-worth.

- **Attachment theory:** John Bowlby's mid-20th-century theory, which argues that all of a person's relationships with other people originate from the initial attachment bonds he forms with primary caregivers as an infant. A disruption in the attachment relationship may prevent a healthy bond from forming, thus making the child vulnerable to depression when faced with future losses and relationship difficulties.

  In infancy, many factors — a drug-addicted parent or an unloving foster home are just two examples — can disrupt bonding and attachment. Children with poor attachment relationships are often left feeling helpless. Helplessness is a hallmark of depression.

✔ **Learned helplessness theory:** Martin Seligman in the 1960s worked with people's experience of and with failure or an inability to achieve what they desire at some point in their lives. Under normal circumstances, most people can keep on keeping on; they don't give up or develop any serious sense of pessimism about the likelihood of future successes. But some people, because of adverse circumstances or a general tendency to view their efforts as worthless, may become depressed in the face of disappointing experiences and come to see insurmountable odds in their path.

✔ **Cognitive theory:** Aaron Beck's 1960s theory has become extremely popular and is well supported by research. Beck proposed that depression is a type of thinking disorder that produces the emotional outcome of depressed moods and the other related symptoms.

Several cognitive "distortions" may be involved:

- **Automatic thoughts:** Automatic thoughts are statements people make secretly to themselves that produce depressive experiences. For example, if you get in your car in the morning and it doesn't start, you may consciously say, "Dang, just my luck." But unconsciously, you may be having an automatic thought (that you're not even aware of having), "Nothing ever goes right for me."

- **Mistaken assumptions and self-other schemas:** The assumptions and self-other *schemas* (beliefs about who you are in relationship to others) that you assume to be true — as well as your views of the world, yourself, and the future — greatly influence how you move in the world. Beck introduced the *cognitive triad.* Each point in the triangle contains a set of beliefs that reflect a negative evaluation of oneself, a hopeless view of the future, and a view of the world as excessively harsh.

- **Cyclical thinking:** A final component of the cognitive view is the cyclical nature of depressive thinking. For example, if you believe that you can't do anything, then you won't exactly be fired up when you approach a task; your motivation is affected by your belief about your abilities. Then, you probably make minimal (if any) effort because of your lack of motivation, and, in turn, "prove" to yourself that you really can't do anything right. This twisted and self-confirmatory bias in thinking often leads to depression.

Treating depression

Several effective treatment approaches for depression exist. Antidepressant medication, including famous medications as Prozac and Paxil, works for some people. Psychotherapy, specifically cognitive-behavioral therapy and interpersonal psychotherapy, is also helpful for many people. Research also indicates that "activity" — staying physically active and generally busy — makes an effective antidote to depression. Some studies even indicate that regular physical exercise can be as effective as medication in alleviating symptoms of depression according to the self-reports of subjects, but more research needs to be done before this is considered a mainline treatment. The common standard of practice is to utilize both medication and psychotherapy.

Riding the waves of bipolar disorder

Bipolar disorder used to be known as *manic-depression* can be characterized as a disorder of severe mood swings involving both depression and *mania* — a state of excessively elevated or irritable mood lasting for approximately one week and co-occurring with the following symptoms:

- Inflated self-esteem or grandiosity (coming up with a solution to end starvation and creating peace on Earth, all before tonight's dinner reservation)

- Decreased need for sleep (feeling rested with three to four hours of sleep a night or feeling of not needing sleep at all; there's just too much to do!)

- Extreme need and pressure to talk

- Racing and rapid thoughts

- Extremely short attention span

- Drastically increased activity level (engaging in a lot of projects or mowing the lawn at 2 a.m.)

- Excessive engagement in pleasurable activities that have potentially damaging consequences (gambling your house payment, spending sprees, sexual excursions)

An accurate diagnosis of bipolar disorder requires a person to experience at least one episode of mania in his life and currently be experiencing a manic, depressed, or mixed episode (both depression and mania). A person needs to experience both depression and mania — hence the concept of severe mood swings — to earn his bipolar stripes, so to speak.

People suffering from bipolar disorder usually have several recurring episodes over the course of their lifetimes. Manic episodes can be particularly damaging because when someone is in the throes of mania, it's not uncommon to amass extremely large debts, incur broken relationships, or even engage in illegal or criminal acts.

Bipolar disorder is akin to being on a roller coaster of extreme emotion (sometimes sad, sometimes happy) beyond all proportion, but these mood swings do not occur within a day or even within a week. Bipolar disorder refers to extreme mood swings that occur over a long period of time — such as four mood episodes (either depression, manic, or mixed) within a ten-year period. An episode can last anywhere from one week to multiple years.

Depression drug?

Antidepressant medication is one of the most widely prescribed medications in the United States. What's the story with that? Is everyone in the US depressed? I think it comes down to a great deal of public awareness about depression — and television advertising for these drugs doesn't hurt either. But it's important to remember that certain forms of psychotherapy can be just as effective as medication in the short-run and perhaps more beneficial to a person's long-term well-being than medication. In other words, the best "drug" for depression may not be a drug at all.

Some people have what's called *rapid cycling* — they may experience four or more episodes within a one-year period. Rapid-cycling individuals have an especially tough experience because each bipolar episode can be quite disruptive, and there's no time to get their life back together between episodes.

Revealing bipolar disorder's causes

The most popular theories on the causes of bipolar disorder — specifically, mania — are biological. Research has implicated neurochemical abnormalities in the specific parts of the brain that involve the neurotransmitters dopamine and serotonin. There is little other conclusive evidence.

Long before biological studies, however, psychoanalysts offered their explanation: Mania is a defensive reaction to depression. Rather than feeling overwhelmed with depression, a person's mind makes a switch of sorts, turning that extreme sadness into extreme happiness. The symbolic equivalent to this idea is laughing when someone you love dies. It's a severe form of denial. When a manic patient is seen in psychoanalytic-oriented psychotherapy, the main focus is this defensive hypothesis.

Stress, too, is thought to play a role in intensifying the mood episodes within bipolar disorder. Stress doesn't necessarily cause mania or depression, but it can make matters worse or speed up the arrival of an approaching mood episode.

Treating bipolar disorder

Currently, the first line in treating bipolar disorder is medication. A class of drugs known as *mood stabilizers* is used to stabilize a person's mood and reduce the likelihood of future episodes. Common mood stabilizers are Lithium and Depakote.

Supportive psychotherapy can also be part of treatment, mainly to help people deal with the negative consequences of manic behavior and come to terms with the seriousness of this illness. Cognitive-Behavioral Therapy (CBT) is being used increasingly to help people with bipolar disorder manage their behavior and identify early warning signs of an upcoming mood episode.

For more information on bipolar disorder, read *Bipolar Disorder For Dummies* by Candida Fink and Joe Kraynak (Wiley, 2012).

Being Scared

Euphemisms abound when it comes to the most common class of mental disorders, the *anxiety disorders*. "Stress," "worry," "nerves," "nervousness," and "fear" are all everyday terms for this condition. *Anxiety* is a sense of generalized fear and apprehension. When someone is anxious, he is generally fearful. Fearful of what? That depends. Identifying what scares a person helps psychologists determine what kind of anxiety disorder he may have.

Normal worrying aside, anxiety disorders are probably the most common type of mental disorder. But is worrying actually a mental disorder? Remember, all behavior and mental processes exist on a continuum of normalcy. Worry can be so intense or bothersome to the worrier that it reaches the level of a disorder in need of professional attention. Worried about being a pathological worrier yet? Relax, take a deep breath, and read on. There's more to cover before you start jumping to conclusions and running for help.

Scared sweaterless

People can fear or worry about all kinds of things. When someone is extremely afraid of a particular thing or situation, even if she knows it poses no real danger, it's called a *phobia*. There are different types of phobias. Social phobia is the fear of people. Agoraphobia is the fear of being outdoors, away from home, or in crowded places. Angoraphobia is fear of sweaters and heavy winter coats. Just kidding about the last one, but hundreds of phobias are out there. Here are a few notables:

- ✔ **Acrophobia:** Fear of heights
- ✔ **Claustrophobia:** Fear of closed spaces
- ✔ **Nyctophobia:** Fear of the dark
- ✔ **Mysophobia:** Fear of germ contamination
- ✔ **Zoophobia:** Fear of animals or a specific animal

Some of the most common anxiety disorders include:

- **Generalized anxiety disorder:** Excessive and persistent worry about many different things
- **Posttraumatic Stress Disorder (PTSD):** Reexperiencing traumatic events that were life threatening, hyper or excessive physiological arousal and avoidance of trauma-related places and people
- **Obsessive-compulsive disorder:** Obsessions (recurring thoughts) and compulsive behavior (driven to repeat an activity like hand-washing)

In this section, I focus on one of the most common anxiety disorders; it's known as *panic disorder.*

If you live in a bad neighborhood and you're afraid to leave your home at night, that's not a phobia; that's realistic (or rational) anxiety! On the other hand, some people are afraid to leave their homes, and it's not because they live in a bad neighborhood. The people I'm referring to suffer from a phobia of large, open, or crowded places called *agoraphobia.* Agoraphobia is typically associated with a major anxiety disorder known as *panic disorder* — a condition in which a person experiences recurring panic or anxiety attacks and a fear of future attacks.

The *DSM-5* definition for a panic attack is "a discrete period of intense fear or discomfort, in which four (or more) of the following symptoms developed abruptly and reached a peak within 10 minutes":

- Palpitations, pounding heart, or accelerated heart rate
- Sweating, trembling, or shaking
- Shortness of breath, feeling of choking, or chest pain
- Nausea, dizziness, or lightheadedness
- Feelings of unreality or being detached from oneself
- Fear of losing control or going crazy or dying
- Numbness, tingling, chills, or hot flashes

A person who has recurrent panic attacks may be suffering from panic disorder if he worries incessantly about having more attacks, has unrealistic fears of the implications of the attack, or has significantly changed his behavior as a result of the attacks. A hallmark of panic disorder is fear that the panic attacks are a signal of some major illness, such as a heart attack, losing one's mind, or dying. This symptom can be very serious because it can lead to excessive stress. Worrying about dying can be pretty stressful and may well be a factor in triggering the very illnesses a person is actively dreading.

The most common change in a person's behavior is the development of agoraphobia. This state involves an intense fear of being in places or situations in which it may be difficult to get away or to get help if needed. Common examples of situations associated with agoraphobia are riding in elevators, standing in a large crowd, traveling on a crowded subway car, or even driving in thick traffic.

This is only the first half of agoraphobia, though. The other part involves the person avoiding these potentially trapping situations and, often, confining himself to his home. This symptom can be extremely stressful for the person suffering from panic disorder and for his family members as well. What kind of life can you have if your spouse or parent won't leave the house? Severe marital strain is not uncommon for people with panic disorder.

Revealing panic disorder's causes

At least two excellent explanations of panic disorder exist; there's David Barlow's *biopsychosocial approach* as well as the *cognitive model.*

Barlow's main idea is that panic attacks are the result of a hyperactive fear response within the brain under stress. Certain individuals possess a physiological vulnerability in which their nervous systems overreact in some situations. This biological vulnerability is paired with the psychological vulnerability that's caused by exaggerated beliefs about the dangerousness of certain bodily sensations and the world in general.

The cognitive model (Beck, Emery, & Greenberg, 1985) is similar to Barlow's model, but it puts more emphasis on the person's beliefs. The basic idea of the cognitive model is that panic attacks are the result of a misattribution of normal bodily sensations that leads to increased fear, which in turn exacerbates the sensations, which leads to more misattribution. It's a vicious cycle. A person interprets something that he feels is life threatening or dangerous, and this makes him worry, which intensifies both the feeling and his fear of it.

Treating panic disorder

Panic disorder is treated by mental health professionals with both medications and various forms of psychotherapy. Antidepressant medications known as tricyclics can reduce the occurrence of panic. Benzodiazapines, a class of "relaxing" drugs, are also used for some people to reduce the likelihood of anxiety symptoms getting "out of control" and blossoming into full-blown panic.

Behavior therapy is usually an important part of treatment for panic patients. It sounds kind of cruel, but behavior therapy basically involves teaching relaxation techniques and then, in small-step increments, exposing patients to situations that formerly triggered panic. The exercise teaches participants how to endure a panic attack until it subsides. More importantly, it works. Patients become calm in situations that initially triggered strong anxiety.

Cognitive therapy can teach sufferers to change their thinking in ways that reduce their tendency to misperceive or misinterpret bodily sensations and blow them out of proportion. The intent of cognitive therapy is to change "what if thinking" to "so what thinking" through education about physiological processes and available sources of help.

Understanding Young People's Problems

Mental disorders affect children and adolescents at rates similar to adults, which is about 1 in 5, or 20 percent, according to the United States Surgeon General. Kids are not exempt from mental problems; they experience many of the same disorders that adults do, in slightly different numbers. For example, rates of depression in people under the age of 18 years old are similar to adults, but the occurrences of schizophrenia in the under-18 set are much lower than for adults. Schizophrenia is considered fairly rare in children. Anxiety disorders, on the other hand, may be the most common disorder of childhood; incidences among kids are similar to occurrence rates for adults.

Although children and adults can experience the same mental disorders, there are some disorders that are more likely to show or "turn up" during childhood; they're typically recognized in a person before she reaches adulthood:

- **Intellectual disability:** Characterized by abnormally low intellectual and adaptive skills such as self-care and communication abilities

- **Learning disorders:** Problems related to acquiring, manipulating, and using information, including dyslexia and mathematics disorder

- **Motor skills disorders:** Insufficient development of coordinated physical activity

- **Communication disorders:** Difficulties with expressive and receptive speech

- **Oppositional defiant and conduct disorder:** Characterized by behavior that violates the rights of others such as aggression, criminal behavior, and bullying

- ✔ **Feeding and eating disorder of infancy and early childhood:** Abnormal eating in terms of amount, intake method, or some other feature such as ingesting nonnutritive substances, known as the disorder *pica*

- ✔ **Tic disorders:** Involves the presence of involuntary vocal or motor movements and includes Tourette's disorder

- ✔ **Elimination disorders:** Includes encopresis (the soiling of clothing with feces) and enuresis (same problem only with urine)

- ✔ **Attention deficit/hyperactivity disorder:** Characterized by abnormal levels of activity and deficits in concentrating, attending, and impulse control

- ✔ **Pervasive developmental disorders:** Involves disorders of severe deficits in communication, social functioning, and behavior, including autism

Dealing with ADHD

Are you always on the go, unable to sit still, constantly messing with things, struggling to think before acting or doing something foolish, spacing out frequently, and having a hard time finishing things? These are common examples of behaviors and symptoms of *Attention Deficit/Hyperactivity Disorder* or ADHD.

ADHD used to be called *ADD* or Attention Deficit Disorder, but it's been officially recognized as ADHD for at least 20 years. The actual diagnostic symptoms of ADHD are divided into two categories: symptoms of hyperactivity and impulsivity and symptoms of inattention. Individuals can display predominant symptoms in one of the two categories and meet criteria for the diagnosis. Or, they can have symptoms in both and be considered a "combined type."

Here's rundown of the symptoms associated in each of the two categories:

- ✔ **Hyperactivity and impulsivity:** Fidgety, squirmy, can't stay seated, runs and climbs excessively, can't play quietly, always on the go, talkative, can't wait, interrupts, and is intrusive

- ✔ **Inattention:** Difficulties with paying close attention to details, making careless mistakes, difficulty sustaining attention, not appearing to listen, poor follow-through and finishing things, loses things, is distractible, and forgetful

ADHD can range in severity from very mild to severe and is not typically diagnosed before the age of 4 years old. Boys are more likely to have ADHD, but it shows up in girls, too. The most common treatment is medication, typically in the class of psychostimulants (such as Ritalin or Straterra), but behavior modification and psychosocial interventions are also important parts of treatment. Specifically, the approach popularized by Russell Barkley and in the work of Dr. Arthur D Anastopoulos uses psychosocial interventions that include behavior modification components, parent education, child education, and counseling, if necessary.

Wait a minute, did that say "psychostimulants"? That's right, the medication used to treat ADHD functions as a brain stimulant. It's the concept of adults using coffee to stay up and work or study. People tend to concentrate a little better when they're a little wired.

Although it seems counterintuitive, the underlying neuropsychological deficits of ADHD are consistent with the use of a stimulant medication. Essentially, the symptoms of ADHD are the result of the less-than-optimal functioning of the frontal lobe of the brain, deficits in its functions known as *executive functions*, such as planning and organizing. The frontal lobe and its executive functions play a critical role in inhibition and impulse control, organization, attention, concentration, and *goal-directed behavior*, which is knowing how to stay on target to meet a goal, even if that goal is simply picking up your socks.

For people with ADHD, the frontal lobe is "underpowered" and not up to its tasks, thus leaving the rest of the brain disorganized, impulsive, overly active, and prone to a bit of wandering. Stimulant medications address the power shortage, give the frontal lobe a boost, and slow down Joe ADHD to focus him and increase his impulse control.

The cause of this frontal lobe power deficit has yet to be fully identified but research shows a strong genetic component and the role of some sort of negative developmental event or exposure that results in underdevelopment of the frontal lobe and executive functions.

Living in a world of her own

> *I am much less autistic now, compared to when I was young. I remember some behaviors like picking carpet fuzz and watching spinning plates for hours. I didn't want to be touched. I couldn't shut out background noise. I didn't talk until I was about 4 years old. I screamed. I hummed. But as I grew up, I improved.*
>
> — Temple Grandin

Temple Grandin is a relatively famous adult woman who has *autism,* a neurodevelopmental disorder characterized by deficits or abnormal language development, abnormal social skills and development, and repetitive and restricted behavior. Actress Claire Danes starred in a TV movie about Temple Grandin made in 2010 that featured her life, her struggles, and her success. Ms. Grandin, who holds a PhD in animal science, is considered by many as a spokesperson and advocate for those with autism and engages in numerous speaking engagements every year to increase awareness of this condition.

Autism, usually recognized by the age of 3 to 4 (although signs and symptoms can manifest and show up earlier) consists of symptoms and deficits the following three areas:

- **Impairment in social interaction:** Deficits in nonverbal social behavior such as eye contact and gestures; failure to develop peer relationships appropriate to age level; a lack of spontaneous seeking to share enjoyment, interests, or achievements with other people; and lack of social or emotional reciprocity

- **Impairments in communication:** Delay in, or total lack of, the development of spoken language or, in individuals with adequate speech, impairment in the ability to initiate or sustain a conversation with others; stereotyped and repetitive use of language or idiosyncratic language such as repeating incessantly or odd intonation or word usage; and deficits in varied, spontaneous make-believe play or social imitative play

- **Repetitive and stereotyped patterns of behavior, interests, and activities:** Intense preoccupation with one or more stereotyped and restricted patterns of interest that is abnormal either in intensity or focus; inflexible adherence to specific, nonfunctional routines or ritual; stereotyped (persistent repetition of a behavior with no obvious purpose) and repeated motor mannerisms (such as hand or finger flapping or twisting, or complex whole-body movements); and persistent preoccupation with parts of objects

Autism is a complex neurodevelopmental disorder that can range from mild (often called *high-functioning autism*) to severe. A cause for the disorder has yet to be identified, but research findings are promising. For example, genetic research is progressing. No "autism gene" has been identified, but much has been learned about the underlying cognitive and neuropsychological aspects of autism. Two areas in particular stand out: *neural connectivity models* and *theory of mind* models.

It is thought that the brain in individuals with autism develops and is organized differently from the brain in children with typical development (see Chapter 3 for content on how the brain is organized and works). Research findings are complicated, showing that autistic people have some underdeveloped areas as well as some overdevelopment — and even larger brain volume. Taken as a whole, researchers propose that the brain in autism interacts and communicates with itself in unique and disordered ways that differ from activity in typical individuals. From this perspective, autism can be considered a disorder of neural organization and integration.

Thinking that someone you're looking at or talking to has a "mind of his own" is known as "theory of mind" (abbreviated TOM). Most people believe that other people have a mind just like their own, which helps them understand the world from another person's point of view. Consistently, research and clinical work show that individuals with autism have deficits in TOM. In other words, people with autism do not assume the existence of an "other's mind" and, as a result, display social and communication deficits. Their difficulties with understanding facial expressions and gestures, anticipating the actions and of others, engaging in conversation, and showing social and emotional reciprocity may be a consequence of TOM deficits. But, as with genetics, TOM deficits have yet to come through as the "silver bullet" of underlying deficits that account for or produce the entire syndrome of autism.

One thing is for certain; in many respects, autism is a lifelong disorder. Yet there's significant hope for those who get early and intensive intervention. As a neurodevelopmental disorder, the course of autism can likely be altered in a significant and positive direction. A comprehensive interventions approach that broadly addresses a child's neurodevelopment and development have been developed, researched, and show encouraging results. These approaches use a "teaching" approach of sorts to facilitate the normal development of children and address developmental delays. Here are four of the most well-researched and exciting intervention approaches for autism:

- ✔ **Applied behavior analysis — Discrete trial teaching (DTT):** DTT is a specific teaching technique in which the principles of operant and classical conditioning are used to present children with massed learning trials that are very intensive (find details on ABA in Chapter 16 and information on operant and classical conditioning in Chapter 8). DTT is most associated with the work of Dr. Ivar Lovaas (1927–2010)).

- ✔ **Pivotal response treatments (PRT):** PRT is considered an ABA intervention, but it differs from DTT in that it tends to be more play-based, uses naturalistic reinforcement within the operant conditioning paradigm, and focuses on increasing the motivation of the participant to optimal levels. PRT is associated with the work of husband-and-wife psychologist team, Drs. Robert and Lynn Koegel of University of California, Santa Barbara, who first developed their work in the 1970s.

- ✔ **Early start Denver model:** Developed by psychologists Sally Rogers and Geraldine Dawson in the early 2000s, the early start Denver model combines the PRT approach and a "developmental model" in which experiences identified as critical in child development are used to guide the intervention and its curriculum.

- ✔ **Verbal behavior approach:** Dr. Mark Sundberg developed the VB approach in the early 2000s to help children with autism learn how to communicate and speak. Although not considered a comprehensive intervention approach for all developmental areas, the verbal behavior approach is widely respected as a sophisticated and well-designed intervention for communication and language development.

Part V
Building a Better You

Discover and see the validity in the wide variety of human experiences in my article "Exploring Human Differences: Culture, Gender, and Sexuality" at www.dummies.com/extras/psychology.

In this part...

- ✔ Dig deep into psychological testing and assessment to find out how psychologists determine whether people have problems and suggest what can be done about them.

- ✔ Get familiar with the differences among traditional "talk" psychotherapies: psychoanalysis, behavior therapy, cognitive therapy, and other popular forms of psychological treatment.

- ✔ Discover behavior therapy and cognitive therapy, widely used forms of therapy that take a simpler and less mysterious approach to psychological problems.

- ✔ Check out humanistic and existential therapies that focus on the core issues of being a person and how a person deals with these issues.

- ✔ Find out about the growing field of health psychology and its approach to stress, illness, coping, and human psychological strength and resilience.

Chapter 14

Assessing the Problem and Testing the Psyche

People go to a psychologist or other mental health professional usually because they're experiencing strong negative emotions or facing difficulties in their everyday lives. Just like when visiting a general physician, a person goes to a psychologist's office with a complaint, issue, or problem. A lot of times, the individual is looking for answers because he's unsure about what's really going on. The psychologist listens and tries to assess the full extent of the problem, attempting to gain a full sense of the patient's situation. If the psychologist gets the problem wrong, she won't be able to fix it.

It's like this: I recently bought a new computer, took it home, set it up, and everything seemed great. I was excited to get on the Internet and start surfing around. But when I tried to connect, it didn't work. You can imagine my frustration after spending north of a thousand dollars on a brand-new computer that wasn't working right. I spent three frantic days trying to figure out what was wrong, changing cables, calling the Internet service provider, and talking with the store that sold me the computer. Nothing I did and no one I talked to fixed the problem.

Finally, my wife pointed out (three days later) that I had plugged a cord into the wrong jack in the back of the computer. She simply placed the cord where it belonged and connected with ease. I had incorrectly identified the problem and was therefore clueless about how to fix it. I figured that because I was a scientist I had thoroughly ruled out all possible causes and variables. Boy, was I wrong.

This chapter introduces you to the process and procedures psychologists use in clinical evaluations. Those include taking history and gathering information about the nature of the presenting problems of clients and patients. Psychological assessment and testing, two things psychologists are particularly trained well to do, are discussed, including a review of the different types of tests and evaluations a psychologist conducts.

Naming the Problem

The first step toward any solution is to recognize and clearly define the problem. Psychologists use specific tools and techniques for that very purpose. Here's how it typically goes: A person visits a psychologist and the conversation begins with an exploration of the patient's *presenting complaint* (the issue that motivated the patient to seek therapy). The discussion then gets into a more thorough information-gathering process:

> **Psychologist:** Tell me, Mr. Smith, what seems to be the problem?
>
> **Mr. Smith:** How am I supposed to know? You're the doctor.

The "What's the problem?" question sometimes annoys patients because they often don't know what's going on; they're seeking help from a professional and expect the psychologist to have the answers. But without a thorough investigation of the patient's situation, any mental health professional can only perform expensive guesswork. The two most common approaches to clinical assessment are formal interviews and psychological testing. I describe these processes in this section.

Documenting history

There may be as many interview techniques in the psychological world as there are individual psychologists out there. Everyone has a different way of getting at the relevant information. So what is the relevant information?

Most shrink-to-patient encounters begin with a discussion of the patient's basic issue, the initial complaint or *presenting problem*. Very few people who come to a psychologist describe their problems according to the criteria established in the *Diagnostic and Statistical Manual,* the manual published by the American Psychiatric Press that most US psychologists use to diagnose mental disorders. Presenting problems tend to be vague or convoluted.

Early communication problems between the psychologist and the patient are not necessarily because people don't understand themselves. Rather, it's usually more an issue of vocabulary; doctors and patients use different words to describe the same problems. You say to-*may*-to, and I say to-*mah*-to. You may say you can't sleep or stop crying, and I say you're depressed.

To begin exploring a person's psychological problems, a psychologist often gathers information about the patient's family, friends, co-workers, and other major relationships in order to better understand her social, educational, and occupational functioning. Did the patient graduate from high school? Has she been able to stay gainfully employed?

Often, although people begin therapy with a lot to say and get off their chests, they're overwhelmed and sometimes have a hard time knowing exactly how to describe their experiences. Therapy isn't always so cut and dried, but psychologists typically try to structure the first interview with the following steps:

1. **Clarify the presenting problem.**

2. **Gather a history of the patient's life.**

   Is it an autobiography? In a way it is, except that only specific areas are covered. The most relevant aspect in a psychological interview is the history of the presenting problem. When did it all begin . . . ?

3. **Explore the patient's physical health.**

   An assessment of the patient's physical health and history is always important in the history-taking process mainly because many psychiatric or psychological problems can be an aspect of certain physical illnesses or conditions. That is, a psychological problem may actually be a symptom of an underlying medical condition. For example, a person may think he or she is having a panic attack (psychological) but may in fact be having a heart attack (medical/physical illness). When was his most recent physical? Does she have any major medical problems? Is he taking any medications? Does (or has) she abused drugs or alcohol? Does he have an altered state of consciousness that requires medical assessment or treatment?

4. **Gather a thorough history of any psychological problems.**

   A psychologist wants to find out if the patient has ever suffered from depression in the past, attempted suicide, or been treated for a mental disorder in a psychiatric hospital or other type of setting. Do any family members have a history of mental illness? Is he thinking about hurting other people? Certain pieces of information are extremely important to find out if the patient's safety is at risk. A prudent professional always takes the time to assess the most serious aspects of a case first, and no issues are more serious to a psychologist than suicide or a patient's potential for violence.

Examining mental status

Throughout the initial interview, the psychologist looks for specific behavioral, cognitive, and emotional indicators of psychological disturbance. This is called a *mental status examination (MSE)*. Typically, the psychologist observes these 11 mental status areas:

- ✔ **Appearance:** Grooming, hygiene, physical characteristics, and unusual features are observed. If someone has an unusual appearance — severely underweight, disheveled, or bizarre or inappropriate grooming, for instance — outside of cultural or subcultural norms, it may be worth discussing.

- ✔ **Behavior:** Some of the most striking signs of disturbance come from the way people act.

  - **Body movement:** Body movements such as fidgeting, fast movements, slowed movements, or strange gestures may be relevant. Nervous individuals may fidget a lot. Depressed patients may sit slumped in their chairs. Someone with a paranoid delusion that the CIA is following him may get up and peek out the curtains every five minutes.

  - **Facial expressions:** Facial expressions can sometimes reveal how a person is feeling. A sad, mad, immobile, or frozen expression, for example, can indicate specific moods.

- ✔ **Speech:** Two disorders in particular, schizophrenia and bipolar disorder, include disturbances in speech:

  - **Schizophrenia:** A patient's speech may be disordered, jumbled, or difficult to understand. He may seem to be speaking a foreign language, using words and phrases that don't seem to make sense. For example, I once received an anonymous phone call while volunteering at a homeless shelter. When I asked the caller if I could help him, he replied, "Stick the pin in the cushion. You called me. What do you want? The letters make me crazy . . . light bulb . . . beat the drum . . . stick the pin in the cushion . . . what do you want?" This is an excellent case of disordered speech.

  - **Bipolar disorder:** The rate and pace of speech can be abnormal in people with bipolar disorder. Patients in a manic episode, for instance, can speak very fast and act as if they physically need to keep talking. They may jump from one topic to another.

- ✔ **Mood and affect:** *Mood* describes the predominant emotions being expressed by the patient. Is she sad, happy, angry, euphoric, or anxious? *Affect* refers to the range, intensity, and appropriateness of a patient's emotional behavior. Is she mildly sad or intensely sad? Does she feel anything other than sadness, or does she seem to have a full range of emotions? Another common observation of affect is called *mood lability*. How often and easily does mood change? Is she hot one second and cold the next?

✔ **Thought content:** What people think about is relevant to any clinical evaluation. Bizarre thought content, such as delusions, can be telltale signs of the presence of a mental disorder. Less bizarre but sometimes equally disturbing thoughts, such as obsessive preoccupations and intrusive ideas, can also be signs of severe anxiety. Thoughts of death and violence are relevant to assessing suicidality and violence potential.

✔ **Thought process:** Different ways of thinking can sometimes be clues to a mental disorder.

- **Tangential thinking:** Often a sign of thought disorder, tangential thinking is characterized by a wandering focus and the tendency to go off on tangents that are only minimally related to the topic currently being discussed.

- **Clang associations:** These are serious indicators of thought disorder. When someone ends a sentence with a word, and the sound of that word triggers another thought, related to the conversation only by the sound of the last word uttered, the thought process is known as a *clang association.* "I came home from work the other day, and the car was in the driveway . . . highway's are crowded. Loud noises bother me . . . tree." This type of disordered thought is unorganized and hard to follow; it doesn't make sense.

✔ **Perception:** Perceptual problems consist of hallucinations. Patients can experience auditory hallucinations (voices), visual hallucinations, olfactory hallucinations (smells or odors), gustatory hallucinations (tastes), or somatic hallucinations (strange bodily sensations, such as feeling like bugs are crawling under the skin). A very serious auditory hallucination is when patients hear a voice or voices telling them to hurt themselves or someone else. These are sometimes called command hallucinations.

✔ **Intellectual functioning:** This status can be casually observed by paying attention to the patient's vocabulary, general quantity of knowledge and information, and abstract thinking ability. However, trying to figure out someone's intellectual functioning based on observation alone is highly subjective and should only be used as a starting point for further assessment.

✔ **Attention/concentration and memory:** Pay attention to whether a patient is distracted during the interview and struggling to concentrate on the task at hand. Short-term memory can be checked by asking the individual to remember a few things and checking with her a few minutes later. How well she recalls her history and provides historical information offers a measure of long-term memory. Many disorders present attention problems and memory deficits.

✔ **Orientation:** Does the patient know where she is? The season? The time? Ascertaining whether a patient knows where she is in time and space is an important part of the MSE. Many serious medical conditions and neuropsychological disorders manifest signs of disorientation.

To each his own animal

If you see a middle-aged gentleman wearing a pair of famous mouse ears with a mouse nose, teeth, and whiskers in a coffee shop, you may wonder if he's mentally ill. It's a free country, but most people would agree that this appearance is unusual. Middle-aged men don't normally dress up like mice. So when someone treats every day like Halloween, it's worth asking about. No judging or jumping to conclusions; it's just worth checking out.

✔ **Insight and judgment:** Does the patient understand that she may be mentally ill? Does she understand the relationship between her behaviors and mental processes and a psychological disturbance? Insight is important for assessing how motivated a patient is going to be during treatment and whether compliance issues are likely to interfere with illness management or recovery. Addressing a patient's judgment involves looking at the soundness of the decisions she makes and the degree of impulsivity and planning that goes on before she takes action. Judgment is especially important when assessing for dangerousness, violence potential, or suicide risk.

Checking Under the Hood with Psychological Testing

These days, any number of different disciplines are involved in the treatment of mental illness and working with people with mental disorders. Psychological testing, however, is considered the sole domain of psychologists. Although some professionals, such as school counselors and learning disability specialists, conduct psychological testing, their testing is limited in scope and to a specific problem. Psychologists are thoroughly trained in all aspects of psychological testing and are the primary professionals in this area.

Psychological testing is part of the entire psychological assessment process. *Assessment* is a set of scientific procedures used to measure and evaluate an individual's behavior and mental processes. Psychologist Anne Anastasi (1908–2001), a past president of the American Psychological Association and a distinguished researcher in psychological assessment, defines a psychological test as an objective, standardized sample of behavior or mental processes. Tests can formalize data based on observations. Nearly all topics in psychology can be measured with a test.

Testing formats include surveys, pencil and paper tests, exercises and activities (like putting a puzzle together), interviews, and observation. Testing in psychology is not much different from testing in other fields. A blood test is a means of measuring an individual's T-cell count, for example. A personality test is a way to measure some specific aspect of a person's personality. Psychological testing uses the same idea; it just focuses on the subject matter of psychology, behavior, and mental processes.

A test is objective if it meets acceptable standards in three important areas: standardization, reliability, and validity.

Standardizing

Anne Anastasi considers a test properly *standardized* if it has a uniform procedure for administering and scoring. Control of extraneous variables allows for maximum accuracy. In other words, if I give a test differently to two different people, then I can't very well trust the results because I've violated the principle of control in science.

Establishing a norm for a test is another step in standardization. A *norm* is a measure of the average performance for a large group of people on any given psychological test. For example, the average score on the Wechsler Adult Intelligence Scale, 4th Edition, is 100. This average score establishes a point of comparison for the test taker's scores to be referenced to. This is called *a norm* and is a standard by which to compare people. Norms are established by administering the test to a large group of people, or several groups, and measuring the average performance and range of performances, something called *variability*. So, if I develop a test to measure problem solving. I would establish a norm or comparison group by going out and giving my test to thousands of people and documenting their performance and the range of performances. This comparison group is used to compare the scores of any individual taking the test to the thousands of other people who took the test and allows me to determine how well or how poorly any one individual test taker did in comparison to all the other people who took the test.

Relying on tests

Reliability is consistency across different testing occasions, test providers, settings, or circumstances. A reliable test should give the same result regardless of the circumstances. An inconsistent test is not reliable and therefore not very helpful for psychological testing. If I give the same person the same test on two or more occasions, will he get the same or comparable score? If the answer is yes, then the test is reliable. If I test a person, and another psychologist uses the same test on the same person, the results should be comparable; this is called inter-rater reliability. A test needs to prove reliable before being put to use by professionals. In fact, psychologists are ethically bound to use reliable tests and instruments because they are being entrusted to provide accurate and useful information. An unreliable test is not able to deliver in that regard. A psychologist wants to know if a person's test performance is due to their own characteristics and not to the setting, circumstances, or situation. The psychologist would not be measuring what he thinks he is measuring if a test weren't reliable. An example of reliability used in test development is *test-retest reliability*. This involves giving a test and then giving it again later (not too soon, of course, because you don't want practice effects) and then seeing if the scores are close or similar.

When it comes to psychological testing, I've often had patients object that a test was unreliable and that it didn't prove or measure a darn thing. They may have had a point, but only if the test was unreliable.

Trusting tests

How do you know that a test you're using is really measuring what it claims to measure? You may think that you're measuring intelligence when you're really measuring English-language aptitude. This actually happens quite often when tests are improperly used with people for whom the test has not been *normed* — which means that its statistical properties haven't been established with a large population of individuals similar to the people to whom it will be applied. Tests used with people who were not part of the group the test was normed on are highly suspect and most likely invalid.

When a test measures what it claims to measure, it's considered *valid.* The validity of a test is established by comparing the test with an outside measure of the psychological topic in question. If I have a test that claims to measure depression, I must compare my test findings with an already established measure of depression such as the Beck Depression Inventory.

Keep in mind that many, if not most, psychological tests measure things that are unobservable in the way other factors in other fields are. T-cells can be physically seen and therefore counted under a microscope. But intelligence cannot be viewed in the same manner. Intelligence is presumed to exist as it manifests itself in a measurable form on a psychological test. Therefore, the scientific basis on which psychological testing is formed is of utmost importance.

Psychological testing is a little more sophisticated than asking a few questions and counting up someone's responses. It's a scientific endeavor. Because of the complexity of psychological testing, most professionals argue that use of tests should be controlled — only qualified examiners should use them. The risk for potential oversimplification or misinterpretation is just too high when an untrained administrator attempts to diagnose a person's mental status through testing.

Plus, if the tests are spread around indiscriminately, people may become too familiar with them and be able to manipulate their responses; thus the tests would lose their validity. Instead of measuring someone's intelligence, for example, the psychologist may end up measuring a subject's skill at remembering the test questions and answers that reveal the traits he wants to show.

Testing Types

Numerous types of psychological testing exist. Five of the most common are clinical testing, educational/achievement testing, personality testing, intelligence testing, and neuropsychological testing. Each of these different types of tests looks at a different type of behavior and/or mental process.

Clinical testing

Clinical psychologists (psychologists who work with mental disorders and abnormal behavior) typically use clinical testing as a way to clarify diagnoses and assess the scope and nature of a person's or family's disturbance and dysfunction. Specific tests are designed to assess the extent to which a patient may or may not be experiencing the symptoms of a particular disorder. These are *diagnostic tests.* A popular example is the Beck Depression Inventory, which is designed to assess a patient's level of depression.

Behavioral and adaptive functioning tests are two types of clinical tests that determine how well a person is doing in her everyday life and whether she exhibits specific problem behaviors. A common instrument used with children is the Child Behavior Checklist, which is designed to assess the extent of a child's behavior problems. Another commonly used clinical test is the Conner's Parent Rating Scale, which detects attention deficit/hyperactivity disorder (ADHD) symptoms.

In addition to disorder-specific inventories and tests, a wide variety of tests designed for other purposes lend themselves to the diagnostic process. Intelligence tests are designed to measure intelligence, but they can also show signs of cognitive dysfunction and learning disabilities. Personality tests are designed to measure personality, but they can also provide helpful insight to the types of psychological problems an individual is experiencing.

Educational/achievement testing

Educational and achievement tests measure an individual's current level of academic competence. Glen Aylward, chair of the Division of Developmental and Behavioral Pediatrics at the Southern Illinois University School of Medicine, identifies three major purposes of this type of testing:

- ✔ Identify students who need special instruction.
- ✔ Identify the nature of a student's difficulties in order to rule out learning disabilities.
- ✔ Assist in educational planning and approach to instruction.

A typical educational/achievement test assesses the most common areas of school activity: reading, mathematics, spelling, and writing skills. Some tests include other areas such as science and social studies. A popular achievement test in wide use today is the Woodcock-Johnson Psychoeducational Battery, Revised. The test consists of nine subtests, measuring the standard areas of instruction but in more detail (mathematics is broken down into calculation and applied problems, for example).

Educational/achievement testing is widely used in the school systems in the United States and Western Europe. When a child or older student is having a hard time in school, it's not unusual for her to take an achievement test to get a closer look at her basic skill level. Sometimes, students have a difficult time because they have a learning disability. Part of identifying a learning disability is assessing the student's achievement level. Other times, a student struggles because of non-academic difficulties such as emotional problems, substance abuse, or family issues. An achievement test sometimes helps to tease out these non-academic problems.

Personality testing

Personality tests measure many different things, not just personality. Numerous tests are designed to measure emotion, motivation, and interpersonal skills as well as specific aspects of personality, according to the given theory on which a test is based. Most personality tests are known as *self-reports*. With self-reports, the person answering questions about herself, typically in a pencil-and-paper format, provides the information.

Personality tests are usually developed with a particular theory of personality in mind. A test may measure id, ego, or superego issues, for example, if it originates from a Freudian view of personality development.

Getting down with MMPI-2

Perhaps the most widely used personality test in the United States is the MMPI-2, The Minnesota Multiphasic Personality Inventory, 2nd Edition. Almost all American psychologists are trained to use the MMPI-2, which is considered to be a very reliable and valid instrument. A patient's results from a MMPI-2 test provide rich information about the presence of psychopathology and level of severity, if present. The test's results also reveal information about the emotional, behavioral, and social functioning of the test taker. A lot of psychologists use the MMPI-2 as a way to check the accuracy of their observations and diagnoses.

The MMPI-2 test consists of 567 individual items and produces a score on nine clinical categories or scales. If a score is over a specific cutoff, it usually gets the attention of the psychologist administering the test. Psychologists consider such scores to be of clinical significance. The MMPI-2 covers a wide variety of areas, including depression, physical complaints, anger, social contact, anxiety, and energy level.

Projecting to the deep stuff

Projective personality tests are a unique breed of test. When most people think of psychological testing, these kinds of tests come readily to mind. The stereotype involves sitting across from a psychologist, looking at a card with smeared ink or a picture of somebody doing something on it, and answering questions like "What do you see here?"

(You can take a free, mock personality test at www.dummies.com/extras/psychology.)

Projective personality tests are unique because they're based on something called the *projective hypothesis,* which states that when presented with ambiguous stimuli, people will project, and thus reveal, parts of themselves and their psychological functioning that they may not reveal if asked directly. It's not like these tests are trying to trick people, though. The idea is that a lot of folks can't exactly put words to or describe what's going on mentally and emotionally because of psychological defense mechanisms. Some people are not conscious of their feelings. Projective tests are designed to get past the defenses and penetrate the deep recesses of the psyche.

Perhaps the most popular projective personality test and maybe even the most popular psychological test of all time is the Rorschach Inkblot Test (RIT). The RIT consists of ten cards, each with its own standard inkblot figure. None of these inkblots are a picture or representation of anything. They were created by simply pouring ink onto a sheet of paper and folding it in half. The only meaning and structure the cards have are provided by the projections of the test taker himself.

Intelligence testing

Intelligence tests may be the most frequently administered type of psychological test. They measure a broad range of intellectual and cognitive abilities and often provide a general measure of intelligence, which is sometimes called an *IQ* — intelligence quotient.

Intelligence tests are used in a wide variety of settings and applications. They can be used for diagnostic purposes to identify disabilities and cognitive disorders. They're commonly used in academic and school settings. Intelligence tests have been around since the beginning of psychology as an established science, dating back to the work of Wilhelm Wundt in the early 20th century.

The most commonly used tests of intelligence are the Wechsler Adult Intelligence Scale, 4th Edition, (WAIS-IV) for adults and the Wechsler Intelligence Scale for Children, 4th Edition, (WISC-IV) for children. Each of these tests contains several subtests designed to measure specific aspects of intelligence such as attention, general knowledge, visual organization, and comprehension. Both tests provide individual scores for each subtest and an overall score representing overall intelligence. (You can take a free, mock intelligence test at www.dummies.com/extras/psychology.)

Neuropsychological and cognitive testing

Although not a new field, tests of neuropsychological functioning and cognitive ability, related specifically to brain functioning, are rapidly becoming a standard part of a psychologist's testing toolset. Neuropsychological tests have traditionally been used to augment neurological exams and brain imaging techniques (such as MRIs, CT scans, and PET scans) but they're being used more widely now in psychoeducational testing and other clinical testing situations.

The technology of scanning techniques picks up on the presence of brain damage, but neuropsychological tests serve as a more precise measure of the actual functional impairments an individual may suffer from. Scans say, "Yep, there's damage!" Neuropsychological tests say, ". . . and here's the cognitive problem related to it."

Neuropsychological testing is used in hospitals, clinics, private practices, and other places where psychologists work with patients who are suspected of neuropsychological impairment. People suffering head trauma, developmental disorder, or other insults to the brain may need a thorough neuropsychological examination.

A popular neuropsychological test is actually not a test at all but a collection of tests called a *test battery.* The Halstead-Reitan Neuropsychological Test Battery includes numerous tests that measure neuropsychological constructs such as memory, attention and concentration, language ability, motor skills, auditory skill, and planning. The battery also includes an MMPI-2 and WAIS-IV test. Completing the battery requires several hours, and it's never done in one sitting, so going through a neuropsychological evaluation can take several weeks and be costly. However, when conducted by a competent professional, the testing can yield a tremendous amount of helpful information.

Many neuropsychological instruments are available; some are comprehensive, like the Halstead-Reitan, and some are designed to measure a specific function such as language or attention. Whether a neuropsychological evaluation is conducted using a comprehensive instrument or a collection of individual instruments to create a profile of neuropsychological strengths and weaknesses, the following areas of neuropsychological functioning are typically assessed:

✔ **Executive Functions:** Focusing, planning, organizing, monitoring, inhibiting, and self-regulating

✔ **Communication and Language:** Perceiving, receiving, and expressing self with language and nonverbal communication

✔ **Memory:** Auditory memory, visual memory, working memory, and long-term memory

✔ **Sensormotor Functions:** Sensory and motor functions, including hearing, touch, smell, and fine and gross muscle movements

✔ **Visual-Spatial Functions:** Visual perception, visual motor coordination, visual scanning, and perceptual reasoning.

✔ **Speed and Efficiency:** How fast and how efficient thinking is

Keeping Them Honest

An important tip that a psychologist doesn't typically find out about in graduate school is that not everybody coming in for an evaluation or assessment is honest. What? No way! Hard to believe, maybe, but it's true. Unfortunately, some people who seek a psychological assessment and evaluation, or have been ordered to get it, engage in what psychologists call dissimulation and malingering.

Dissimulation in assessment occurs when a client conceals, distorts, and alters his true abilities, concerns, and other characteristics for various motives. Dissimulation is deception. Within the assessment context, a person may dissimulate by concealing or distorting some deficit or disorder by "faking good" or "faking bad." *Malingering* is a "faking bad" process in which a person deliberately feigns, fakes, or exaggerates symptoms or deficits.

Why would someone want to "fake good" when getting a psychological assessment or evaluation? This most often occurs when the results of the psychological assessment are being used for some sort of selection or screening process such as employment, background check, parenting evaluation in a divorce proceeding, or risk assessment.

When I worked in forensics (see the free online article "Exploring Human Differences: Culture, Gender, and Sexuality" at www.dummies.com/extras/psychology for details on forensic psychology), one of the duties I performed was to assess the violence risk of prison inmates convicted of serious violent crimes who were approaching a parole evaluation. My job was to estimate how likely it was that an individual would commit more violent crimes or offenses if freed. My evaluation played a big part in whether an inmate was granted parole, so these people had plenty of incentive to present themselves as a low risk and "fake good."

On the other side, why would anybody want to make herself seem to be mentally ill? Plenty of reasons exist for presenting such a picture, but most often it's for money. A common "faking bad" scenario is when a person tries to demonstrate an inability to hold down a job and therefore qualify for compensation without working (such as Social Security benefits) during an employment disability evaluation.

It's not all just about money, though. When someone's arrested and accused of a crime, she can sometimes get away with a lighter punishment — or even be found not guilty — if a mental disorder is to blame. This is a gamble that some accused people are willing to make, and "faking bad" is the road to take.

The bad news for the dissimulators and malingerers out there is that psychologists have tools, methods, and specialized techniques of evaluation and assessment that are specifically designed to sniff out deception, poor effort, exaggeration, and dishonesty. Many test instruments themselves have built-in components and scales to measure dishonesty factors. Special interview techniques and lines of questioning can help with this as well. In fact, in the business of forensic assessment, there is good money to be made on being an expert in picking out the fakers, and these professionals pride themselves on being able to detect deception.

Chapter 15

Getting Comfy on the Couch

. . . .

. . . .

1've often wondered how many therapists' kids invite their parent to speak at career day at their school. "My mom is a therapist. She helps people, I think. She sits around with people, and they talk about their problems. Sometimes they cry, and sometimes they get mad." It's true that some careers seem easier to describe than others. A lot of people are familiar with the concept of *psychotherapy,* or just *therapy,* even though they may have a difficult time describing exactly what psychotherapy is.

It seems like there are hundreds of definitions for psychotherapy. Lewis Wolberg, a prominent psychoanalyst from New York, defined psychotherapy as a form of treatment for emotional problems in which a trained professional establishes a relationship with a patient with the objective of relieving or removing symptoms, changing disturbed patterns of behavior, and promoting healthy personality development. The symptoms addressed are assumed to be psychological in nature.

J. B. Rotter of the University of Connecticut gives another good definition: "Psychotherapy . . . is planned activity of the psychologist, the purpose of which is to accomplish changes in the individual that make his life adjustment potentially happier, more constructive, or both." I think a good conversation with friends over a pizza can promote a happier life, so what's all the fuss about? Psychotherapy is more than just a conversation between two people; it's a professional relationship in which one of the participants is an acknowledged healer, helper, or expert in psychological, interpersonal, or behavioral problems.

Help comes in many forms, and psychologists haven't cornered the market in helping people wade through the psychological mess of life. All kinds of people, places, and things can be therapeutic, heal, or enhance one's sense of well-being. Marriage, music, literature, great works of art, love, religion, a good movie, the birth of a child, and a beautiful sunset can all be therapeutic or healing. But psychotherapy is a unique activity that's specifically designed to be therapeutic or curative for psychological problems.

In this chapter, I describe specific forms of psychotherapy. Each type of therapy has its own goals, although all of them have a lot in common, and each of them emphasizes specific psychological issues such as emotions, thoughts, or behaviors. Here, I explore the best-known form of psychotherapy: *psychoanalysis.*

Finding Out What's Really Going On

Psychoanalysis is a type of psychotherapy that's been around for over a century. Different variations of psychoanalysis exist, but the basic form, *classic psychoanalysis,* was introduced by Sigmund Freud in 1896, and further developed by numerous others, including Otto Fenichel, Anna Freud, Melanie Klein, Heinz Kohut, Otto Kernberg, and others.

Psychological problems, including emotional, behavioral, and cognitive difficulties, are the general focus of psychotherapy. Finding a theory to explain a client's or patient's psychological problems is a critical component of psychotherapy. From that, a psychologist can formulate and implement therapeutic techniques and treatments. Similarly, psychoanalysis offers a unique view of problems and potential solutions.

Psychoanalysis is based on a comprehensive set of theories and ideas that center on psychological and personality development, personality structure, the structure of the mind, and relationship development (see Chapter 9 for more about psychoanalysis). As a system of thought, psychoanalysis gives rise to psychoanalytic explanations of psychological problems and how to treat them.

Psychological problems manifest as *symptoms,* which are defined as signs or indicators of a disease or disorder. According to psychoanalysis, when people have problematic reactions to events in their lives, symptoms emerge that indicate the presence of an internal and unconscious conflict. Stress can lead to symptoms as events trigger unresolved conflicts from a person's early development or childhood; certain events can also stimulate the use of *defense mechanisms,* or ways of coping that can also lead to problems.

Consider the following example. Robert recently suffered an injury to his back and, as a result, has been in excruciating pain, can barely move, and is pretty much confined to his room or home. He's had to rely heavily on his wife for virtually everything, including dressing, bathing, and even using the toilet. Eventually the issue is resolved and Robert gets back on his feet again. But, he begins to act differently, displaying mood swings, withdrawing socially, and, most shockingly, accusing his wife of having an affair. Robert's symptoms appear to be manifesting as abnormal mood, social difficulties, and paranoid thinking (flip to Chapter 13 for more on abnormal psychology).

Psychoanalysts never take a symptom at face value. Below the surface of Robert's everyday thoughts, feelings, and actions boils a chaotic brew of inner conflict. Robert's everyday stressors are observable; anyone can see he's been in pain and more dependent on his wife than ever before. But psychoanalysts look below the surface of his everyday thoughts, feelings, actions, and awareness for the internal, unconscious, and deeply rooted sources of his symptoms.

A neat thing about professional therapists is that they already have some ideas about what's going on before you even come to their office. They get out a little crystal ball and tarot cards and predict that a man with Robert's problems is going to walk through the door at any minute. No, that's a psychic, not a psychotherapist. Therapists don't usually have a crystal ball, but they do have a theoretical system that explains why people develop psychological problems and where their inner conflicts come from.

Problems like those Robert was experiencing (pain and dependency) happen. When strained, here are some symptoms that can emerge:

- **Regression:** Freud stated that people are vulnerable to regression when under stress (such as the stress caused by pain and dependency), a psychological return to an earlier stage of development. Certain events can trigger unconscious impulses and memories that you've forgotten or are completely unaware of. When this happens, you may be at risk for regressing. When you regress, you act younger, often childish. Temper tantrums, ignoring reality, and living in a fantasy world are examples of regression. Do you stick your fingers in your ears and repeat, "La la la la la la" so you can't hear someone talk? Regression!

- **Impulse control:** When your impulses and desires to seek pleasure without regard for reality are stirred, you may use defense mechanisms to keep them from getting out of control. You don't want all those powerful and primitive impulses overpowering your more mature and reality-based personality. These impulses can boil to the top, either because of stress or because you haven't been able to successfully deny their power. That's when defenses kick in and psychological symptoms can emerge. These symptoms can be the product of specific defenses working against impulses, including the following common defense mechanisms:

  - **Repression:** keeping impulses and desires out of your awareness so you don't act on them and they don't destroy your life. Repression requires a great deal of mental energy.

- **Hypochondriasis:** the preoccupation with having a serious disease. George Vaillant, an American psychiatrist at Harvard, proposed that hypochondriasis provides people with an opportunity to complain and then reject other's efforts to help. Hypochondriasis allows an individual to feel misunderstood because no one can find anything wrong with the person and, therefore, cannot help him. Everyone else seems like they're being insensitive and uncaring about the individual's needs.

- **Acting out:** enacting or behaving with the direct expression of an unconscious impulse or desire without having to consciously acknowledge feeling a particular way.

Doing Analysis

What if psychoanalysis was a sport, and it had its own Monday night television show? Just for fun, imagine that it was more popular than Monday-night football. I hope I didn't lose any of you football fans; stay with me. "Welcome to Monday Night on the Couch. I'm Dr. Clearview, and with me is my partner, Phil Good. Tonight we bring you a session of the psychoanalysis of John Smith. If you remember, Phil, Mr. Smith felt pretty bad when he left his last session with the Dr. Freud. . . ."

What would these announcers possibly have to commentate on? You may be surprised. There's a lot going on in therapy. In fact, one of the ways that therapists learn how to do therapy is by watching others do it and then dissecting what they see. The therapists-in-training watch therapy training videos or observe live therapy from other rooms.

Would you know psychoanalysis if you saw it? It may help to think about psychoanalysis from these four different perspectives:

- ✔ The logistics
- ✔ What the patient does
- ✔ What the analyst does
- ✔ The overall process of the analysis

I dig into each of these perspectives in this section.

Taking a load off

No discussion of psychoanalysis would be complete without discussing the *couch*. The image of a patient lying on the couch is one of the most popular of psychoanalysis. In this well-known scene, the analyst sits upright in a chair, out of the patient's line of sight, for technical reasons related to the task and goals of the therapy itself. The truth is that psychoanalysis does not need to take place on a couch; but, to be truly "classic," a couch is great.

Getting practical

The logistics of psychoanalysis are easy. The patient sets up an appointment, goes to the office, and meets the analyst. The two talk about the fees and schedule. Typically, classic psychoanalysis involves anywhere from four to six sessions of therapy each week, but most people can't afford this many sessions. Therefore, many psychoanalysts have learned to perform a scaled-down version with only one to two sessions per week. Sessions last about 50 minutes in both classic and the shorter version of psychoanalysis. After getting acquainted, the patient and analyst get to work.

The patient talks; the analyst listens and comments. A patient is encouraged to discuss anything that comes to mind and not to filter or edit what comes out. The analyst lets him ramble a bit but periodically emphasizes something the patient says in order to increase awareness of a topic or trend.

The typical length of classic psychoanalysis is five years or so. Yet most people don't stick with it for that long because a variant of truly classic psychoanalysis has emerged to serve many people. I describe this variant approach in the section "Transferring to the New School" later in this chapter.

Keeping an eye on the ball

The process of psychoanalysis has several goals:

- ✔ To further the development and maturation of personality

- ✔ To help the patient become fully aware of her inner conflicts and how these conflicts contribute to her difficulties

- ✔ To help the patient become aware of how her coping mechanisms (known as *defenses* in psychoanalysis) operate and how she distorts reality, including relationships

✔ To help the patient experience a more meaningful life overall

✔ To help the patient develop more mature defenses

✔ To help the patient develop healthier ways and means to express her impulses and desires

All of these goals have something in common — enhanced *awareness.* If nothing else, psychoanalysis is an exercise in increasing one's awareness. Awareness sits at the core of the analytic process, and it's one of the curative aspects of psychoanalysis. Change happens by uncovering unconscious conflicts so people can consciously address and work on their issues. After all, if you don't know what the problem is, you can't fix it.

Being (the) patient

Remember that psychotherapy, in general, and psychoanalysis, in particular, are defined by professional relationships that function toward specific goals. The roles of each participant in this relationship are specified to achieve the desired goal of improved well-being. In other words, psychoanalysis calls for certain ways of behaving. But it's not as strict as I may make it sound.

It may seem obvious, but the psychologist expects the patient to come to appointments on time and pay his bills. These practices are important for maintaining the professionalism of the relationship; it isn't just two good friends chatting about life.

Expectations need to be appropriate as well. Some patients enter therapy with a "fix me" attitude or a "give me all the answers" demand — as if just showing up and talking about some problems is enough to achieve change. Let me tell you: That's not going to get the job done. The amount of work that goes into being a patient is often wildly underestimated. Patients sometimes leave therapy early in the process because things get too difficult or they're required to put in what they perceive to be too much effort.

It's not like a psychoanalyst is going to ask you to drop and give her 50 push-ups in the middle of the session. But a patient needs to be ready to think critically about the things being discussed in the analysis. Sydney Pulver, clinical professor of psychiatry at the University of Pennsylvania School of Medicine, provides a good summary of common expectations that psychologists have of patients:

✔ Notice how unconscious material arises during the session.

✔ Be willing to experience strong emotions and face negative memories.

✔ Focus on understanding the process of how the relationship between the therapist and patient produces change.

There should be a disclaimer at the beginning of all therapy stating that the therapy may not be all that fun, and it may even be downright painful. No pain, no gain, I guess.

Perhaps the most important task that a patient in psychoanalysis is asked to do is *free association.* As the analysis begins, the therapist instructs the patient to lie on the couch and begin talking about anything and everything that comes to mind — no matter how absurd, silly, or embarrassing it may be. The idea is to get in touch with unconscious material by not editing what one thinks about and verbalizes. This process can be pretty difficult; it sometimes takes a while to get the hang of it. The only rule is to talk about whatever comes to mind, which provides the patient and the analyst access to hidden conflicts and impulses.

Sometimes it's hard to remember all the things discussed in therapy. Take a pen and some paper! A lot of good information comes up during therapy, and it's a shame to forget it. Write down important points and topics. Take notes. This can help maintain the gains outside of the therapy room.

Getting down to analyzing

So let me get this straight: If I'm a patient, I'm going to pay a psychoanalyst, and I'm the one who has to put out all kinds of effort. What's the sense in that? I'm sure military recruits think the same thing when they first get to boot camp and have that tough-nosed drill instructor in their face, putting them down and challenging their commitment. The drill instructors will tell you that it's in the recruits' best interests. And, yep, that's the gist of therapy, too. Psychoanalysis is a far cry from boot camp, but patients are asked to believe that it's all in their best interest to work hard and feel the burn, so to speak. Fortunately, analysts participate heavily in the process. Patients and analysts both have some tough duties in therapy.

Here are some expectations that patients have of the analyst:

✔ Be empathic and communicate a certain level of care for the patient, a professional level of concern.

✔ Be aware of her own inner conflicts. That way, the focus in the therapy session is on the patient's problems and not on the analyst's difficulties. If the analyst's problems start to dominate the session, the analyst should seek immediate consultation with her own therapist, a colleague, or a supervisor.

✔ Remain objective and morally neutral with regard to the patient's problems. Classic psychoanalysts used to be expected to be a "blank screen" and to introduce as little of their own personalities as possible into the process. That way, whatever the patient free-associates about is related to the patient's inner conflicts and not a reaction to the actual person of the analyst. This is a "pure" approach; most analysts today do not adhere absolutely to this. It's okay to be a little more interactive with the patient in order to facilitate change and have a more personal connection than a blank screen.

✔ Work respectfully with the patient's anxiety, not overwhelming or overstimulating him. When a patient comes to therapy, he may be experiencing a great deal of fear about what's going to happen during the sessions. The analyst shouldn't push the patient too hard or too fast to talk about things that he may not be ready to talk about. There's a reason that people are not aware of their inner conflicts, and a good analyst respects this, pacing her comments accordingly.

A good analyst learns to listen with what T. Reik, in 1948, called a "third ear" to find the unconscious conflict within each statement of the patient. An analyst can also observe unconscious conflict in the material of dreams, jokes, and slips of the tongue. The analyst is supposed to notice these signs of unconscious conflict and make appropriate comments when the timing is right. Analysts attempt to understand what is going on at all three levels of the patient's consciousness: the unconscious, preconscious, and conscious. For more on levels of consciousness, see Chapter 4.

What the analyst actually chooses to comment on and when he makes comments depend on the particular conflicts of the patient. The analyst makes *interpretations,* explanations that add to patients' knowledge and awareness about themselves and the connections between their inner conflicts and current problems. Interpretation is the primary tool in the analyst's toolbox. Many psychoanalysts consider interpretation to be synonymous with psychoanalysis itself because it's their best means for increasing a patient's awareness.

Analysts don't just interpret any little thing in therapy; it could get pretty ridiculous. Imagine someone saying to a patient, "So, I noticed that you folded the tissue I gave you into fourths and not thirds. . . ." An analyst interprets and highlights a patient's unconscious material that's just below the surface of consciousness to push the patient toward awareness, letting her arrive at the insight on her "own," with a bit of gentle guidance. It's not as fun if the analyst gives you all the answers!

Sydney Pulver identifies at least five types of interpretation:

✔ **Resistance interpretations:** Pointing out the things the patient is doing to resist the process of analysis and change

✔ **Transference interpretations:** Pointing out when the patient relates to the analyst in a way that's similar to earlier relationships the patient has had

✔ **Extra-transference interpretations:** Pointing out when the patient is relating to other people in a way that's similar to the patient's earlier relationships

✔ **Reconstructions:** Pointing out the patient's thoughts, emotions, and behaviors that may "fill in" incomplete memories the patient may have

✔ **Character interpretations:** Pointing out maladaptive behavior that seems to be a core aspect of the patient's personality

Seeing the overall process

After the logistics are negotiated, the patient and analyst know their roles, and the therapist prepares an appropriate approach, therapy begins. In an ideal world, psychoanalytic therapy progresses through a series of specific stages:

✔ Resistance

✔ Transference

✔ Working through

✔ Termination

Beginning with resistance

In the initial stage of therapy, the analyst gathers information regarding the patient's history, emphasizing relationships and family interactions during childhood. The patient goes through the process of discussing his problems with the analyst, a task that may seem easier than it actually is.

As a patient continues to talk and free-associate, conflicts begin to emerge. The analyst listens for the presence of deeper conflicts. The more the patient's conflicts begin to bubble to the surface, the harder the patient usually works to keep them out of awareness and defend himself from the disturbing content. This psychological defense is accomplished, in part, by a process known as *resistance* — a form of noncompliance with the psycho-analytic process of increasing awareness and of making the unconscious conscious. All patients resist at least a little, some more than others, depending on how defensive they are. The more threatening the unconscious material, the stronger the resistance.

Resistance behavior can be as simple as missing appointments in order to avoid discussing one's problems or as complicated as developing new symptoms to keep the analyst away from the deeper material. Resistance is usually the first obstacle to the analytic cure. An analyst can count on a patient's resistance because the whole theory of psychoanalysis hinges upon the idea that people's problems center on their unwillingness to fully address their issues. Through the process of interpretation and commenting on the resistance, a therapist helps a patient move past resistance.

Here's how it may go: The analyst gently attempts to draw the patient's attention to the idea that his habit of showing up late may relate to a deeper, unconscious reason for his action. Is he avoiding something in therapy? This can be a turning point in the analysis, depending on how the patient responds to the question:

- He may get defensive and insist that the analyst is fishing or jumping to conclusions.
- He may admit to the attempt at avoidance.
- He may get angry with the therapist and accuse her of being too nit-picky.

No matter how the patient responds, the analyst's comments are an attempt to get at something deeper.

As analysis progresses and the patient's resistance fades, the patient begins to settle into the process, more easily free-associating and *regressing* into earlier levels of psychological development. The patient begins to act in ways and speak about things from his earlier life, letting childhood conflicts and impulses emerge more fully in response to the interpretations of the analyst and the setting of the analysis itself. The analyst and patient get deeper into their archaeological dig of the patient's mind, and more and more is revealed.

Developing transference

Sometimes patients get angry when their analyst points out certain things. They may stop talking or accuse the analyst of being overly critical or nit-picky. Why does this happen? After all, isn't it the analyst's job to point out things about the patient if she thinks they may be related to unconscious material? If the patient reacts by accusing the analyst of being overly critical, the reaction may be something slightly more complex than just a simple act of resistance. The patient may be engaging in *transference*.

Transference occurs when a patient begins to relate to the analyst in a way that's reflective of another (typically earlier) relationship. It's a distortion of the real relationship and interaction between the patient and analyst.

Many people have had some experience with the concept of transference. Ever heard the term "baggage"? In today's usage, it commonly refers to bringing relationship problems and issues from previous relationships into new ones. Say you're out on a first date and you run into a co-worker at a restaurant. He stops by the table and says hello. You introduce your date and the co-worker to each other, and then say you'll see the person tomorrow at work. Your date then proceeds to question you about who that person was and whether you've been intimate with him. He generally acts jealous and insecure about your friendly interaction with this person. That's baggage.

It's your first date, so you may be confused about where the jealousy is coming from. Luckily for your date, you've just read *Psychology For Dummies* and understand that his behavior is probably a type of transference from a previous relationship. But you're on a date, not in a therapy session, so you make a mental note to lose this person's phone number — stat!

When a patient starts acting toward an analyst in a similar way, the analyst interprets the behavior as representing a kind of reenactment of some other relationship. The analyst points out the distortion, helping the patient become aware of when it happens and how it influences the patient's perceptions of people. This process is intended to help patients become fully aware of their distortions, how they relate to people based not on the people themselves but on their own baggage.

Working through

Transference happens over and over again; each time, the analyst interprets it with the goal of increased patient awareness. The analyst and patient work on each episode of transference in a stage of therapy known as *working through*. Old conflicts are brought to light and the patient addresses them, learning how to recognize these incidents and relate to the analyst in a more realistic and undistorted way. Transference does not interfere with the patient-analyst relationship, and the patient is well on the way toward ending his analysis by this stage of therapy.

Terminating treatment

As a patient's distortions diminish, awareness increases, and symptoms subside, the therapist and patient decide on a date for terminating therapy. This involves another layer of working through that focuses on addressing thoughts, feelings, and distortions related to separation in relationships. Saying goodbye is hard for some people, but it can be even harder for others. If a patient has significant conflict with being separated from his parents or other important relationships, there may be more resistance, transference, and working through to be done before the analysis can finally end.

Transferring to the New School

So far, this chapter has focused on classic psychoanalysis. And although the basic process and mechanisms remain at the core of conducting psychoanalytic therapy, numerous revisions and adaptations have been made to the classic form. The main difference between the newer forms of psychoanalytic therapy and its classic predecessor is the emphasis on the relationship and interpretation of transference.

Psychoanalyst Harry Stack-Sullivan introduced an *interpersonal* focus to psychoanalysis in the 1920s that emphasized the real relationship dynamics between patient and analyst. Freud emphasized what was going on inside the patient's deep unconscious, but the interpersonally oriented analysts instead began to focus on what happens in the relationship. These psychologists interpreted incidents of transference as deriving from the interaction — not solely from within the patient. That is, the analyst may actually act in certain ways that remind the patient of earlier, conflicted relationships, thus setting the wheels of transference in motion.

The key for the newer psychoanalysts is the relationship between the therapist and the analyst and how the patient interacts with others in relationships — reenacting earlier conflicts in their styles of relating to others. Psychoanalyst Franz Alexander (1891–1964), a professor of psychoanalysis at the University of Chicago, introduced the concept of the *corrective emotional experience* to depict a situation in which the analyst relates to the patient in a manner that the patient did not experience growing up, helping the patient to overcome his developmental impasse. If a patient's conflicts are assumed to be the consequence of poor parenting, the analyst's job is to, in a sense, re-parent the patient. Therapy, then, becomes a new type of relationship — one that the patient has never had and that can help him relate to people in a healthier and more mature manner.

Shorter versions of psychoanalytic therapy, known as *brief dynamic therapies,* also exist. This abbreviated process is much more active, and the therapist attempts to push the process along by being more targeted. The therapist and patient focus on highly specific goals related to a certain interpersonal problem, and thereby change the patient's problematic circumstances. Instead of talking about relationships in general, the therapist and patient target a specific relationship such as spouse to spouse or parent to child.

Are we there yet?

Does psychoanalysis actually work? Do people get better, or do they end up seeing their therapist indefinitely? A large study conducted by *Consumer Reports* in 1996 found that people who engage in any form of psychotherapy report feeling generally better as a result, regardless of the type of therapy. (This of course is a relatively old study but is considered by many researchers to be one of the most extensive on this topic and is still referenced to this day.) But psychoanalysis is typically a long form of therapy, and today, many people don't have the time or the money to invest in such a long and expensive enterprise. Some studies show that people do get better with psychoanalysis when compared to people who get no help at all.

Chapter 16

Changing Behavior, Changing Thinking

There are few things in life that I hate more than shopping for a car. If I'm looking for a blue two-door, compact pickup, the salespeople show me a white four-door model. If I want a sports car with front-wheel drive, they show me the latest, greatest, four-wheel-drive sports utility vehicle. I walk onto the lot thinking I know what I want, but somehow I leave thinking that I want something different.

Now imagine a similar experience in the context of going to a therapist. Mr. Ramirez is having marital problems, and one of his children is acting up at school. He knows that he wants help with his marriage and his child. But, when Mr. Ramirez meets with the therapist, something strange happens. He wants to talk about his marriage, and the therapist wants to talk about his childhood. He wants to talk about his kid, and the therapist wants to talk about his dreams. This guy may walk away from the encounter with "car-shopping disorientation disorder," not knowing which way is up and what he really came to therapy for.

Jay Haley criticized therapy approaches that seem to ignore a patient's real concerns and insist that her real problem is something else that's related to some underlying or hidden issue waiting to be uncovered and analyzed. Psychoanalysts, for example, may be criticized as seeing the unconscious as the cause of any problem, even if it's fear of flying. "The power of the airplane and your fear of flying represent your father and an unresolved Oedipal complex." Say what? Do I really need seven years of psychoanalytic therapy to get over my fear of flying? I'd rather take the bus.

This chapter introduces two general classes of therapy that can probably pass the "Haley test." *Behavior therapy* and *cognitive therapy* and combined iterations of the two are very widely used forms of therapy that have a simpler (but not simplistic) view of psychological problems. Behavior therapy focuses on behavior. Pretty simple, huh? So, if Mr. Ramirez went to a behavior therapist, the focus would be on the behaviors occurring within his marriage. Cognitive therapy focuses on thoughts, so a cognitive therapist would focus on the thoughts that Mr. Ramirez is having about his marriage and his kid. These approaches take a simpler and less mysterious approach to patients' difficulties than psychoanalysis, for example.

Weeding Out Bad Behavior with Behavior Therapy

Behavior therapy emphasizes the current conditions that maintain a behavior, the conditions that keep it going. This form of therapy focuses on the problem, not on the person. A psychology professor who I once had, Elizabeth Klonoff, likened behavior therapy to a weed-pulling process. She stated that psychoanalysts attempt to pull the weed up by its roots so that it'll never come back, but behavior therapists pluck the weed from the top, and if it grows back, they pluck it again. Of course, this makes behavior therapy sound more inefficient than it actually is. The idea is that in behavior therapy the developmental or childhood origins of a problem are not necessarily as important as the conditions that keep it going. In that sense, if you change the maintaining conditions of a behavior, then you have in essence "uprooted it," as long as those conditions don't recur. For example, who cares how you started smoking? The important part is the factors that keep you smoking.

Basing therapy on learning theories

All behavior is learned, whether it's healthy or abnormal. Behavior therapy is based on the learning theories of Ivan Pavlov's classical conditioning, B. F. Skinner's operant conditioning, and Albert Bandura's social learning theory. Here's how these theories understand learning (see Chapter 9 for details):

- ✔ In the classical-conditioning sense, *learning* refers to associations formed between events or actions.

- ✔ In the operant-conditioning sense, *learning* refers to the process of increasing the likelihood of a behavior occurring or not occurring based on its consequences.

- ✔ In the social learning theory sense, *learning* refers to discovering things by watching other people.

These days, it's pretty hard to argue that smoking is not bad for a person's health. I think most people now accept the unhealthy aspects of smoking as fact, but some just choose to ignore this information. Smoking is a good example of an unhealthy behavior that is learned. Cigarette advertisements associate sexy people and having fun with smoking (classical conditioning). Nicotine gives a pleasurable, stimulating sensation (operant conditioning). Teenagers sometimes learn to smoke by watching their parents, older siblings, or peers smoke (social leaning theory).

Classical conditioning and behavior therapy

Behavior therapy treats abnormal behavior as learned behavior, and anything that's been learned can be unlearned — theoretically anyway (see Chapter 13 for info on abnormal behavior). A key feature of behavior therapy is the notion that environmental conditions and circumstances can be explored and manipulated to change a person's behavior without having to dig around their mind or psyche and evoke psychological or mental explanations for their issues.

A classic case cited by proponents of behavior therapy to support this approach is the case of *Little Hans*. Little Hans was a boy who was deathly afraid of horses. A lot of children like horses, so his fear seemed at least a little strange. Why was Hans afraid of horses? According to psychoanalysis a mental or psychological explanation was that Hans's fear of horses was a displaced fear of his powerful father. The behaviorists had a simpler explanation.

Hans had recently witnessed a number of extremely frightening events involving horses. On one occasion, he saw a horse die in a carting accident. This event made Hans very upset, and it scared him. The behaviorists proposed that the fear Hans developed from watching the horse die and from witnessing the other frightening, horse-related events had become classically conditioned to horses. He had associated fear with horses.

Remember how classical conditioning works? Here's a little summary, but check out Chapter 8 for details.

Unconditioned Stimulus (Accident)→Unconditioned Response (Fear)

Conditioned Stimulus (Horse) + Unconditioned Stimulus (Accident)→Unconditioned Response (Fear)

Conditioned Stimulus (Horse)→Conditioned Response (Fear)

What do you get? Fear of horses à la classical conditioning. The beauty of this explanation comes from its implications for treating Little Hans's horse phobia. According to behavior therapists, if he learned to be afraid of horses, he could learn how not to be afraid of horses. This type of result can be accomplished with a behavior therapy technique called *systematic desensitization,* which I cover in the "Exposure-based therapies" section later in this chapter.

Operant conditioning and behavior therapy

What about operant conditioning? What role does it play in behavior therapy? Take a look at anger, for example. If I get my way every time I get angry, I'm being positively reinforced for that behavior; therefore, I'm more likely to keep using anger in this way. This is a common explanation for a child's behavior problems. If a child behaves in a manner that is not acceptable, her parents may be inadvertently reinforcing that behavior by providing attention to her that they may not provide in any other way.

An example of a negatively reinforced behavior is seen when an individual gives in to peer pressure. The ridicule a teenager endures for not going along with the crowd can be hurtful. He may give in to peer pressure just to put a stop to the ridicule (the removal of a painful stimulus).

Having a difficult time being assertive is a great example of a behavior, or the lack of that behavior, that is maintained through punishment. If I live in a home where I'm laughed at or otherwise punished for being assertive and speaking my mind, I'm far less likely to be assertive in other situations. I've been punished for being assertive. Lacking assertiveness can be a serious problem, and it often leads to feelings of victimization and resentfulness.

Behavior that is reinforced is more likely to happen again and again. If my angry outbursts for a sandwich get rewarded with a sandwich then I'm just going to keep on yelling. If my child's tear-ridden tantrums get him out of homework then I can expect a tantrum each time the books get cracked. If I try to talk about my feelings with my parents and they ignore me, I'm going to keep those feelings to myself. If I'm punished for speaking my mind, then I'll keep those thoughts to myself. Simply put, you get behavior that you reward; you don't get behavior you don't reward (or punish).

Social learning theory and behavior therapy

Humans learn by watching other people. A common problem in marriages involves fighting over money. This is sometimes a consequence of watching our parents fight over money, engaging in nonproductive, emotionally hurtful, and frustrating exchanges over who's to blame for spending too much or not earning enough, for example. *Modeling* is a form of behavior therapy that is used to teach people new behaviors by showing them how to behave in a healthier way. I may ask that the husband begin a conversation with me about money and I can model, or show, the couple how to discuss money in a healthier manner. This only works, however, if the therapist knows how to model healthy behavior!

Behavior therapy, behavior modification, and applied behavior analysis

Broadly speaking, therapy conducted using the principles of classical and/or operant conditioning without particular concern for psychological or mental explanations is considered *behavior therapy*. Behavior therapy has also been called *behavior modification (B-Mod)* and is also known as *applied behavior analysis (ABA)*. In many ways B-Mod and ABA are the same exact thing, therapeutic interventions that alter behavior through the application of the principles of classical and operant conditioning.

Honestly, not being a historian or sociologist, I am not exactly sure how the concepts of B-Mod and ABA became known as they did in their separate forms. As both an undergraduate and graduate student in California, I was always taught B-Mod but later on in my career I was exposed to ABA. As far as I can tell, different psychologists, researchers, and therapists in different parts of the country at different times in the 20th century developed different names for essentially the same therapy approach. Keep in mind that hard-core practitioners of ABA may suggest that ABA is a more comprehensive approach to behavior change that includes a specific set of data collection techniques, data recording, and applications beyond clinical psychology such as employee behavior in the workplace. Another thing that may, in fact, set ABA apart is that at its outset, it was specifically concerned with problem behavior such as aggression and self-injurious behavior that you often see in individuals who suffer from developmental disabilities, intellectual disability, or autism (for more on autism see Chapter 13.) Ultimately, however, I believe it really boils down to the old, "You say "to-*mah*-to," I say "to-*may*-to." So, you say ABA, I say B-Mod.

Assessing the problem

The simplicity of the behavioral approach to psychological problems is made possible with an equally simplified (but not easy!) set of practices. Behavior therapists put a lot of emphasis on the scientific method and its focus on observable changes and measurement. The therapy techniques and activities are well planned out, highly structured, and systematic. The therapist is viewed less as a holder of some divine truth and more as a collaborative partner in the behavior-change process. The patient is expected to pull his own weight outside of therapy, as well as in the therapy session itself, by completing homework assignments designed to change behavior in the real world and to further the progress made during each session.

In keeping with a systematic and scientifically based approach to psychological disturbance, behavior therapists begin by conducting a thorough assessment of the patient's problem. Here's a simple outline of the basic steps of *behavioral assessment:*

1. **Identify the target behavior.**

   Step one involves taking a thorough look at the problem the patient originally presents to the therapist. Behavior therapists use a special technique called an *ABC analysis* to analyze the initial problem. The ABC analysis is an evaluation of the events that happen before, during, and after a *target behavior* (the patient's problem behavior).

   A. *A* stands for the *antecedents* of a particular behavior, the things or events that happen just prior to the target behavior. A common problem that behavior therapists encounter involves couples that argue excessively, so it serves as a good example. The particular antecedents of interest in the case of such a couple may be the time, place, and surrounding circumstances that immediately precede each argument.

      Time: When each of them gets home from work

      Place: Dinner table

      Circumstances: Talking about each other's day at work

   B. *B* stands for behavior, as in the target behavior. In the case of the bickering couple, the target behavior is the act of arguing, itself.

   C. *C* stands for the *consequences* of the behavior, or the events and general circumstances that occur after and are a direct result of *B*. In the case of the arguing couple, the *Cs* may be that both individuals get mad and stomp off, the man goes out for a drive, or the woman leaves the house to take a long walk.

2. **Identify the present maintaining conditions.**

   Spiegler and Guevremont define the *present maintaining conditions* as those circumstances that contribute to the perpetuation of the behavior. They identify two specific sources:

   • **Environment:** Conditions from the environment include time, setting, reactions from others, and any other external circumstances. This would be the who, what, when, where, and how of our arguing couple.

   • **Patient's own behavior:** The patient's contribution includes his or her thoughts, feelings, and actions. This would be what each partner is thinking, feeling, and doing before, during, and after the arguments.

Exploring functions and outcomes

Functional Analysis of Behavior (FAB) is a more formal version of the behavioral assessment process. FAB (or FBA as some people call it) involves a specific approach to ascertaining the *function* of a particular behavior as it relates to the ultimate outcome it accomplishes. A behavior results in something happening and that something is the driving force behind the behavior. A child throws a tantrum because it works in accomplishing something for that child, maybe escape from the dreaded shopping trip with grandma. So the function of the tantrum is to escape the store.

The following are the most typical functions of behavior identified in an FAB:

✔ **Access to tangible rewards:** Hitting gets me the toy I want.

✔ **Escape or avoidance of aversive stimuli:** Screaming gets me out of doing chores.

✔ **Attention from others:** Calling you names gets you to pay attention to me.

✔ **Automatic reinforcement:** Scratching my skin relieves the itch.

After the patient and therapist figure out the function of the behavior, the therapist can formulate an intervention that may involve helping a person ascertain the desired function in a more appropriate manner, such as talking quietly instead of screaming.

3. **Establish the specific goals of therapy in explicit terms.**

   The original therapy goal may be to stop arguing. However, this description is a little too vague for a behavior therapist's liking. A more precise measure of the target behavior may consist of identifying specific numbers, occurrences, or lengths of time of the arguments. So, instead of the couple simply trying to stop fighting, a more fitting target behavior is to reduce their fighting to once a week.

Trying different techniques

Two of the nice things about behavior therapy for both the patient and the therapist are its clarity and structure. Behavior therapists can use a variety of highly structured treatment techniques to approach their patients' problems. Spiegler and Guevremont identify three classes of behavior therapy techniques: reinforcement-based therapy, decelerating therapy and extinction, and exposure-based therapy.

Reinforcement-based therapy

Reinforcement-based techniques of behavior therapy are based on the principles of operant conditioning, specifically the use of positive reinforcement.

Bribing for basic school skills

I worked with autistic children by using applied behavior analysis, and one of the most challenging aspects of the therapy was finding reinforcers. The treatment consisted of using reinforcement to increase the children's functional behaviors, such as communicating, socializing, playing, and learning basic school skills (recognizing letters, numbers, and colors, for example). The process consisted of teaching the target behaviors and reinforcing the children when they successfully performed them. But if the reinforcers had no reinforcing value, forget it.

Some children liked certain kinds of food or candy, so that's what was used for them. Some liked certain toys or other objects, so those items were used too. If it improved their functioning, it was used. Some days, candy worked; other days it was toys. One child liked it when I pretended to bonk my head on the table, so I used that as a reinforcer. Hey, whatever works, right?

You may be thinking that all of this sounds like bribery. It is in a way. Sure, I bribed the kids to perform the goal behaviors, but think about the alternative. If I didn't use reinforcement, the kids wouldn't have learned these skills that have the power to improve the quality of their lives. I'd choose bribery over neglect any day.

After a thorough behavioral assessment, the therapist and the patient(s) follow these steps when participating in reinforcement-based therapy:

1. **Identify a list of reinforcers to be used in the therapy.**

   This is a crucial process. Anything that's likely to increase the probability of a desired behavior occurring again can be used as a reinforcer.

2. **Determine how and when to administer the reinforcers.**

   Continuous reinforcement is the best way to get a quick jump on changing a behavior. Continuous reinforcement involves the patient receiving reinforcement every time she performs the target behavior. When the patient begins to consistently perform the new behavior, the reinforcement can be *faded* and only given once in a while, even randomly. This is the best way to keep a behavior going.

3. **Begin shaping.**

   Shaping is a procedure in which successful approximations of the target behavior are reinforced in order to *shape,* move, or guide the patient toward the desired target behavior.

If the problem is studying and the target behavior has been identified as studying two hours a night without interruption, the student may be reinforced after studying for increasingly longer intervals leading up to the two-hour mark (20 minutes, then 30 minutes, then one hour, and so on) during the shaping process.

4. **Create a formal contract that outlines all of the agreed-upon features of the treatment plan and clarifies when, how, and where the target behavior is to occur.**

5. **Conduct periodic reassessments throughout treatment to monitor the patient's progress toward the goal.**

Adjustments are made, as necessary, in the reinforcement procedures.

6. **End therapy.**

When the patient achieves the target behavior and maintains it for the desired length of time, therapy ends.

Deceleration and extinction therapies

Never cry wolf — most of us are familiar with this ancient warning. If I yell out for help too many times when I don't need it, I won't get help when I really do need it. But how long does it take for people to realize that I'm full of it? Don't they know that I only keep crying wolf because they keep running to help? Basically, their response reinforces my crying-out behavior. It's all their fault! All they have to do is ignore my pleas and stop running to my aid. That'll get me to stop.

Collect your tokens, win a prize!

One of the more advanced forms of reinforcement-based therapy is the creation of a token economy. A *token economy* is a structured system of reinforcement that uses *tokens,* symbolic reinforcers that represent more tangible reinforcers, to increase the likelihood of a target behavior occurring. The best example of a token is money. Money in and of itself is useless, except maybe for the paper it's printed on. (The paper can start a nice fire or be used as pillow stuffing.) The power of money comes from what it can bring us or what it represents — the ability to purchase tangible goods.

Token economies are often used in situations that require individuals or groups to follow a particular set of instructions or rules. Patients in a psychiatric hospital, for example, are often given points or other tokens for following institutional rules or performing one of their patient-specific target behaviors. In many cases, these tokens can be redeemed once a week at a snack or gift exchange. Some systems use tokens to help patients work toward leaving the hospital on small trips or excursions with the eventual goal of discharge in mind. This form of therapy is an excellent example of shaping.

The process of withholding or eliminating reinforcement, thus eliminating the response, is known as *extinction*. A long time ago, behaviorists figured out that a behavior stops when reinforcement stops.

Spiegler and Guevremont classify treatments that utilize the phenomenon of extinction as *deceleration therapies*. When the reinforcer that maintains a behavior is either withdrawn or withheld, the behavior eventually extinguishes. Deceleration therapy is conducted in much the same way as reinforcement-based therapy: Target behaviors and reinforcing conditions are identified. The main difference between the therapies is that reinforcers are withheld instead of given.

One of the best-known examples of deceleration therapy is the dreaded *time out*. Time out has become one of the most widely used disciplinary techniques by parents. The idea behind time out is that the undesirable target behavior of a child (or anyone for that matter) is being maintained by either the reinforcing social attention the child receives as a result of the behavior or some other reinforcer inherent in the situation itself, such as getting a toy away from another child.

When little Johnny performs the target behavior, he's taken to a designated time-out area, thus removing him from whatever reinforcers are present in the situation. Also, no potential reinforcers should be present in the time-out area that could provide the child with reinforcement while on time out.

Time-out tips

I've heard a lot of parents say that time out doesn't work, but I often wonder if they're actually doing it right. Spiegler and Guevremont point out four conditions that help make time out more successful:

✔ Time-out time periods should be brief (five minutes or less), and the child should know how long the time period will last. A lot of parents leave their children in time out for too long. Younger children only need about one minute of time out for every year of their age — 4 years old: four minutes. Simple.

✔ No reinforcers should be available during the time-out period. Using the playroom as a time-out area is not recommended. That's like suspending a kid who hates school to begin with. Thanks!

✔ Time out should end when the time is up and the child is behaving appropriately. If he or she is still acting up, extend time out for another designated time period.

✔ Time out shouldn't be used by kids as an escape to get out of doing things that they didn't want to do in the first place. It requires some skill to determine when a child is manipulating the use of time out for this purpose. If children attempt to pull this trick, make them do whatever they were trying to avoid when they get out of time out.

Exposure-based therapies

There are several different types of therapy known as *exposure-based therapies* that involve "exposing" a target behavior to new conditions in order to reduce its occurrence. *Exposure* is another word for reassociating or relearning a target behavior with another behavior that results in the cessation of the target behavior.

Have you ever tried to smoke a cigarette while in the shower? It's pretty hard to do. I once worked with a guy who managed to come up with a way to pull it off. (Interested? Sorry, I won't support that habit by giving you the details.) Anyway, I'm guessing that most of us find that smoking and water don't mix. These two actions are incompatible. Finding a behavior that interferes with a target behavior is a good way to stop the target behavior from occurring.

There are different therapy techniques that make use of this incompatibility concept. When two behaviors occur at the same time, the stronger behavior prevails. Water always wins over cigarettes. The behavior-therapist jargon for this concept is *reciprocal inhibition* or *counterconditioning*. Therapy that makes use of reciprocal inhibition or counterconditioning is designed to weaken the classically conditioned, negative target behavior. When you expose cigarettes to water, smoking is pretty hard to pull off. *Counterconditioning* is the operative mechanism of all exposure-based therapies.

Perhaps the best way to explain how counterconditioning drives exposure therapy is to talk about one of the most popular forms of exposure therapies, *systematic desensitization (SD)*. SD is most commonly used to treat phobias, like fear of public speaking, social phobia, or some other specific phobia. Therapists have also used it to successfully treat panic disorder accompanied by agoraphobia. There are several types of exposure-based therapies based on the systematic desensitization principle:

- **Covert sensitization (imaginal exposure):** The "learning" or associating is only occurring in the patient's mind and not in real life.

  The procedures that Wolpe and Jacobsen developed are very similar. Therapists teach patients how to enter a state of deep relaxation. Then they ask the patients to imagine themselves in the fear-producing, phobic situation, while maintaining their state of relaxation. When a patient's anxiety level gets too high, the therapist asks the patient to let go of the image and continue to just relax.

  When this process is repeated over and over again for several sessions, the fear response to the situation is diminished because the state of relaxation is competing with the original fear of the situation or object. Instead of fear, the patient now associates relaxation with the fear-inducing situation or phobic object.

✔ **Graduated-exposure therapy:** When a patient learns to perform his feared behavior in a real-life situation, he or she is engaging in *in vivo sensitization*. Usually, this form of desensitization is done gradually, hence its name. If I'm afraid of flying, my therapist may start with me watching movies about flying (of course these should be movies about flying that don't include a crash or some kind of airline disaster). Then I'd go to the airport; then I'd sit in the terminal; then go on an airplane. There's a gradual move toward the eventual goal of flying, but not until I've done a lot of preparatory work and discovered how to relax during subsequent stages.

✔ **Flooding:** This form of therapy involves exposing a patient to his or her fear-inducing situation or object for a sustained and prolonged period of time. The patient's anxiety goes through the roof, so this can kind of sound like torture. If you're afraid of snakes, jump into a tank full of them. You'll either die or get over your fear of snakes! There's no gradual exposure here. Just jump into a pit of snakes and get over it already!

It gets better! The patient is not only exposed to his worst fears, but he's prevented from running away, leaving, or engaging in whatever escape behavior he's typically used in the past to avoid the fear. This is called *response prevention*.

Flooding sounds horrible, but it's actually one of the most powerful forms of behavior therapy. If a patient trusts her doctor, it can be a quick way to get over some powerful and debilitating phobias. It may seem cruel, but patients must consent to all treatment, and typically, people aren't forced to go to any kind of therapy, unless it's by the courts. (For more on the role of therapy in the criminal justice system, see Chapter 14.)

Getting in good with germs

A good example of flooding (see the "Exposure-based therapies" section in this chapter) comes from treating people with germ phobias. Let's say that I was afraid of germs and catching diseases from trash cans. I managed to fill my entire apartment with garbage because I was too afraid to touch the trash in order to take it out. It was getting pretty rank in there, and my landlord was threatening to evict me. Luckily, I found a good behavior therapist in the neighborhood, and he agreed to help me.

When I met the therapist, he told me that he was going to do the therapy in my apartment. I thought that was pretty cool. When the therapist showed up, he explained that he was going to cure me of my germs-from-trash phobia. He pointed out a pile of trash and told me to jump in it. "Say what?" I said. "You heard me," he replied, "jump in it!" The rest is history. I jumped in the pile of trash and began to roll around. After my garbage swim session, the therapist refused to let me take a shower until the next day. I complied, and I no longer fear trash.

Keep in mind that this is not a true story, and it's a pretty extreme example of flooding, but it's not that far from the truth. Therapists who use flooding ask their patients to completely expose themselves to the things they fear the most. Believe it or not, it actually works!

Applying Some Soap to Your Mind with Cognitive Therapy

Alcoholics Anonymous uses the term "stinking thinking" to describe the kinds of thoughts that a recovering alcoholic has when he thinks negatively and contemplates taking a drink. The simplicity of this statement should not be mistaken for a lack of wisdom. The power of thought should never be underestimated.

Cognitive therapy is a popular and well-researched form of psychotherapy that emphasizes the power of thought. From the perspective of cognitive therapists, psychological problems such as interpersonal difficulties and emotional disorders are the direct result of "stinking thinking." In other words, maladaptive thought processes or cognitions cause these problems. "Stinking thinking" can have a tremendous impact on our psyche because people analyze and process information about every event that occurs around them and their reactions to all of these events. Maladaptive thinking can go something like this:

> **A** (losing my job)→**B** (my thoughts about getting fired)→**C** (my emotions and subsequent and more exaggerated thought processes about the event)

People's reactions are the product of how and what they think about a situation or event. In many situations, such as the experience of loss, an insult, a failure, or encountering something scary, it's only natural to feel some negative emotion. Negative reactions are not necessarily abnormal. It's only when emotional and behavioral reactions become extreme, fixed, and repetitive that people start down the path of psychological disturbance.

Exploring distorted thinking

Sometimes thinking can be biased or distorted, and this can get people into trouble. Cognitive therapy approaches reality from a relativistic perspective: An individual's reality is the byproduct of how he or she perceives it. However, cognitive therapists don't view psychopathology as simply a consequence of thinking. Instead, it's the result of a certain kind of thinking. Specific errors in thinking produce specific problems.

If you lost your job, it would be natural to think, "I need to find another job." But you would be distorting reality if you thought, "I'm never going to find a new job." This kind of pessimistic thinking is bound to produce a stronger than usual negative emotional reaction. There's a world of difference between "I need a new job" and "I will never get another job."

Peale is so positive

Norman Vincent Peale's *The Power of Positive Thinking* (Ballantine Books) is now one of the most famous self-help books on the market. Peale's basic idea is that positive thinking produces positive results in people's lives. He believes that our thoughts play a central role in the production and maintenance of behavior.

Aaron Beck identified six specific cognitive distortions that lead to psychological problems:

- **Arbitrary inference:** This distortion occurs when someone draws a conclusion based on incomplete or inaccurate information. If a couple of scientists are asked to describe an elephant, but all they can see of the elephant is what's visible through a small hole in a fence, each scientist's elephant description will probably be different. One scientist looks through the hole and sees a tail. Another looks through and sees a trunk. The first scientist describes an elephant as an animal with a tail, and the other says that it's an animal with a trunk. Neither one of them has the complete picture, but they both think that they know the truth.

- **Catastrophizing:** My grandmother used to refer to this distortion as "making a mountain out of a molehill." Beck defined it as seeing something as more significant than it actually is.

- **Dichotomous thinking:** Most of us know that thinking only in terms of black and white, without considering the gray areas, can get us into trouble. When I categorize events or situations into one of two extremes, I'm thinking dichotomously. While working in prisons, I've found that inmates often separate people into two groups — friend or foe. "If you're not my friend, you're my enemy."

- **Overgeneralization:** "My boyfriend dumped me; no one loves me." This is an example of overgeneralization — when someone takes one experience or rule and applies it across the board to a larger, unrelated set of circumstances.

- **Personalization:** One of my favorite movies is *Tempest*, the 1982 move directed by Paul Mazursky starring John Cassavetes, Gina Rowlands, and Susan Sarandon. Toward the end of the movie, the main character thinks that he summoned a storm that capsized his enemies' boat. Personalization occurs when someone thinks an event is related to him or her when it actually isn't.

> ✔ **Selective abstraction:** I once knew a guy in college who believed that women always laughed at him when he walked by them on campus. Little did he know that most of the women probably didn't notice his existence. They were most likely laughing at a joke or some other funny situation that had nothing to do with him. He arrived at a conclusion by taking their behavior out of context.

The theory underlying cognitive therapy is beautiful in its simplicity. If psychological problems are the products of errors in thinking, therapy should seek to correct that thinking. This is sometimes easier said than done. Fortunately, cognitive therapists have a wide range of techniques and a highly systematic approach at their disposal.

Changing the way you think

The goal of cognitive therapy is to change biased thinking through logical analysis and behavioral experiments designed to test dysfunctional beliefs. Many thinking errors consist of faulty assumptions about oneself, the world, and others. Cognitive therapy usually goes something like this:

1. **The therapist and patient perform a thorough assessment of the patient's faulty beliefs and assumptions and how these thoughts connect to specific dysfunctional behaviors and emotions.**

   Christine Padesky and Dennis Greenberger, in their book *Mind Over Mood* (Guilford Press, 1995), provide the patient with a system for identifying these thinking errors, which cognitive psychologists commonly call *automatic thoughts* — thoughts that occur automatically as a reaction to a particular situation. The patient is asked to keep track of specific situations that occur between therapy sessions and to identify and describe in detail his reactions to those situations.

2. **The therapist and patient work together, using the automatic thought record, to identify the cognitive distortions mediating between the situations and her reactions.**

   This often-difficult process can take anywhere from several weeks to several months, but at the end of the process, the distortions have been thoroughly identified.

3. **The therapist and patient work collaboratively to alter the distorted beliefs.**

   The therapist and patient collaborate in a process of logical refutation, questioning, challenging, and testing of these faulty conclusions and premises. This effort attempts to make the patient a better thinker and break him of the habit of poor information processing.

Depressing thoughts

One of the best-known applications of cognitive therapy comes from Aaron Beck's *cognitive therapy of depression*. Beck proposes that depressive symptoms, such as a sad mood and a lack of motivation, are the result of cognitive distortions based on three very specific beliefs that the patient holds about himself, the world, and the future. Beck called these beliefs *depressogenic assumptions,* and they exist in a *cognitive triad.* The cognitive triad of individuals suffering from depression consists of the following basic beliefs:

✔ I am inadequate, deserted and abandoned, and worthless.

✔ The world is an unfair and harsh place. There's nothing in it for me.

✔ There is no hope for the future. My current troubles will never go away.

These beliefs interfere with reasonable and healthy adaptation and information processing concerning events in the patient's life. The challenge for both the patient and therapist is to come up with ways to identify, challenge, and alter these beliefs in order to reduce their impact on the patient's emotions and motivations.

Playing Together Nicely: Behavior and Cognitive Therapies

Albert Ellis was the founder of a combined form of therapy that borrows from both behavior therapy and cognitive therapy. *Rational emotive behavior therapy,* or REBT, is built on the premise that psychological problems are the result of irrational thinking and behavior that supports that irrational thinking; therefore, they can be addressed by increasing a patient's ability to think more rationally and behave in ways that support more rational thought.

Ellis is a charismatic psychologist whose style and personality accentuate the main ideas of REBT. Rational emotive behavior therapists believe that most of our problems are self-generated, and that people upset themselves by clinging to irrational ideas that don't hold up under scrutiny. The trouble lies in the fact that many people don't scrutinize their thoughts very often. People make irrational statements to themselves on a regular basis:

"I can't stand it!"

"This is just too awful!"

"I'm worthless because I can't handle this!"

These are examples of irrational thinking. Rational emotive behavior therapists define these statements as irrational because they argue that people can actually handle or "stand" negative events. These events are rarely, if ever, as bad as people think they are. Also, people often hold themselves to rules of "should" that increase their guilt for being overwhelmed, sad, anxious, and so on. "I shouldn't get angry." "I shouldn't care what she thinks." "I shouldn't worry about it." Ellis used to call this "shoulding all over yourself." REBT therapists vigorously challenge statements like these.

The challenging posture of REBT should not be taken as harsh or uncaring. REBT emphasizes the same levels of empathy and unconditional acceptance as many other therapies. REBT therapists are not necessarily trying to talk patients out of feeling the way that they feel. They're trying to help patients experience their emotions in a more attenuated and manageable fashion. There are healthy levels of emotion, and then there are irrational levels of emotion. The goal of therapy is to help the patient learn how to experience her emotions and other situations in this more rational manner.

The behavior-therapy aspects of REBT involve the patient engaging in experiments designed to test the rationality or irrationality of his beliefs. A therapist may ask a patient who is deathly afraid of talking to strangers to approach ten strangers a week and strike up a conversation. If the patient originally thought that he was going to die from embarrassment, the therapist may begin their next session with, "Nice to see you. I guess talking to strangers didn't kill you after all, did it?"

REBT takes the position that two approaches can bring about changes in thinking — talking with a therapist and rationally disputing irrational ideas, and engaging in behaviors that "prove" irrational ideas wrong. Ellis states that people rarely change their irrational thinking without acting against it. Their thinking won't change unless their behavior changes.

Being Aware with Acceptance and Mindfulness-Based Therapies

Therapy is certainly about change. Change your behavior. Change your thinking. Behavior and cognitive therapies are consistent with this. But change is hard, right? I've failed at change and I'm pretty certain you know somebody who has as well. Change is a multibillion dollar industry. Just peruse the "self-help" section of the local bookstore. But what do you do with all this failure to change? How can you change your failure to change? This is exhausting to write about, let alone live with.

Luckily, a group of therapies classified broadly as "acceptance and mind-fulness-based" therapies have been developed that put the issue of change front and center. At the core of these therapies is the concept of *acceptance,* defined within the therapies as helping patients stop struggling with the change process and helping them experience their lives, emotions, thoughts, and behavior in a direct, nonjudgmental, open-minded, and accepting manner. Two well-researched and popular forms of acceptance and mind-fulness based therapies are *ACT (acceptance and commitment therapy)* and *MBCT (mindfulness-based cognitive therapy).*

According to these therapies, a patient's lack of acceptance of his life, emo-tions, history, and so on is part of the problem; it is part of the pathology for which they visited a therapist for in the first place. Rather than change behavior as in behavior modification or thoughts as with cognitive therapy, there is an emphasis on changing the way a patient approaches his behavior, thoughts, and so on. A patient is changing the way he views and interacts with his issues, history, and problems. It's kind of like stepping back, or step-ping away for a different perspective, a nonjudgmental perspective.

The *mindfulness* component involves being aware of the real and present moment and staying open to the ongoing thoughts, sensations, and feelings without trying to change, alter, or modify them. Facing these things with acceptance and mindfulness is therapeutic. Stephen Hayes, a key developer of ACT, states that certain aspects of how human language works results in avoidance, rather than acceptance and mindfulness. People "talk" to them-selves and about themselves, others, and the environment in ways that lead to avoidance and a lack of acceptance.

But it isn't all about acceptance. A key decision point for therapists is whether and when to help patients accept or change at any given point or with any given situation. This decision is based on evaluating situations or circumstances using two criteria, changeability and justifiability:

✔ **Is the situation changeable?** If something is not changeable, such as the death of a loved one, then focusing on changing that situation would not lead to psychological health. If a situation is changeable, such as whether or not you can stop drinking soda, then it should be a focus of change. Change what can be changed, accept what cannot. Can anyone say *Serenity Prayer?*

✔ **Is the reaction justifiable?** The "justifiable" aspect of a patient's thinking, emotions, or behavior involves an analysis of whether or not a patient's reactions are in proportion to and related to an actual event or situation or if they are out of line or overreactions. If a reaction is not justified, then solving the problem that triggered the reaction doesn't make sense because there was no real problem to solve, just an overreaction. If the situation or circumstance is changeable, then change it; if not, then adopt an accepting attitude toward it. If your reaction is justifiable, then accept your reaction or change your reaction. If it is not a justifiable reaction, then just accept the reaction, non-judgmentally and mindfully.

You're Okay, Now Change: Dialectical Behavior Therapy

Dialectical behavior therapy, the brainchild of Dr. Marsha Linehan, is a therapy approach that combines the behavioral, cognitive, and mindfulness approaches. DBT was originally developed for individuals diagnosed with borderline personality disorder who were engaging in self-injurious behavior (such as cutting themselves) and who were at high risk for suicide. Since its inception, however, DBT has been used with a much wider range of problems and patients and is considered one of the most well researched and empirically based therapies in clinical psychology.

DBT is considered a very comprehensive intervention that includes individual therapy and a range of consultative approaches to a client's problems and skill-building approaches (such as social skills training). In many of its behavior and cognitive approaches, it's not necessarily all that unique from other behavior and cognitive approaches. One aspect that certainly sets DBT apart, however, is the inclusion and centrality of acceptance and mindfulness components.

A key acceptance and mindfulness feature of DBT is found in the name of the therapy itself, *Dialectic.* Dialectic refers to the broad concept that reality is interconnected, made up of opposing forces and forms, and dynamic and constantly changing. A dialectic view of things would hold that something can be two seemingly contradictory things or in two contradictory states at the same time. A patient can both want to change and not want to change at the same time. The central dialectic in DBT is focused on the opposing forces of acceptance and change. Patients are taught how to change and are expected to change but are also taught how to and are expected to work on acceptance of themselves, their past, and the world.

DBT respects and responds to the all-too-often reality that people coming to therapy can feel pushed too hard to change and as a result will drop out of therapy early. Focusing too much on change may be emotionally overwhelming, feel invalidating, or even feel shaming. It is critical to strike a balance between acceptance and change. This balance is sought and achieved with a variety of techniques including training in mindfulness. Dr. Linehan outlines the following key components of mindfulness:

- ✔ **Observing:** Simply experiencing the present moment, thoughts, emotions, bodily sensations, and so on
- ✔ **Describing:** Describing the present moment without judgment
- ✔ **Participating:** Throwing oneself into an activity without self-consciousness

DBT mindfulness involves paying attention to the current, moment-by-moment reality and in a non-reactive manner, responding to the facts rather than the patients' own thoughts, emotions, or other reactions. This engenders acceptance, facilitates effective problem solving, and reduces avoidance. The patient has to be willing not to resist reality and to resist engaging in "as if" or "it shouldn't be this way" thinking, or insisting something is true or real when in fact it is not. This willingness then facilitates more effective problem solving and reduces reactivity over time.

Chapter 17

Being a Person Is Tough: Client-Centered and Existential Therapies

A 35-year-old woman, I'll call her Mrs. Garcia, had recently attended her mother's funeral and was having a difficult time going back to work and interacting with her family. She went to her family physician for fear that she may be depressed. Instead of putting her on medication, her family physician referred her to a psychologist.

Consider the following opening exchange between Mrs. Garcia and the psychologist:

> **Therapist:** Hello, Mrs. Garcia, nice to meet you. Dr. Huang had mentioned that you've been having some trouble going to work and that you recently attended your mother's funeral. Please, sit down.
>
> **Patient:** Thanks. First of all, I want to say that I'm a little uncomfortable with this. I've been through psychoanalysis before, and I didn't like it. My doctor was too impersonal and cold.
>
> **T:** I'm sorry that you had a bad experience. Just so you know, I'm not a psychoanalyst. Would you like to talk about that experience?
>
> **P:** Not really, not now anyway. I've been feeling pretty bad lately, really ever since my mother became ill. I'd go and help my sister take care of her and leave feeling this sense of doom and gloom. But I didn't really feel sad about the fact that she was dying; she had suffered for a long time, and I accepted that her death would probably be a relief. It was her life, not her death, that seemed to be bothering me.

T: Her life was bothering you. You had accepted her death. Tell me more. You did not approve of her lifestyle?

P: Kind of. It was like she was living for everyone else, the boss, my father, us children, the grandchildren. I felt really bad about judging her, especially when I began to realize that I was living the exact same life.

T: You've been living the same way as your mother?

Mrs. Garcia's feelings and experience are illustrative of the kinds of issues that practitioners of *humanistic* therapies (client-centered and existential) are concerned with. She's questioning her life, her very identity, her sense of self. Who is she really living for? Is she being true to herself? Humanistic therapies approach human difficulties with the core tenets that humans are dignified, have choices, and struggle with life's inevitabilities (death, illness, conflict, and so on), but have the freedom to make changes and address these difficulties with appropriate support.

Although each of them made unique contributions to the theory and practice of psychotherapy, the big names in humanistic therapy such as Carl Rogers, Rollo May, and Irvin Yalom all had one thing in common. Each of them saw great potential in all of us. They believed that all people strive for maximum development of themselves and their potential and take responsibility for their lives.

Many of the forms of psychotherapy I introduce in this book (psychoanalysis in Chapter 15 and behavior and cognitive therapies in Chapter 16) have been criticized for being too technical, sterile, or out of touch with the real experience of the patient or client. They've been accused of making too little room for the *real person*. The therapies discussed in this chapter all have the *personhood* of the patient seeking help as a central theme.

This section introduces humanistic and existential therapies that focus on the core issues of being a person and how a person struggles with, through, and around these issues.

Client-Centered Therapy: Shining in the Therapist's Spotlight

Take a minute to do a little exercise. Get a piece of paper and a pen and make a list of all the people you admire and hold in a positive light. Who's on the list — teachers, spouses, celebrities, parents? What about yourself? Are you on your list of people you positively regard? Would you be a member of your own fan club?

In this big, chaotic world of billions of people, sometimes it seems like I don't matter, like my individual identity is so small, so insignificant. Yet I walk around with the sense of being an individual. Sometimes I feel so independent that I actually feel lonely and isolated, like no one cares about me. "What about me? Don't I matter?"

Carl Rogers cared. Rogers (1902–1987) is perhaps one of the most famous psychologists of all time, nominated for the Nobel Peace Prize and considered on par with Sigmund Freud. His influence on psychotherapy has been profound. He put the person back into the process, attempting to understand and value each of his patients as unique individuals with real problems and not just as abstract theories and models. You can say one thing for sure about Carl Rogers's *client-centered therapy* — it placed great value on the *humanness* of each and every patient. Rogers believed that all humans inherently strive toward the fullest development of their capacity to maintain an optimal level of survival. It's kind of like the US Army slogan, "Be all you can be."

Growth is a big buzzword for client-centered therapists. A patient's personal growth is foremost in the therapist's mind and central to the therapy process. Every time I read something from a client-centered perspective or something that Carl Rogers wrote, I start reflecting and asking myself, "Am I growing?" If you count my waistline, the answer is definitely yes. As far as that personal growth and expanding abilities stuff . . .

What does Carl Rogers's belief in the inherent worth of each of his patients have to do with helping them get better? Are client-centered therapy patients paying for someone to like them, to value them? Maybe, but that would be a gross oversimplification. It's more than an "I'll love you until you can love yourself" therapy or "I'll accept you until you can accept yourself."

The healing or helping mechanism in client-centered therapy is found in the process of the therapist working to understand the patient's unique experiences, thoughts, behaviors, and feelings. As the therapist strives to understand where the patient is coming from, the patient learns to experience herself in a new, and more productive, life-enhancing way.

Understanding theory of the person

Why would Carl Rogers think that making a genuine connection with his patient and really trying to understand what it's like to be that particular individual has a helping or healing effect? The answer to that question may seem obvious: All of us like to feel understood. (See Chapter 10 for more on the importance of relationships.) Having people get what you're about seems to give you a sense of well-being, a feeling of being more alive and present against the backdrop of a dark and uncaring world.

Wanting to be understood

Although he's not considered a client-centered therapist, Eric Fromm introduced a concept that attempts to explain why being understood is so important to everyone. Fromm believed that people all make constant attempts to check their perceptions and experiences against the perceptions and experiences of others, particularly people whose opinion is of value. You may have heard of the concept of a *reality check* — like asking someone if she just saw the UFO land in the field next to the highway. "Did you just see what I just saw?" If the other person saw it too, you experience something Fromm called *validation.* Validation is the experience of having someone concur or support your experience of reality. Validation brings a sense of presence; it makes you feel like you *exist.* According to Fromm, without validation, people would feel as if they didn't exist.

Have you ever talked to someone when she wasn't getting what you were trying to say, like she didn't understand you? This type of experience can feel pretty bad. In situations like this and many others, you can feel disconnected and, in extreme cases, isolated.

Why is being understood or understanding others so difficult at times? Rogers believed that each and every person has a unique frame of reference from which he experiences the world. Think about it. Someone else in this world may look just like you, have the same name, and be exactly like you in almost every other way. Biologically, identical twins even share the same genetic code. But even identical twins are not exactly alike. They are, in fact, two separate people. I like to look at it this way. No other person can occupy the same physical space that I occupy at the same time I occupy it. And they can't occupy the same mental space either! In the abstract, people can "walk a mile in my shoes," but in the literal sense, only when I'm not wearing them.

Developing a sense of self

You're unique! Our individual experience is specifically separate from others', and as you differentiate your experience from the experiences of others, you begin to develop a sense of self, a sense of who you are. A sense of self depends first, however, on how other people see you and relate to you. As children, experience is intertwined and merged with the experiences of parents, families, and caregivers. They serve as an experiential guide of sorts, providing the first models of understanding and experience in the world. Later, you begin to differentiate your experience from the experiences of others.

This *experience-differentiation process* is only possible, however, within an environment of positive regard and support from those around you. If I see a UFO, and the other person doesn't, he may still support me in my experience by saying that he doesn't see the UFO, but that doesn't mean I didn't see it. If he wasn't supportive, he may say, "You're crazy! You don't see a UFO!" More realistically, I've often witnessed a young child who gets hurt or upset and goes to a parent for comfort only to have the parent say, "You're not hurt.

You're okay." This situation is the opposite of validation; it's an *invalidating* experience. The child may get confused, thinking, "I feel hurt, but Daddy says I'm not. Am I really hurt or not?" Pretty confusing stuff for a kid.

Dealing with differences in self-perception

Rogers called the experience of oneself, as it depends on the views of others, the *conditions of worth*. As long as people continue to meet the conditions of worth set up by others, they'll do fine. But when they don't receive unconditional acceptance, they can get into trouble and experience distress. They may then start seeking the *conditional acceptance* of others because they've yet to experience their own *unconditional acceptance*.

When seeking conditional acceptance, a person lives a lie of sorts, adopting a confusing and undifferentiated experiential approach to living. If her experiences are different than the experiences of those around her, she may distort her own thinking, feelings, or behavior in order to be in line with those of others. She may walk around with a belief that, if she thinks, feels, and behaves in accordance with the people around her, she'll get the positive regard she is longing for.

Even if people don't receive unconditional acceptance, they still have this underlying sense of individuality and uniqueness. When there's a disconnection or inconsistency between your experience of yourself and your experience of yourself as you distort it to be in line with other's views, you're *incongruent*. This involves having two views of yourself: how you actually are, and how you think others think you are. Rogers believed that what lies at the core of psychological maladjustment is the incongruity between your total experience and your distorted self-concept. This incongruity leads to feeling estranged, disconnected, and not whole. You're then only living out part of your full being and therefore not fulfilling your basic need to experience, enhance, and expand your being.

As a person travels along this compromised path, he may use different defense mechanisms to keep up the act. He may selectively process information about himself, others, and the world so as not to overturn the apple cart of reality. For example, a lot of families have a "black-sheep" member who stands out. At times, this person may deliberately do something that goes against the grain in order to stay in line with his family-derived self and the image that everyone has of him. Sometimes, he can stick to this plan in such a rigid manner that he may actually lose touch with reality.

Reconnecting in therapy

One of the main goals of client-centered therapy is to help the patient reintegrate different versions of the self: how the patient sees himself and how he thinks others see him. At the center of this process is perhaps Rogers's most important contribution to psychotherapy — *unconditional positive regard.*

This involves accepting the patient as a person without judging his experiences, feelings, thoughts, or behaviors in a moral sense. The therapist does not want to repeat the invalidating experience that the patient probably went through growing up or continues to go through.

Client-centered therapists engage in what Rogers called *reflection* — communicating to the patient that they hear what the patient is saying and that they're trying to understand where the patient's coming from. Rogers emphasized *accurate empathy*. Therapists who adopt this concept stay away from imposing their own understandings and structures on the patient's experience. This helps patients begin to see how they've distorted their own experiences without introducing any new distortions in relation to the therapist's expectations.

The therapist *reflects* you back to yourself by being attentive and describing to you the self that you're presenting to him. During this process, your self-awareness increases, and you start to see yourself in a way that you've never been able to before. The client-centered therapist is kind of like a mirror or a *self-amplifier*.

Another huge contribution Rogers made to psychotherapy was the introduction of his six *necessary and sufficient conditions* that must be in place for therapy to be helpful:

- ✔ A professional, respectful, and accepting relationship formed between the client and therapist.

- ✔ A patient's willingness to be vulnerable and to experience strong feelings, such as anxiety, and the therapist's ability to motivate the patient to seek and stay involved in the therapy relationship.

- ✔ Genuineness — the client is expected to be "freely and deeply" himself, not distorting how he feels or what he thinks.

- ✔ Unconditional positive regard.

- ✔ Accurate empathy.

- ✔ Perception of genuineness — the therapist has to be a real person (with feelings, thoughts, and behaviors of his own), not just a person playing a role, acting, or pretending for the sake of the client.

Rogerian, or client-centered, therapy has been around in one form or another for about 60 years now. The ultimate question for any form of psychotherapy, psychological intervention, or medication is whether it works or not. Research into the effectiveness of client-centered therapy has typically investigated the specific "necessary and sufficient" conditions.

Most studies, including one conducted by Beutler, Crago, and Arezmendi, have shown that three of the six conditions, empathy, genuineness, and prizing (unconditional positive regard), are valuable but not necessary or sufficient (on their own) to bring about therapeutic change. That is, a therapist doesn't have to possess or do these things in order to be helpful. Orlinsky and Howard, however, found that warmth, empathy, and genuineness facilitate the therapy process. That is, therapy may go a little better if the therapist creates these conditions. It doesn't seem to hurt, so why not?

Being at Peace with Your Being: Existential Therapy

In the 1960s, the *Tibetan Book of the Dead* became really popular among members of the counterculture (you know, hippies). The book is a Buddhist instruction manual for what to do when you die — go toward the light, don't go toward the light, that sort of thing. The book and its subject matter captured a lot of people's imaginations, as death always comes to us. Death seems to have a profound effect on the quality of our lives. Whether a person is facing death himself or dealing with the loss of someone important to him, the looming presence of death almost invariably stirs up strong emotions.

A group of psychologists from the school of *existential psychology* places death center stage among the most important issues to discuss in psychotherapy. In addition to death, they view some issues (anxiety, freedom, and choice) as very basic to human existence and at the core of much of what is called *psychopathology* (psychological problems). In a way, the existentialists cut straight to the chase concerning therapy by placing ultimate importance on deep philosophical issues such as:

- ✔ Anxiety
- ✔ Guilt
- ✔ Death
- ✔ Time
- ✔ Transcendence

Why all this morose fascination? Existential therapists, such as Rollo May (author of the famous book *Love and Will*, published in 1969) and Irvin Yalom, professor emeritus at Stanford University, shared a philosophical perspective that was deeply dissatisfied with the focus of much of psychoanalysis and other forms of therapy. They believed that our most important issues were ignored, or at the very least indirectly addressed, by forms of therapy such as psychoanalysis and cognitive-behavioral therapy. Specifically, they saw behavior therapy (see Chapter 16) as an overly narrow and technical exercise that didn't respect the struggles that humanity faces. They wanted to do therapy with a real person sitting across from them, examining his or her real concerns and deepest issues. It seems like they didn't want to be distracted by theories and models that dehumanized therapy, which at its heart is a basic human process.

Existential therapy is more of a philosophical position than a specific technique. It does, however, make some unique contributions to technique, as I discuss later in this chapter. At the center of the philosophy is the assumption that all human beings have a core experience of "I am." This experience is our basic sense of being alive and striving toward being.

If you ever want to take a road trip into hardcore philosophical obscurity concerning the issue of being or not-being, read Jean Paul Sartre's *On Being and Nothingness*. It's like a computer instruction manual for existential philosophy.

Hanging out with your hang-ups: Death, guilt, and anxiety

People are all striving to realize their truest sense of being, the truest sense of ontological existence. *Ontology* is a branch of philosophy that concerns itself with determining what is real in our universe. I feel real. Hopefully, you feel real, too. If you and I are both real, there's common ground to speak about the sense of ontological existence and sense of being.

There's always a catch, though. If there's going to be being, there has to be not-being. The ultimate not-being experience is death. When a person faces death, his own or someone else's death, he experiences anxiety over the thought of not-being, of not being around anymore.

Normal and neurotic anxiety

Existential therapists tend to focus on the differences between a patient's normal or healthy anxiety and what they call neurotic anxiety. *Normal anxiety* comes from striving to be and facing threats to our being. Wait a minute, normal anxiety? Before I started learning about the existential approach, I always thought that anxiety was pretty much a bad thing. It feels pretty bad, and it can get in the way of doing a lot of things.

Healthy anxiety is anxiety that is proportionate to the situation and not out of control. Therefore, healthy anxiety doesn't need to be repressed because it's manageable and realistic. It's also constructive and helpful. If I'm appropriately anxious about my test, I may just sit down and study in order to pass it. My anxiety can motivate me. Many people can relate to anxiety being at the core of a lot of what they do. "No problem," say the existentialists, as long as your anxiety is working for you and it's not overblown.

Neurotic anxiety has two qualities that work against our realization of being and cut us off from fully engaging the world around us:

✔ **It's disproportionate to the situation at hand.** Fearing that they may fail, a lot of college students get worked up and anxious about taking big exams. For many people, failing an exam is a big deal, but being anxious about the exam is fine, as long as they don't get carried away. Anxiety becomes a problem when it becomes disproportionate to the situation. If you're so anxious that you think you're going to die if you fail, the anxiety has definitely become a problem, and existentially speaking, it's out of whack.

✔ **It's destructive.** Staying with the exam example, all that anxiety may make students physically ill. If they're sick, they can't study. If they don't study, they fail. Their anxiety was counterproductive. Neurotic anxiety should be tolerated as it comes up, but it should be eliminated to the greatest extent possible. People also tend to repress, or "stuff," neurotic anxiety into their unconscious in an attempt to cope with it. The anxiety is painful, and when something is painful, they try to forget it exists.

Normal and neurotic guilt

Like anxiety, guilt is a key existential phenomenon. Guilt is an important concept in our society and, probably, in most others as well. The existentialists aren't priests who seek to absolve their patients of guilt; instead, they help their patients focus on issues of guilt as they relate to the full experience of being.

Guilt may be normal or neurotic. *Normal guilt* arises from two situations:

✔ **Failing to properly engage in ethical behavior:** This type of guilt comes up when you actually do something wrong according to your own and your social group's ethical and moral standards. Guilt is a normal and healthy emotion.

✔ **Failing to live up to our own expectations:** This one is often downplayed in psychotherapy. Individuals often talk about letting other people down. A lot of people actually come to therapy because they've let someone down through infidelity, physical abuse, and so on. But what about your own standards for yourself? How are you supposed to feel when you let yourself down? Guilty!

Neurotic guilt is guilt that comes from our fearful fantasies of having done someone harm that actually didn't happen. Are you afraid to tell someone what you really think for fear of hurting her feelings? That's nice. Are you afraid that you've hurt someone's feelings even when you're sure that you didn't? That's a *fantasized transgression* — a created or imagined trespass that never occurred.

Being in the here and now: Time and transcendence

When I think of the concept of *being,* I always think of smoke-filled coffee shops with beatnik poets sporting goatees, berets, and sunglasses and spouting poetry about the nobility of a cockroach.

They're alive, man!

Their legs are so short that they can't help but be down to earth.

They scurry around with zest and zeal, never worrying about money or pride.

They're just looking for their next meal.

Sorry, I couldn't help it, but my little existential poem does illustrate the idea that there's a genuineness in the simplicity of the cockroach. They seem focused on what really matters; to them, it's food. They're not distracted by neurotic guilt or anxiety. They are what the existential therapists call *being-in-the-world.*

Existential therapists try hard to understand the experience of their patients and how they accomplish "being-in-the-world." There are three important levels of this being:

- ✓ **Umwelt:** Being among or within one's environment and the external world of objects and things
- ✓ **Mitwelt:** Being within one's social world
- ✓ **Eigenwelt:** Relating to oneself

Being is maximized when people are in touch with each of these levels to a sufficient degree, engaging with each level without neurotic anxiety or guilt (see the preceding section for details on anxiety and guilt). Remember the cockroach — he ain't guilty, man!

Being-in-the-world includes the experience of time. *Time* is an absolute fact of life. It's an existential given. Time goes on whether or not you try to resist it. The key for the existentialists was for people to learn to live in the present and the immediate future. They shouldn't waste their time worrying about the past. They should commit to the present, realizing that time only moves one closer to his or her inevitable death and that life is what one makes of it. Make life, or it will make you, I guess.

Another important existential issue that serves as background for the actual practice of existential psychotherapy is the concept of transcendence. If you weren't depressed before you started reading this chapter, you may be now. All this talk about death, time, anxiety, and guilt isn't much fun. It's not all hopeless, though. The existentialists see a way out. *Transcendence* involves trying to realize our being. It's the act of living one's life without being overly anxious or ill, and striving to transcend the past and grow toward the future.

Being flexible with your time

A quick story: My wife and I went to Paris, France, to see some paintings. We went to the Salvador Dalí museum to check out *The Persistence of Memory* and a couple of his other works. When we arrived, it wasn't there! It was in a gallery in St. Petersburg, Florida. We couldn't believe it. St. Petersburg? Come on!

Anyway, my fascination with this painting comes from Dalí's representation of time using flimsy clocks draped over different objects like the way you drape dirty clothes over the back of a chair. I'm no art critic, but I took that to symbolize the flexibility of time — it's not brittle; it doesn't break; it only bends. Time drapes over everything, and nothing escapes it. Well Mr. Dalí, the existentialists would have probably agreed.

The human imagination and the ability to think abstractly are powerful tools in this cosmic struggle. To *abstract* something is to remove it or extract it. A person can take herself beyond the limits of her immediate situation with the ability to think of or imagine herself as outside of these limits. An individual's ability to separate herself by thinking creatively creates a psychological space of sorts. She can envision possibilities. As long as a person is able to imagine alternatives and other possibilities, she can continue to strive toward being. This power is crucial to the existential concept of freedom. It also sounds like hope to me.

Facing freedom, isolation, and meaninglessness

As if addressing anxiety and guilt isn't enough, existential therapy also takes on a patient's struggle with four more existential issues: death, freedom, isolation, and meaninglessness. Just when you thought you've gotten away from a discussion of *death,* it comes right back. I've often wondered if the existentialists were obsessed with death. In therapy, they emphasize that psychopathology and problems in living are the result of a patient's inability to transcend the idea of death. There's no escaping it. You're conflicted — you want to live, but you know you're going to die. Knowing that you are going to die may lead to despair. You may think, "If I'm going to die, why should I even try?" Existential therapy helps patients face the fact of death without despair.

After working in jails and prisons, I've come to really cherish one thing — my freedom. Existential psychologists emphasize the importance of the concept of *freedom* in a patient's life. They don't believe that some absolute structure to the universe is waiting to be discovered. Humanity makes up the structure as it goes along. For some people, freedom feels burdensome. Freedom requires that people take responsibility for all their actions, and it means that they've got nobody but themselves to blame when things go wrong. The good part: They can take full credit when things go right!

Just in case you thought you may catch a break from the existentialists and not have to face every single crappy fact of life, they throw in *isolation* for good measure. A lot of people find shelter from the harshness of the world in companionship. At the core, people realize that they are essentially alone and they'll die alone. Individuals try to overcome this fact by attempting to *merge* with others. When a person seeks a merger in the extreme, he engages in disingenuous relating, using other people as a means to an end (ending isolation). When someone's identity is so dependent on others, he may find himself feeling as if he doesn't exist without the other person. He longs for recognition. "Get over it!" say the existentialists. "You're alone, and there's nothing you can do about it!"

What's the meaning of life? Don't go to an existential psychologist for the answer to this question. Each person is expected to create his own meanings, to construct something out of this meaningless mass of confusion. When someone adaptively and creatively uses his will to build meaning for himself, he's on the right track.

> **Patient:** I've wanted to get a new job for a while, but I can't seem to find anything.
>
> **Therapist:** Have you been looking?
>
> **Patient:** Not really.
>
> **Therapist:** Then how can you say that you can't find anything when you're not looking? Do you really want another job badly enough to actually look for one?
>
> **Patient:** I don't know. I think I just want to be treated with more respect at work.
>
> **Therapist:** Then what you really want is respect, not another job.
>
> **Patient:** Respect is important.
>
> **Therapist:** To whom?
>
> **Patient:** Respect is important to me. I want it.

After the patient becomes aware of what he wants, the therapist helps him remove any obstacles or blocks to action. The therapist also points out that the patient makes decisions every day, even when he doesn't realize it. If you're standing in your own way, move over. Here comes the existential express: I'm a lean, mean, existential fact-facing, decision-making machine.

Letting go of defense mechanisms

When you use defense mechanisms to protect yourself from what can sometimes feel like an abyss of existential truth, you can get into trouble. Sometimes, you can do the following:

- **Develop an unconscious sense of being special or omnipotent to ward off the unknown:** Irvin Yalom points out that this development may lead to being selfish or even paranoid. I once knew a man who thought he was Jesus Christ. I told him that I had just met Jesus Christ in a previous therapy session with another patient, and I was pretty sure there could be only one. He insisted he was the one. There must have been a lot of emptiness or meaninglessness in this patient's life.

- **Believe in an ultimate "rescuer":** Too much indulgence in this kind of thinking can lead to dependency. This is a no-no in existential therapy. It's a cop-out and serves as a poor excuse for facing the existential facts. Man, the existentialists won't even let me carry around my almighty teddy bear, Snuggles. Sorry, Snuggles, I guess I'll just have to go it alone. The existentialists take all the fun out of everything.

Claiming responsibility

With all their talk about being, you may begin to wonder if the existential therapists ever do anything but philosophize. Existential therapy incorporates core issues into therapy and uses them to guide the focus of the therapist in treatment. Existential therapists

- Help their patients to act willfully and responsibly in the face of the existential facts.

- Listen for existential themes and point them out to patients when they suspect one is lurking underneath a trivial dilemma or psychological symptom.

- Explore these existential themes and point out the patients' compromised and maladaptive ways of coping with them.

- Set out to help patients develop more adaptive coping behaviors.

- Expect patients to create their own lives and worlds through action and choice.

- Expect patients to exercise their will in making decisions without being too impulsive or compulsive.

Acting impulsively and compulsively are not active approaches to living in an existential sense. Active approaches are thoughtful, deliberate, and responsible actions, and active approaches are what existentialists look for.

Existentialists emphasize responsible action without the need to defer to someone around us to make our decisions. Because of this, existential therapists can sometimes be frustrating to a patient because the therapist refuses to get into a caregiver—care receiver interaction.

If you have trouble "owning up" to the circumstances of your life and accepting responsibility for them, existential therapy may help. It includes an expectation of owning one's experiences, including feelings, thoughts, and behaviors. One way to demonstrate this ownership is for patients to learn how to say *I,* instead of *you,* when talking about their experiences. Check out this example:

> **Patient:** There are people in your life who you love, and when they hurt you, it sticks with you.

> **Therapist:** I want you to practice saying *I* instead of *you.* For example, instead of saying, "There are people in your life," try saying, "There are people in my life who I love, and when they hurt me, it sticks with me."

> **Patient:** There are people in my life . . .

> **Therapist:** Good. How does that feel?

> **Patient:** It kind of makes you feel sad.

> **Therapist:** It makes me feel sad?

> **Patient:** No, it makes *me* feel sad.

> **Therapist:** You feel sad.

> **Patient:** Yes.

I hope I haven't painted too bleak of a picture of existential therapy. The truth is that existential therapy is one of the most hopeful therapies out there. It doesn't sound like it at first because it kind of works in reverse. Instead of using hope in external things, such as other people and supernatural forces, it points patients inward, helping them generate hope from small actions. With each step a person takes, she is exercising the hope that the ground will not fall out from under her. It's a leap of faith facilitated through willful action. By taking patients down to the bare bones of existence, the existentialists show them how every thought, feeling, and behavior is an act of will that demonstrates the presence of their being — their striving to exist and survive.

Chapter 18

Stress, Illness, Growth, and Strength

In This Chapter

▶ Living under pressure

▶ Keeping it together

▶ Getting sick

▶ Being healthy

▶ Flexing your mental muscle

▶ Staying positive

When I was a college I could stay up all night studying, take exams the next day, and then go to work as a busboy in the evening — without even thinking about breaking plans with my friends at night. I could just keep going and going. When I hit the work world, I could work as a jail psychologist during the day, teach community college at night, and do mental disability testing on the weekends. I must have worked more than 100 hours every week. But something changed as I got older. I slowed down. I couldn't pull all-nighters. Working 100 hours a week and holding down five jobs was just no longer possible. With age came additional responsibilities and preferences for how I spent my time.

"Life" was happening around me and to me, and I came to know stress illness, and the challenges of everyday life in new and sometimes-upsetting ways. I found myself looking for sources of energy, strength, replenishment, and inner reserve.

Then it dawned on me that I'm a psychologist, and psychological science probably has something to say about these issues. This field of research studies stress, illness, coping, and resilience. I wish I could report that reading up on these issues in the psychological literature gave me everything I needed to fix myself, but that's not the case. However, psychological science does offer a great deal of information about these matters.

In this chapter, I introduce the concepts of stress and coping and the growing field of health psychology to describe psychology's approach to stress, illness, coping, and human psychological strength and resilience.

Stressing Out

Every year around the same time I get sick. It never fails. Come October, I've got a cold. Is it the weather? Is it a cosmic curse? At some point I made a connection between my getting sick and stress. In school, it was the stress of midterms. Now, it's the stress of the holidays. Everyone gets stressed about different stuff, and sometimes the stress makes people become physically ill.

Psychologists have worked hard over the years, trying to figure out what triggers stress. Within the last 20 years or so, they've started to use their knowledge of human behavior and mental processes to learn more about what makes people sick and how people cope with illness.

What is *stress?* When most people talk about stress, they refer to the things or events that cause worry, anxiety, and strain — work, money, bills, kids, bosses, and so on. The strains and pace of modern life seem to get the best of most people at one time or another. Often, even the gadgets that people get to make their lives easier end up complicating things. Stress can be defined as a person's subjective experience of being overwhelmed, burdened, or run down.

Considering ways to think about stress

Formal definitions of stress range from descriptions of bodily reactions to different ways of thinking about stress. In his 1997 book *Stress and Health: Biological and Psychological Interactions,* William Lavallo defined stress as a bodily or mental tension to something that knocks people off balance, either physically or mentally. Conversely, when a person has *equilibrium,* he's maintaining a balance between the external world and his internal world. Walter Cannon, an American physiologist at Harvard Medical School, in 1939, called this concept *homeostasis.* So basically, people feel stressed when they're out of homeostatic balance.

Hans Selye, an endocrinologist at the Université de Montréal and Nobel Prize nominee, gave one of the most famous theories of stress. His theory was based on something he called the *general adaptation syndrome (GAS).* The idea is that when someone is confronted with something that threatens either her physical or mental equilibrium, she goes through a series of changes:

- ✔ **Alarm:** The initial reaction to the stressor. The brain and hormones are activated in order to provide the body with the necessary energy to respond to the element causing stress.

- ✔ **Resistance:** The activation of the body system best suited to deal with the stressor. If the stressor requires that you run — if you're being chased by a pack of wild dogs — then your nervous system and hormones make sure that you've got enough blood pumping to your legs to get the job done. Plus, extra energy is provided to your heart so it can pump blood faster. It's a beautifully designed system.

- ✔ **Exhaustion:** The final stage. If the bodily system activated in the resistance stage gets the job done, your trip down GAS lane ends. If the stressor continues, you enter this final stage. When you're exhausted, your body is no longer able to resist the stress, and it becomes vulnerable to disease and breakdown.

The body is not the only thing at work when you're stressed. Numerous cognitive (thinking) and emotional responses are also going on. Arnold Lazarus, a South African psychologist known for his work on behavior therapy, stated that during times of stress, an individual goes through a process of emotional analysis. It's kind of like having a little psychologist inside your head. You ask yourself to determine the current significance of the problem and its importance for the future. How does this stress work? You make two important *appraisals,* or evaluations — known as *primary* and *secondary appraisals.*

In most stressful situations, something important is at stake, or at least you think it is; otherwise, you wouldn't be stressed about it. The evaluation of what is at stake is the primary appraisal of the situation. At this stage, situations are classified into one of three categories:

- ✔ **Threat:** An example of a threatening situation is a situation that requires a response. If I'm standing in line at the grocery store and someone cuts in front of me, I'm not forced to respond. But if a guy grabs me by the shirt and threatens to kick my butt if I don't let him in front of me, I have to respond in one way or another. Like run!

- ✔ **Harm-loss:** A harm-loss situation may involve getting hurt in some way — physically, mentally, or emotionally. A blow to my pride may be seen as a harm-loss situation. It's relative.

- ✔ **Challenge:** I can also look a threatening person straight in the eye and see the perceived threat as a challenge. Instead of seeing the situation in dangerous terms, I may see it as an opportunity to try out those judo lessons I've been taking.

After figuring out what's at stake, I take stock of the resources I have available to deal with the situation. This is secondary appraisal. I may take a look at my previous experience with this type of situation. What did I do when this happened before, and how did that turn out? Most people also take a look at how they feel about themselves. If you see yourself as a capable person, then you're likely to become less stressed out than someone who thinks less of their capabilities.

Stress can be viewed as something more than the actual situation; a person's reaction depends on how he looks at the stressor. Stress is not a situation; it's a consequence of how a situation and a person's response to that situation interact. I can react differently to the same situation. For example, If I'm called on to pitch for the final out in the bottom of the ninth inning in the World Series I could get all stressed out because I dread failing, giving up the game losing home run. Or, I could look at the situation with excitement because I have the opportunity to pitch for the last out and the win. The situation didn't change, but my reaction to it did. One leads to the experience of stress, one does not.

Stress can also be a product of how much control a person thinks she has over events and situations. Stress arises when people lack an adequate response to a situation, and the consequences of failure are important. Seeing yourself as having little or no control can have negative psychological and physical consequences.

On the other hand, feeling like the "master of your domain" may help keep stress at bay. I remember a cartoon from my childhood called *He-Man;* He-Man had this phrase that he yelled out when he was getting ready to kick butt: "I have the power!" It would be nice if I could just yell that out and be ready to take on the world. In 1982, George Mandler, professor emeritus at the University of California, San Diego, defined *mastery* as the thought or perception that things in an individual's environment can be brought under her control. Sounds like He-Man to me.

Stressing to the types

So, stress isn't just a situation. It's the coping process and a result of how you think and feel about a situation. That explains why some stimuli are stressors and some are not, and why some people get stressed out by certain things that don't affect other people. However, some situations are pretty stressful for nearly everyone. Here are some things that most people find stressful:

- ✔ **Extreme stressors:** Events that occur rarely and that have a severe and dramatic impact on routines and access to normalcy, such as natural disasters, human-made disasters (such as an oil spill), war, terrorism, migration, and watching others get hurt

- ✔ **Developmental and psychosocial stressors:** Events that occur as you grow and change, including marriage, childbirth, raising children, caring for a sick person, and being a teenager

✔ **Common stressors:** Things you deal with in daily life — urban living, daily hassles (like driving to work), job pressure, and household chores

Psychologists Holmes and Rahe in 1967 created a list of stressful events called the *social readjustment rating scale*. They took different stressful events and assigned a point value to each of them — the higher the point value, the more stressful the event is. Here are the top five:

Event	*Point Value*
Death of a spouse	100
Divorce	73
Marital separation	65
Jail sentence	63
Death of a close family member	63

If you're wondering what the bottom-five stressful events are, they are (in descending order of stressfulness): change in number of family get-togethers, change in eating habits, vacation, Christmas, and minor violations of the law.

Getting sick of being worried

I've heard people say that they thrive on stress or that they do their best work when they're under pressure. Yet research shows that this is not true for most people. Stress can have very serious effects on people; and usually, if you *do* work well under stress, you'll do even better when you're not under stress.

As researchers learn more about stress, a psychological and biological phenomenon, the connection between stress and illness — both psychological and physical — has become impossible to deny.

Psychological

One of the most well-known psychological results of exposure to extreme stress is *posttraumatic stress disorder (PTSD)*. PTSD can occur when a person is exposed to a life-threatening situation or a situation that may involve serious injury. War, car accidents, plane crashes, rape, and physical assault are all examples of situations that may cause PTSD. The symptoms include emotional numbing, guilt, insomnia, impaired concentration, avoidance of trauma-related events and memories, and excessive physiological arousal (hyperactivity due to fear). Many Vietnam War and Iraq War veterans returned home with PTSD. During World War I, PTSD was called *shell shock*.

Have you ever wondered what it must be like to be a firefighter, police officer, or emergency physician? I mean, all the death and destruction they see every day has to be stressful. And, according to research, it is. People in very stressful occupations have been found to be at increased risk for *secondary traumatic stress disorder (STSD).* The symptoms of STSD are exactly like those of PTSD, but instead of the sufferers themselves facing a life-threatening or harmful stressor, people with STSD receive "vicarious exposure" to stressors. In other words, they're around people who are exposed to life-threatening and harmful situations all the time, and it takes a toll. People who witness an event and feel fear, horror, or helplessness may be at risk for developing STSD.

Physical

Hans Selye looked at the connections between stress, mental problems, difficulties adjusting, physical health problems, and disease. He found that the same things that help people cope with stress sometimes lead to disease. When the body and mind react to stress, the reactions don't diminish right away. In fact, when Selye performed experiments with stressed-out pigeons, he found that a lot of the pigeons died after his stress experiments, even if they coped well when the stressor was active. Selye identified several conditions that he called "diseases of adaptation," including peptic ulcers, high blood pressure, heart incidents, and "nervous disturbances."

Based on the work of Selye and others, it's been discovered that stress can lead to physical health problems or illness in several ways. An indirect link between stress and physical health problems may involve people who engage in potentially physically harmful behaviors as a means to cope with stress. A lot of people drink alcohol when they're stressed. Drinking alcohol can be harmful to your health, especially if you drink and drive. Another dangerous behavior often associated with stress is increased cigarette smoking. I've heard plenty of patients talk about smoking as a way to relax. But it's so unhealthy!

Another link between stress and physical illness comes from the new and exciting field of *psychoneuroimmunology,* the study of the connection between psychology and the immune system. Researchers have long suspected that there's a connection between the two systems, and there actually is. High levels of stress and intense emotions can suppress nervous system functioning. There isn't a clear-cut diagnosis of all the ins and outs, but the suspicion is that the cost of the body's coping reactions to stress is paid in part by the immunity department.

Ever heard of the flight-or-fight response? Walter Cannon showed that exposure to extreme stress causes people to decide whether they're going to take off running or stand their ground and fight. It sounds animalistic, but you can also look at it as a choice between walking away or yelling at someone. Either way, these protective actions require energy. Arguing and running from someone can be tiring! So, the brain sends signals to the heart and the hormone system that causes blood pressure to increase. The heart races, respiration quickens, and sugar levels in the blood rise. When these changes occur, all of the body's vital resources are devoted to the moment. Resources from other areas are used for the immediate purpose of fighting or fleeing.

The hormones that kick in when you're in fight-or-flight mode are epinephrine and cortisol — both have immunosuppressive effects. If higher than-normal levels of epinephrine and cortisol are present in the blood stream, then the immune system doesn't work as well. It kind of makes sense, if you think about it. If a bear is chasing you, probably the last thing on your mind is getting the flu. Forget the flu; you can't get the flu if that bear rips your head off! Save the head, and you can deal with the flu later.

You're probably saying, "Yeah, but I haven't been chased by a bear in at least five years, so why does it seem like I still get sick from stress?" You get sick for the same reason that I used to get sick during every midterm-exam week in college. These are stressful times! But it's not the same kind of stress that running from bears every day would produce. Modern stress is typically chronic and low grade. It's always there, constantly gnawing away at the immune system because the fight-or-flight system stays on medium alert most of the time. So instead of going from no alert (relaxed) to high alert (bear attack), most people are on medium alert (daily hassles, work, bills, kids, and so on) all the time. It slowly takes its toll on the immune-system functions.

Relationships between stress and specific diseases seem to exist. Strong negative emotions such as anger, chronic hostility, and anxiety are associated with hypertension, ulcers, rheumatoid arthritis, headaches, and asthma.

A risk to the heart

People with the *Type A personality* — a personality pattern characterized by an aggressive and persistent struggle to achieve more and more in less and less time — are the real go-getters of the world. They're the corporate executives who build a Fortune 500 company from the bottom up in a matter of years, the millionaire workaholics, and the hyper-competitive college students driven by perfection. Type A people tend to be very impatient and view almost everything as urgent.

You may be thinking, "So what? These people can be very successful, right?" Yes, but they also generally have a higher risk of suffering from *coronary heart disease* — hardening of the arteries, angina, and heart attacks. But before you quit school and make relaxing walks on the beach your full-time job, remember that the relationship between Type A personalities and developing coronary heart disease is not one-to-one. The research shows an *increase* in *risk;* developing these health problems is not inevitable.

Risk means that these folks need to take precautions and be aware of contributing factors and warning signs. Read up on coronary heart disease if you're worried; check out *Heart Disease For Dummies* by James M. Rippe, MD (Wiley, 2004). And if you're really worried, go see your family physician.

Coping Is No Gamble

Stress, stress, stress — everyone's got it. So what can you and I do about it? This question brings me to the concept of *coping,* the response to stressful and upsetting situations. Sometimes a person's coping strategies can make things better (as in getting healthy from exercising) and sometimes they can make things worse (if your way of coping is to blow your paycheck at a casino). There are many different ways of coping with stress; some are good and some are bad.

Even though bad coping skills can lead to problems, having no coping skills can lead to vulnerability and, sometimes, more problems. That's why on occasion, using bad coping techniques is better than not coping at all.

Discovering how to cope

Most psychologists classify coping behaviors into two big categories, *approach processes* and *avoidance processes.* Approach coping is more active than its avoidance cousin; approach processes resemble a take-charge kind of response to stress.

Common approach coping responses include:

- **Logical analysis:** Looking at a situation in as realistic terms as possible
- **Reappraising or reframing:** Looking at a situation from a different perspective and trying to see the positive side of things
- **Accepting responsibility:** Taking charge of your part in a situation
- **Seeking guidance and support:** Asking for help (see the next section "Finding resources")
- **Problem solving:** Coming up with alternatives, making a choice, and evaluating outcomes
- **Information gathering:** Collecting additional information about the stressor so you can more easily cope

Avoidance coping strategies are less active and involve coping in less direct ways. Here are some common avoidance coping strategies:

- **Denial:** Refusing to admit that a problem exists
- **Avoidance:** Evading possible sources of stress

- ✔ **Distraction or seeking alternative rewards:** Trying to get satisfaction elsewhere like watching a funny movie when feeling sad or enjoying recreational activities on the weekend to cope with having a bad job

- ✔ **Venting or emotional discharge:** Yelling, getting depressed, worrying

- ✔ **Sedation:** Numbing oneself to the stress through drugs, alcohol, sex, eating binges, and so on

Finding resources

Coping is more than just the actions that a person takes in response to stress. The way an individual copes also depends on the resources available to him. After all, a billionaire who loses her job may experience a lot less stress than a suddenly unemployed day laborer who makes $30 a day and has a family of five.

A person's response to stress is a complex reaction that depends on her coping skills, environmental resources, and personal resources. Any life event that a person encounters is influenced by the interaction of the person's ongoing life stressors, social coping resources, demographic characteristics, and personal coping resources. Further, the person's cognitive appraisals of the stressor influence her health and well-being in both positive and negative ways.

An *integrative approach* considers three factors when attempting to predict the health outcome of a particular stressor:

- ✔ The resources an individual possesses prior to encountering a stressor or stressful event

- ✔ The event itself

- ✔ The appraisal of the event

An individual's ability to resist stress is called *resilience* — the outcome of the interaction between an individual's *personal* and *social resources* and his coping efforts. Personal coping resources include stable personality traits, beliefs, and approaches to life that help us cope:

- ✔ **Self-efficacy:** Your belief in yourself and that you can handle a situation based on your experience

- ✔ **Optimism:** Having a positive outlook on the future and expecting positive outcomes

- ✔ **Internal locus of control:** Your belief that certain things are within, not out of, your control

One type of environmental resource that is helpful in coping is *social resources,* which aid in coping by providing support, information, and problem-solving suggestions. Good social resources include family, friends, significant others, religious and spiritual organizations, and sometimes even co-workers and supervisors. Other environmental resources include money, shelter, health services, and transportation. These things can make all the difference in the world when someone's attempting to cope with stress.

Going Beyond Stress: The Psychology of Health

Psychologists don't stop at the intersection of stress, disease, and coping. They're also attempting to apply what they know about human behavior and mental processes to the problems of health in general. They're looking for ways to keep people physically well and trying to find out how people's behavior contributes to illness. Psychology researchers work in the field of *health psychology,* the psychological study of health and illness.

Health psychologists work in many types of settings, ranging from universities (conducting research) to clinics and hospitals, which involve the direct care of patients. Their main activities include preventing illness, helping people and families cope with illness, and developing programs for health-related behavior change and maintaining a healthy lifestyle.

Preventing illness

Health psychologists engage in three types of illness prevention:

- **Primary:** Preventing an illness from occurring in otherwise healthy people. Examples of primary prevention programs are childhood immunization, condom use, and HIV-awareness campaigns.

- **Secondary:** Focusing on the early identification and treatment of a developing illness or disease. Secondary prevention programs include breast cancer awareness campaigns and the promotion of self-examinations for testicular cancer.

- **Tertiary:** Helping people cope with already developed diseases and preventing them from getting worse. Tertiary prevention programs include helping people reduce high blood pressure, quit smoking, and treat obesity.

Making changes

Have you ever kept a New Year's resolution to start doing something healthy — exercise more often, take a yoga class, eat better, get more rest, wear your seat belt? Why not? If you're being honest, I bet you're thinking it was harder than you thought it would be. Take a minute to think about what keeps you from doing what's most healthy?

A common problem with health-related behavior is people not sticking to the course they know is right. Part of this problem falls under the heading of *compliance* — whether or not someone follows through with a physician's recommendations and treatment or his own health-related plans. But what determines whether or not someone engages in health-promoting behavior to begin with? Some people make it look so easy. They go to the gym regularly. They eat right consistently. They don't smoke — ever.

Some people do unhealthy things than others for numerous reasons. For starters, a lot of people won't start or stick with a health-related behavior if substantial barriers are in the way. It's too easy to give up if something or someone makes it hard. Perhaps you don't go to the gym because it's too expensive, or you don't sleep enough because you don't have a nice set of pajamas. Money is a commonly cited barrier to engaging in healthy behavior. Another reason people don't *just do it* is that the health-related behavior may cut into something more fun or necessary. If I go to the gym, I'll miss my television programs. If I eat right, I'll have to go to the grocery store, and then I'll have to cook, and then I'll never finish any of my other household duties.

Commitment to change is most often brought about when a person believes that he can make a difference. A lot of people have a *fatalistic* attitude toward their physical health — the "you go when you go" philosophy. They don't see their behavior as contributing to their health and, therefore, don't bother to change.

This mind-set is also known as having an *external locus of control* — thinking that control over something rests outside of oneself. Having the belief that the power to change a situation or event resides inside yourself, that it's under your control, is called an *internal locus of control.* When someone feels that he can control something, he's more likely to try and do something about it.

After you've changed, either because of external rewards or because of your belief that you can make a difference, how do you maintain those changes? It's easy to quit smoking, for example, but staying smoke-free is another story. You can maintain a commitment to healthy behavior by first examining the pros and cons of changing and not changing. Your ability to develop an accurate tally depends on having access to reliable information. Confusing or conflicting health messages don't quite do the job.

Getting the message in the information age

People like to call this period of time the "Information Age." No question, there's a lot of information out there. At times, the world seems to suffer from an information overload. With all of these facts, figures, and opinions floating about, who and what information do you tend to believe? Do those stop-smoking ad campaigns really work?

Media campaigns usually are only effective when they inform people about something they didn't already know. By now, though, almost everyone knows that smoking is harmful to health. People didn't always know about the health risks associated with smoking, and when that information finally became public knowledge, smoking rates dropped. But a lot of people kept smoking anyway, and many people actually picked up the habit after the warnings were put out there. Then again, many people feel that the mainstream media is not trustworthy. I've even heard people say that the idea that smoking causes cancer is bogus.

A number of factors influence people's tendencies to listen to and believe a particular source of information. Research on *persuasion* — getting somebody to do something he may not do on his own accord — has supplied psychologists with much of their knowledge in the area of source believability. Who do people believe?

For a message to be persuasive, it must grab your attention, be easy to understand, and be acceptable and worthwhile. You also have to be able to remember it. If you don't remember the message, who cares what it said? Persuasive arguments tend to present both sides of an issue, making the arguments look fair and unbiased. Fear-inducing messages work best when attainable steps are mentioned along with the scary stuff.

Decisions to engage or not to engage in healthy behavior are based on many factors, including your beliefs about the behavior and your locus of control. Researchers Hochbaum, Rosenstock, and Kegels, working in the US Public Health Services in the 1950s, came up with the *health belief model* to demonstrate the psychological processes someone goes through when making health-related decisions. The model is based on beliefs about the following:

- ✔ **Severity:** How bad can the illness or disease get if I don't do something about it?

- ✔ **Susceptibility:** How likely am I to get sick if I don't engage in healthy behavior?

- ✔ **Benefits outweighing costs:** What's in it for me, and is it worth it?

> ✔ **Efficacy:** How effective will my attempts at change be? I don't want to work for nothing.

The answers to these questions play a role in determining the likelihood that a person will do the healthy thing. If I arrive at a high severity, high susceptibility, high benefits-over-costs, and high-efficacy conclusion, then the likelihood that I'll choose the healthy option goes up. Otherwise, the healthy path may not seem to be worth the sacrifice and effort.

Intervening

What's the next step after you decide to do something about your unhealthy lifestyle? What can you actually do to get the ball rolling? A health psychologist or other health professional can design *interventions* that help you change and then maintain that change.

Behavior modification is a powerful method of behavior change. The most basic, yet very powerful, form of behavior modification is to use punishments and rewards for either not engaging or engaging in the target behavior. For example, if I schedule myself to run three times a week at 5:30 p.m. and I don't do it, then I have to clean the kitchen and bathroom, and do the laundry that night. If I comply, I get to treat myself to a nice dip in the spa. The trick with this technique is to enlist a partner to keep you from cheating on your rewards and punishments. I may decide to skip the laundry and go in the spa even if I don't run. A partner helps keep you honest.

Cognitive change is a process by which I examine the mental messages I give myself that may prevent me from changing a behavior or maintaining a change. Everyone has *automatic thoughts* — thoughts that they don't realize automatically go through their minds in certain situations. I may tell myself that I really want to run three times a week, but I also may be having the automatic thought, "You'll never do it; you never follow through with anything." Well, thanks for the positive reinforcement, me!

The good news is that automatic thoughts can be replaced with positive self-statements. This process takes a lot of practice and encouragement from other people, but the conversion is usually worth the hard work.

This section only begins to scratch the surface of health psychology and stress-related issues, but I hope this overview of the subject whets your appetite for more knowledge about living a less stressful and healthier life. Remember to relax, believe in yourself, and don't avoid things. And reward yourself when you follow through with this advice!

Harnessing the Power of Positivity

Some people criticize psychology as "negatively focused" with all its focus on therapy and pathology and learning disabilities; they say it's always trying to fix people and groups. Well, a group of psychologists in the late 1990s and early 2000s, headed by the well-known psychologists Martin Seligman and Mihaly Csikszentmihalyi, introduced an essentially new branch of psychology known as *positive psychology*. Positive psychology is defined as a science of positive subjective experience, positive individual traits, and positive institutions that improve quality of life and prevents pathologies.

Positive psychology as a science of human strength covers a range of topics:

Emotional intelligence	***Creativity***
Optimism	Self-efficacy
Wisdom	Compassion
Gratitude	Altruism
Courage	Toughness
Meaning	Humor

Since its inception, research programs have taken positive psychology into the realms of business, sports, the military, and stress and illness. The military has sought the help of positive psychologists to alleviate stress and bolster the hardiness of its troops. Patients with terminal illnesses seek help in finding hope and courage in the face of death. Creative professionals want to be more innovative.

A central organizing concept in positive psychology is the idea of optimal living, characterized by two opposing poles of success: *flourishing* and *floundering*.

Flourishing (and its opposite, *floundering*) is synonymous with positive mental health as opposed to mental illness or disorder. Imagine going to a psychologist for a mental health check-up or wellness visit instead of the traditional "what's wrong with me?" focus. This can happen on a yearly basis the same way some people visit a medical doctor for an annual physical — not because they're sick but because they want to get a checkup. Call it a *mentacal* (ment-*uh*-cull). Okay, so I need to work on the name, but you get the point.

Psychologist C. L. M. Keyes, professor of sociology at Emory University in Atlanta, Georgia, identifies the following dimensions of flourishing/mental health:

- ✔ **Positive affect:** Emotional well-being

- ✔ **Avowed quality of life:** Satisfied with life

- ✔ **Self-acceptance:** Positive attitude toward oneself

- ✔ **Personal growth:** Seeking challenges

- ✔ **Purpose in life:** Meaning

- ✔ **Environmental mastery:** The ability to select, manage, and mold one's environment

- ✔ **Autonomy:** Guided by one's own standards

- ✔ **Positive relations with others:** Calm, trusting relationships

- ✔ **Social acceptance:** Positive attitude toward others and human differences

- ✔ **Social actualization:** Belief in people's potential for growth

- ✔ **Social contribution:** Seeing one's daily activities as useful to others

- ✔ **Social coherence:** Interest in society and social life

- ✔ **Social integration:** Belonging

Flourishing as a concept is used by some psychologists in therapy as a guide in determining broad, more lifestyle-oriented goals for therapy clients or patients as they set goals for themselves in life. It can be used as an informal metric of client well-being, pointing therapist and client toward areas in need of improvement. However, it is not a formal component of therapy and is not considered part of formal diagnosis. That is, therapy focusing on flourishing, as opposed to treating a mental disorder, is not typically reimbursed by third party payers such as insurance companies. Professional therapy provided by a psychologist would not necessarily focus on flourishing as a primary goal in therapy but could include, interweave, and use the concept within therapy in providing direction for personal growth to a client in a general manner. This crosses over a bit into the realm of *life coaching* or advice giving, roles that therapists typically do not engage in. However, if a client asks for this service and consents to it, understanding the psychologist's training and expertise in this regard, then what happens between two consenting adults can be considered generally acceptable.

Acquiring the Bionic Brain

Something happens to me nearly every day at around two in the afternoon. After a busy morning of report writing, therapy sessions, e-mails, phone calls, testing, and other doings of a psychologist, I "hit a wall." That is, I slow way down, have trouble concentrating, and become much less productive. After doing some reading, I realized that maybe my brain glucose levels are lower at this time and my brain isn't firing on all cylinders. I started eating a little protein snack and hydrating a little better, which seems to perk me up. My brain needed a boost, I guess.

Athletes train to get stronger, faster, and more agile. Musicians practice to get more fluid and precise. But what if you want to get mentally quicker, more agile, stronger, more precise, or just plain smarter? This is an area of psychology known as *cognitive* enhancement, defined in 2008 by psychologists Nick Bostrom and Anders Sandberg as the amplification or extension of core capacities of the mind through improvement of external information-processing systems.

Many forms of cognitive enhancement are being researched, and some have been around for a very long time. In essence, education is a form of cognitive enhancement. Other forms include mental training, medications, transcranial magnetic stimulation (TMS), relaxation techniques, neurofeedback, and biofeedback.

Some techniques that are being investigated in animals (not on humans) include genetic and prenatal and perinatal processes such as gene replacement and fetal supplementation in mice.

Before you go out and buy that *Baby Einstein* DVD collection for your unborn genius, know that there has been absolutely no data to support that any "make your baby smarter" program has ever actually made a baby smarter.

Doing smart drugs

I once had a gig doing learning disability and psychological assessments for a local university, and I witnessed something interesting. A whole bunch of students were actually looking for me to diagnose them with ADHD! It didn't take me long to figure out why. The doctors over at the university health center would not prescribe a psychostimulant to a student without an official diagnosis of ADHD. Now, these students weren't looking to get "high" off Ritalin or Strattera, and they weren't necessarily looking to sell the pills. But they were looking to boost their attention and concentration skills so they could excel academically.

In these modern times, medications and pharmacology are an integral and widely accepted part of life. Medications that are designed and used for cognitive and neuropsychological improvement and/or enhancement are called *nootropics*.

Many ethical and moral objections exist to using drugs to enhance mental performance, and some people see them in the same way they think of using steroids or performance-enhancing drugs in sports; it's cheating. That's a huge discussion. But, for a moment, consider that a person with a learning disability, brain injury, or other cognitive deficit could take a medication to improve his mental functioning. Is this any different than taking medicine for other types of ailments?

The fact is, this is already happening — sometimes in overt ways and often in indirect ways. An indirect way of using medication to improve thinking comes from the use of antidepressant medication. Anyone who's ever been severely depressed can attest that the condition comes with a mental fog of sorts (something professionals call *pseudodementia*) that accompanies the depressed mood and feelings of guilt and lack of pleasure and motivation. Antidepressants help ease this cognitive dullness.

Medications that enhance or otherwise assist in cognitive processes include the following:

- ✔ **Stimulants:** Used for increased attention and short-term memory and includes such drugs as Adderall, Vyvanse, Atomoxetine (Strattera), and good old-fashioned caffeine

- ✔ **Cholinergics:** Used as memory enhancing-drugs; examples are Aricept and medical cannabis

- ✔ **Dopaminergics:** Used to increase attention and alertness and includes such drugs as methylphenidate (Ritalin, Concerta) and modafinil (Provigil)

The list of known or suspected nootropic drugs is much larger and expanding. However, I must point out that the number of prescriptions written for these drugs for actual nootropic purposes is still fairly limited. It would seem that physicians may be somewhat hesitant to go down the rabbit hole of drug-induced or assisted cognitive enhancement.

Hitting the limits of the skull

Just as mental training, neurofeedback, and drugs can enhance cognitive processes, so to can devices such as cochlear implants, computers, smart phones, and even Post-it Notes. The field of technological devices that enhance cognitive processes is known in some circles as *cognitive prosthetics* or *neuroprosthetics*.

Many scientists show incredible interest in the promise and possibility of the field of cognitive prosthetics. Some fairly well-established devices are already available, including *speech production devices,* mobile phone or mobile technology software programs that "talk" for individuals who cannot or do not speak, *memory aide* software programs, and even voice-activated and -prompted GPS route and guidance systems.

Perhaps one of the most interesting approaches to cognitive prosthetics comes from work being done with *brain-computer-interfacing* in which external computer and/or other digital devices are directly wired into the brain and controlled directly by brain activity. Studies reveal that when electrodes are inserted into the brain of a primate or human, even those with fairly profound neurological damage, control of a computer cursor is possible. Doesn't sound like much at first, but think about it; controlling a computer interface by just thinking about it is downright telepathic almost — and pretty cool!

Part VI
The Part of Tens

For a rundown of ten fascinating ways the Internet and psychology are intersecting, head to www.dummies.com/extras/psychology.

In this part...

- ✔ Get a mental health check-up and discover lots of tips on achieving and maintaining good psychological health.

- ✔ Have a look at some of the greatest silver-screen treatments of all kinds of thorny and fascinating psychological issues, from *Psycho* to *The Matrix*.

Chapter 19

Ten Tips for Maintaining Psychological Health

*T*here's no magic formula — and no standard — for being a psychologically healthy person. Is psychological health simply the absence of mental disease or mental illness? If so, a lot of people are perfectly healthy from a psychological standpoint. Is the absence of physical disease the same thing as being physically healthy? Some people think that there's more to being healthy than being disease-free. Unfortunately, this chapter doesn't give you all the answers to these questions. In fact, it probably creates more questions than answers.

Psychologists are not necessarily in the business of deciding the values of a society. A lot of scientists think that values are beyond the scope of science, that values and morals are too subjective and personal to be reduced to scientific analysis. But some psychologists believe that psychological health is as close to a universal value as any. After all, who doesn't want to be healthy?

Psychology has uncovered a lot about human thinking and behavior over the years, and it would be a waste not to try to apply some of that knowledge to the human quest for well-being, happiness, and health. I agree that psychologists may be overstepping their bounds when they advocate a particular set of values.

But, as a professor of mine once said, "That's an empirical question, isn't it?" What he meant is that opinions can be evaluated empirically, and one opinion can be judged with respect to another as long as agreed-upon criteria for evaluating the opinions are in place. In other words, researchers may actually be able to evaluate the "good life" with psychological science as long as they can all agree upon a definition of what the good life is. For example,

I may agree that a good life is one in which my needs are met without much effort and I'm relatively free to do what I please. With that, researchers can scientifically evaluate circumstances, behaviors, and thought processes that lead to such conditions. If researchers can agree upon a standard, they can investigate what contributes to the achievement of that standard.

Because this chapter is providing tips for psychological health, I need to set a standard. So here it is: I define psychological health broadly as *optimal living*. This is a safe position because individuals can tweak the meaning of optimal living to fit their own values.

My use of the term optimal living in this chapter takes a *subjective* view of psychological health. For years, psychologists have studied the concept of *subjective well-being*. This concept refers to my sense of personal well-being and happiness without reference to the views of anyone else. It represents my personal values, and it may or may not be in harmony with others around me.

Some philosophers have argued that it is morally preferable to hold values that correspond with the values of others or, at the very least, to hold values that don't impinge upon or impact the values of others. Subscribing to a value system that doesn't impact the values of others is the "different strokes for different folks" approach.

Another definition of psychological health is perhaps more objective. This definition holds that psychological health centers on behaviors and mental processes that lead to the ability to adjust and function well in one's life. This view can also be subjective to some degree. For example, you may adjust quite well to prison, but this adjustment may involve behaviors that can be considered quite unhealthy in other contexts. But, for most people and societies, the norms for good adjustment and functioning often involve surviving within the typically acceptable rules and boundaries of a community.

At the very least, psychological health involves being happy. I've never met a person who didn't want to be happy, even if being happy to him meant being miserable. You can't escape the desire to be happy. That reminds me of a joke:

> "Hit me, hit me!" says the masochist.
>
> "No!" says the sadist.

Enough of the philosophical, let's get down to practical suggestions. The following ten tips for maintaining psychological health are equally important. No one is more important than the others; that's why they are not numbered.

Accept Yourself

A lot of popular psychology and self-help books tell us to "love ourselves." It's not a bad idea. Severe dislike for oneself is often associated with extreme guilt, shame, and depression. Don't underestimate the power of believing in your abilities and valuing your uniqueness.

Too often, people lead inauthentic lives that are defined by others as they strive for acceptance. Self-acceptance is a crucial ingredient for motivation and positive emotion, and accepting yourself even leads to more acceptance by others. Accepting yourself is not the same as thinking you are perfect.

Strive for Self-Determination

When I feel like the captain of my own ship, I'm more interested in life, more excited about life, and more confident. My motivations are a complex mix of the things I truly want for myself and things I've adopted from significant others over the years.

Feeling as if I have some control over the decisions that affect me is crucial to psychological health. When I'm in controlling, punitive, or dominating environments, my sense of importance and freedom suffers.

Sometimes you need to adapt to the desires and values of others. In these situations, you can still retain a sense of self-determination if you agree even slightly with what you're adapting to. What if you want to paint your house bright purple, but the city won't let you? Well, if the officials can agree to lavender, then you probably don't feel so pushed around. It's rarely (if ever) a good thing for people to feel like they're being told what to do when they don't agree with the directive.

Stay Connected and Nurture Relationships

Sometimes it seems like modern lives are lonely. Everyone speeds around in their cars or stares into computer screens all day, isolated from other people and busy with the details of their own lives. I've often felt like I have to sacrifice productivity at work in order to socialize. I hear people make similar comments all the time, "I just don't have time for friends and family." Here's a tip: Make time!

In these times of mega-cities and super-suburbs, it can be hard to stay close to friends and family. The age of the small town filled with extended family is all but gone. Small towns are out there, but most people don't live in them. Despite these conditions, there is a benefit in working to maintain closer proximity to people who matter. The huge growth in mobile phone, Internet, and social media use may reflect both the desire to stay connected and an attempt to do so in a fragmented and fast-paced world.

Having friends and family around is nice, but it's only a good thing if the relationships are good. Some people can't wait to get as far away from certain people as possible. Feeling emotionally connected and supported by your relationships is just as important, if not more important, than simple proximity. People need intimate relationships that they can count on when times are hard. They need trustworthy romantic partners who value the same things.

Here are some other helpful hints for maintaining good relationships: Practice forgiveness, be tolerant, communicate honestly, express yourself, balance independence with dependence, and act responsibly toward others — and nurture their values, desires, feelings, and wishes.

Lend a Helping Hand

When you reach out to others in need, you often get a sense of mastery over my own circumstances, and you're working to foster positive social conditions. Lending a helping hand helps the intended beneficiaries, and it also helps the individuals who offer the assistance. I won't mention that there's a nice tax break in it too. Win, win, win.

Find Meaning and Purpose and Work Toward Goals

Feeling like life is meaningless is a hallmark of depression. One of the drawbacks of modern society is the sense of alienation that can come from working day in and day out with only the next workday or the next paycheck as a reward.

It's crucial to have meaningful personal goals. Research consistently finds that the process of working toward goals is as important as the goals themselves. At times, goals can be too lofty, and people can set themselves up for disappointment because they can't reach them. This defeats the purpose of setting goals in the first place. Realistic and meaningful goals are helpful. Having goals is not the same as being perfectionistic. Perfectionists set themselves up to fail because no one is perfect. Being a little kind to yourself and understanding that you're going to make mistakes in life is part of accepting yourself, and it's good for your psychological health.

Find Hope and Maintain Faith

Research has consistently shown that having a deep sense of spiritual faith can be a protective measure for dealing with loss, illness, and psychological disorders. When things seem dark, it really helps to have a sense of hope and optimism about the future and a belief that goals can eventually be achieved.

Having a *positivity bias* helps to override fear and maintain motivation. Being biased in this way is kind of like seeing the world through rose-colored glasses. Pessimists may claim that they're more in touch with reality, but a little positive illusion never hurts.

Find Flow and Be Engaged

Professional athletes talk about "being in the groove" when they've had a good game. *Flow* is the experience of feeling totally engaged, involved, engrossed, and focused in an activity or experience. Living a happy life is a matter of learning to maximize and control inner experiences in order to feel harmoniously engaged in the activity for its own sake.

I once heard a piece of Buddhist wisdom: If you are thinking about resting while sweeping the floor, you are not truly experiencing life as it exists. When you sweep, sweep. When you rest, rest. Find flow!

Enjoy the Beautiful Things in Life

The ability to appreciate beauty is *aesthetics*. There's a lot of negativity and ugliness in the world — wars, disease, violence, and degradation are all around. Depressing, right? Being able to appreciate the beautiful things is a saving grace in a world that's so often unattractive.

The experience of beauty is personal and one that no one else can define for another person. You may see the beauty in a famous painting or the sun shining through the clouds. When I see a well-executed play in football, it brings tears to my eyes. "That's beautiful, man!" Sniff, sniff.

Even things that are imperfect and incomplete can be beautiful, particularly if you are a practitioner of the "wabi-sabi" worldview derived from Buddhism. Finally, an excuse not to clean the house!

Struggle to Overcome; Learn to Let Go

Challenge and adversity are undeniable facts of life. Being able to effectively cope with challenges is crucial to maintaining psychological and even physical well-being. Each person has a variety of skills and techniques used to cope with stress and adversity. Here's the best general advice for coping with adversity: Cope actively within situations that you have some measure of control over, and cope passively within situations that you don't have control over.

Active coping involves taking actions to improve a situation such as looking for a job when you're fired instead of just saying, "Oh well, I guess I just wasn't meant to have a job." In situations that you can control, such as many health-related problems, taking action consistently leads to better outcomes and better psychological functioning.

Passive coping involves processes of psychological and emotional acceptance. When a person you love dies, you may run yourself ragged trying to shake or diminish the feelings of loss and sadness. But eventually, you have to accept the reality of the situation. Accepting reality when you cannot change it is a good example of passive coping. Forgiveness is another one.

Don't Be Afraid to Change

Morihei Ueshiba, founder of the martial art aikido, wrote a book called *The Art of Peace*. His secret to living a peaceful life was the core principle of Judo: Go with the flow! When you are rigid and inflexible, you are more likely to experience resistance and strain yourself in trying to maintain your posture. When you are flexible and willing to change a behavior that is not working, you are more adaptable and better adjusted. It takes courage to change your ways, but it is vital for health and well-being.

Chapter 20

Ten Great Psychological Movies

So what makes a good psychological movie? The definition of a psychological movie is a film that directly addresses a psychological topic or mental disorder and/or utilizes psychological concepts or a psychological theme as part of the plot.

My ratings of the movies covered here are based on a five-cigar rating system. Sigmund Freud was quite the cigar aficionado, and receiving five cigars would have sounded great to him. For our purposes, five cigars is a great film, and one cigar is a bad psychological film. Each film can earn one cigar for each of the following criteria:

✔ Accurate depiction of a mental disorder and accurate portrayal of a person suffering from a mental disorder, including the subjective experience

✔ Accurate depiction of the structure, process, and function of mental health treatment including psychotherapy and medication

✔ Interesting and thought-provoking presentation of psychological science, research, or theory

✔ Use of psychological principles and knowledge to anticipate, predict, and get inside the mind of the characters in the film necessary on the part of the viewer

One Flew Over the Cuckoo's Nest

One Flew Over the Cuckoo's Nest was released in 1975 and based on Ken Kesey's book of the same name. The film, directed by Milos Forman, stars Jack Nicholson as Randle P. McMurphy, a man who is involuntary committed to a mental hospital.

The thing that makes this movie a real contender for the Golden Cigar is the question of whether Nicholson's character is really mentally ill. The film is a commentary on the mental health system during the time period within which the movie is set and how the system was used as a means of social control. Is Nicholson's character mentally ill, or is he just a pain in the neck who has a problem with authority? There's no doubt that Jack stands out and bucks the system every chance he gets, but does that make him sick? Maybe he just has a real zest for life.

For the acting, social commentary, and existential dilemma, I give this film five cigars! Definitely check this one out, and for more discussion of the issues brought up by this film check out Chapter 3's sections on medication and Chapter 13 on abnormal psychology.

A Clockwork Orange

A Clockwork Orange, based on the book by Anthony Burgess and directed by Stanley Kubrick, was made in 1971 and stars Malcolm McDowell as Alex DeLarge, a young troublemaker and delinquent. McDowell and his gang of three friends engage in various crimes and shenanigans, such as fighting, vandalism, skipping school, and the like. One night, they steal a car and go for a joy ride. They commit a horrific home invasion, raping a woman and brutally beating her husband. McDowell gets caught.

This is where the psychologically interesting part begins. McDowell is put through a rigorous behavior modification program that utilizes a technique called *aversion training.* After learning takes place, every time McDowell's character is exposed to violence, he becomes violently ill. Therefore, he is compelled to avoid engaging in violence in order to avoid getting sick.

The film seems to pose a number of questions: Do we really want to resort to such tactics in reforming our criminals? Are we doing more harm than good? Is the level of violence in a society a function of a collective aversion to it or more a matter of the strong preying on the weak?

For the macabre nature of the film and its use of behaviorism, not to mention the social commentary on violence in society, I give this film five cigars! For more on behavior therapy check out Chapter 16.

12 Monkeys

12 Monkeys, directed by Terry Gilliam (1995) and starring Bruce Willis, Madeleine Stowe, and Brad Pitt, takes place in a post-apocalyptic world in which Bruce is sent back in time to stop whomever spread a virus that destroyed the world. The psychological crux of *12 Monkeys* is the question, "What is real?" How do we know if someone is really delusional or not? How can we prove that God really does speak to some people? Willis and Stowe develop what looks like a mental disorder known as *folie à deux,* a shared fantasy or delusion by two or more people.

The acting in *12 Monkeys* is great. Brad Pitt's portrayal of a person suffering from schizophrenia (check out Chapter 13) is pretty good. The questioning of reality is a complicated topic, but *12 Monkeys* pulls it off. Five cigars!

Ordinary People

Ordinary People (1980), directed by Robert Redford and starring Timothy Hutton, Jud Hirsch, Donald Sutherland, and Mary Tyler Moore, is about a teenage boy recovering from depression and a suicide attempt following a boating accident that took his older brother's life. This is an excellent story about how complex grief and depression can be and yet how much can be accomplished by taking things slowly and making them simple.

The acting is superb. The depiction of a mental disorder is excellent. Only one problem costs this movie a cigar. Psychiatrists rarely, if ever, do psychotherapy nowadays. Psychologists, social workers, and marriage and family counselors conduct most psychotherapy. Four cigars! For more about trauma check out Chapter 13.

Girl, Interrupted

In *Girl, Interrupted,* a 1999 film directed by James Mangold, Winona Ryder plays a depressed and suicidal young woman who's admitted to a mental hospital. She's reluctant about being there and resists many of the efforts by the staff to help her "get better." The movie contrasts the characters' lives and afflictions as a way to demonstrate that middle-class suburban angst is small potatoes when compared to other more serous illnesses. At the same time, the film doesn't minimize Ryder's difficulties, but instead it appears to place them in perspective. Developing a new perspective is a turning point for Ryder's character; her life is simply being *interrupted.* She won't let her life end in the institution due to a failure to deal with her problems.

The moral of the story is that Ryder's character was fortunate to have made it out alive, merely taking a detour into mental illness instead of permanent residence. It's a very personal story. It's a story about hope and the harsh reality of some people's lives (for more about life's "issues" check out Chapter 17). Five cigars!

The Silence of the Lambs

This is the movie that made everyone want to go out, join the FBI, and become a *profiler*. Directed by Jonathan Demme, this 1991 film stars Jodie Foster and Anthony Hopkins in a psychological thriller that gets you inside the mind of a serial killer. Foster's character, Clarise Starling, is an FBI agent who must deal with a famous psychiatrist/serial killer named Hannibal Lecter, played by Anthony Hopkins. The movie centers on their interactions and the psychological games they play with each other in order to get what they both want. Hopkins plays doctor with Foster's psyche, and Foster asks Hopkins to look inside and use his self-knowledge to help her catch a serial killer.

The movie's strength is not so much in its portrayal of a mentally ill psychiatrist, but in its insight to how the human mind works and how we become who we are. The tragedy of Foster's childhood makes being a profiler her destiny. The serial killer's (Buffalo Bill) quest for transformation into his true self drives his horrendous murders. The real anomaly is Hopkins's character. He seems to represent both the good and the bad aspects of the human psyche. He helps Foster, both as consultant and as healer, but he also demonstrates depravity and demonic insanity through acts of murder. It's as if he is both the giver and the taker of life. His powerful knowledge of the human mind easily turns into a tool for murder.

Hannibal Lecter represents what a lot of us fear — that those we trust to help us can also hurt us. Five cigars! (For more discussion about psychopathic personality and forensic psychology, check out see the free online article "Applying Psychology for a Better World" at www.dummies.com/extras/psychology.)

Sybil

Sally Field stars in this classic 1976 made-for-TV movie, directed by Daniel Petrie, about multiple personality disorder (MPD). Field, playing Sybil, is a reclusive young woman who appears to be shy and quiet, but under the surface a chaotic tangle of personalities swirls out of control. She ends up in the care of a doctor who begins to treat her for multiple personality disorder.

The scenes in which Field and her doctor are in therapy are very dramatic and disturbing. They're intense! Sally Field's performance is very powerful. It's actually pretty hard to watch someone act so strangely. It gets a ten on the "Hair on the Back of My Neck Standing Up" scale. It gives me the willies!

As Sybil switches back and forth between personalities, the therapist begins to gain some insight as to how Field's character could have become so ill.

Field's character was horribly sexually and physically abused as a child. The film presents the professionally popular idea that MPD is the result of the personality splitting off from itself in order to defend the core personality from the reality of the abuse. It does a good job of respecting this notion and stays a true course, not yielding to the temptation to get too "Hollywood."

The strength of *Sybil* rests on three pillars: Sally Field's acting, the emotional intensity of the therapy scenes, and the portrayal of the hypothesized cause of multiple personality disorder. Five cigars! To learn more about psycho-therapy check out Chapter 15.

Psycho

No list of great psychological movies would be complete without Alfred Hitchcock's 1960 film *Psycho.* Anthony Perkins stars as a depraved psy-chopath with a strange delusion that involves dressing up like his mother. Perkins's character appears to suffer from a split personality in which part of his personality is his mother. How weird is that? The "psycho" in *Psycho* only kills one person in the entire movie, small potatoes by today's standards, but Hitchcock's use of suspense and surprise are superb.

Psycho introduced the American public to the idea of a psychopathic killer, a man with a warped mind. On the outside, Perkins's character is meek and socially awkward, a boy in a man's body. He enjoys the voyeuristic thrill of an occasional peep at his motel customers. The suggestion is that under-neath that calm exterior is a deranged killer waiting for his opportunity. But the key psychological component in *Psycho* is Perkins's twisted relationship with his mother. He is the quintessential "momma's boy," unable to go out into the world on his own and enjoy the pleasures that he fantasizes about. Freud would have been proud of this twisted version of Oedipus in which Perkins's mother, rather than the father, is the castrating threat. Perkins's rage appears to be the product of his failure to be the king of his own castle, so to speak.

Psycho is a classic. Don't bother with the remake with Vince Vaughn; go rent the original. Five cigars. (For more about psychopaths, check out the free online article "Applying Psychology for a Better World" at www.dummies.com/extras/psychology.)

The Matrix

The Matrix (1999), directed by Lana and Andy Wachowski and starring Keanu Reeves, Laurence Fishburne, and Carrie-Anne Moss is an apocalyptic film in which a "master computer" has taken over the world and the minds of all humans and created an alternative reality. Humans are kept alive in a farm of sorts, where the energy from human bodies keeps the technology powered.

The master computer has taken over the minds of all humans by linking them into a virtual reality matrix in order to sustain their minds and mental functioning after finding out that without the matrix-derived mass delusion the human body would die, thus eliminating its power source. However, a group of people have managed to "break free" from the matrix and "come back" to reality, waking up to a world in which most humans are fuel and the master computer hunts them down.

Are you surprised to see this movie on this list? Some critics and viewers consider *The Matrix* to be a good "action" film, and some say it is quite mediocre. But, this movie explores the concepts of virtual reality, artificial intelligence, machine intelligence, consciousness, and human-machine/human-technology relationships. The matrix itself is suggestive of the Internet and how it is often mistaken for reality. Are people becoming disembodied minds in this Internet age? Is this a form of mental slavery in which human minds and desires are subject to manipulation by more powerful, massive, and complex intelligences such as corporate marketers and spin masters?

The Matrix is thought-provoking and taps into some very contemporary and complex areas of psychological study and research. Five cigars! (For more about consciousness check out Chapter 4 and for more about technology, check out the free online article "www.Psychology" at www.dummies.com/extras/psychology.)

The Boost

The Boost (1988), directed by Harold Becker, is a movie about addiction. James Woods stars as a typical guy with a wife and a career whose recreational drug use spirals out of control, tearing his life apart. Woods's acting is absolutely incredible. His portrayal of addiction as a cunning, baffling, bewildering, and powerful disorder is spot on! This is not a "pretty" movie and it makes no bones about the darkness of addiction. Powerful movie. Addiction is not glamorous. Five cigars.

Index

•••

• H •

• I •

• T •

About the Author

Adam Cash is a practicing psychologist and Clinical Director of Specialized Psychology Solutions, a psychological services clinic in Palm Springs, California. He specializes in child psychology, autism, developmental disorders, learning, cognition, and neurodevelopment. He's taught courses in developmental psychology, methods and statistics, substance abuse treatment, and abnormal psychology. Although Dr. Cash's clinical work focuses primarily on children, he once worked extensively with adults and was a full-time forensic psychologist, specializing in prison psychology, violence risk assessment, and sex offender assessment, and he served as an expert witness in trials related to competency-to-stand-trial and not-guilty-by-reason-of-insanity cases. Dr. Cash has developed a specialty focus on psychotic disorders such as schizophrenia and post-traumatic stress disorder. He is the author of *Wiley Concise Guides to Mental Health: Posttraumatic Stress Disorder* (2006). Dr. Cash has expertise in psychological assessment and has conducted several thousand evaluations. He provides medico-legal evaluations for disability and conducts assessment. He is most proud of his marriage to his beautiful wife, Liyona, and the home and family they've built together.

Dedication

To my wife, Liyona, and my beautiful children. Thank you for your love and purity. You are the light; may I stay in it always.

Author's Acknowledgments

I am very grateful to Jenny Brown and Lindsay Lefevere for approaching me to revise the first edition of this book. I would also like go back and thank the team from the first edition as well, Tonya Maddox Cupp and Greg Tubach. Without them, this second edition would not have been possible. Thanks, too, to the children, families, patients, and employees that I work with. I'm grateful for the opportunity to be a part of your lives.

Publisher's Acknowledgments

Acquisitions Editor: Lindsay Lefevere

Project Editor: Jenny Brown

Copy Editor: Nancy Reinhardt

Technical Editors: Professor Robert Howard Ingleby Dale, Dr. Sue O'Rourke

Art Coordinator: Alicia B. South

Sr. Project Coordinator: Kristie Rees

Cover Image: ©iStockphoto.com/cloudnumber9